A Ronin's Tale:

An Odyssey of Manhood

By Nick Osborne

©2024 Nick Osborne

All rights reserved. No part of this book, in part or in whole, may be reproduced, transmitted or utilized in any form or by any means, electronic, photographic or mechanical, including photocopying, recording, or by any information storage and retrieval system without permission in writing from Ozark Mountain Publishing, Inc. except for brief quotations embodied in literary articles and reviews.

For permission, serialization, condensation, adaptations, or for our catalog of other publications, write to Ozark Mountain Publishing, Inc., P.O. box 754, Huntsville, AR 72740, ATTN: Permissions Department.

Library of Congress Cataloging-in-Publication Data

A Ronin's Tale: An Odessey of Manhood
by Osborne, Nick – 1978-

This book delves into the mysterious complexities of manhood, and the elusive pursuit to be courageous, particularly when immersed in adversity and self-doubt.

1. Inner Peace 2. Metaphysical 3. Self-Help
I. Osborne, Nick – 1978- II. Metaphysical III. Title

Library of Congress Catalog Card Number: 2024939411
ISBN: 978-1-962858-11-3

Cover Design: Victoria Cooper Art
Book Set in: Multiple Fonts
Book Design: Summer Garr

OZARK
MOUNTAIN
PUBLISHING

PO Box 754
Huntsville, AR 72740
800-935-0045 or 479-738-2348 fax: 479-738-2448
www.ozarkmt.com
Printed in the United States of America

For my parents, Howard and Denise.

And for everyone on the search. Be easy with yourselves, and enjoy the ride.

Acknowledgments

The hero's journey has convinced me above everything else that the people who cross our path come with a purpose. They come bearing messages and wearing different costumes. They come to uplift us with love, or to destroy us with hurt. But regardless of how they show up, they carry the torches that illuminate what we need to see. Their presence in our lives is not by accident.

To my dear family, immediate and extended: The bonds we share, in all forms, is the highlight of my life. I am proud of our clan—from the gypsies and outlaws, to the angels and saints.

To my faithful friends: There are too many of you to list, but I would like to acknowledge my closest ally, Troy Lewiston. I couldn't have asked for a better running mate this life. Here is to our adventures, brother; the ones we've conquered and especially the ones yet to come.

To my teachers of the wisdom traditions, whose brilliance and counsel gives my life meaning: Joseph Campbell, Maharishi Mahesh Yogi, Robert Bly, Aaron Kipnis, Malidoma Some, Phyllis Curott, Dolores Cannon, Tat Wale Baba, and Jim Morrison. To my mentors at Lees-McCrae College, Humboldt State University, and the University of California at Davis. You nurtured curiosity and held me accountable for my thinking. I would also like to thank the Maharishi School of the Age of Enlightenment for planting seeds of a profound reality that I continue to tap into and admire.

To the University of Illinois at Urbana-Champaign: thank you for entertaining me for eight years, and no hard feelings.

To the team at Ozark Mountain Publishing, and my editor, Deborah Upton: My deepest appreciation for believing in my work and of the utility of my story. And a heartfelt praise for putting out nonlinear works that disrupt the matrix and enliven the soul.

To the craftsmen who tempered my sword and instilled grit: salutations to the brave men and women of the United States Coast

Guard. A deep bow to Professor Art Bier and Sensei Sal Belahi of the Kobudokan Dojo; and sincerest gratitude to the prodigious and humble warrior, Dyllon Muniz, of Ground Zero Mixed Martial Arts; and to Danielle and Brady Hill at Impact Fitness. Thank you all for the stoke you bring to my life.

And lastly, to the women I've loved. Each of you made me a better man.

Contents

Preface: The Search for the Source — i
Part 1: The Ordinary World
Chapter 1. The Upgrade — 3
Chapter 2. Toward the Heroic — 8
Chapter 3. Unfamiliar Soil — 10
Chapter 4. Invisible Teachers — 22
Chapter 5. Patterns — 30
Chapter 6. The Call — 35
Chapter 7. Put Up Your Dukes — 37
Chapter 8. Follow Your Bliss — 45
Chapter 9. To Utopia — 49
Chapter 10. Wild Man's Cage — 61
Chapter 11. Go West, Young Man — 68
Chapter 12. The Invocation — 80
Chapter 13. Initiation — 82
Part 2: The Special World
Chapter 14. The Wasteland — 99
Chapter 15. Guides — 105
Chapter 16. Tribe of Misfits — 107
Chapter 17. Leg Cramps and Lady-Boys — 125
Chapter 18. The Cabin — 137
Chapter 19. Journal Entry, Saigon — 139
Chapter 20. Happy Birthday — 142
Chapter 21. Grittier Flavors — 155
Chapter 22. Under the Sheets — 159
Chapter 23. Father's Day Email — 173
Chapter 24. Island Messengers — 175

Chapter 25. Boyhood Magic	180
Chapter 26. Moving Toward Center	184
Chapter 27. Small Doors, Big Doors	186
Chapter 28. The Purge	199
Chapter 29. Dark Microscope	202
Chapter 30. Elixir Theft	226
Chapter 31. Familiar Giants	228
Chapter 32. The Surgery	232
Chapter 33. The Ordeal	245
Chapter 34. Shiva's Playground	247
Chapter 35. Embrace the Suffering	264
Chapter 36. The Sweetness of Death	270
Chapter 37. Good-bye, Hero	276
Chapter 38. Let Go of the Raft	278
Chapter 39. Next to the Fire	294
Chapter 40. Prasad	296
Chapter 41. The Reward	312
Chapter 42. Ayurveda	314
Chapter 43. Love	330
Chapter 44. Chocolate	332
Part 3: The Return Home	
Chapter 45. Homecoming	347
Chapter 46. These Shadows	350
Chapter 47. Be Artists	367
Afterword: Reintegration	370
Bibliography	378
About the Author	379

Preface

THE SEARCH FOR THE SOURCE

Surfers talk about chasing the stoke, an elusive but present force that gifts profound meaning and inner fire. When that passion is ignited, its presence is raw and undeniable. The insignificant noise goes silent, and the breath comes easily. There is satisfaction facing something with teeth. Something unknown and dangerous. Something you have to respect and that humbles. Maybe the stoke is another dimension, or something the mysterious ones dole out when we're open for it. Regardless of how it shows up, my life lost the stoke.

Each of us, at a moment in time, go through what is colloquially known as a crisis. We get our turn at bat where an unknown circumstance submerges with such force that we doubt our stable, well-regulated life. The wheel of emotions spin off axis in these times, and we question God. The nostalgia of easier days and hope for a better future loom. But these crises also bring truthful vitality to the moment. An opportunity to feel extremely alive, ready to drink from that source where potency flows unrestrained. My crisis eventually came, but yellow flags had cautioned for a while. They hit in quieter moods, like traffic, or alone at a bar. Sometimes seated at my altar in meditation and other times in bed with a woman I wished wasn't there. A rot-gut cocktail of boredom and desperation served neat. The truth is, the juice had dried up awhile back and I was merely existing, coloring inside the lines. But I sensed I wasn't alone.

The mortality rate for men in U.S. society is six times higher than that of women. Men kill themselves at a rate that is nearly four times more than women. White men between the ages of forty-five and fifty-four kill themselves more than any other group. It's a strange paradox that among those who earn the most money and enjoy the most privileges is a hidden hopelessness. Although cultural beliefs whisper that a midlife crisis comes for each of us, maybe it's more accurately a concealed gift to recalibrate the soul. A shake-up from a deep slumber that somehow convinces us that a lackluster existence is acceptable. When my career unexpectedly ended, security—and a woman I loved—crumbled with it. I was called back to the trail into the unknown. The last of my belongings sold, I sat on the cold hardwood floor of my condo, staring at its naked walls. I bought the damn thing only fourteen months earlier with the intention to root, yet here I was at forty, single, alone, and without any sense of my future. Most men define themselves, at least in part, by what they do. A title, a role, an emblem of one's contribution and significance. Who was I now?

Despite an overabundance of schooling and credentialing, and even a successful stint in the military, my unknown validation was hiding somewhere in the Orient. Although a novice, hobbyist martial artist at best, the tentacles of naive boyhood fantasies and images of training with enlightened masters in the jungle still clung to my soul even at forty. More truthfully, I needed a challenge; a shove into unknown frontiers that required body and mind commitment. I needed a gut check to see if I still had grit. What masculine currency did I hold, and how much of it mattered? Was I capable of confronting certain tests; the truthful kind that discomfort and push the soul past its edge?

I didn't buy into the admonishment that masculinity was toxic, but I was sympathetic that some men were barely existing and subsequently acting out. I reflected on the hard-edged alpha wolves from the military and other circles I witnessed, their impenetrable armor that kept most conversations to sports and sexual conquest. I considered the androgynous café philosophers at the university where I worked, parading around campus in skinny jeans and tweed suits, activist stickers adorned to their expensive laptops and electric vehicles. There was something about both camps I didn't trust. The voices of women I respected reverberated; an admonishing chorus of the man-boys in their lives. Men who were emotionally unavailable. Men who played videogames and hid in their man caves. Men they were raising. *Comfortable men don't grow.* I took stock of the message as it intercepted one of my evening meditations. Then I concluded that I was among the guilty. Something sacred fell out of my satchel as I ascended the career ladder. A necessary fire was extinguished. So my crisis told me it was time to get uncomfortable and go find the matches.

The Search for the Source

A week before everything unexpectedly crashed at work, my new passport arrived. I flexed its spine and sniffed its unmarked pages, reminiscing of backpacker escapades and the days of stoke. Old ghosts of my past. Strangely, about six months earlier, I sipped coffee in my palatial university office and researched martial art camps in Thailand. I went online and looked at backpacks just for the hell of it. Then images of the Himalayas, where colorful prayer flags encircled high summits. These became part of a mysterious ritual. My soul had already left. I sensed Joseph Campbell smiling from above. Indeed, the divine sends messages.

> God is the same everywhere. It is men who make him different.[1]
>
> —Tat Wale Baba

It is not my place to tell others what to believe or worship. A path to the holy is a most personal one. But I do hold that a path is needed, nonetheless. Going through the complex highs and lows of a lifetime without some form of spiritual anchor is a guarantee for suffering. Suffering in the hardest ways. Suffering in that there is no counter explanation or awareness into the significance of the hardships that arise. To make sense of it all, and by doing so, to feel less fearful by what unfolds. To come through the experience changed, with newfound wisdom. Maybe even faith. As Brazilian Jiu Jitsu legend and wise man Rickson Gracie states, "If you don't have a spiritual connection, you can't dance on the razor's edge."

My father is a lifelong seeker who began his spiritual quest in the Catholic tradition. He followed this path from primary school through college at St. Mary's. While in college, the turbulent 1960s sent shockwaves through different parts of the country, but it was California's Bay Area, where my parents were raised, that received a hefty dose of the medicine. It was in those parts that concentrated elixirs were divvied up and expressed through activist and artistic expression. Psychedelics flirted specks of other realities, while bands like the Grateful Dead and Jefferson Airplane served in shamanic capacity to awaken groups of young people eager to turn on and open.

---

1 V. Daczynski, *Tat Wale Baba: Rishi of the Himalayas* (Yogi Vince Books, 2022).

It became a mystical oasis, prompting droves of seekers west to find their tribe. Old structures collapsed, while new ones were erected. The buzz to plug into the Source and feed off its magic was realized. It was the same energy; this sense of a reality beyond reality that led my parents to transcendental meditation, and eventually, to its commune in the Midwest where I was raised.

Consideration that a divine force exists can change one's relationship to the events that unfold in their lifetime. Instead of feeling like a victim, hardships become teachable moments. Meditation is one medium to take time away, to unplug from the chaotic circus of daily living and re-center. It's through this place of stillness that wiser voices come through. If we go there often enough, profound insights awaken, and peace becomes available. At the very least, it lessens the grip of the matrix and all the crazy shit that lands on our plate.

The story line of our lives is just like the Fool of the tarot. While undergoing a *hero's journey,* the Fool confronts a series of tests in pursuit of knowledge and liberation. The lifechanging moments show up as heartbreak, illness, or loss of name and status. The tarot is a framework and curriculum from the ancient ones that speaks to the necessary challenges imposed by the journey. Our interior gets rattled, while the parts of ourselves that no longer serve our development are stripped away so that better parts emerge. We have to get dirty on the journey. We have to come face to face with the things that scare us, and our poisonous patterns, otherwise the pearls of authentic transformation aren't delivered. It's the humbled soul that listens.

For those who believe in the existence of the Source, pursuing it becomes a lifelong mission. The people who cross our lives, as in the tarot, come bearing messages. They serve as teachers and as mirrors. There are no coincidences. Even death loses its power since the soul has been progressively dying and being reborn all along. For those lucky enough to hear the music of the divine symphony, to see the mosaic on the serpent's scales, suffering lessens. The dark forest becomes just as significant as the astral light. The gods and demons take tea together.

I have been on the Search for as long as I can remember. The meditation, the vast interest in world religions and mysticism, nature, alone time, and more recently, the martial arts. All represent different strands that plug me in. The wanderings through foreign lands and the palpable obsession for experiences, especially dangerous and sexual ones, were part of my schooling. If a person is born this way, or if they stumble upon the destiny to explore these roads, there is no other choice but to go forward. To live a life devoid of this pursuit will render a soul impotent. I believe wholeheartedly in the Source. This is my story, chasing it.

Part 1

The Ordinary World

The Hero's Journey

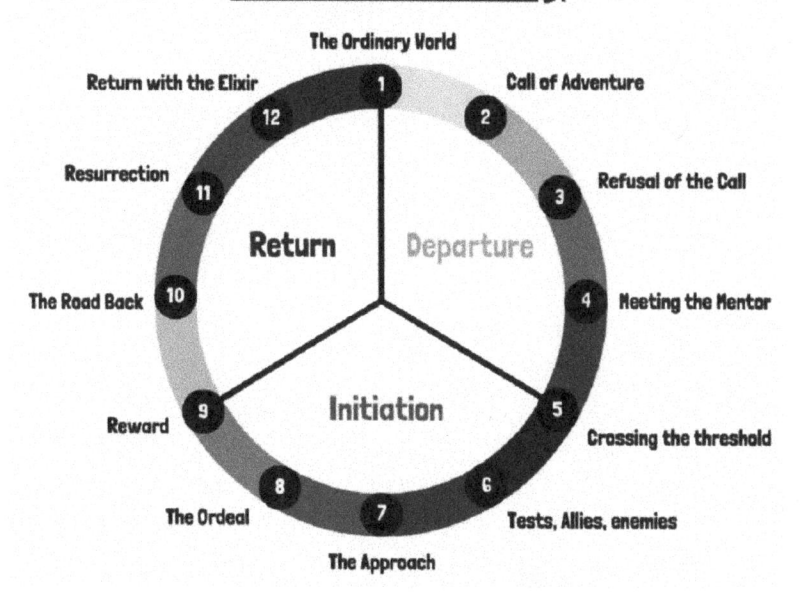

- 1. The Ordinary World
- 2. Call of Adventure
- 3. Refusal of the Call
- 4. Meeting the Mentor
- 5. Crossing the threshold
- 6. Tests, Allies, enemies
- 7. The Approach
- 8. The Ordeal
- 9. Reward
- 10. The Road Back
- 11. Resurrection
- 12. Return with the Elixir

Departure / Initiation / Return

A decline in courage may be the most striking feature that an outside observer notices in the West today. The Western world has lost its civic courage ... Such a decline in courage is particularly noticeable among the ruling and intellectual elite, causing an impression of a loss of courage by the entire society.

—Aleksandr I. Solzhenitsyn[2]

---

2 A. Solzhenitsyn, "A World Split Apart," *Solzhenitsyn's Commencement Address Harvard University.* June 8, 1978.

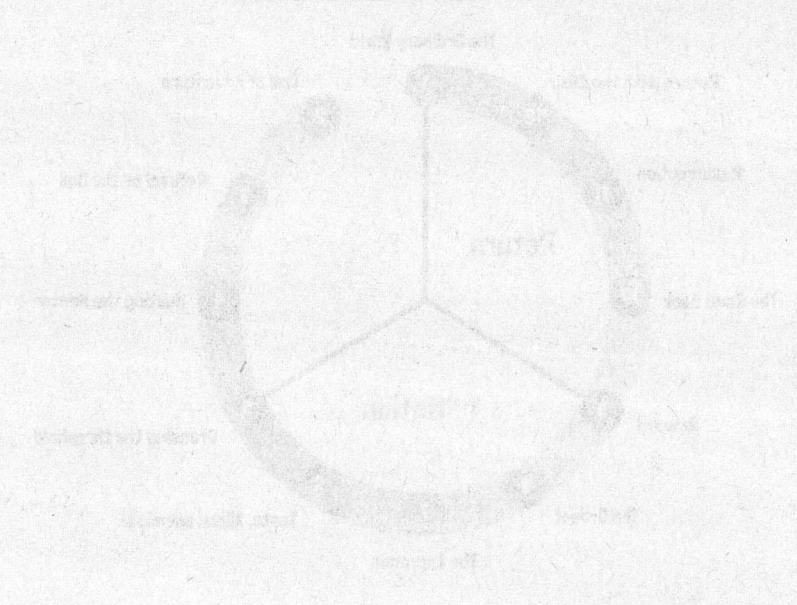

Chapter 1
THE UPGRADE

April 2019, Missouri

"Over here, sir." The slight handwave motioned me toward a sterile brown counter, as I removed my gold Ray Bans.
"Well, aren't you a tall drink of water. Where you flying to, hon?" The voice was warm and accented.
"That's a good question," I answered as I grinned.
"Well, let me rephrase that. Where you flyin' *today*?"
I pulled my passport from my back pocket. His manicured and pointy fingers typed quickly; his nails looked after professionally.
"Mm hmm. There you are. Ooh ... San Francisco. One of my favorite places on this whole earth. They say the locals don't like it though when people call it 'Frisco or San Fran." His blue eyes pierced through thick black lashes.
"Yeah, I heard that too. But a lot of those people pay five dollars for a cup of coffee."
A hearty chuckle came from the well-groomed agent, as his slender but athletic body shook side to side like a jovial Jamaican woman I once met at a homeless shelter.
"Well, five dollars is a *cheap* cup of coffee 'round here."
Behind, the airport queue was surprisingly sparse. A young Asian couple texted, while a tall regal man about sixty with a full head of silver hair and expensive satchel waited his turn. There were two other agents hurriedly putting people through the tedious process of air travel.
"Your ticket is one way, sir. A California boy?"
"Another good question. Was born there and lived most my life there," my words trailing.

"But ..." he interrupted.

"But life put me in other places. Sort of homeless now. Or a man wandering without a home I guess is more what it is."

His fingers returned to the keyboard and more typing. He looked at the lone bag on the scale and asked if I had any flammables, weapons, or narcotics. Those were all left at my father's house in Iowa. The bag weighed just over twelve pounds. About 90 percent of everything I owned.

"Ooh. A vagabond. I bet those dimples get you a free spot on a couch, though, or maybe even a bed."

He was fishing.

"The accent. That doesn't sound Midwest," I said.

"Oh no. Not local. Sort of a wandering gypsy, like yourself."

"Wandering from?"

"Alabama. Well, born in Kentucky but raised in Alabama, so that's what I claim. But I like it here much better. It's not *California* mind you, but it suits me just fine. For now, anyway."

He began again, but his eye wandered hurriedly to the right as he leaned closer.

"You see that man over there in that hideous black suit? The one that looks like a mall security guard?" He motioned cautiously toward a short balding man with a trimmed goatee and gut that suspended his tie several inches above his navel.

"That's my boss, and he's a ... well, pardon the curt tongue, but he's kind of an asshole, frankly. Do me a favor and get a bit animated."

"Animated?"

"Like talk with your hands and act a bit frustrated. But not too much that it draws security over. We're supposed to have folks ticketed and through in under three minutes. It's one of our *strategic priorities* this year," he said, rolling his eyes.

I smirked and spoke gibberish; my hands arced circularly, as they often did when giving lectures.

"What is taking you to Frisco, or to the City by the Bay or whatever it is? With all those crazy homeless, it needs a new name, like ..."

"It's actually just a stopover," I interjected. "I'm headed overseas. I have family up north, and a few old haunts to visit."

"Overseas?" he asked quizzically. "It sounds so serious the way you say it. Are you some kind of diplomat? An agent, or a spy? I guess with all those tattoos you're not a diplomat. And those broad shoulders and arms, maybe CIA or something."

The Upgrade

"Or something ..." I repeated. "Hold on, let me shut this off," I said, turning off an invisible mic on the lapel of my black Under Armour polo.

"What's taking you there and for how long? And where to? Oh my gosh, questions questions!"

He wasn't hiding his excitement.

I knew this question, or ones like it, would become a regular part of life in this new reality. There's a certain level of worth affixed to profession. Just a few months earlier, I was among the prestigious academic ranks of high social nobility. And now? A lowly unemployed bum with most of his life's belongings stuffed into a Patagonia duffel sack. Size medium, no less. I considered the self-employed or temporarily retired rap for my story, but another part was disconnected from that noise. I would take each moment as it came and maybe the truthful answer of what was happening would reveal itself. In its purest form, I had recently died and had more dying to do.

"I lost my job. Well, I didn't really lose it. I was fired."

"Fired?" he said. The typing paused.

"Oh, you poor dear."

"Well, technically, they're going in a 'new direction' and after eight years my services were no longer part of that direction. Long story. Lots of drama. Even some local news for the public gossip mill."

Then nodding left toward the mall security guard, I added, "And quite a few assholes."

"Mm hmm." He nodded back, confirming a story all too familiar.

"Well, anyway. I sold everything I own. Just about everything I own. Decided it's time to travel, trek, study martial arts, and just ... wander. Southeast Asia. Thailand to start, then Vietnam, then who knows. Make it up as I go along."

"Oh, my goodness!" he gasped, clapping his pristine hands together. "And you're serious. I mean, you're really doing this?"

"Getting rid of my cell phone, too." I nodded. "Actually, going to forget it in the bathroom before I fly out."

"You're joking?" he asked incredulously.

"Fresh beginning. Or maybe it's already begun, and this is just another chapter and a more exciting one," I waxed philosophically.

"I would personally die without my phone. But seriously, this is just great. I must put well over two hundred people through this line every day and most of them have this look."

"Look?" I asked.

A Ronin's Tale

"Hold on ..."

Scanning behind there were no more travelers in the queue. The other agents eyeballed their phones, lost in the cyber abyss of texting and most likely fantasies of happier circumstance. I've flown in many airports across the globe. Even as a child there was an excitement walking through the electric doors, getting blasted by the artificial lights. Overpriced food and beverages and the aggressive angst of others didn't sink those feelings. Airports ultimately meant freedom. They were symbolic of awaiting adventure.

"There's this look I see on most people. It's a look of ..." he moved his right hand and snapped.

"Hypnosis? Defeat?" I offered.

"Sort of. It's a look, almost as if this is all there is. Yeah, that's it. It's a look of, 'I'm not happy or fulfilled or even content, but I've accepted that's just the way it is.' It's a look of ... *accepted hopelessness.*"

The stout man with the goatee and clipboard circled closer to the desk and was within earshot. He clumsily pulled papers from his binder and shuffled them.

"I appreciate the assistance, and sorry about that confusion. Ever since Iraq I have difficulty with ..." My words trailed off as the supervisor lapped clockwise and away.

"You're terrible. I probably should let you go, or we might end up chatting 'till you miss your flight. Well, Mr. Osborne ..."

"Actually, it's *doctor*," I corrected with a dimpled grin, before adding, "But call me Nick."

"Are you a real doctor?"

"No, I just play one on TV. I actually failed high school chemistry. I have a doctorate, though, and worked at a university until ..."

"The new direction."

"Exactly. For the record though, I didn't sleep with any students."

Another chuckle.

"Well, that's good, I guess. And for the record, I barely passed chemistry, too. The arts were more my thing. I should probably get back to the other strategic priorities. Gee whiz, young man, I think I could chat with you longer. On Facebook?"

"No." I laughed.

"I kinda figured, but thought I'd ask. Well, may your adventure be a good one," he added, returning my passport.

"I have a feeling it will be. Maybe it really is a beginning."

"Or maybe ..." he paused thoughtfully. "Maybe it's a reward. Like good karma in the bank that you get to withdraw and start spending."

I meditated on his words for a moment.

"I like that."

"Here is your ticket, good doctor. I see you're not part of our frequent flyer program, but I've upgraded you anyway. A lot of empties on your flight to Typhoid Town. I'm James, by the way. Most people call me Jimmy, but I'm James here."

I offered my hand and Jimmy returned a strong grip with solid eye contact. A product of the South, for sure. We nodded to each other, reveling on a subtle joke the universe tells those receptive enough to listen. It was the start of something. It was April 2019 in Kansas City International Airport, and the first time I'd ever flown first class.

Chapter 2

Toward the Heroic

August 2017, A Classroom in the Midwest

Welcome to campus. I created this course specifically for student veterans transitioning to the university. Many students I worked with over the years confided that they didn't relate well to being in a First Year Experience course with a bunch of eighteen-year-olds. Therefore, this class is only for veterans. In this course, we will delve into principles and insights that come from what are known as "wisdom traditions." Wisdom traditions center on the development of our inner self. The things we don't typically reveal outside to the world but that have a profound impact on us.

Why is this important? During your time at the university you will be immersed in empirical, or what is known as rational knowledge. Things you memorize, things you test and conduct experiments on. This is, of course, a fundamental part of college. However, in addition to scientific inquiry, it is also important that we consider this other elusive knowledge that is tied to our happiness and health. If we think about our society in the United States, there are many great things here, like a high standard of living, freedom, and opportunities. But there is chaos, too, yeah? We have significant rates of depression, anxiety, and feelings of loneliness as reported by different polls. As a culture, we work more and sleep less. Stress and stress-related illnesses are growing, as is our addiction to technology and different substances. Pharmaceutical use is big business here, as more people become medicated in an effort to find peace. So, when we take all this into consideration, wisdom traditions might caution that in spite of our prosperity and power, there is a significant deficit here that diminishes our quality of life. How each *of us navigates and moves through this duality varies, but each of us has to deal with it in some capacity no matter what.*

To help us along, we're going to learn about one of my personal heroes, Joseph Campbell. Mr. Campbell was a scholar of world religions and mythology. He argued that among all major religions, and even among the spiritual beliefs of lesser known "primitive societies" are stories that are similar in nature. At the heart of these tales is a Hero who embarks on an important life-changing journey. He undergoes a systematic process of transformation, as he advances through its various stages. The journey is not an easy one, and it pushes the Hero to his breaking point, only to culminate with him symbolically dying so that he is reborn more powerfully upon completing his mission. The Hero's Journey is a metaphorical system of our lives and of the human condition, such as how we negotiate a myriad of experiences, confront fear and tragedy, while finding meaning and a stronger inner self from the process. Through the path of adventure comes profound self-discovery. It is a popular structure, found in many pieces of literature and film. George Lucas, for instance, was a fan of Campbell and based his famed **Star Wars** trilogy on his work. Perhaps it is not by accident that so many popular films portray the hero's journey: Rocky, Indiana Jones, *the* Hunger Games, *and on and on.* For us, we're going to dissect it through The Karate Kid.[3] It should also be emphasized that the Hero is not exclusively male, nor is he bound to a specific culture or era.

---

3   *The Karate Kid*, Columbia Pictures, June 22, 1984.

Chapter 3

Unfamiliar Soil

The Beginning

> The very basic core of a man's living spirit is his passion for adventure.[4]
> —Christopher McCandless

A spiritual walkabout or pilgrimage is not a new concept. For thousands of years, seekers have journeyed to significant places for healing, perspective, or as a symbol of devotion. The first portal that opened and teased what the adventurous path looked like came from a dingy warehouse of all places. It was the beginning. The market was my first real job aside from cutting lawns in the neighborhood. I lied and said I was sixteen, and after changing my birth date by a year, the portly manager with the sparkling eyes passed me a green apron. The cavernous tin warehouse shook like a quake when trains rolled by, the tracks adjacent to the parking lot. I didn't know what whole foods were in the nineties, but the foreign smells and wares piqued curiosity. Large vats of olive oil hung off rusted crooked shelves next to loaves of focaccia bread. Dusty sacks of rice and mung lentils with Hindi script were stacked in a corner like military sandbags next to yellow jars of ghee. The real aromatic pitch came from the loose herbs. Customers scooped the mysterious goods into tiny plastic baggies, then wrote the bin numbers on little circle stickers so they could be weighed. Turmeric, coriander, cumin, and lavender. Sometimes a Townie friend stopped by.

---

[4] J. Krakauer, *Into the Wild* (Anchor Books, 1997).

They'd plug their nose and gasp, asking how I could work in such a place. They didn't see it as I saw it. A perfumed otherworld. A peephole into something vast and beyond our midwestern town of nine thousand. Vito the owner was a tall, lanky fellow from Italy. Lengthy black hairs protruded from his oversized nostrils. Like my parents, meditation and a quest for enlightenment drew him to the small town. His much younger girlfriend, his mistress at one point, was in my father's class years earlier. My breathing changed around her, and I'd sometimes hold a box in front of my green apron to conceal my pulsating erections.

"Nico, over here." Vito waved toward the produce.

"Nico, I want you to sweep and mop over this monstrosity. Then organize the fruits and veggies so they are colorful. I want them *colorful*, you know, *happy*."

He stood with pinched fingers in the air as if giving a sermon from a lectern.

"I want the customer to see this color and to see this vibrancy and to feel happy. Okay?"

A surge of heat rose into my throat and neck being summoned by the boss. Then he tapped me on the shoulder and told me I was a good employee before placing pints of ice cream into a khaki-colored canvas bag. His girlfriend met him at the register where he opened both tills and placed handfuls of cash into his pocket before walking away, hand in hand with my crush. On some afternoons, his nephew, Alonzo, who had recently moved to town and didn't speak a word of English, watched us as a quasi-manager. We nicknamed him the Lion because of his long flowing mane. His shirts, with yellow pit stains, were at least a size too small with different colored paint smatterings on them.

"He is one of those *artist types*, you know, Nico. He will starve," Vito confided as I inserted medjool dates into little baggies.

The Lion's sleeves clung tightly to his somewhat muscular arms where a red heart tattoo with an arrow going through it sat prominently. He flirted with all women, from twelve to those hunched over with a cane. He provided hours of entertainment to my posse who also worked at the market. Sometimes the Lion came in with a black eye. A souvenir from a Townie. While weighing dried fruit near the office door, I listened intently as Vito admonished him in Italian. The feverish exchange often ended with one of them storming out and shouting the last word, throwing whatever was in reach.

Vito was the first person in town to have foreign films. A hodgepodge of VHS tapes scattered on a wall without any semblance of order. They were from all over, but mostly Europe. Sex-starved women from the meditation commune avoided eyes as they sheepishly placed their film jackets onto the counter with their little baggies of herbs on top. I watched a few of those films, taken back by the frontal male nudity and realistic sex scenes. They didn't have special effects, but there was a truthfulness of the emotional highs and lows of the human condition in them. And scenery. Landscapes that whispered that there was a world out there, a mysterious and exciting one filled with passion. And it called.

You pay attention to your surroundings on unfamiliar soil. You carry yourself a certain way to detract unwanted attention. Oversold and cramped minibuses teach patience. Septic rooms with bed bugs slow things, forcing you into the moment. The road bestows a responsibility to find peace with yourself. It demands it, actually. If you trek long enough, mysteries unfold. People show up for a reason. You step on the wrong boat only to meet a companion for a nonattached fling. Most of my travels over two decades were alone. There is a tribe who understand what it means to venture faraway with few belongings. Most do not understand it, though. For them, such an undertaking is irresponsible or too lonely to fathom. Some venerate the road with naïve romanticism. Exotic sites, free of congestion. A perfect selfie spot for Facebook. But they don't understand the dues. They don't consider warm diarrhea on a squat toilet without paper or rolling into a seedy jungle town run by Narcos.

Southeast Asia is a good place to start and where I lost my vagabond virginity. It's a colorful playground with blurry undefined lines, a forest primed well for the Wild Man to roam. The Wild Man is that primordial beast that lives inside all men. He feels something profound in nature, his spirit lifted by smells of fire smoke and pine. He relishes going without a wash or shave, the grime under his nails, markings of pride. At times he reveals himself fiercely from the murky depths, having no issue telling us when we're giving into fear, taking the easy route, or being weak. The Wild Man reminds us of the special need for guy time. To be challenged regularly, and to rise beyond self-pity. He incarnated long before political correctness and victim culture. Although not a barbarian by any means, or even violent, he is unapologetic in his rawness, directed toward having a mission and possessed by purpose and experiences. He calls bullshit when the intellect tries to calm or outwit him. And he likes to explore, especially where sex and danger lurk. He is a teacher that guides us on the Search. A shapeshifter found in all cultures. If a man has never met his Wild Man, his existence is likely impotent.

I first met the Wild Man when I left high school at sixteen, but it was a couple years later in Bangkok that he began to show me things. Iced buckets of Chang beer flowed freely next to obnoxiously loud clubs. Nearby, darkened alleys pushed ecstasy tabs from the Golden Triangle up north. Thousands of intrepid searchers wearing backpacks meandered through the carnival streets, as a man with a food cart sold skewers of scorpions and jungle bugs. Voices called from all directions merging into a single pulse. The scene psychedelic, with temptations and vices for everyone. And women. Lots of them. Women of different shapes and colors, with different dialects and hairstyles. Some with tattoos. Some even with cocks and balls. Notorious as the sex tourist mecca, an estimated 150,000 workers make their living turning tricks in a nation devoutly Buddhist. Hookers in miniskirts flash sultry smiles and broken English to passerby lurkers on the same block as monks in bright saffron robes. The vampires come out at night.

At twenty-four I got my ticket to the underbelly with my closest friend, Troy. It was my first international excursion, in a tight middle seat. Troy had already popped his cherry on a study abroad to South America, divulging tales of fiery Latin women and evading Colombian kidnappers. I had student loans and was preparing to move west for graduate school. The money should have gone toward more sensible things. But I needed this trip. There were parts of the world that drew me, the force of the pull inexplicable. As a boy, we meditated each morning at my alternative school in the commune. After meditation I spun a globe during free time. My finger traced over the scratchy blue-and-green surface, stopping on various countries. The Orient called more than the others.

The third-class hot box arrived just as shallow rays broke the darkness. We'd left Malaysia nearly a full day earlier, a narrow wooden bench the only available seats on the Bangkok-bound train. Quarter-a-piece beers and the prospect of loose vixens and mischief soothed our numb asses. Older women with wrapped faces pushed broomsticks through the battered open windows. Small baggies of noodles and dried fish dangled from their hooks. The intense temperature mixed with industrial pollution created a hazy mist that lingered in the throat. Smells of sweet incense wafted above sacred shrines next to piles of decaying meat and garbage. Scooters whizzed by through symphonies of horns, sometimes with entire families on board, a mother sideways, an infant clutched to her chest. Not wasting any time, we decided to hunt for contraband from a smiley Tuk Tuk driver our first evening in the infamous Khaosan backpacker's ghetto. The motorized auto rickshaws found throughout Asia are notorious con artists known for inflated prices and calculated hustles. But they also hold court for obtaining most things illegal.

******

"Alright, so we're in a jeep, and right out there is the ocean," I said, pointing into the black.

"North or south?" Troy asked.

"South. Maybe San Diego, or somewhere in LA."

"Hmm. Okay."

"You see it, yet?" I asked, somewhat impatiently.

"Hold on." Troy looked outside his grimy window into the shadowy night, then let out a loud fart which made us laugh hysterically.

"Did you hear the Lion got punched by some dude from Van Buren?" I asked.

"I kinda figured something went down ..." Troy said. Then he paused and added excitedly, "I'm coming on. It's creeping, but I'm definitely feeling it."

More giggles filled the cab of his silver Beretta. A slight paranoia crept in though, prompting me to look behind, then scan the front again. It was still just blackness.

"Yeah, I feel it," Troy said.

"This is awesome, man. It's like it's right out there. It's just calling to us, you know?"

Troy turned toward me, his usual soft eyes replaced by a raw wildness. If an older version of ourselves swept into the cab to confide the adventures ahead—the women, the treks around the world, the near-death and jail experiences—our jaws would have dropped. But at sixteen, we swam in more innocent waters, protected in the womb of a random Iowa alley, though cognizant that something more expansive was seated there beside us.

"We need music. How about some Tom Petty, or *black hole sun*?"

Troy fumbled through his glovebox and retrieved a tape. We were about to paddle out.

Unfamiliar Soil

I discovered marijuana my sophomore year in high school. Well, technically that's when I started smoking it. I knew about it years earlier since my extended family grew for decades in California. During one particular visit to Mendo, a cousin prepared a nondescript ride for Hollywood to hook up the film industry elite, while my uncle supervised and dropped trade secrets.

"*Always* wash your car as soon as you hit pavement. A dusty one screams grower. And make sure all your lights and signals work."

Most of their vehicles smelled like coffee grinds and patchouli oil. As things legalized, other clusters of relatives got into the trade. Weed and I matured together. I watched it move from an underground culture of guerrilla growers to boutique dispensaries describing their offerings as "heady and relaxing, with hints of citrus and floral." I was drawn to the mysterious green tobacco when my older cousins smoked it in the woods at the holidays. They were doing something wayward, but that was the appeal. Eventually I was entrusted into their circle, and stories leaked. The helicopters that hovered above the yurt at night were narcs. Around harvest season, gangs from cities down south drifted upward and broke into homes, beating zip-tied growers and taking their crops. Sightings of shady figures were spoken in serious tones by the adults. A rumor that one-percenter biker clubs buried bodies for a fee was told more than once. My grandfather, a quiet man that never cursed or spoke ill of others, confided that people disappeared up north.

One summer marijuana just kind of appeared at a party in the cornfield. By fall, I bought my first eighth. Dressed in a dark hoodie, I met Will at a park three blocks from my house. He was bunked on acid, giggling on a swing set. I heard him first, then made out the silhouette as my eyes adjusted to the darkness. He'd put on weight since I'd seen him last, and as I moved closer I spotted his goatee.

"Hey, man, long time," he said as we slapped hands.

"Yeah, it's good see you," I said, not fully sure of the weed-dealer-consumer etiquette.

A friend of a friend said Will was living about an hour south with his birth father who owned a strip club, but occasionally he'd come to town and was always flush with substances. Someone else said Will was schizophrenic and in and out of different mental hospitals. I reached into my black sweats then handed him twenty-eight dollars which took five hours to earn at the market. I was short two bucks and fumbled through my pocket for change. Will just laughed and gave me a side-shoulder hug. Our older sisters were in the same class.

"No worries, man. Remember, weed should be shared."

"You still wrestling?" I asked.

He slid the baggie over, his dilated eyes fixated intensely. I looked around the onyx parking lot and slid the contents into my hoodie without inspecting it. Dr. Dre's *Chronic* had blown up a couple months earlier. Trucks on oversized rubber drove around the town square, bass vibrating through the windows. Even in the Midwest the streets of Compton were alive. Black culture and all things gangster tsunamied through unexpected places in the early nineties. I was carrying drugs, now. I strutted home with an unfamiliar swagger.

Not long after the park deal, Will ran through the hallways of our high school, screaming incoherently. I was seated in Spanish class when Senora Martinez peeked outside the classroom, then locked the door. A frightened look cascaded over her chipmunk face. Will had been expelled a while ago. I don't know the specifics of that run, but a guttural sound echoed off the pristine white walls near the cabinet with the wrestling and football trophies. Ironically, they were crowns that Will contributed to in a previous existence. After high school, his name came up here and there. I saw him once when I returned to Iowa on military leave. He was a good forty pounds heavier, and he mumbled to himself at the end of the bar, alone. I avoided eyes, but he caught mine. Small talk; incoherent ramblings that didn't make sense, me trying to direct the conversation to something positive like his standout athleticism. The real questions though, the ones about what the hell happened, were never posed. And then a year after that awkward reunion I found out Will died. His sister was working in the hospital when the 911 call went through. My first dealer.

******

Troy and I cooled ourselves under a rickety fan, as a swath of mosquitos circled my sweaty brow. A cocktail of travel weariness and the anticipation of Bangkok's underbelly fueled our rapid heartbeats. Obnoxiously loud music rattled off the thin walls as Khaosan sprung to life just blocks away. I sat on the edge of the bed to put on clean socks, and balanced being in the moment, while another part drifted back home. More memories circled in.

The shabby bucket seats of the Beretta were sticky. The interior smelled like warmed garbage with a dead body underneath, and shit was scattered everywhere. But Troy's boyish good looks and charm assured him a certain latitude, so much so, that his many girlfriends never seemed to complain about rolling in the unholy litter box. We sheepishly grinned at the alley, both of us feeling the anticipation of what was to happen. I pulled out a pinch of Will's sacrament, and our grins widened. We didn't know how to roll joints, so I steadied the green substance on top of a soda can with a hole punched in the side. The makeshift pipe, another nugget gleaned from my grower family, was crude but got the job done. These alley missions, as we called them, sometimes produced a shared hallucination. Instead of Iowa, we were paddling through the rugged waters of a random California break, surrendering to its ethereal magic. We wasted hours in those alleys, ruminating on the places we would eventually see, sensing the voyages that beckoned. On the Search. A sacred bond forged at sixteen. We talked about Thailand. And eight years later we landed.

The Tuk Tuk driver had tracks on his arms and pockmarked skin. The local methamphetamine, *yaba*, is a favored drug among the three-wheeling pirates. A cigarette dangled from his blackened teeth, and most of the smoke exited his nostrils. On his dash, a golden Buddha figurine sat prominently atop a lotus, watching us.

"You want girl, sexy massage, sucky-fucky? I know good place," he said.

Before we answered, his script continued.

"Gemstones? I get you good price. Take home, sell, make money … no problem, I take you now."

We settled into the cramped plastic bench seat of the Tuk Tuk, then directed the driver toward one of the many tourist temples, unsure of our plan. We were in a young man's paradise, though not completely immune to its consequences. A week earlier, we watched a team of undercover Malaysian police officers spring out of the shadows and beat a man close to his death. He had drugs in his backpack. The officer that approached us afterward unemotionally stated the man would be hanged. A simple possession in this part of the world could forever change our lives. But we didn't give a shit. The consequences didn't register. Our senior year in high school, a small mob of us streaked our town's grocery store. Not long after, Troy and I outran several cops as we scurried across the gazebo of our town's main square during a festival with our cocks and balls flapping in the humid breeze. Before the Internet made deviance accessible, we cooked up hydrochloric acid bombs from the scratched recipe book of our friend's older brother and put them in mailboxes. Then we'd drive by bars and spray overly served factory workers unwinding from the night shift with eggs and water. It was all for a chase, and the prospect of arrest or a beating. Troy and I fused our brotherhood around missions, and here we were in our early twenties still under its hypnotic charms. Troy broke the ice.

"Uh …" he stuttered. He leaned closer to the driver and whispered.

"Can you, uh, get us some herb?"

"HERB?" the driver yelled, excitedly. "HERB? What is HERB? What HERB mean?"

Troy and I looked at each other.

"Uh, can you get us some smoke?" I added delicately, motioning a finger to my mouth.

"SMOKE? Oh … smoke! You want smoke! I sell you five baht each," he said, pulling two cigarettes from a dingy packet resting on his lap. His leathery hands bore distinctive wear wrinkles and light-colored sores.

"No, no. Cannabis, weed, pot, marijuana, ganja …" we continued, our illicit lexicon in bloom.

The driver's foot lifted from the pedal, causing the entire Tuk Tuk to jerk forward. Then his eyes veered off the bright road and stared coldly at us through the rearview mirror.

"GANJA! GANJA! You want GANJA?" he rocked back and forth in his seat, his eyes squinted and fierce.

"ILLEGAL! Cannot have! ILLEGAL!" he repeated.

I stared at the Buddha, rocking on the dash, then looked away.

Troy and I sank further into the uncomfortable bench with its steadfast metal bar pressing firmly into our backs. We opted for silence. Moments later the driver spoke softly.

"Illegal … but can get."

The stifling energy waned, as his shabby blue flip-flop pushed the accelerator earnestly.

I looked over at Troy, who was already looking at me. We were in it now.

"Can we get a joint?" I whispered to the driver.

"Joint?" he replied, his head cocked. "Do not understand."

I picked up one of his cigarettes.

"This much?"

He grunted, then pulled his flip phone from a pocket. I stopped looking at the Buddha altogether.

Unfamiliar Soil

Sweat beads descended slowly down my neck. I wiped my forehead with my wrist. Periodically I sat upward from the seat, my cotton t-shirt peeling off my torso as if opening a grilled cheese sandwich. Quick Thai emanated from the front. Our driver spoke rapidly, "Chi chi chi." Then he nodded. His flip phone snapped closed.

We veered off the heavily trafficked road, the smell of exhaust lessened. Communication ceased entirely, as we approached a quiet side street. Small food stalls with rudimentary lighting silhouetted a dozen Tuk Tuks parked on both sides of the road. A collection of fifteen to twenty people, all Thai, sat on short plastic stools eating rice noodles with fetid fish sauce. Metal chopsticks stood erect inside stainless containers in the middle of each table. Our driver turned around for the first time and looked us in the eyes.

"Three hundred baht," he said, motioning to his open hand.

I pulled three crisp notes with the Thai King looking back at me from my wallet, the equivalent of about ten dollars.

"Wait," he commanded.

The driver disappeared. I scanned the street, noting the unblinking sets of eyes fixated on us. About ten minutes passed, though it could have been shorter, when our driver emerged into the light.

"Get out," he said.

Tiny chill bumps clustered around my arm and the back of my neck. A faint premonition of undercover Thai officers exploding off plastic stools with weapons drawn haunted the moment. Throughout my life, intuition saved me from a handful of disasters. The premonition continued. We would be ordered out of the vehicle and harshly put on the diseased street, face first. From there we'd be taken to a local district station and interrogated, and then left in a squalid cell for hours. If lucky, a bribe would be pitched discretely with a moderate percentage gifted to our driver.

We awkwardly dismounted the Tuk Tuk. The driver held something, partially concealed behind his right leg. Through the glare of the streetlight, it gave an appearance that he was missing an arm. Then the driver's arm moved into view, as he motioned to his hand and simultaneously dropped a scrunched napkin onto the ground.

He pointed over his shoulder.

"Khaosan Road there. You walk. Less than ten minutes."

The whir of his Tuk Tuk jarred me to a flinch, as a plume of exhaust dissipated over Troy and I. The hard, unblinking gaze from the tables was surely still there but it was the silence I found most troubling. I walked toward the napkin, that inner voice pleading to leave the area immediately. Technically we were still in the clear. We could keep walking, grab some noodles, and casually head back to Khaosan. Someone from the hostel, a more experienced trekker, would have some ganja or at least knowledge of how to play the game. As incoherent thoughts unraveled, dominos pushed. I stooped down to tie my shoelace, then instinctively touched the napkin with my fingertips. It had a waffled texture. The Wild Man was here. Moving slowly, I rose with the contents and slid the bundle into my pocket while sending a brief prayer to Will. After an extended exhale, we walked in the direction we were shown, unsure of the route to our guesthouse but moving simply to clear away the lingering spirits. My first night in Bangkok.

A year later I would return to Thailand, but on a solo mission. A spontaneous itinerary change ushered me toward Cambodia, through the bustling and septic streets of Phnom Penh where scores of limb-missing beggars sat idle on dilapidated rugs. Bits of story; Easter egg style hunts for lost soccer balls in a jungle riddled with landmines. I eventually meandered to a coastal spot, quieter and remote, where I skinny dipped with a young veterinarian student in rough seas, before having sex with her in a teak guesthouse owned by an alcoholic Frenchman. His ear propped against our door.

Just weeks earlier, I sat in my girlfriend's apartment near Lake Merritt in Oakland. She was in the shower; I was in the living room perched in a contouring leather chair that swiveled, pricing flights to Asia. It was supposed to just be a curious look, but I waited until she was out of the room, and I could hear the water. The evening before, we feasted on a collection of perfectly spiced Indian food at a place in the city that took some effort to get reservations. Afterward, we tasted forty-dollar-a-glass pinots in the Sea Cliff neighborhood for some charity thing she was loosely connected to. An Oscar-winning actor known for his short height and even shorter temper peed next to me at the small gala. We stared hard at each other, not uttering a word as the pinot descended down the pisser. I swiveled in the chair, balancing my wallet on my lap. More spins, pricking open memories of teacup rides at the local fair, just as a congratulatory email for a nonrefundable ticket topped my inbox.

I clicked the email, feeling an expansive energy open my throat and chest, just as Kali walked into the room with a towel wrapped around her smooth dark-skinned waist. A steaming coffee in hand and another white towel snaked around her head accentuated her goddess features. Her oval brown eyes gave a cagey look, then pierced. The relationship had finished a while ago, or perhaps it never really started. But now that truth was sealed. My Wild Man, unable or unwilling to return to his cage, trumped both of us. I wanted to express it; to share it with her and try to make sense that this invisible presence was pulling me, but instead, I simply looked back and nodded slowly. Moments later, her steaming mug with the crest of her women's college embroidered in the middle breezed by my head and shattered against the wall. The invisible teachers were summoning me.

Chapter 4
INVISIBLE TEACHERS

August 2017, A Classroom in the Midwest

There is something about the hero's journey I want us to consider because it's a fundamental theme that appears often and with great significance. And, you have to humor me here since I grew up in a meditation commune and I have some granola in me. But take a moment, and just consider what I am about to tell you. It doesn't mean you have to believe it.

There is a theme we keep running across that suggests there are forces in play when the Hero is on the journey. Forces that go beyond freewill and choice. For instance, the right person appears out of nowhere and gives direction or delivers a profound message just when the Hero needs it most. Some might call it God or Nature or Synchronicity, while others might just call it coincidence or dumb luck. Regardless of how we think about it, let's agree that there is something there with an invisible presence that makes a powerful contribution to the story. It propels the Hero forward on his quest, but it also reveals the interconnectedness and vast mysteries of the universe.

In The Karate Kid, we see Mr. Miyagi show up after Daniel has endured a series of beatings and bullying. We have seen Mr. Miyagi throughout the film, but he doesn't present as a martial art teacher. He is a simple maintenance man living a humble life. After one particularly brutal attack, Mr. Miyagi intervenes and wipes out a group of Cobra Kai, exhibiting this whole other side of him. The story shifts at this point and he begins to train Daniel in karate. Daniel has been unwittingly called to an adventure through a medium of being bullied, while this invisible presence sends an elderly maintenance man to guide him. In *other words, if we follow this belief, Daniel was destined to have these unfortunate circumstances occur so that he would meet Miyagi. But why? What is behind all of it?*

Let me share a few real-life examples related to these unseen forces. In the 1920s, Joseph Campbell drove his car from New York to California to bum around for a while. He was in a stage in his life where he was rudderless and continued on to Hawaii, following his bliss. On a return boat voyage to California, he met a woman and maintained a long-distance correspondence through letters and postcards. He decided one day to surprise Idell and showed up unannounced at her door. She was delighted to see Campbell and persuaded him to take a road trip to visit her sister and her sister's husband, who was a writer. It turns out that the sister's husband was John Steinbeck, and he hit it off wonderfully with Campbell. Campbell was introduced to many of Steinbeck's friends, including several characters highlighted in Cannery Row. Enjoying his newfound companions and bohemian lifestyle, Campbell stayed in California for a year having all sorts of rich adventures, then returned to New York to work at a prep school for boys. Eventually, the Call surfaced again, and he set off on a new journey. Campbell talked about those days in California as a magical time. He didn't intend to stay there for a year but his friendship with Idell launched him into this unique circle of companions, which further brought deep experiences to him. One could argue that Campbell was a bum during this phase and that he was wasting time that could have been applied to earning money and building a career. But he didn't speak of it that way. The unseen force was at work, and he accepted its guidance knowing that wisdom would come from the process. He trusted it, and that trust to follow one's inner voice and to take solace knowing that the invisible presence will protect is what nurtures the Hero on his journey.

Another story, but this one personal. Fast forward to 2008. I am living in California and I'm a doctoral student working at the Department of Veterans Affairs. About fifteen months earlier, I returned home after nearly a year in the Middle East with the military, so I had some money saved and, like Campbell, I was feeling restless. I decided to backpack for a month and chose a spot in Central America because it's cheap and I heard it's nice. My first day in San Jose, I am weary from the long flight and lack of sleep. It's still morning and if I succumb to fatigue, my entire sleep schedule will be thrown off for a few days. I hand the lady with the gentle face my passport at the guesthouse and then drop my *belongings in my room before wandering outside. It's a ritual I do while traveling, to check in and then walk without any set plan or destination, simply following my instincts. After a solid half hour of sauntering, I come across a park that has a similar vibe as a cemetery. Beyond the aged and rusting steel fence it has rolling hills tucked under a canopy of unfamiliar trees with large green leaves. A symphony of noisy birds welcomed me. The previous evening rain made everything lush and vibrant, the flowers fragrant and projecting something unexplainable and otherworldly. I hear Spanish spoken by different groups and I walk with a strong coffee just taking it all in. I feel drawn to a certain part of the park away from the main area, and I head over there. Do you ever notice that some spots feel better than others? For example, you go to a restaurant and certain seats just feel better than other ones, and you're not sure why? Anyway, I felt that same pull toward this deserted part of the park. As I walked closer, this beautiful woman in her twenties caught my attention. There was something about her, a sensation, like she was familiar in some way, maybe even a face from a dream I once had. Sensing my gaze, she looked up and stared back, giving a smile that just melted me. This blanket of warmth and kindness swept over, and it wasn't a sexual response, but more a recognition of someone I knew and who cared for me. It's wild, right? Here I am in some random park in another country that I just stumbled upon literally hours after landing, and now I am the creepy American tourist obsessing on this beautiful local. But kidding aside, there was something invisible that I sensed in the moment. A force. An inner voice confirmed this is not only happening, but it is supposed to happen.*

The woman rises from the concrete bench and greets me as if she's been waiting for some time. Her smile up close is even more radiant, and her short black hair and clothing, especially the purse she holds, give off a sophisticated style and intuition that she's prosperous.

"Buenas dias, senorita," I begin, "Yo soy Nick. Soy de Estados Unidos," I offer while pointing to myself. It's all I had really; I basically exhausted what I could recall from two years of high school Spanish.

We stand there for several minutes playing the inevitable skit and hand gesture game that accompanies world travel. I'm giddy as if on a date, laughing nervously and still trying to process if this is really happening. Through disjointed communication we laboriously reveal drops to each other and I'm able to make out that she's four years younger than I am and was born and raised in San Jose. She is a student, and hopes to become a dentist, pointing to my braces and smiling that

Invisible Teachers

she likes them. We laugh more and struggle through another ten minutes of conversation, and then she takes my hand and clasps it in hers. We walk through the park, and she speaks softly in Spanish the entire time. She points to different markings that look like old ruins or burial points of some kind, then rolls her eyes when an obnoxious shriek wafts from the tree canopy above.

"Stupid bird. Noisy noisy," she laments.

We exit the park and continue in an unknown direction. Our hands still clasped together while we inch leisurely along the sidewalk. A few times on our walk she turns her head toward me and smiles. We giggle, and I shake my head.

"Food?" she asks.

"Comida?" I nod back. We smile again, and she looks away and mutters something quietly.

They seat us near a large window overlooking the sidewalk. The usual commotion of a busy and vibrant city exists outside, yet there is a deep peace and easiness around me. I think back to my upbringing in the meditation commune, and our guru, Maharishi, responding to a question about what it means to find the right spouse. He says boldly that most people choose the wrong spouse, then he sits quietly with his eyes closed. A minute later he speaks:

"There must be three things for a relationship to be healthy and to work. Deep easiness, deep easiness, deep easiness."

She orders small platters with different kinds of beans and sausage, and it's the first time I have had sweet plantains. Fresh corn tortillas and scrambled eggs come out in regal stainless containers. A wooden contraption sits in the middle of the table with what looks like a giant sock in between it. The sock resembles a stocking you would hang off a mantle, next to a Christmas tree. I point to the mysterious object and make a face at her. She looks past me and points to the sock and rattles to our waiter, who nods. A moment later the waiter returns and places fresh ground beans inside the sock and meticulously pours water from a kettle with a skinny curved spout. Steam rises from the sock. I blow on the medicinal brew.

The food overpowers and settles quickly. I yawn. Then again. After my third one she laughs and says, "Sleepy boy, bed for you."

I rise and take out my wallet, but she quickly moves toward me and places her hand on top of it.

"No. My gift."

We didn't speak much at breakfast, the language barrier too difficult.

A Ronin's Tale

A distant thought from the back row dances around that she might be a prostitute, and I will be hit with a large bill for her companionship. But something rises above those thoughts. I trust what's happening, even though it doesn't make much sense.

At my guesthouse, she presses her lips against mine briefly and then kisses my cheek. We hold a smile for a moment before she leaves. I soon fall fast asleep. Hours later, the communal phone outside my room rings. The guesthouse manager speaks quickly. I think I hear her say my name, or something close to it. Then silence and footsteps. A knock on my door.

"Mr. Nick, are you awake? Mr. Nick, you have a phone call."

I open the door and Mrs. Flores motions me to follow. She's an attractive older woman and gracefully picks up the lime-colored phone dangling on a long, tangled cord. I recall a similar tangled cord lifetimes earlier when my older sister, Becki, spoke to boys in the kitchen.

"Mr. Nick. The woman you met earlier today in the park, Ms. Isabel, would like to speak with you and I will translate."

I nod.

"She says that she enjoyed meeting you today. She says that she had a feeling earlier in the week that she was going to meet a man, a foreigner, and that he would be a good man with spiritual powers. She believes that you are this man. She says that you should go to Puerto Viejo on the Caribbean side."

Mrs. Flores's dark brown eyes look into mine as she turns her head, still cupping the phone to her ear. The motion suggests I should respond.

"Please tell Ms. Isabel that I also enjoyed meeting her, and that I will give her my email so that we can stay in touch."

Mrs. Flores relays the message and then laughs along with Isabel. Isabel's laughter penetrates through the phone.

"Ms. Isabel says that would be nice. She says that she would like to see you again and to also stay in touch."

"Can you please ask her why I am supposed to go to this town?"

After translating, Mrs. Flores shifts away from the wall, turning her back toward me. She speaks in a quieter, hushed, almost concerning tone before repeating, "Si, si, si."

"She does not know if there is someone you are supposed to meet, but she said she feels very strongly that you must go there."

I vaguely recall reading about the town several weeks earlier. The book mentioned a murder of two women who were backpacking nearby

Invisible Teachers

and about the town being a hotspot for narcotrafficking.

"Mrs. Flores, please tell Isabel that I will consider what she said and that I will look forward to speaking again at another time. Bunes noches, senorita," I said.

Mrs. Flores hurriedly finished the conversation with Isabel, and then swung around abruptly as the lime phone clasped into the receiver making an audible pop.

"Mr. Nick?" she began.

I turned and saw her eyes, even darker than just minutes before, staring fervently.

"Mr. Nick, I advise you to not go to Puerto Viejo. It is not a good place for a foreigner to go, especially alone."

"I read about the drug dealers and the ..."

Mrs. Flores immediately waved her hand up and down, shaking her head.

"No, no, no. Not that. They are not the problem. The problem is that there are many brujos and brujas wandering around there. Do you know that term, yes?"

I nodded.

"Witches."

"Yes. It is a place of black magic and lost souls. Powerful people put curses on foreigners, then demand money to release the curse. The curses are real. You are a big man, yes, but it won't keep you safe. You will draw attention to yourself, and you are a kind man who trusts easily. It is better you see the touristy places. This country is very safe, but ..."

My first day in the town, a young American from the East Coast who was on the same bus got caught in a riptide. A few expats wrinkled from the sun and presumably from hard living talked about the dangerous surf over sweating beers. There wasn't much emotion in their voice about the college student whose lifeless corpse was unceremoniously dumped into the back of a golf cart on the beach. Then, a few days after I settled in, a Gringo walked into the guesthouse I was staying at and sat beside me.

"I've seen you around. You look like a veteran," he said, offering his hand.

We shook hands and bullshitted for a bit. I noticed a prominent facial scar, and he casually dropped that he served in Vietnam. His nose looked cancerous from the sun, and he snorted heavily and often, like his sinuses were out of whack. I don't think anything of it until he left *and the woman behind the bar tells me I've met their resident celebrity. Resident celebrity? I ask. Turns out that he was the main figure of a surf book. She adds proudly that High Times magazine was just in town to interview him. All of a sudden it hits. I just met the guy from a book I read more than a decade ago. I was a poor undergraduate living in the mountains of North Carolina. I spent a lot of time reading near a stream outside my studio. The book was an outlaw odyssey about two best friends who were drug smugglers and surfers. One of the main guys, a Vietnam veteran with a facial scar, ended up moving to Central America to surf, but wound up becoming a full-blown drug addict. As it turned out, I was staying at the hostel of another main figure from the book, whom I'd been chatting with unbeknown for several days.*

Is this all coincidence, or dumb luck? I end up having dinner with the veteran, and a few times during the meal he snorts coke off the table right there in this breezeway hut where we hear waves breaking nearby. I asked him questions—what was his transition from Vietnam like? What was it like in a foreign prison? We talked about the sacred bond between best friends, and I remember thinking a lot about my best friend, Troy, when reading the book. We also spoke about how many men are drawn to take risk throughout their lives, even if the consequences are devastating. There is a dichotomy that longs for the completeness of a stable career and healthy relationship, and even a family, perhaps. But there is this other energy, too, that longs for freedom and adventure. To be untethered and wild. There is an element of danger, and even outlaw-ness that seduces certain men, like a witchy woman who is mysterious and beautiful, but will only bring heartache in the end. The tendency to chase these energies can naturally lead to horrible decisions that drive away healthy relationships, get us locked up, or even killed. Here I was, face to face, listening to a shadowy figure that made an impression on me long ago. I recorded something in my journal that he said at dinner.

> It wasn't 'Nam, man. My entire life I chased shit that scared me. Insane fucking waves, flying planes loaded with kilos. I looked it all in the eye, even when it was black and sinister. Maybe because it was black and sinister. It scared me, and that excited me. There was like a wild animal inside. Sometimes I handled it, sometimes I didn't. But it was always there.

Invisible Teachers

During our evening, a few times the man looked sternly into my eyes and mentioned, almost demanded, that I study martial arts. He was incoherent at times, talking about reptilian forces and demonic energies in his town, but he was lucid with the fight talk.

"Listen. You need to study fighting. I can see it in you. I can see it all over you, man. It's like your soul is telling me to tell you this. You need to be a fighter, man. You need to do that training."

I confided that I messed around with different arts when younger and in the military. Ironically, a strong feeling had recently surfaced. It urged me to take it up again, and right before I headed to Central America, I even toured a few dojos. It was strange that in the midst of our conversation he delivered this message.

So, let's bring it all together now. In real life, the hero's journey is seldomly clean. It's messy and complicated, just like our own lives. There's pain, too. When I was with the resident celebrity, I felt that I was in the presence of a truly broken man. A lost soul clinging to an existence that had immeasurable suffering with this strange mix of folk celebrity. The journey is not focused on outcomes as much as it's focused on inner transformation and the cultivation of wisdom. In other words, how one looks at the circumstances of their life as an experience for growth is critical. You get divorced, or you serve time in prison, or you come back from war with emotional scars. Can these be positive experiences in the long run? Or are these fates an imprisonment of constant sorrow? Do we choose to become victims and build an altar to our wounds? Does Daniel accept that being bullied is his unfortunate fate, or does he begin the hard work of transforming himself? If you buy into the belief of the hero's journey, then the force is real. It always reveals things and sends messengers. Always.

Chapter 5

Patterns

April 2019, Bangkok

> The shadow, especially the shadow of death, is the greatest teacher for how to come to the light.[5]
>
> —Ram Dass

A dome of light cascaded above the frenzied skyline, serving as a torch for our descent. Drops from a slight drizzle ran down the fogged oval-shaped window. As we taxied toward the international terminal, smatterings of workers cruised over in miniature flatbed trucks, their colorful lights spinning frantically. They wore bright yellow raincoats and moved efficiently. The stillness inside the cabin waned, as weary travelers began their slow movements back to life. A ping of cell phones chimed through the silence. I yawned audibly, then peeked outside again. Had it really been sixteen years?

I was in my mid-twenties the last time my feet touched Asian soil. It made sense then; do your adventures young because you won't always have the opportunity. Seize it. Yet here I was at forty, under unclear circumstances, trying to sort out my new reality. Somewhere unbeknown to me, the arc of my path veered off the hardtop surface. As I got into my thirties, friends coupled up and settled. Eventually I became the solo bachelor at weddings and work functions, occasionally receiving comments about it. My contemporaries, secure with families and home repair projects, were surfing different waves. Most were

---

[5] R. Dass, *Dealing with Fear*. Accessed from the Ram Dass Foundation on June 3, 2023. www.ramdass.org.

content with dad bods and weekends around the house drinking beer and watching sports. But settling wasn't something I did well. It was different landing in Bangkok at forty, though. It felt less exciting and free. And temptations and opportunities to go dark and completely change the purpose of the journey were everywhere.

Certain parts of the world poke our patterns and temptations with a stick. They offer a place to purge the dark, shadowy energies we pretend are not inside us. They spring to life in these places where the boundaries are fuzzy. Vegas blesses this way, as do the red-light districts of most cities. But a person doesn't have to travel far to see what's inside them. A couple times each semester I met with a ridiculously educated woman, demure but classy in her early sixties, and who was universally respected on campus. She had a maternal wisdom and knack for navigating the university circus and academic turf wars, in which I found myself often tangled. One evening, over too much wine, she confessed that after her divorce she went online for several months and had ravenous casual sex with random men. She held her eye contact as bits of her story leaked, not an ounce of shame or embarrassment noted. Just a matter-of-fact ownership of each word. Each of us holds onto secrets, while we keep our collection of masks dusted and pristine.

Day three in Bangkok, the jet lag wanes as my patterns pop out of the can and dance feverishly. I am back on Khaosan Road. European kids with dreadlocks who look like they haven't eaten or bathed in weeks sit sleepy-eyed and hungover at outside tables. Some nurse big bottle Chang beers. Hustlers guard the corners, whispering their illegal wares while handing out postcards of temples. It's just as stifling as I remember. Stinks, too. I meander toward the end of Khaosan and aimlessly turn the corner without a destination in mind. A few touts approach, but I firmly wave them off. Cheap noodle stalls with steam rising above plastic bowls line the street, along with feral dogs. A stainless container with communal chopsticks anchors a pile of tissue napkins. I smile, recalling the weed mission with Troy. Eventually I'm on a massage block with "no prostitution" signs prominently displayed in the windows. Then I found myself walking through shadier neighborhoods where average-looking women and beautiful women entice morbidly obese and balding Western men. They cajole and flirt, luring like black widows toward the tinted doors of their web.

"Hey you, sexy man. Let me give you sexy massage," an anonymous face bellows.

My entire life I've been drawn to darkened doors. Troy and I walked through a set in Tijuana shortly after high school. Then again, near the Soi Cowboy on our first Thailand run. Scores of half-naked women with numbers affixed to their G-strings like cattle gyrated against poles with phony smiles. Others just stood there with blank expressions, stoned on glue or pills. A sickly sensation washed over each time, exhilaration diluted by potent overtones of melancholy.

Nearby, two pasty middle-aged men with sunburned arms, hoop earrings, and faded tattoos sit with their drinks. One dons a soiled low-cut tank top with a colorful Thai elephant on the front. The elephant a sign of good fortune. The other is shirtless. It's a little after nine in the morning and there's a good chance they haven't been to bed. A sign for cheap Viagra suspends above the cluster of parlors. The rooster crows and I recognize its urgings. I will justify a beer before I start the hard work at the fight camps. An innocent toast to my freedom, and a celebratory drink in honor of the journey. After a few more big bottles, I will rationalize a massage to loosen the limbs and prepare for the hard training ahead. Strictly rejuvenating, I'll tell myself. Then another drink, more colorful this time, with an umbrella in it. And another massage, but this one in a different neighborhood. From there, the Wild Man will run down the mountain with an axe and severed heads in his hand. There's no telling where he will take me or what calamities will unfold. But calamities will unfold, that much I know. I have a bit of money and a lot of free time. The Wild Man's charms and my shadow temptations still cunning, even at forty. I got to get rid of this shit. I ponder the time back home and wonder what D is doing.

I peep again at the European pirates, but study them this time. They plunge deeply into their phones, then onward into the carnivalesque road, occasionally interrupted with pulls of their beers. The ritual repeats, and they don't engage each other. I understand the spell, its seductive grip. Especially with prospects of uncomplicated, nonattached sex all around. I briefly leave Asia for a moment, where I'm seated at my favorite bar. I rest my carabiner of keys on its shiny mahogany counter. The televisions broadcast sports and other things I don't care about, but they're muted, so it creates the right atmosphere for brooding. After a day of too many meetings or managing the sour mood swings of a particularly needy secretary, it was my sanctuary. I became friendly with other regulars, retired academics turned professional drunks. The waitstaff and I traded secrets, and soon I knew who was screwing who. The first drinks went quickly with just a few pulls. Full pint IPAs and stouts, 8 or 9 percent alcohol a piece. The second ones quieted the noise. By the third and fourth, specks of hope materialized. The chest tightness subsided. Optimism hovered. Is this happiness? Maybe I'm unrealistic for what I want, and ungrateful for what I have? How many people really love their lives, anyway? Then the juice took a turn. Out went my phone, and with it, any logical centeredness.

Part of the exhilaration is the hunt. The unknowingness of it all. The wait. The anticipation builds the longer the text sits in silence. More drinks navigate me toward where the sultry fantasies hide. The orgasms more powerful when deviance lingers. The booze whispers its conniving wisdom: I'm sure an ex I fucked over would love to hear from me. Maybe she can text some nudes. Better yet, maybe I can swing by just for a minute. An internal shutoff switch came with most of my relationships. A progression of distancing. Rather than communicate what I felt, the pattern was to just slowly disengage and hope they lost interest. My conscience clear that way. I launched texts from that sparkly mahogany, communications that should have never been sent.

There was an older woman, a professor, who lived close by. I'd watch her from my kitchen three stories high. She'd effortlessly hurl a horse saddle into her cramped Civic on Thursdays. Her long blonde hair and southern accent too much. More than once, I taped a note on her front door but retrieved it before she returned home, and I sobered up. Eventually it was laundry on Memorial Day weekend that we conversed and in short order made plans for a beer. She'd been watching me too. It lasted for some years, fiery passion that took me into the belly of confusing chambers. Longing, yet hands pressed upward for distance. We never defined what was between us. It wasn't given a name even though I loved her painfully. Sometimes I had other women. Sometimes she found out. Sometimes my father visited, and I never introduced her. It was crushing behavior, even cruel at times. I didn't see that mug coming from my Oakland girlfriend, but I deserved it in retrospect. There was a chorus standing behind her.

But what I want to know from these pasty Bangkok pirates, unknowingly studied under the Viagra signs, what I *really* want to know is their pain. Even among those of us who had the good fortune of stable upbringings and loving parents, we carry something. Even among those of us well educated and paid the handsome dollars, we, too, carry something. Each of us under the weight. A cross to bear. A universal truth. So here I am on Khaosan, swimming near the fast current, listening to the voices of men I know as they hurry their kids to baseball practice and stain the porch. Voices that tell me how lucky

A Ronin's Tale

I am, how they wish they could trade places. Every damn one of them mentioning the prostitution. But it's the longing of someone waiting for me at home that lingers feverishly. Crawling into a warm bed with D, intertwined in unabashed union. I ruminate on this as I stare at a mass of signs, glowing electronic neon pussy. The inner voice was much different this time around.

34

Chapter 6
The Call

Fall 2017, A Classroom in the Midwest

It begins in the Ordinary World. The Ordinary World is similar to the daily grind. It's the reality where we just go through the motions on autopilot. We go to work and strategize our next promotion. We hang with friends, maybe we have a love interest. Kids get ushered to school and test boundaries. We go to the gym and see our favorite bands in concert to maintain sanity. Amazon packages arrive and we think about things like vacation destinations, our 401K, and whether or not we'll afford that nicer home in the future. Certain dates on the calendar take on special meaning and are cause for celebration. And of course, we plaster pictures of our great lives on social media, so the world knows how badass we are. But on our nightly walk, or those quiet moments sipping tea in bed, noisy thoughts beckon. We wonder if we're still attractive, sexy, and have "it." We wonder if we are living productive and successful lives. Naturally, we compare ourselves to others, sometimes assuming they have it better or easier. A heaviness looms.

In the Ordinary World, something inside is not fully at peace. Something in our internal world feels off center. A chaotic routine makes it harder to see. Some see their patterns, though; the hardwiring within that reveal limiting thoughts and unhealthy behaviors. Drinking too much, neglecting self-care, mistreating others, flirting with married people. Thoughts arise that things need to be different, and changes need to be made. Then things shake up and the wind changes direction. According to Campbell, the Hero is asleep and must be awakened. He senses something is lost and goes to find it.

A Ronin's Tale

For our **Karate Kid** *hero, Daniel, the Ordinary World was moving from New Jersey to Los Angeles with his mother. His father died when he was young, and he and his mom are working-class poor. The Ordinary World is starting over at a new high school, finding his place to fit in, such as making the soccer team, while also meeting a woman he likes. But he's also dealing with something very real and commonplace. Bullies. And he's not just being bullied by one person. A gang of intensively trained karate practitioners make his life hell. It starts at a beach party his first weekend in town and escalates from there.*

Campbell tells us that the hero's journey begins with the Call to Adventure. The Call happens in a lot of ways. Often times, the Hero is an unwilling participant and doesn't immediately identify that something great is taking place. In other words, he doesn't see that he's on a journey per se or about to start one, and he certainly doesn't see that profound experiences and teachings await him. Do you think Daniel sees wisdom when he gets his ass kicked, or when he's booted off the soccer team? When we're humiliated in our own lives, do we see this as a positive thing? An opportunity for growth? Or do we feel like victims? Do we seek vengeance against our aggressors? Do we retreat to unhealthy patterns?

There are circumstances that transpire in the Hero's life that propel him onto the journey. Again, pay attention to that invisible presence that pulls the puppet strings and moves the chess pieces, so the Hero is called to the Adventure. Remember, there are no coincidences according to Campbell. The occurrences that unfold, the people who enter and exit our lives, both good and bad, come for a purpose. Let's consider what he says:

> The call to adventure signifies that destiny has summoned the hero.
>
> We must be willing to get rid of the life we've planned, so as to have the life that is waiting for us. The old skin has to be shed before the new one can come.
>
> Hell is life drying up.
>
> The hoarder, the one in us that wants to keep, to hold on, must be killed.
>
> Destruction before creation.[6]

---

6   Diane K. Osbon, *Reflections on the Art of Living: A Joseph Campbell Companion* (New York: Harper-Collins, 1991).

Chapter 7

PUT UP YOUR DUKES

April 2019, Chiang Mai, Thailand

> I'm a relatively respectable citizen. Multiple felon perhaps, but certainly not dangerous.[7]
> —Hunter S. Thompson

There is a profound essence in low-budget martial arts films that involve the resurrection of the hero. There is the inevitable beating and humiliation the hero endures, often orchestrated publicly. Only through such shame can he be stripped to his bones; exposed and forced to sift through his layers. This place of uncomfortable stillness nurtures humility and guides the hero toward an introspective interrogation. Most men I know, whether they admit to it or not, sit with the *enough* questions. They grapple and arm wrestle them in their own way: Is my career enough? Do I earn enough? Am I tough enough? Have I slept with enough women? The endless elusive thoughts are supposed to, in some mysterious way, produce a definitive outcome of where one stands. But the internal grilling poignantly stems from a more profound question, perhaps the most truthful one: *Am I worthy of love?* The lifeline of self-love and love of others gets harder to grasp when we fall into a routine, especially one that breeds complacency. The rope cuts and burns, the strands unravel. Eventually all that's left is a scar and a story.

Stumbling home on a Thursday, the mounting career drama and work battles buzzed feverishly. I wasn't sleeping much. Earlier in the

---

[7] H. Thompson, *Fear and Loathing in Las Vegas: A Savage Journey to the Heart of the American Dream* (Warner Books, 1982).

week I was selected for a committee tasked with identifying a new mascot. The previous one, deemed offensive and subsequently banned, created intensive divides within the community. Bumper stickers revealed which tribe one affiliated with. For two hours without pause, venomous musings on patriarchal privilege, cultural appropriation, and whether or not we were inclusive enough permeated the overfilled room. Progress, already moving at a snail's pace, was soon abated entirely by some disgruntled voice. I recognized several in the group. I'd read their colorful quotes in the paper to cancel Halloween, another racist and misogynistic event. One of the louder voices in the bunch decreed that having university law enforcement was creating a police state atmosphere on campus. I sat in silence.

 I struggled back to the apartment, stopping to pee in the shadows of a neighbor's lawn near fragrant lilacs. Leaning the key into the aged wooden door with streaks on its foggy glass, I braced myself against the narrow stairwell and zigzagged upward, my hands steadying along the walls. On each step, I thought of the professor I loved who was presently not speaking to me. Eventually inside my topside cavern, I sank into my new leather sofa. An ominous dread lingered. It wasn't the echoes of the committee moral police, or my secretary who knocked on my office door each morning before I could hang up my coat, but rather, it was a sensation that my life could stay this way indefinitely. Routine. Bland. Lifeless. It didn't matter that I had a respected career or income. Something was sacrificed for it. Something significant extinguished an inexplicable fire. I steeped in the spoil momentarily, then shot-gunned a series of texts. Flirtatious attempts to charm, one after the other, they arced like mortars to the unsuspecting in my little black book. The hooks sat in the miscellaneous ponds with anticipation, though the satisfying chime never came. I checked work email, then placed the phone on the table and stared at it. The solitude deafening, I rose to pee.

 Half a dozen pints applauded, urging me toward the bedroom. With a mash of incoherent thoughts, my hands swam underneath a pyramid of stacked boxes, searching for a hard rectangular case. My fingers soon recognized its scratchy surface and pulled it from the closet. Inside was Duke, my weighty .357 magnum. A six-shot hand cannon. Not quite what Dirty Harry carried, but a tough little brother. I picked Duke up and inspected closely, sniffing his satisfying metallic and oil cologne around the cylinder. I bought him online during a similar evening of drunken loneliness.

 I descended the back stairwell. A foggy mist swept eerily

overhead. The lack of streetlights and cars muted the already soundless neighborhood, where university elite rested on fair trade cotton and high thread counts. I looked around timidly, seeing only blackness, then raised Duke. I thought of the committee. I thought of the legions of meetings packed within my schedule one after the other, each centered on inflated victim stories. Then images of corrupt politicos stopping by unannounced with requests for photos with my veterans slithered in.

"We need more chrome and moan, Nick. You know, wheelchairs, prosthetics, brain injuries. That's what tugs at the heart strings and gets the big checks," a campus leader whispered.

My career had become nothing more than showmanship; a never-ending performance of empire building camouflaged in bullshit buzzwords of the month, like *transparency* and *inclusivity*. I took a full breath, feeling the rolling beat echo throughout my chest. The crickets chirped, egging me on. Delicately, I squeezed Duke's long double-action trigger, the anticipation building like the liberating ecstasy just before orgasm. Within seconds my ears rang painfully from the thunderous boom. An aroma of gunpowder wafted out the barrel as a cacophony of agitated dogs pierced the blackness. The truthfulness of post-orgasm clarity. I shook from the chill, wondering where the bullet would eventually land, contemplating the damage it could inflict. The police were sure to hover through, even shine their big spotlights in the crevices. A front-page piece on the local beat guaranteed. I felt the stale breath of the tipping point breeze my back. The rope was starting to cut.

******

Outside Black Canyon Coffee, I wait with my lone Patagonia bag between my feet. The driver is supposed to be here. I unzip my medium-sized duffel, an electric pea-green color busier than the image shown on Amazon. I confirm the pick-up point on the email, then glance at the packing list for camp. My new hand wraps are secured in a zippered mesh compartment on top of the duffel. A black pair and a gray one. When they were delivered to my condo, I was selling most of my possessions to strangers off Craig's List. The small yellow envelope uplifted me. I squeezed the plastic baggie and sniffed its chemical perfume. A spell was cast. I wondered where these wraps would travel. Would they have blood on them? Would it be my blood or someone else's? There

A Ronin's Tale

is primal energy in martial practices, but it's much more than senseless violence or bravado. It's symbolic of facing fear, triggering something within our wiring that prioritizes survival. And each of us has a war inside. It's not surprising that in the midst of extreme wokeness, mixed martial art culture is exploding. A cathartic balance. The wraps deserve their place on top of the duffel, like a crown.

I don't have a phone, or even a number for the camp. Collections of travelers and locals mill about inside the tiny airport. Their luggage assorted; cardboard boxes wrapped heavily with tape, designer knockoffs that wheel. My eyes scan a pair of oversized backpacks affixed to young, fatigued adventurers. Taxi and touts lurk outside, circling the steamy asphalt like hungry sharks. I order a coffee and contort into the uncomfortable plastic booth, drifting back to my former life.

It's better overall, but still comes in waves in certain moments. I'm transported to the office of my former supervisor, exactly one week after my fortieth birthday. An older woman, a few years junior to my parents, with hair shorter than mine. Her back pointed toward me, she speaks authoritatively, sternly, and points to a small table in the middle. Usually uncomfortably warm, there is a palpable coolness in the room. A good friend who has been at the university longer than I've been alive sits at the table. I glance at the tiny polo player on his crisp green sweater as he fumbles with a manila folder, avoiding eyes. I stare out the large window onto an empty field, recalling the many times I've walked it over the past eight years. My friend is a fixer for the department, the person sought to handle delicate situations quietly. I hadn't seen him in a while. His reluctance to meet for coffee or a beer over the past months now making sense. A voice, not sure if it's hers or his, says that someone from human resources is outside.

A wiry man with broad and muscularly defined shoulders hurries into the coffee shop. He dabs at his sweaty forehead and looks around. Our eyes meet and hold for a second. He grabs my bag, which could weigh more than him and speedily ushers us to a black SUV, the website of the fight camp prominently plastered along the doors. The sprint forces a sequence of deep breaths, foreboding what is soon to begin. The drive to camp is nearly forty-five minutes from the airport. People scurry by on scooters and compact cars. A congested Sunday, but the scene less hectic than Bangkok. I think about Sundays in my former life. The afternoon sun moving to early evening as the start of a new week hovers like a poltergeist. A heaviness fills the condo. I check work emails from my phone, then peek at the calendar. An obsessive ritual of

Put Up Your Dukes

compulsive checking, sometimes on the toilet. I unpack groceries and stare at dates on the crunchy peanut butter jar and a box of condoms. Where will I be when these expire? Will I be back on the Search, feeling the juice of adventure?

The fire season is ending in Chiang Mai, but the air is still thick and muggy. Through the foggy haze, I glance toward a billboard with the camp's emblem, as we exit the busy road. A trepidation boils. It's really happening. I suspend in time to gym classes and competitive events at barbecues. Tall and sturdy, there are expectations. Throughout high school I dodged organized sports, opting to lift weights and have my afternoons free instead. As at most schools, toughness and sports were kissing cousins, and whether or not one was branded a pussy was largely rooted in its relations. Without the athletic angle to go off, my stature was a big unknown. That is, until my sophomore year on a biting Friday in December.

It was a frigid, windchill evening, on the town's main square when my mettle was tested. Our obligatory weekend hunt for girls and the warming prospect of female companionship fueled our polar expedition. Heath steered his mom's red Tercel wagon into an open spot, as the others in our party parked beside and hid their beers. About two dozen of us congregated around colorful electric candles, an illuminated Menorah, and nine plastic reindeer. It was unclear what kicked it off or who he was, the agitated figure that emerged mysteriously. I placed him some years out of school by his weathered features and mature facial hair. He started with Heath, shoving him multiple times until one of the candle cords tripped him off his feet. He sucker-punched another kid I sat near in study hall, then wove in and out of the clustered groups, scrutinizing each male in his path before choosing a victim. When he circled toward me, my heart leapt into my throat. I recalled a moment a few summers back, accosted by some roughnecks on the basketball court, who proceeded to humiliate and wail on my neighbor friend. But on this particular night, I braced for something ominous, as it was my turn to sit in the crosshairs. Instinctively, my gloved hands clinched, then balled as the figure's dilated pupils met mine and a circle organically formed around us. He scowled and hissed, the stench of his cigarette breath raw as he delivered a firm push and I braced. But by the grace of baby Jesus, who watched nearby from the manger, a score of wild haymaker punches miraculously landed and knocked the menacing foe to the ground, where he stayed. It was my only fight in high school.

A Ronin's Tale

A decade later in the military, I took up combatives, a prescribed and regular training of hand-to-hand combat. It was one of my favorite aspects of the military, and on the occasions where we donned gloves and mouthguards and were let loose, my size and strength allowed me to dominate. I would eventually adopt a dedicated martial arts practice at a traditional karate dojo, where my size and strength again allowed me to rise quickly through the belt ranks. After some years training at the dojo, I saw a flyer for a free trial at an MMA school and decided to test what I knew.

For the better part of a week, men half my size pummeled me. I was clueless on the ground, eating punches and submissions, one after the other. A middleweight who fought on the local circuit and was a good fifty pounds lighter, tripped me to the mat, then casually toyed as I threw everything at him and gassed out. By the following Saturday, I limped to my leather sofa and inspected my bruised shins. I couldn't extend my elbows or twist my neck, but that wasn't as troubling as the realization that I had no idea how to fight. I had coasted for far too long with a false sense of my abilities. After this humbled awakening, I began a mysterious ritual researching fight camps in Southeast Asia. Although riding high on the waves of consistent work promotions, I poured over the fight camp websites and their illustrious pictures, drunk on scenarios where I tendered my resignation to embark on my own version of *Kickboxer*. The need to be tested in some meaningful way was all I thought about.

******

Dust from the freshly graveled road kicks into a cloud, as the black SUV corners hastily. We traverse more turns before the driver eases off the pedal. Soon after we're parked near a collection of newer motorcycles and I'm motion sick. The camp is situated on four acres with sixteen individual bungalows scattered about. A neatly maintained stone path snakes across various foot bridges with koi fish below. I drift to special weekends as a young boy, walking through the Japanese Tea Garden in Golden Gate Park. We sip jasmine tea and snack on seaweed crackers. The mystery of the Orient whispered even then.

An open-air training hall sits prominently in the middle of the camp with expensive black mats coating the floor. A dozen leather bags hang from tall wooden beams. Half the bags are long and skinny, the others round and shaped like teardrops. Industrial steel fans

Put Up Your Dukes

stand erect in strategic spots in each of the corners. Black-and-white portraits of stern-faced fighters and their championship belts gaze off the wall. Outside the training hall collections of tires, pull-up bars, and rusted equipment sit undisturbed. Healthy palms and plush green fields encircle the perimeter with tucked-away residential streets and prosperous homes adjacent to the property. The setting is more serene than I anticipated; a quietness resembling a monastery occasionally broken by the fainted cadences and regimented yelling echoed from a nearby military installation. Indeed, this is warrior country. A smiley Thai woman in a red tank top with the camp's iconic logo greets me with a cold fruit juice and moist towel. Her English exceptional, she gestures to a chair, as I dab the damp towel against my sweaty brow. I take a long sip of the refreshing mango concoction as she moves closer with a binder. She instructs me to look through it while she scans my passport. Close to her office a large sign hangs above the door: NO REFUNDS. I see it again, on a sheet of paper in the binder, and she instructs me to put an initial beside it.

"Ah, new blood, yeah?" says an English accent.

I look up and see a slightly pudgy man with curly ginger hair. His skin is freckled and pasty.

"Yep. Just got here."

"Cheers. I'm Warren. States, eh?"

"Yes. Accent pretty obvious?" I reply, trying to conceal that I'm not in a mood for conversation.

"Nah. You just got that American look, mate. Anyway, you're probably tired so I'll let you get to it."

I rise to properly greet Warren, impressed by his social wherewithal to not engage. As I stand, he quickly puts both hands into a fist and bounces slightly.

"Put up your dukes, mate. Let's see whatcha got," he challenges and laughs, before extending his hand.

I shake it firmly, then ask if the training is difficult.

"Hardest thing I've ever done, mate. Hardest by far," he says.

"But I'm part of the PlayStation generation. Lost a good twelve kilos in two months, though ..."

Warren doesn't look like a warrior, a thought that produces relief and disappointment. He shares that dinner will begin in an hour and taken at a communal table, where I'll meet the other "lads," as he calls them. I retire to my bungalow to organize my belongings, as two lizards cling to the wall watching. There is no television, and the Internet is intermittent like the hot water. I look at my watch. In my previous life I would be headed into a committee meeting. A white mosquito net drapes over the queen-sized bed reminding me of a ghost.

Chapter 8

Follow Your Bliss

Fall 2017, A Classroom in the Midwest

The journey always begins with the call to adventure, or simply, the Call. Campbell tells us that the Hero is asleep, and the purpose of the guide is to come along and say,

> Look, you're in Sleepy Land. Wake. Come on a trip. There is a whole aspect of your consciousness, your Being, that's not been touched. So, you're at home here?[8]

    Referencing the late German philosopher Arthur Schopenhauer, Campbell tells us that when we look back on our life at old age, it will have unfolded like a beautiful story. It's as if our lives are a plot with one surprise occurring after another. Characters dance in and out, sometimes bringing chaos in their wake. Of course, when we go through some of our experiences it is pure madness and just a mess. It can be painful, too. But eventually we understand there was an order. A perfection to it all.
    What is scariest to Campbell is living life inside the Wasteland. This is the place where one lives inauthentically. It is a reality where people, intentionally or unintentionally, lay trips on one another and an unhealthy dose of "Thou Shalt." For instance, a father who wants his son to take over the family business when everything inside the son is pointed toward a different calling. Jim Morrison, one of my shadow

---
8   Osbon, *Reflections on the Art of Living*.

heroes, was the son of a naval admiral who was in the Gulf of Tonkin when Vietnam began. Sit with that for a moment.

Maybe another father was a star athlete in high school but wasn't good enough for college. His son, therefore, inherits his father's wound, as unhealthy pressure takes over. There are interesting documentaries about parents that enroll their children in expensive athletic camps and hire nutritionists and personal trainers in an attempt to make their child a famous athlete. Or what about those creepy beauty pageants for incredibly young girls? At what point does this go too far and become cruel? At what point does the unresolved inadequacy of a parent get passed to their child?

Campbell also cautions that working exclusively for money and title is part of the Wasteland. Think about people you know with high-paying jobs, but chaotic lives. Are they fulfilled? Perhaps. But they may also be totally burned out by their routine, or have hearts that long for something much more sacred than what they're doing. It is easy to romanticize that others are happier. It is easy to put life on hold and convince ourselves it will get better in the future. It is easier to stay in an unhealthy relationship than to let it go and face the inevitable pain and solitude that will ultimately lead to richer happiness. But what happens when we totally abandon what these deeper voices tell us? A crucial thing Campbell emphasizes is to honor what our interior, or inner guide, says. To constantly listen. The Hero has to possess enough conviction to not get caught up in the regret or fear of others in order to hear his own song. He must possess the fortitude to answer the Call, but he must also trust what comes from it and the different masks the teachers wear; the good, the bad, and definitely the ugly.

Naturally, there is reluctance, to leave friends, family, the comforts and safety of home and community. There is danger if one takes a worthwhile adventure. Think of films where the wimpy kid is chosen for an important quest and the first thing he does is shake his head, "There must be some mistake ..." In these circumstances, he refuses the Call. When these moments show up and we refuse them long enough, does the opportunity eventually pass? In other words, do we miss the boat by giving in to fear and that's that? And sometimes the journey chooses us regardless. The decision makes itself, as it does for Daniel.

A pivotal transition in the film is when Daniel endures his worst beating at the Halloween dance. He randomly learns that the leader of the Cobra Kai, Johnny, is in the bathroom crouched in a stall. Daniel sneaks over and turns on a hose dousing Johnny in an attempt at revenge.

Follow Your Bliss

Successful with this, he runs out of the dance and tries to escape the Cobra Kai mob, but eventually they catch him outside his apartment complex. Unable to defend himself and beaten nearly unconscious, we see Mr. Miyagi jump from the shadows of a chain fence and effortlessly destroy Daniel's attackers. All of a sudden something much more profound is revealed. At this point, we only know Miyagi as a simple handyman. But as he nurses Daniel back to recovery a conversation ensues, and we learn that Miyagi is from Okinawa and descended from a powerful karate lineage. He's a karate master. Throughout the evening, Miyagi convinces Daniel to search for a solution by visiting the Cobra Kai dojo.

The following day they visit the dojo and meet the head instructor, Mr. Kreese. This is a rational choice, is it not? When bullying takes place, we call the offender's parents or schedule a meeting with the principal. In this case, we talk to the Cobra Kai chief. But the mythological world doesn't run on things like linear time or reason. Other laws of nature govern the unfoldment of one's life. At the dojo, tempers escalate, and Miyagi understands that the bullying stems from the influence Kreese has over his students. They've been walking the wrong path. Before we know it, Miyagi and Kreese have entered into an agreement that Daniel will fight in the coveted All Valley Karate Tournament a few months away.

Our Hero refuses the Call. Daniel leaves the dojo yelling at Miyagi, proclaiming a list of reasons he shouldn't compete at the All Valley. What is at the heart of this refusal? Fear. Daniel is afraid. I'm theorizing here, but he is probably without a lot of confidence. He doesn't have a father figure we know of who can assist him in grappling with questions about manhood or offer him healthy masculine mentoring. He doesn't even appear to have friends. Daniel shows us what is a very real part of the human condition—"I am scared, I am overwhelmed, I feel alone, and I am without control in my life." Refusing the Call humanizes the Hero. It tells us this person is not impervious to pain or to their emotions. They are not superheroes, but rather they are just like us. We will expand on this point further in the next lecture, but what does Campbell cautiously warn when we fail to answer the Call?

> If someone has had a sense of the Call, the feeling that there is an adventure waiting for him, and if he doesn't follow it, then life dries up. And then he comes to that

condition in late middle life, where he's gotten to the top of the ladder, and found that it's leaning against the wrong wall. For the person who has the guts to follow their bliss and answer the Call, doors open.

What will they think of me? That must be put aside for bliss.[9]

---

9   Osbon, *Reflections on the Art of Living*.

Chapter 9

To Utopia

April 2019, Chiang Mai, Thailand

When a cult grows up it becomes a culture.[10]
—Jan Shipps

We would rise early and run. Run. That was the consensus around the table with the lads.

"Not that bad, maybe like five kilometers," one of the nameless faces said. I do the math and realize that is over three miles. Damn. In yet another previous life, I checked into my new unit. It would be home for nearly half a year, as we prepared for our deployment to the Middle East. The rail-thin commanding officer's fiery gaze looked me up and down as I rendered a salute and formal greeting. He scrutinized carefully, evaluating the crispness of my gig line before he nodded at a chair. I heard he wasn't an easy customer to please. It was a solid half minute of gaze before he opened his mouth. I scanned the walls of his office, noting a vast array of pictures of different marathons, including Boston. There was a certificate with times written down, along with gaudy medallions suspended from colorful ribbons.

"I expect my officers to run, and to run fast," he began, matter of fact.

I hate running. Pudgy Warren said the camp run was just a warm-up. Afterward it was back to the open-air hall for the real exercise.

---

10 A. Cameron, *Cult or Culture? How to Avoid the Kool-Aid Effect.* Cult or Culture? How to avoid the Kool-Aid effect (linkedin.com), April 10, 2017.

49

A Ronin's Tale

Eventually, we'd transition into formal training. Ninety minutes, start to finish. Then another session in the afternoon. I digested what I could, discretely examining the vast shin bruises and puffy knuckles of my contemporaries. I posed questions carefully, cautious of showing my hand. The intel officer in me studied each man beyond his black-and-blue markings. What is *his* story? I was curious what prompted the men to camp, but more truthfully fixated on where I stood on the pecking order of toughness and physical aptitude. Most of our tribe were missing, I was informed. One name among the missing surfaced several times. The mood shifted. The group at the table wasn't intimidating, but they were younger and lean. Could probably run, too. An accented man with receding hairline and pockmarked acne scars made it sound like we were going to war. He emphasized arriving at class hydrated and salting the food at each meal. A couple others said it wasn't that bad. The butterflies flapped regardless, even at forty. I politely excused myself after forcing down a couple bites of curried rice and meat, then retired to the bungalow. It was no longer a dreamy lifeline of exotic enchantment and fantasy. A fun story to share over a beer to friends who were possibly concealing their truthful thoughts of my new life path. But here I was. Sweating. The queen-sized bed comfortable, and the oscillating ceiling fan providing just enough breeze. I studied its circular path, occasionally interrupted by the scurrying tap of lizards. I sank further down the recesses of the consciousness ocean, contemplating the seeds of this obscure warrior odyssey. Then thoughts came.

******

Jeff and I shot hoops at an elementary school six blocks from home. The remaining relics of summer, the charming time when days and weekends blend was on its death spiral. I did my best to preserve the last of the magic, evading thoughts that eighth grade was close by. Jeff, who lived down the street with his father, was a year older and off to the public high school in a couple days. He was feeling even more of the punch, so evening basketball became our therapeutic ritual to keep the banshees away. An ambitious toss from half-court arced miserably, missing the rim entirely and bouncing the ball far onto the grass. As Jeff went to retrieve it, a weathered Monte Carlo pulled sharply into the lot ahead, the screech of heavy metal blaring from its muffled speakers.

To Utopia

A truthful voice urged to run. But I stood frozen, glancing curiously at the Townies inside. The two faces stared momentarily before the driver revved the gas pedal, causing the parked muscle to shake and vibrate furiously. It had one of those loud mufflers that shrieked and waned like a cutting saw. I recognized the driver with his spiky, dyed-blond hair that was long in the back and shaved on the sides. He only wore hairband t-shirts, and he wore the Def Leppard one most, usually underneath an acid-washed jacket without sleeves. Sometimes he took quarters from the hands of smaller kids outside Mi-T-Mart, a gas station with the only videogames in town. The other one, who dismounted from the passenger's side was stockier, but I'd never seen him before.

Jeff was from a meditating family, too, but they couldn't afford the tuition at Maharishi School. I was only there because my father was a teacher and that included free tuition. The Townies walked briskly, the stockier one looking around mischievously. Within seconds, Spiky Hair kicked the ball, and I watched it soar into the distance along with my peace. The other one pushed Jeff to the ground.

"You like that, don't you, 'Ru boy? Yeah, yeah, 'Ru boy!" He snarled after he spoke, his face distorted.

Jeff was pinned to the ground, feebly struggling against the bigger boy. His breath was audible, and my own breathing accelerated, weighting my chest. The menace balled his fist and cocked it back like a gun. I watched that fist, anxiously awaiting its release. Jeff's hands shot upward to shield himself, as strange sounds emanated throughout the humid evening.

"Start floatin', 'Ru boy! C'mon now, let me see you float ... levitate for me!"

Jeff whimpered and shifted on the ground, doing his best to keep his hands upright. I heard him whimper like that before, usually when his dad was in a rage. The boy with the fist bluffed a punch several times, but didn't commit. Instead, he turned and looked at me.

"Hey, pussy, what school do you go to?" he demanded.

I scanned the neighborhood, hoping adult eyes were upon us. I considered a cutting sprint across the field, but there were two of them and running wasn't my forte.

"MSAE," I stuttered.

"WHAT?" he barked.

I repeated it, the affliction in my quivering voice unmistakable.

"Say it again. Say the full name, and I'll let you go."

My mouth opened, but the words were tangled.

"Uh ... Maharishi School ..." I squeaked.
"The WHOLE thing, retard! Say the WHOLE THING!"
"Um, of the Age of Enlightenment."
Spiky Hair let out a belly roar, a guttural glee that overwhelmed me with shame. His sidekick raised his knee off Jeff's belly, then stepped closer.
"Oh, so you're a 'Ru boy, too? A Maharishi floater guru, eh?"
His right hand still clinched, I instinctively backed away. Spiky stepped between us.
"Nah, leave this one alone. His sister is Becki Osborne."
A momentary pause sang through the universe. The stocky boy stood in place, shaking his head.
"No freakin' way, man. This bean-pole pussy is related to *Becki*?" he said incredulously.
Spiky nodded. I looked down at the cracked cement on the court.
In the fullness of the moment, with the humiliation buzzing on overdrive, I longed for armament. I summoned upward for a gun, a knife, a baseball bat with nails protruding from it. Anything. Not a cell inside hesitated in the want to inflict serious and grave bodily injury on these punks. But instead of the gratifying weight of weaponry in my shaking hands, I stood firmly rooted in panic, awash in helplessness.
"It's a good thing you got a hot sister, 'Ru boy."
Before they turned to walk away, the stocky one paced closer.
"Better watch your ass. You'll see me again."
Then Spiky scurried over to Jeff and belted him forcefully. The audible impact made Jeff shriek out desperately, as blood and hot tears descended down his nose and cheeks into the freshly cut grass. It was the first act of violence I'd ever witnessed. Those six blocks to our neighborhood took some time. Neither Jeff nor I spoke a word.

******

Fairfield was mentioned first on my fifth birthday. Bubbles the clown made balloon animals for neighborhood friends and cousins after we got worn out on the Slip n Slide. We removed our wax mouths with funny teeth and fangs, as my mom poured Hawaiian punch into small Dixie cups. Sugar was a rarity in our home, so I felt strangely guilty washing down the Darth Vader cake with the punch. We sat under a shady oak in the middle of our lawn to open presents. Somebody got me a ninja outfit, and Dad promised to order more throwing stars from the martial arts catalog next to my bed. Later in the day, a man I'd never seen before pulled into our gravel driveway in a rickety Honda hatchback. The man was tall and sickly thin, and he wore a cream suit. A quality of importance shrouded him, as my parents greeted with their hands clasped in a sort of prayer-like fashion. Mom had cleared off a table inside, and the stranger placed various things on it. Some of the items smelled strange. In the middle, a gold-framed picture of an old man with a long gray beard sat prominently staring through gentle eyes. Flowers and fruit were brought into the room and placed reverently next to the picture.

"Happy birthday, Nicholas. What a joyous and special day it is for you, yes?"

My parents stood in the doorway looking on, smiling.

"Has anyone explained to you what is going to happen today?"

I shook my head. The man's soothing voice spoke steadily, deliberately. His hazel eyes sparkled.

"Who's that?" I asked, pointing to the picture.

"Ah," the man laughed. "That is his Holiness, Maharishi."

I moved my lips attempting to repeat the peculiar name.

"His full name is Maharishi Mahesh Yogi, but he is mostly known as Maharishi. And this other man over here was his teacher, Guru Dev."

I stared into the picture. The man reminded me of a wizard. His teacher had a stern face and sat in a strange posture on top of a tiger skin. I wondered if he killed that tiger.

"Is he like Jesus?" I asked quizzically. I knew a little about Jesus from my dad's mother, my British nana, who was a devout Catholic that went to church every day. The man laughed heartily, along with my parents.

"He has similar qualities to Jesus. But he is different. *Maha* means great, and *rishi* means teacher. When you combine the words together it means great teacher. *Maharishi* is a title given to a great teacher. A person who knows things, like mysteries and secrets of the universe. And today you will be taught the wonderful Word of Wisdom that he developed."

My father sensed my confusion, stepped closer, and whispered, "It's like Luke Skywalker, Nick. He was able to do all those amazing things because he had *Siddhis*, special powers like what you're going to receive today."

A Ronin's Tale

A poster from *Star Wars* hung over my bed. Just a few months earlier I sat mesmerized at a drive-in theater as the forces of good and evil battled. A wooden light saber made from a sawed broom handle and wrapped in twine rested near the poster.

"Yes, that is a good comparison," the man added. "Luke Skywalker spent time with his teacher, Yoda. You can think of Maharishi like Yoda."

He paused briefly, then added, "And you can think of the Word of Wisdom like the Force, a special power to use throughout your life."

I looked at the Maharishi again, expecting to catch a smile or a wink.

"Shall we get started? Are you ready to accept the powers of the *mantra*?"

Before the ninja craze went mainstream, I was an early devotee. My parents were relaxed about R-rated movies and took me to see *Revenge of the Ninja* weeks earlier. Shoddy acting and gratuitous violence aside, it was a holy experience. I knew that ninjas meditated before going into battle and possessed supernatural abilities. In kindergarten at Penngrove Elementary, I drew a picture of a man in black pajamas with a face mask and sword. We were assigned to draw what we wanted to be when we grew up. Confused and likely concerned by the severed heads in the drawing, my parents were called to speak with my teacher, Mrs. Lindsey. My kung fu uniform hung freshly pressed in the closet, while a dozen ninja stars protruded from the barn outside. Now, the special powers from a Yoda-like master bequeathed. All signs confirmed that my warrior's path was unfolding beautifully.

The man lit a candle in front of the Maharishi and began singing in a language I'd never heard before. He motioned me to place the freshly washed fruit and flowers onto the altar. Then he dropped a pinch of rice, that clinked against the brass cup. Sandalwood fumes swirled off the yellow incense sticks around the *prasad* transporting me somewhere ancient, but familiar. It was as if I'd experienced this before. He chanted several more minutes before he sat on a chair and crossed his legs.

"Nicholas, I am now going to give you the mantra. The Word of Wisdom. It is important that you never share this word with anyone, even your sister or your parents."

I looked behind, my parents no longer in the doorway. It was just the thin man and me in my room. His tone remained soft, but an apparent seriousness loomed. I looked at the man, then nodded that I understood and would honor the discrete code of the secret warrior knowledge.

To Utopia

A strange word exited his lips; it was more like a sound than anything else. He said it again. And again. He instructed me to repeat it aloud and then again silently in my mind, over and over. He told me that I could do it on a walk or in my bedroom, and that I would feel deep joy and happiness the more I did it. He even said that over time I would achieve great Siddhis and eventually be able to levitate off the ground. I sat in disbelief, as an adult from the realms of truth telling confided that my life would have all sorts of mystical experiences. I was stoked. After sitting with the insightful man, my parents returned to the room with two pieces of cake. He mentioned something about Fairfield, and they smiled. Then all of them left for the kitchen while I sat alone at the altar staring at the great teacher.

******

When meditation halls with large golden domes are erected, and mostly vegetarian white folks from the coasts show up to hop on foam, a midwestern town of fewer than ten thousand is bound to take notice. About an hour southwest of Iowa City is Fairfield, situated among rolling cornfields and well-manicured farms. In the center of town, a gazebo and perfect square of restaurants and eclectic shops provide everything from sustainable building supplies to organic scented candles and Ayurvedic herbs. Strong breezes in warmer months invoke smells of pig waste that permeate the air from nearby hog lots. Summer months bring live music with brass instruments. On the surface, Fairfield is just another nondescript midwestern village that runs on a slower pace and provides an inexpensive place to raise a family. Most doors are still unlocked at night, and most children ride their bikes freely through old Victorian neighborhoods. But underneath the Norman Rockwell americana, Fairfield is a spiritual enclave with an unorthodox history.

Transcendental meditation, or TM for short, was brought to the United States in the 1950s by its principal founder and guru, Maharishi Mahesh Yogi. Throughout the 1960s and '70s, TM ascended on college campuses through the rise of the counterculture and hippie movement. All things Eastern and spiritual were in, and top-shelf celebrities like the Beatles propelled the technique's popularity. My parents discovered it in the early seventies in Berkeley. Today, millions of people globally have learned TM. In 2012, Oprah's jet landed a few miles north of town. Although Fairfield attracts a wide populace of stars and seekers, most have no idea what the early years were like or what is in the soil.

In 1974, just a year before Maharishi went on *The Merv Griffin Show*, the TM leadership, or *Movement*, purchased a near four-hundred-acre campus of the bankrupt Parsons College. The vision was to create an ideal community where meditation took place twice a day in large groups. According to Maharishi, the material world by itself is rife with suffering and chaos. Lasting peace and bliss, the ultimate goal of our soul's journey, are forfeited by stressful existences and unhealthy routines. Therefore, through a systematic practice of TM, practitioners disassociate from the noise and raise their consciousness. If enough people meditate in a group, its effects ripple beyond their area, spreading coherence to other places and even reducing crime. To sustain a permanent community of meditators, two meditation halls with golden domes were erected on the campus.

In late 1983, more than seven thousand meditators converged in Fairfield for the "Taste of Utopia" assembly. The euphoric realization that an ideal community was really happening spread across TM centers around the country. Less than a year later, my family would make the trip to be part of the utopian vision. Ironically, we lived in a trailer court on the campus called Utopia Park. My father was hired to teach at the Maharishi School of the Age of Enlightenment. Every morning in Ms. Jackson's first-grade class we did the Word of Wisdom. Afterward we studied the Science of Creative Intelligence, or SCI. SCI included a list of sixteen principles from Maharshi, such as "The Nature of Life is to Grow"; "Water the Root to Enjoy the Fruit"; and "Do Less and Accomplish More." Displayed throughout the aged three-story brick school were the many SCI principles we wrote on oversized poster boards with fruit-scented markers. Sometimes we spoke of their meaning, while other times we expressed them through theater or painting.

On occasion Maharishi orchestrated a conference call, creating mass excitement and frenzy. Every adult had their story of when life changed for them, their awakening moment. Some stood, tears descending down their cheeks, recounting their journey into a microphone as Maharishi lauded our accomplishments and breathed fresh air onto our path. The golden domes were packed with hundreds of devotees, each seated on comfortable pieces of foam. Our parents soaked in Maharishi's every word, while the children ran freely in the dome's basement, making forts and playing tag. The Movement was growing, and we were the architects.

Like moths to a flame, clusters of people showed up from Europe, India, and Africa. International faces spoke earnestly of Maharishi's global vision to create world peace. We were embodying *Vasudhaiva Kutumbakan*, "the world is one family." Most meditators worked and lived on campus in simple dwellings like trailers and dorm rooms and ate in a communal facility called Annapurna. The dining hall had a room off to the left designated for Silent Dining, where nobody spoke. There was a commissary for families, not unlike what you would find in a communist locale. On Saturday mornings we rummaged through stacks of yellow crates with gallons of milk dangerously close to expiration. Bruised and blemished fruits and veggies were available, sometimes eggs. There was always an abundance of unsalted butter and stale cereal.

Although young, I sensed that we were part of something big. Soft-spoken administrators confided at school that we were being groomed for future world leadership, and that the knowledge we received was sacred and from the Veda. Some afternoons the academics ceased, and the entire school went outside for kickball, or a nature hike around the campus. Long before everything new age became mainstream, we were exposed to yoga, Ayurveda, sustainable farming, and organic food. Even Vedic astrology was part of our lifestyle, as parents bragged in the commissary line about their child being some reincarnated sage. Birthday cakes were made of carob. Birthday songs included wishes for heaven on earth. Nobody wore black.

Not long after we settled into Utopia Park, I wandered the campus's many dwellings and wooded perimeter. Weathered dormitories that reeked of mildew and sandalwood housed clusters of single meditators segregated by sex. In the common areas, plants and quartz crystals sparkled on windowsills. The vast windows welcomed radiant sunshine that graced expensively framed pictures of Maharishi. Residents placed shoes outside their rooms on thick orange carpet. In the middle of campus, a Japanese-style bridge suspended over a shallow pond with turtles and narrow white fish. Sometimes there were snakes. The grounds were vibrantly green and wily, with overgrown grass and cattails. Tall oaks stood confidently above smatterings of historic stone and brick buildings leftover from the Parsons era. It was like the grounds of an elite New England boarding school mixed with the unkempt wildness of the third world. In many ways, if the world shrunk to a village, the campus's demographics and standard of living would be close. Rusted cars that shot black smoke from mufflers held on by wire coat hangers stayed parked for years. Even a dilapidated sailboat sat unmoved for over a decade. I wasn't alone in my explorations for long. Utopia Park had dozens of children eager to explore. Hide and seek occupied our free time, and every evening between five and seven, we were left unattended as our parents hopped on foam in their quest for enlightenment. A Frenchman I knew, who pronounced certain words funnily, had an Atari. We spent mornings in his trailer playing Pac Man, afternoons waging war with our G.I. Joes, and then finished with a campus safari. Years later, he took his own life while I was overseas with the military. It wasn't all blissful and utopian.

Divisions within the Movement were apparent even as a child. The economically privileged and those who enjoyed personal time with Maharishi called the shots. Some loyalists had been with Maharishi from the beginning, spending time in India and traveling the world as his prominence grew to a larger stage. They carried themselves with a flair of importance and were quick to quote him. Judgments were doled out based on a person's perceived level of commitment, or how "on the program" they were. Even pronunciations revealed subtle clues. Among the diehards, Maharishi was referred to as "Ma Harshi." Those even more devout scaled the diction closer, simply calling him "Marshi." My parents, being among the ranks of the impoverished worker bees, stuck to the traditional four-syllable speak, "Ma-ha-ri-shi" common to the campus proletariat.

Egos hovered in subtle ways, as glorious accounts of profound meditation experiences were bragged to others. Sometimes skirmishes leaked into the rumor mill. Some names surfaced after being spotted eating meat at local restaurants or attending talks by other gurus and mystics. Marital infidelities occurred. A ten o'clock bedtime was expected as part of the ideal routine. My mom, who had once been an airline stewardess and model in the Bay Area, didn't adapt well to the lifestyle. She stashed bottles of wine when company visited, and never warmed to starting and ending her conversations with "Jai Guru Dev." My dad, however, was elated by this utopia. A devout Catholic and altar boy most of his youth, he loved the knowledge he was receiving and never missed a meditation. At times, a palpable tension radiated inside our trailer.

In addition to the diehards, there were legions of the socially awkward, clad in pastel clothing and ill-fitted suits. Meditation and other types of self-help organizations are magnets for the odd. One woman rode her bicycle through town in a down jacket, ski goggles, and a bright red scarf. It was the middle of summer. Most men were sickly thin, devoid of muscle and assertiveness. Their strange fishing-style hats were beige in summer and the sheepskin ones in winter looked straight from a Russian gulag. But these qualities somehow produced an endearing charm, too. It produced acceptance and a feeling of safety. We roamed our campus without danger. And MSAE produced many creative and brilliant minds, including a famous actor. But there was also a disproportionately high number of drug users and broken souls in our young ranks. Misfits, perhaps given too much freedom and praise, and not enough direction. I learned later that a moderate number of my campus generation did time in jail for various offenses or suffered from mental illness or substance issues.

Spending formative years in a spiritual commune hinted that there was more to reality than simply making a living, buying stuff, and gauging success based on one's profession. We meditated regularly as children, taking time each day to go inward. Our daily routine centered on staying positive and avoiding negativity. While meditating there was peace and an inner silence. There was a divinity on campus and within the Movement; a holy presence that protected like a shield and guided like a wise parent. Maybe the Force was real. But as I grew into my teen years gaps also showed, and my utopia began to crumble.

My second-grade teacher, Mr. Angelo, handed me back my drawing of a tank shooting bullets. With a bright red marker, he drew a large heart around the tank and ammunition.

"It's so wonderful, Nicholas, that you want to drive a love tank and spread love throughout the world," he shared with the class.

When I protested and told him that I planned to join the military and kill communists, he lamented, "Oh, Nicholas, the only defense a nation needs is Maharishi's Global Peace. That's the only work that matters."

Being nurtured among the new age and surfing waves of their continuous praise created an unhealthy softness. It wasn't uncommon for grown-ups on campus, aside from Mr. Angelo, to suggest that America do away with its police force and military because TM was the only defense it needed. But the laws of polarity also prevailed, forcing Fairfield to grapple with forces on the other end of its pendulum. It was hardest on us kids.

In those early years, the nonmeditating citizens were rightfully concerned about the presence of a Hindu guru and flock of outsiders showing up in their town. To the locals, TM was a cult. At MSAE, I wore a uniform of khaki slacks, white dress shirt, and bright red tie. It was not uncommon to walk home and hear a "Townie" hurl an insulting "Ru" (slang for Guru) dagger from a porch or passing car. Sometimes they chased us. Stories of violence occasionally surfaced, then eventually I witnessed Jeff's broken nose. I stopped attending MSAE at fourteen when my parents divorced and my father quit teaching. I no longer received free tuition, so that meant public school among the Townies.

Public school was a crossroads in my development. On campus, the safe routine of the ordinary world shielded like a protective cocoon. I skated by academically. I basked in the praise of teachers and effeminate administrators, one even telling my parents that I could lead the Movement in the future. Things were easy, but the ease couldn't overcome the strange awe and trepidation I felt around masculine Townies. Something vague, but wise, intuited that a dark forest was waiting. There was a gentleness I carried from the commune, a sword with a brittle blade that was decorative rather than battle-ready. These feelings grew over the course of a summer, and I eventually accepted that an initiation was imminent.

Chapter 10

WILD MAN'S CAGE

Fairfield, Iowa, 1994–1995

> Adolescence is like having only enough light to see the step directly in front of you.[11]
> —Sarah Addison Allen

I motion my fingers back and forth like a composer, as the tribe of lizards scurry across the walls. There is a soft, almost hypnotic rhythm to their dash. At one point in the symphony something jumps on my bed, startling me. I dwell on previous excursions in Asia, witnessing spiders the size of my hand. I check under the bed, then take a small swig of water. The melatonin from earlier was a dud. It's humid already, too. I will have to ride this out and face the first training session on whatever rest I can muster. It isn't the first time, though.

******

The evening before public school, the brain circuitry spun unfiltered. I obsessed on whether or not I could unlock my locker and transit between classes within three minutes. At MSAE we dawdled. We'd hang at the lockers chewing about girls or trading baseball cards. At most, one of the soft-spoken skeletons would appear from a nearby classroom and

---
11   Allen S. Addison, *The Girl Who Chased the Moon: A Novel* (Bantam Books, 2011).

project his voice as authoritatively as he could,
"Gentle reminder, boys, we should head to class at this time. Please disperse."

There were no gentle reminders where I was headed. I thought about Spiky Hair and his crew of assholes. I contemplated gym with farm kids that wrestled and drove stick-shift trucks with gun racks. The ones that killed animals, some with bows and arrows, then brought pictures of their corpses to class. The ones that rode four-wheelers, spit tobacco juice into plastic Mountain Dew bottles, and fought at parties in the cornfield. That's where I was headed. At least Becki would protect me.

I was a fifteen-year-old sophomore my first year at Fairfield High, falling quickly into an eclectic circle of athletes, partiers, and a musician. Becki having a throne on all the homecoming and prominent courts assured me an invitation to most things cool. Halfway through the year, my very first friend from Utopia Park resurfaced after a lengthy absence. Canadian Derek was a couple years older and often in rooms that were smaller and separate from his classmates. While writing out the SCI principles, he'd put the licorice-scented marker to his nose and close one nostril, then mimic a loud snort. His eyes would go wide as he hopped upward and gyrated wildly. He was the only student that invoked what outsiders would call anger among the Movement echelon.

Eventually he got the boot from MSAE, his single mother apprised that he wasn't quite ready to be an ambassador of world peace. So she shipped him back to British Columbia where his commercial fisherman father lived. True to many in Fairfield, he disappeared only to just show up one day, though Derek showed up in a black leather jacket and matching leather pants. With his well-kempt blond hair and firm jawline, he held a striking resemblance to a youthful Daniel Craig. Derek confessed that he was back to work a series of odd manual jobs, though he was vague when I pressed him on it at Mi-T-Mart. He was gassing up a shabby '81 Cutlass he scored for two hundred bucks that had been abandoned on campus. The interior floor was so rusted that daylight protruded next to the gas pedal. I hopped in the war machine, feeling powerful to be in a car without parental oversight. Derek accelerated on curves, fishtailing the Cutlass and screeching its bald tires. We meandered to the part of town with the industrial buildings and factories. A stout man, mid-forties, with a bald dome and curly hair that wrapped around the sides like an ill-fitting clown wig sat on a porch, waiting. His bowling shirt was several sizes too small and reeked of

Wild Man's Cage

Brut and cigarettes. Canadian Derek handed him a wad of folded bills.

I never asked about the origin of the dilapidated furniture, or the Christmas tree. Each time at Derek's a new item surfaced, along with stories crafted on the fly. We decorated the tree with empty cans of Old Milwaukee and condoms. His phony Canadian I.D. put him in his early twenties. Several bottles of bottom-shelf poisons were staged in a yellow crate, like the kind that housed the expired milk at the commissary.

"Nicky! Nicky boy, where are you? Come here, yeah!" Derek shouted from the living room.

He pulled a heroic swig of triple sec, then grinned deviously and chortled. I did my best to confidently chat up a radiant fresh face in the kitchen, as he walked behind and wrapped his arm around my waist. Snoop Dogg mostly, but sometimes Pink Floyd or Steve Miller crackled from the silver stereo.

"Turn that down, turn that down!" he commanded.

Derek angled me forward, his arm still around my waist.

"Listen here, yeah. I've known this tall bastard for ten years, and he's like my brother, eh. So, all you, you're like my brothers, too. Fuckin' right, yeah. So make yourselves at home!"

The dozen or so pairs of eyes flickered, and a couple hands raised their plastic cups before the music returned. Most of our clan were stoked to have a party spot. Then Derek gulped another shot and bellowed.

"Oh, and if any of you babes want to make a man happy, you can do my dishes over there."

Several women looked at the caked monstrosity stacked in the filthy sink, then shook their heads in disgust. Derek snickered and circulated 'round the hovel, greeting each face with boisterous stories of being a champion kickboxer and ranch hand in Canada.

Derek serendipitously surfaced in a time when my posse and I were already concocting a meaningful ritual of sneaking onto the campus to assault the security force. Most weekends evolved into spur-of-the-moment ambushes; illegal fireworks from Missouri and hurled eggs against the underpaid watchmen who patrolled on foot and in a silver Explorer. The low pay and tedium produced consistent turnover, mostly hard-living Townies who smoked generic cigarettes in the shadows of the holy grounds. Occasionally we got a motivated crew that aggressively went on offense, looking for blood.

One evening, Troy and I casually drove around campus musing

about California and imagined surf odysseys. He had recently lost his virginity, and I was close. The seedlings of our unorthodox futures beginning to sprout just enough that we could feel what was ahead. A powerful super soaker water gun rested in his trunk, likely leftover from an earlier raid. After circling around Utopia Park, we doubled back and spotted a new face. The taller-than-average, large figure had a wide neck and menacing bulk of fat mixed with muscle. I knew Townies like him, standout wrestlers and athletes in high school with reputations. I recalled a party that Becki hosted where one of those archetypes knocked a guy cold on our front porch. Most hit their prime in a manner reminiscent of Springsteen's glory days, only to find themselves as young fathers, clutching onto whatever work was available around town. He swaggered side to side, his jingling keys harmonizing our devious mood.

I didn't say a word. I didn't have to. Troy guided the Beretta up a slight hill, the potholed path jostling us back and forth. We pressed a couple hundred yards toward a sea of abandoned vehicles where we could blend. It was imperative we pulled this off. Weeks earlier, we stripped naked and ran through our town's grocery store with half a dozen other vagrants. A chorus of snickers and sneers erupted in the bathroom, as our cocks and balls flapped freely, just outside the produce section. One at a time, the following Monday, the principal's secretary said our names over the loudspeaker during first period homeroom. Some applauses were given, as we converged at the office, awaiting sentencing. Troy and I swore we were done pulling capers for a while. But the opportunity before us was just too cherry to pass up. The gods of the campus produced a challenge with danger.

Most places on campus we could navigate blindfolded. It allowed us to advance in the shadows and burst out calculated sprints between thick trees and the crevices of historic stone buildings. We peeked around corners, concerned the burly man was concluding his rounds. I scanned the student union with the Japanese pagoda roof, but all was still and dark inside. We sprawled low onto the ground, taking tactical advantage of the slight elevation. The pulsating throb of my heartbeat intensified, and my bladder drummed with it. Troy backed away deliberately, then doubled back into a corner. Seconds later I heard what sounded like rain patting gently onto leaves.

"Troy, Troy ..." I whispered. "Troy, get over here. I see him."

Troy finished as efficiently as he could, then slithered back.

"There," I pointed.

Wild Man's Cage

Around the corner of the student union, we saw the Explorer. Then we watched as his large Maglite rocked back and forth on his leather belt. Indeed, he was a big boy.

"Damn. He must've come out the back. We missed him," Troy said.

As I rose to pee, Troy placed his hand on my back, then pointed. The door to the Explorer was ajar, but the man meandered back toward the front of the union. His keys jingled some more, and then he disappeared inside.

"C'mon, now! We do it now," Troy said.

A consummate athlete who wrestled since elementary school, Troy took off in a lightning dash toward the commissary, which was adjacent and slightly sloped above the union. As if placed there by the holiest of divine forces, a semicircle of yellow crates was stacked approximately ten yards from the Explorer. I recognized the smell of sour milk from the commissary weekends. Under the protective blanket of concealment in enemy territory, we waited. I really had to pee.

******

The satisfying earthy perfume of weed greeted, as we gleefully ascended the short steps onto Derek's porch. The cooler chill drove everyone inside, where our pal Steve entertained with his guitar. I scanned the street for undercovers, Derek's home now marked by every law enforcement entity in the county. They pulled his license, too, and despite several days in county jail, he showed no sign of backing down. He thrived on it, actually. Through unknown forces, the last time I was at his home, I ducked out with a girl to make out in her car as an irate father stormed through the side entrance looking for his daughter. True to the earliest hours in Utopia Park, Derek had uncanny ability to summon tornadoes. But we pushed all that aside, entering the clouded room with more new faces and bodies, to accept our welcome as warriors.

"Eh, Nicky boy! Nicky, where have you been?" a pickled Derek bellowed, embracing us.

"It was fucking awesome. One of the best," Troy said.

"Yeah, man, it was epic. Truly epic, actually," I added.

Steve paused the concert, as we settled into the cozy, though filthy scene. Seconds later, our friend Heath exited a nearby bedroom, a cigarette dangling from his handsome devilish grin.

Wait for it, wait for it, my inner voice counted. Then shortly after that, a sheepish-looking girl with a fresh noticeable stain on her shirt emerged, walking briskly for the bathroom.

Some older Africans, most likely international students from the campus, passed a joint on the lopsided couch. I stepped into the kitchen, needing a breath. Derek handed Troy and I a lukewarm beer.

"Tell me. No more teasing, Nicky boy, yeah."

"Okay, okay," I pleaded. "But just you, man. There's too many people out there I don't know. I don't feel like having an audience. It was intense, Derek. I'm still coming down."

"Ah, Nicky boy! Drink, drink, drink. Calm those nerves, eh."

Derek looked at my shirt and pointed, "Blood?"

We sped through the preliminary parts. The beer, cooler than I realized, soothed my hands. Although no longer bleeding, they still tingled.

"Nick pumped the soaker a good ten or twelve times, then crept over and ducked below the passenger side of the Explorer. I saw the whole thing," Troy began.

"My balls were literally in my throat, man. I could hear him get closer; his keys, then I heard his boots crunching …"

"So Nick popped out and was like, 'ARGH' and it scared the shit out of the guy. He literally fell back and gasped, then Nick sprayed him. All over his face and chest."

Troy paused, as the three of us erupted in laughter. A subtle buzz was approaching, my adrenaline beginning to wane.

"I remember him totally freaked out at first, but then this look, this crazed look, like he just turned the channel. He was ready for war. It's like he wasn't scared any longer, just pissed. Enraged. So, he picked up his Maglite and I turned around, but I was laughing so hard I could barely run, then …"

"Well, I cut out from the crates down the hill toward the rec center, and Nick just eats it on the gravel. I mean his feet go out behind him and he just eats it," Troy added.

"The guy starts trucking down toward me, growling, and he throws the damn Maglite. It goes soaring past my head, bouncing off the gravel. Then he yells, 'Sonofabitch!' I knew my hands were fucked, but I ran down the hill wiping them on my pants. I finally got with Troy, and then we saw a group of cops shining their lights everywhere."

Wild Man's Cage

******

The traditional structure of Midwest public school and small-town hell raising was not enough to pacify the growing realization of the Search. Something burrowed inside I couldn't put my finger on, but its existence was wholeheartedly real. The meditation and commune upbringing were somehow connected to it, as was the adrenaline obsession. Though I wasn't sure how it fit, I considered the initiation rites that certain cultures forced upon their young men. Feelings of being trapped on a mouse wheel engulfed my waking thoughts right around the time I learned that I could leave my junior year on account of my advanced standing from MSAE, and still graduate on time. I negotiated with my parents. I pleaded, then mildly begged. Dad did it overseas in his twenties. He also backpacked the Sierras. Mom ran off to the airlines just out of high school. They understood, at least in part. Mine just arrived earlier. I assured them I would be responsible. I would work at the health food store for a few months, then venture out to California to live among our outlaw relatives who grew pot, shit outside, and bathed in solar showers with rattlesnakes nearby.

    I had discovered the Wild Man at sixteen. He was there when the eggs left our hands, cracking against the truck hoods of redneck Townies on the square. He applauded, as Troy and I dashed across that same square during a music festival, our cocks and balls slapping against our legs as we huffed passed the post office, two cop cars on our heels. The recent discovery of marijuana, the sound of a girl's belt slowly sliding off, the lurid purr of her zipper. The anticipation of fights and violence at parties. The Wild Man was constantly cajoling me to swim a little bit further into the darker parts of the ocean. To the murky primitive parts, knowing that if the sharks weren't there or if the land was still in sight, I was a fraud. I felt him pound his chest, and I heard him beat his drum. He was wily and unapologetic as his rattle shook. He pointed toward the forest and laughed. And I knew he would never go away. I knew that I had to walk inside.

Chapter 11

GO WEST, YOUNG MAN

Northern California, 1995

There are some who can live without wild things, and some who cannot.[12]

—Aldo Leopold

Even the local video store smelled like pot. I scanned its massive shelves, an erratic smattering of genres thrown together without order. Then something caught my attention. The Ultimate Fighting Championship (UFC) is now a household name, but in the mid-nineties it was an obscure underground subculture few people knew about. It was one of the first competitions that pitted different martial arts against one another inside an octagon cage. For years, debates ensued on whether karate was the most effective art, or kung fu, or judo, or whatever. Most purists were insensitive to other styles and defensive about the perceived shortcomings of their own art. The UFC sought to answer those questions by hosting a full contact competition, open to all styles without weight classes. Although now much more refined and professional, the UFC launched a rapid evolution of mixed martial arts that skyrocketed Brazilian Jiu Jitsu and exposed the criticality that fighters be well rounded. As I stood reading the back of the video jacket, a boyish-looking man in his twenties with incredibly blond hair, almost yellow, and faint eyeliner brushed next to me. He flashed a smile warmly before looking at the case.

---

12   A. Leopold, *A Sand County Almanac: And Sketches Here and There* (Oxford University Press, 2020).

Go West, Young Man

"That looks interesting," he said, as he dropped a handful of videos into the return box.

He glided past again, before exiting and crossing the street. The mysterious boy-man got into a brand-new Land Rover and sped away. I recognized the figure from somewhere but couldn't place him.

Without ruminating long, the scraggily bearded clerk with tinted John Lennon glasses and tie-dyed t-shirt said, "That cat's ship sure came in, man. Wouldn't mind tradin' places. Get me out of this Mendo bubble. I like his ride, too. Color matches his hair. You can drive that shit into the mountains and just disappear, you know."

I moved closer toward him, into a perfumed cloud of nag champa and weed.

"Who was that guy, I recognize him?"

The clerk coughed into his hand. It was a wet lung-butter hack. He cleared his throat, then looked at me incredulously.

"Probably on a magazine, man. That's Tre fuckin' Cool. Green Day. You know who they are, right? He was the dude in the straitjacket in their video, bangin' on the drums."

Then he added, "I'm in a band."

It was Tre Cool, the prodigious percussionist of a punk band that cross pollenated with enough mainstream appeal to rise to unfathomable glory. A Willits local, he attended high school with my cousins before jumping into the idyllic waters of superstardom. Like many kids from the area, his father was a Vietnam veteran that probably grokked the serene landscape and lack of population that plagued down south. As if reading my mind, the clerk chuckled.

"A lot of weird stuff happens behind the Redwood Curtain, man."

My body began a phase of rapid change in California, as my spirit tempered with it. I worked out regularly at a gym frequented by law enforcement. In the evenings I meticulously trimmed potent Indica buds with my family, while my mornings were spent spotting sheriff's deputies on the bench press. I gained over twenty-five pounds, most of it muscle. Afternoons got wasted at the coast with my journal and books written by others on the Search. The peaceful warrior, Dan Millman, shared insights from his time in Berkeley apprenticing with Socrates. Carlos Castenada regaled his tale of an intensive adventure with the wise Yaqi shaman, Don Juan. My older cousin, Shankara, whom I stayed with for a while, told me about wandering into Mexico and Central America. He visited pyramids and took copious amounts of psychedelics, sometimes waking up on park benches with no memory of

A Ronin's Tale

the previous days. I soon realized that others grappled with the invisible presence that haunted me. The need for tests, and for spelunking into the interior caves. Stepping left of the conventional path meant risk; the quest toward the heroic. But I was grossly naïve in my romanticism of it all. Especially the drugs. I didn't yet understand what descending down the rabbit hole untethered could bring. It kidnapped several in my family. And where I was staying in California, it had a tight grasp on the whole community.

It wasn't long after I settled into the Mendo scene that I came across predators. Asleep on a couch at my aunt's home, a pack of old trucks with loud mufflers came growling up the drive. Doors opened. Voices whispered first, then shouting ensued. There were wolves out there. Not like the Townies back in Fairfield that broke a nose or gave chase, but actual evil. A sickly feeling ruminated throughout my core.

"EH! COME OUT HERE, SHANKARA! COME OUT HERE, NOW, MOTHERFUCKER!"

I sat up slightly on the couch, trying to decipher if I was awake. Lights shone through the curtains, silhouetting different things in the room.

"You don't want us coming in there!" a different voice demanded.

My aunt tiptoed into the living room and peeked from the curtain. Her body language reminded me of Mom.

"Oh Christ," she began. "It's Sonny's younger brother. He's either drunk or on meth. Probably both. Nick, stay there. Shankara can deal with this."

Sonny was a close friend of Shankara's from an early age. They played little league together on the team my uncle Pat coached. A few summers earlier, Sonny told me about some bandit black community deep in the hills that he and Shankara stumbled upon after crashing his truck. Sonny said proudly that Shankara charmed the bandits, and they ended up smoking and drinking with them until early morning. They were given a ride to town and eventually became customers that bought in volume from the family business. Sonny's father was a Vietnam veteran, too, and full-patched member of the Hells Angels. Tales circulated for years that the Angels owned large parcels of land in the county, and that they disposed of bodies for a fee. Swaths of land in Lake and Mendocino counties were rumored to be giant outlaw cemeteries filled with remnants of the underworld. I heard bits and pieces about Sonny's dad and stints in some of California's gladiator prisons. I was dumbfounded given how well-mannered Sonny was. He had been at the house earlier that evening in a polo shirt tucked into chino shorts. His polite acumen and athletic frame seemed more likely found charming clients on a golf course rather than visiting a biker father in prison. Sonny passed me new beers like clockwork. We watched a UFC tape together and he urged me to leave Iowa permanently, even offering a bedroom at his house.

"Kara, now!" my aunt demanded.

"Don't you want to call the sheriff?" I asked, immediately regretting my foolishness.

My aunt looked over, and through the darkness I felt her eyes.

"Not with all the plants. Things are handled differently here," she said curtly. "Kara, I said get out here, NOW!"

Shankara meandered into the living room, shirtless and wearing boxer shorts with purple pinstripes. He looked out the window, then wiped sleep from his eyes and yawned. After a few seconds he said calmly, "I'll go see what they want."

Two of my female cousins and two of their attractive friends who lived at the house came into the living room.

"What the hell, Mom?" my younger cousin, Delana, asked. She walked to a piece of window and crouched down.

"Oh no, it's Sonny's brother."

"You want me to go out there with you?" I asked meekly.

Pausing for a moment, Shankara replied nonchalantly, "No. Better not. That might just make the situation worse. Stay with the girls."

Shankara walked outside shirtless but managed to throw on a pair of Quiksilver board shorts. He went over to the trucks, the mufflers still growling. I joined the women and peered through a vacant piece of window. Through the fog of my breath, I could make out about five or six guys. I thought I saw Sonny among the shadows but couldn't tell for certain.

Sonny's brother spoke loudly, slurring his words. It was unclear what was said but I heard "little bitches and cunts" repeated. After ten minutes, things were quiet until the trucks backed out the drive and peeled out, squealing tires. Shankara walked in coolly and immediately filled a pipe with some green shake on the kitchen table. He took a few hits and then offered a pass, but everyone declined.

"Everything's fine. Sonny told him about the little tune you all were singing in the kitchen earlier. He didn't like it."

"Tune?" my aunt asked confused. "What the hell are you talking about?"

A Ronin's Tale

"Something like Kelly smelly ..." he began.

My cousin Devaki laughed. Delana joined her.

"Kelly smelly below the belly!" they sang in unison. They repeated it again, this time more punctuated, "Kelly so smelly, what in the world is in that belly?"

"Yeah, that one," Shankara confirmed.

"And Sonny went home and told his brother?" my aunt asked in disbelief.

Sonny's little brother was only sixteen and had recently impregnated a fourteen-year-old girl from a nearby Indian reservation. Her name was Kelly, and my cousins, being theatrical and enjoying a goof after the beers and weed, came up with their little jingle. For whatever reason, Sonny went home and told his brother, who'd likely been awake, spinning for several days.

Not long after that incident, Sonny's brother and another guy, cranked out of their minds, beat a homeless man to death near the railroad tracks. With his brother and father serving life sentences, Sonny was the only free man left to carry on the family name.

Most of Shankara's friends were laidback, children of hippies. They had hair to their shoulders, and Adam had massive blond dreadlocks that fell just above his bony waist. Adam had recently moved back to Willits after a brief stint in the East Bay. One night working in a convenience store in Oakland, he was robbed at gunpoint and pistol whipped opening the till. That was enough city for him. Greener pastures literally called. They all grew powerful marijuana and dabbled in construction. Most were in their mid-twenties and surfed and rode dirt bikes. At that time, Troy and I were obsessed with the movie *Point Break*. Being around my cousin and his friends, I cast myself as Keanu Reeves, the clean-cut square personality seduced by the path of the outlaw. And they accepted me, even being a decade younger. Shortly after I arrived, they took me to the Eel River, and we jumped off towering rocks into the cold water below. Some of the rocks went over thirty feet. Looking back, it was a test.

The boys collectively purchased some acres in the tall redwoods that hid from the sun and built an A-frame. Things were damp out there, but the cool coastal fog made everything lush and vibrant. The drive to their land was about twenty minutes from my grandparents, and the curvy isolated Mendocino roads required full attention. Off the main pavement, a smattering of shacks and battered single-wides with "No Trespassing" signs stapled to wooden poles stood ominously silent.

Beat-up vehicles that would never run again sat rusted. There was a dystopian apocalyptic vibe out in the bush. I memorized two padlock combinations to get through the gated barriers. My aunt warned me to backtrack to the main road and call Shankara from Grandma's if I got lost. This was growing country in the nineties when Emerald Triangle herb sold for over three thousand dollars a pound. Many Vietnam veterans settled the area in the seventies to heal from war trauma and to be left alone. They bought land on the cheap and started families. Some locals were downright dangerous, outsiders were suspicious. Bits of soil were boobytrapped. People went missing. Rolling up on some random property unannounced had consequences.

Inside the cabin, Shankara told me about an old logging road that ran close to their property all the way to the Fort Bragg coast. He handed me a Sierra Nevada that I pretended to enjoy, then unfolded a shabby homemade map. The remote road was mostly downhill, a straightforward shot that would take some hours on a mountain bike. His friend, Reef, was about my size and agreed to loan me his thousand-dollar Cannondale. The morning we were set to ride, Shankara was nowhere to be seen. He was more like his father than he cared to admit. The northern California pot culture has its own rules and codes. Justice, too. Time is elusive, as most people just show up to things. Some of the stores in town bartered their goods for pot rather than exchange money. Big brother's watchful eye, and David Icke's talk of a coming New World Order, circulated unabashedly among town folk, fueling an already apparent paranoia. Some didn't trust the schools and subsequently started their own. Kids named Rain, Raven, and River—their sex difficult to determine from their long flowing hair—ate organic snacks and learned about farming the cash crop. Homes consisted of yurts and domes built without permits; power came from generators and solar. A GED carried weight. Yet meditation, incense, and crystals were there, too. Another utopian vision like the campus back home, but the scene grittier. The men harder and scarier.

I gave Shankara an hour before pedaling off alone. My backpack cinched tight and weighted with power bars, long-sleeved flannel, and a gallon of spring water. This was several years before cell phones. I told my grandparents I would crash at the cabin. The words of my grandfather, a quiet regal man who served in World War II and retired as an executive at Adidas, followed me out the door.

"Remember, Nick, people disappear. Pay attention."

The bike shifted smoothly as a friendly sun punctuated through the giants. A satisfying clicking sound reverberated through the silent forest as I learned the gears. The old road smelled of pine. A mild sadness drifted in as I pictured loggers with heavy saws dropping the colossal elders. Birds sang wistful songs. Colorful flowers and opulent ferns marked the rolling hills. I expected Merlin or some other wizard to approach at any moment. The first hour was mostly gentle with only a handful of switchbacks before I came upon the descent. As I approached a patch of clearing, an abandoned bus about two hundred yards above had sunshine reflecting off its mirrors. It seemed impossible that a bus could drive in such terrain, but this part of the country had its own mysticism. I leaned the bike against a tree a little off the path and peed. My grandfather's words faded, as I found my body move up a slightly steep pass toward the bus.

"Hello? Anyone there?" I shouted through my hands.

Silence.

"Hello? H-E-L-L-OOOO!"

The bus was surprisingly sound, without noticeable dents or scratches. On the rear, near the bumper, a Blue Bird sticker was affixed. The factory that made this bus was less than thirty miles from Fairfield. Synchronicity. Always around.

"Who's there?" a growly voice bellowed.

Instinctively I stepped back then raised my hands, as Adam probably did in Oakland with the robber.

"Who's there? I said," the voice more agitated this time around.

"Uh, my name is Nick. I'm biking to Fort Bragg and saw this bus."

There was a brief pause.

"Whacha want, Nick? Do I know you, Nick?"

"Uh, no. Sorry, sir, didn't mean to startle you or invade your place. I will leave now."

I walked backward, keeping my eyes on the bus.

"Givin' up so soon, are ya? Hold on, let me put some pants on."

My heart raced, and my first inclination was to run to my bike and pedal off, but I detected kindness in the mysterious voice. I was trying to piece together that someone actually lived so remotely, when all of a sudden, a short wiry man, probably close to middle age with a strange homemade hat and scruffy beard, emerged from around the corner. He was emaciated like a Ru, with tanned skin and weathered leathery face. His stained t-shirt hung off his narrow shoulders.

"You law enforcement? You look like law enforcement. You have to tell me if you are, you know."

"I'm sixteen."

"Oh, well, you look older, son. You ridin' to Bragg, huh?"

"Yes, sir. Got my bike down behind that tree over there."

"Need water or somethin'?"

"No thank you, sir. I just saw the bus and it seemed out of place out here, so I wanted to check it out."

"Stop callin' me sir, young fella. Name is Sage. That's what I go by."

Sage walked closer. His stature resembled Becki's, placing him only a few inches above five feet. For some reason, images of Charles Manson flooded in, though Sage had gentler eyes.

"Nice to meet you. I'm Nick. I actually live in Iowa close to where your bus was made. I'm staying with family in Willits."

"Is that right? Well, it ain't my bus. Don't know whose it is. But it's mine now. You wanna step inside, and see?"

Throughout my life I find myself in situations where I'm watching a film, shaking my head at the stupidity of the people on screen.

"Sure, I'd love to see it."

I followed Sage to the entrance, its smell transporting me to earlier school days. The inside was gutted of seats. In the center, a rotting plywood table sat with a bag of homemade granola, an incense holder, and differently colored candles. A sturdier table, similar in style, had a flat pillow on it, yellowed by sweat. A neatly folded olive-drab army blanket was on top. Scanning around the bus there was a small backpacking stove with fuel canisters, a red Swiss army knife, and a blue camping plate. A fat-headed flashlight was next to the blanket along with a roll of thin toilet paper. Outside the window, agitated black soil with skinny bamboo sticks were scattered about.

"Garden out there?" I asked, pointing.

"Yep. Grow my own food. Can't trust things in the stores now. Pesticides. All those GMOs. That's why people gettin' sick. Then the vaccines. Your family, they grow?"

"Yeah, but not vegetables."

A hardy laugh exited his sunken face, his smile revealing badly stained teeth.

"You want to try some smoke?"

"Thank you, but I need to pass. I'm not much of a mountain biker, so need all my coordination to be in place."

Another laugh, this time louder.

"Okay then."

A Ronin's Tale

Sage stared at me for a minute.

"You're not from these parts, are ya?"

"No. I was born in Sonoma, but have been living in Iowa for several years. With my family."

"Iowa? Hmm. Corn, right?"

"Yeah."

"Family, huh. Like wife and kids?"

"No, no. Parents. I live with my parents. I'm only sixteen."

"That's right, that's right," he mumbled.

"Sage, how'd you end up here. Like what made you want to live out here in this bus?"

Sage pulled a toothpick from a small plastic container near the table and fiddled with his teeth.

"Well, it's simple. The whole thing is goin' down."

"What do you mean?" I leaned closer to Sage.

"All of it. That's what I mean. Banking, food, the lies and whatnot. And when it does, those cities will turn violent. Real violent, real quick."

"You know, Nick, most people say they'd share what they have with strangers, and some do. But that kinda thinkin' doesn't linger. You go without long enough, your animal brain takes over. We're all just animals, you know. A different species of animal, but an animal species."

"So you're staying in Mendo for a bit, to prepare for this collapse?" I asked.

"Nah, I work south in the cold, then maybe head to Baja. Come from Seattle. Then Portland. Sad cities, they are. Real sad. Goin' to old Mexico, then go right back up to the gatherings. Was in Eugene few months ago, tree sittin'. Got a friend in Ukiah."

"Gatherings?"

"Rainbow. I'm part of the Rainbow Tribe. Descended from the Hopi. I'm a medicine man, too. Speaking of which, let me get some medicine right now."

Sage walked toward the back of the bus where a white sheet draped over fishing line. He rummaged through some things before emerging with two yellow milk crates. I thought of the security guard and his Maglite. Another life.

"Here, have this seat."

Sage sat upright on his crate and steadied an old dictionary on his lap.

"The whole thing, son, is coming down. The Rothschilds, Soros, all of 'em. The jig is up. And when people find out what's really going on, you better believe violence is coming. Reptilians. They're real, and I've seen 'em. Dark souls. Brought heroin and meth to the earth. Swear to God. You know we got cartel in Ukiah, now? So, I'm taking my time movin' south. May just stay here through winter. Pan a little gold, do some growin'. Go to town once or twice a month."

"No trick or treaters, huh?"

"Nope. No visitors. Most people stay to themselves 'round here. People don't get in others' business and that's the way it should be."

Sage's blackened fingers carefully placed the potent herb between organic rolling papers. He rotated the papers back and forth between his fingers to balance the sides, then licked the paper and rolled it a few more times packing it tight. He finished with a small sliver of cardboard that he effortlessly inserted like a filter to help the joint burn evenly.

"They're gonna force everyone to use a plastic card, like a credit card. It'll have your personal information, health stuff, bank accounts. They don't like what you're doin', or if you're a threat, they just push a button and boom, there goes your money. No funds, no credit, nothing. Won't be able to travel too, cuz everyone will have to prove who they are with the retina scan."

"Retina scan?" I asked.

"Mm hmm. It's beyond '84, man. New World Order calling for it. I'm thirty-six now, no wait a minute, I'm thirty-seven. Never thought I'd see this, but it's coming sure as day follows night."

Sage struck a match off the floor and took a long pull from his joint. He held the fragrant smoke, then turned away to exhale toward the opened window.

"Sure you won't?"

"I'm okay. Thank you, though. I actually need to hop back on my bike, but wanted to see the bus. Really glad I met you, though."

"Okay, then. You know where to find me. Just don't tell anyone about the gold or I'll haunt you in your sleep. Medicine men do that. We travel there just as we travel here. You know you're sittin' on a vortex, right?"

"Vortex?"

"Yep. It's where the witches and shamans jump through the tree and down to the lower world. If they're really powerful, they head up into the astral plane. I've only been down. You find the good and bad there. It's all the same, though. Can't have one without the other."

"Sage, it's been a pleasure. Thank you for showing me your bus."

"Don't thank me for nothin', just some conversation is all. Not my bus, neither. Let me fill up your bottle for you. Nice spring close by. Untouched. Cleanest water you'll drink in California. Maybe anywhere. They put fluoride in the tap water, you know."

"I appreciate that," I said, handing over my half empty jug.

The downhill cruise to the coast was tranquil, and I didn't come across any others. The seagulls sang overhead, while the brisk mist of the pacific baptized. The mind was quiet for a change, the world fresh and ready for exploration. It baffled me that people like Sage lived in the woods in the 1990s. My family had told me about these characters for years, but I never fully believed it.

A couple weeks after the ride, I headed north with my cousins to Garberville, at the southern edge of Humboldt County. The Mateel Community Center hosted an American Indian drum circle, then two reggae bands. Adam made us some phony laminated Press passes, complete with lanyards, that got us in for free. Walking into the venue, a collection of people my parents' age in homemade-looking dresses and braided hair danced in trancelike fashion to the thunderous drumbeat. The center smelled of body odor, more natural than offensive. A woman with thick black hair under her armpits painted beautiful unicorns and stars on the cheeks of children. Little baggies with homemade popcorn and fig newtons sold for fifty cents. Then somebody tapped my shoulder.

"Neil, right?"

"Ah, Sage! It's Nick. How are you, my friend?"

The bones of his back cracked delicately as I squeezed him.

"I'm good. Always good. Staying with a friend in a tipi not far from here. You wanna burn?"

I looked around suspiciously, as Sage pulled a zeppelin from a dirty shirt pocket.

He laughed loudly. "This is Humboldt, man. Even the law burns here."

Usually uncomfortable in formal settings, especially with dancing, I was grateful for Sage's medicine, which took immediate effect. I glided around with tightened shoulders at first, slowly increasing my rhythm. Then my chest and throat opened, allowing an unobstructed breath. I took my shirt off completely and flowed uninhibited through the room, moving side to side, and raising my arms as if prostrating to an unseen god. A pulsating serpent-like force surged through my spine and into my hips, shaking me like a cobra. The sensation was overpowering. The reggae produced a remarkable unity, as I embraced strangers and received their loving energy. At one point, Sage patted me on the back temporarily breaking my spell, before disappearing for good. Later that evening, a hippie girl in colorful floral dress and a ring in her nose danced with me. She moved in more closely, occasionally brushing me. Then she took my hand and led me outside to a blue VW bus with a white canvas top. Inside, she feverishly pulled my pants down to my ankles and slid my penis into her mouth while the music echoed off the walls. It didn't take long. We sat there in silence, as I wondered what my friends were doing in Iowa. I thought about the cornfield parties and Old Milwaukee. She invited me to Portland, but never told me her name. I would eventually return to Iowa after nearly five months away. More muscular. More settled. Having peeked behind the curtain, a scaly skin of my past left behind. A rebirth. The Wild Man was out; fearless, determined, unapologetically free. A belly roar echoed through the cosmos.

Chapter 12

THE INVOCATION

Fall 2017, A Classroom in the Midwest

What is a myth? Typically, when we use this word in our culture it implies something untrue, or so supernatural that it doesn't have applicability in our modern lives. It is a word we use to write something off as unbelievable or unrealistic; "Oh, that's just a myth." But according to Campbell, a myth is more accurately a metaphor that is symbolic of the spiritual powers inside us. They don't derive from an ideological system, but rather they come from a life system. In other words, they come out of our deep center and often produce a feeling of truthfulness when we hear them. We relate to what they say. Myths are not concerned with right and wrong answers or facts, but rather they focus on experience. From our experiences we gain insight. A myth is often shared in story form and their characters and themes transcend time and culture. For instance, the stories of knights on quests in Europe contain rich insight into things like virtue, honor, justice, and confronting fear. The knight may feel conflicted; should he stay within the safe womb of the castle walls with his beautiful wife and family, or should he venture outside where danger lurks? Should he stay loyal to his oath, or accept a pot of gold and work for the enemy? Although the story is from a distant time and place, its knowledge contains an essence that is just as appropriate and applicable to a modern-day stockbroker in New York.

When we explore the mythological world, a prominent theme of death and rebirth is revealed. The Hero does not literally die, but rather he is forced through the voyage to confront parts of himself that need to be healed or released; pieces that hold him back or that weaken his ability to break open into a more powerful way of being. A useful

The Invocation

symbol of the hero's journey is a snake that sheds its skin. Initiation and rites of passage are very much a part of this cycle. We walk through a door and have an intensive and profound experience, only to walk through another door changed by it. Are you the same person you were ten years ago? What types of experiences occurred over this time frame that left a scar or indelible mark? What insights did you learn about yourself? To probe this concept further, let's consider something each of us in this room has shared: military service.

The first introduction into the military begins with the ominous initiation of boot camp. You pull onto base late at night, scared and unsure what to expect. As the bus slows, you see a menacing cadre of drill instructors looming outside like sharks. Suddenly there is a reality check that things are starting, and then a commotion of yelling and chaos ensues. The instructor yells something barely coherent before rushing the group to various buildings where you are stripped of your civilian clothing. Uniforms are passed out curtly, your head is shaved clean, and you wait, nervously anticipating what is next. There is a nakedness and humility that comes from this very basic introduction. A stripping down to your core. As training progresses, you learn the tools of your trade such as marksmanship, first aid, tactics, and physical fitness. You move away from thinking strictly as an individual, as teamwork is prioritized. But you also learn stories. You learn about the history, famous battles, and heroic figures from your branch of service. The songs and marching are expressions of this mythology. As boot camp progresses toward the end, a culminating test is required. In the Marine Corps, they do the Crucible. At the end of training, you are no longer a lowly recruit but instead worthy of a title: Marine, Soldier, Sailor, etc. You have progressed through the rite of passage, which is a mini hero's journey, and you now have a place in the tribe. But what has also happened, and this is the important part, is that you are expected to take your place within the tribe with a new set of expectations. The way that you operated and lived as a civilian won't work in the new organization. That part of you was killed so that this new self could emerge. A rebirth.

Chapter 13

INITIATION

August 2004, Cotati, California

> Look fear in the face, and it will cease to trouble you.[13]
> —Sri Yukteswar

Around five, faint shouting from the nearby army base echoed and reverberated off the lizard-free bulkhead. The motivated chants were in Thai, but the rhythmic pace of the cadences was familiar. I hummed along, reflecting that it had been twelve years since I returned from the Middle East, and almost a decade since I wore the uniform. Another lifetime. Special in part, though merely playing a role in a detached other way. The university was similar. I was still searching for a more truthful place.

My arms extended in a deep stretch. Awash in thoughts of the various trainings I'd done during my eight years of service, I reasoned that I was more prepared for camp than I realized. Yes, I was probably older than the others, and yes, I didn't have any formal fighting experience aside from some karate, but I wasn't training for the octagon. It wasn't a duel to the death. It was merely a task; a test, though its rules and rubric elusive. Resolved there would be no more sleep, and sensing other doubts if I stayed in bed, I rose to pee, then chugged two bottles of water. It was just another initiation. *Not your first rodeo, Nick*, the wiser voice consoled.

---

[13] S. Yukteswar, *The Holy Science* (Self-Realization Fellowship Press, 1990).

Initiation

******

There is a pocket of time I clutch to like a reassuring blanket. A period of purity looking back, just as girls were discovered, but before conversations about mapping out a life began. It was the early nineties, and things moved quickly. Sludgy, dreary grunge lyrics vomited coarse and painful angst, while hip-hop and black culture fused with white America. Things got edgier, and jeans started to sag. Each brick on campus holds a memory from that era, as we awkwardly flirted with crafting our place.

Walking to MSAE in spring, the prospect of summer adventures loomed. Sleepovers with friends, and old school Nintendo. Sometimes a stolen cigarette or a magazine with naked women surfaced. Social media and tech addiction nonexistent, as a gang of adolescent boys roamed, fully present. Subtle thoughts of bravery penetrating just above the surface. For the most part, we were on equal footing. Athletic prowess and toughness not yet apparent. Neither were our charms and rankings among the opposite sex. But thoughts concerning where one stands prowled. A transitional moment before tribes formed and each of us was assigned to one.

It's a losing virtue to reason that men ever mature or become immune to the forces of the pecking order. Its stranglehold cinches too tightly. What varies is the costume it wears and how it's confronted. The Wall Street powerbroker is not much different from the guy who lives in his van and free climbs dangerous peaks. Something elusive drives them. Yet even the peace that comes with acquired victories only lingers so long. Inevitably the cycle begins anew. The high wears off and the fiend goes looking.

The week I defended my master's thesis and graduated, my girlfriend and I ended things abruptly. It was a whirlwind military romance that ascended quickly, feverishly, forfeiting rational thoughts for unbridled naïveté. We were long distance mostly, then kicked around the idea of getting engaged, and me moving up to Seattle. But the pain of separation led to other issues, and the relationship dissolved days before my lease expired. Before long I was burrowed in a two-person tent on the dodgy, transient-riddled Humboldt coast. Then, less than a week later my grandfather died.

Driving a couple hours south to be with family, under the canopy of the massive, though forlorn redwood giants, I felt gratitude for his wisdom.

"You have your whole life to work," he said.

I leaned forward at the breakfast table, hanging onto his words.

"When you're my age, you'll look back and wished you'd not taken it all so seriously. That you'd made time for other things."

I was sixteen, and perhaps he sensed my ambivalence about taking a breather from high school and heading to Shankara's cabin to get stoned.

The chalkboard wiped clean again, I ventured off the frigid Humboldt coast to warm at a café in Arcata, then hopped on Craig's List. The universe responded expeditiously with Ray; a middle-aged Latino Gulf War veteran the army booted for his sexual proclivities. Tidy, kindhearted, and cultured from ten years in Europe, Ray now slugged the night shift at the local newspaper as a delivery driver. He was the perfect roommate, and got me out of the foggy heaviness up north, back to the opulent wine country. With my aching heart being tended to, I needed an unstructured time to just be. The defeat of an ended relationship and harrowing thoughts of her fucking another man haunted me. I never met the man. But I didn't need to. He had something she wanted that I didn't, and that's what wounded. My spiral down the pecking order. Demoted. I marinaded in that for a minute, then went searching for redemption.

The main bar was the only establishment in the county where patched biker clubs, known as one-percenters, could openly wear their colors. It opened at seven in the morning and was popular among blue shirts, solo laborers drinking alone under dim lighting. Their bucket of Budweiser for ten bucks lured me in a couple nights a week, but the incentive really came from its cryptic online reviews as the best prospect in town for a hook-up. As a kid, my dad drove us by that bar on the way to preschool. Two decades later its original sign with fire around an eight ball was still untouched. Yellowed Coors signs crooked in the window next to neon glitz. A seedy ominous energy radiated from its black saloon doors. Even on the way to preschool, I looked up from my ninja magazine to check out its scene.

Crystal was the first. A few years older and recently divorced, she reached past for a coaster and ever so slightly brushed my hand. Then she told me she liked my dimples. The usual pleasantries exchanged, flirtations followed. I tailed her home in my red pickup; her two kids at their father's. More awkward small talk in the living room before a kiss that quickly led to clothes sliding off. A big jar of Vaseline sat on

Initiation

her nightstand. I stared at it while on top of her, thinking of my ex. I thrusted away, launching pangs of rage toward her. I wish she could see me now. I wish she could see I wasn't hurting. I hovered outside my body, Crystal watching as a spectator. Both of us, really. The condom spun a couple times before disappearing in the toilet, as I discretely slid the mirror above her sink to see if she was taking medication. Notions of etiquette, the number of minutes I should stick around before fleeing wandered about. As I opened the bathroom door, my clothes were neatly spread on top of a made bed, Crystal in the living room with a lit cigarette. I drove back to Ray's smelling of the prominent awkwardness that only a one-night stand can deliver. The ego temporarily raised by another notch, the heart meanwhile empty and despondent.

Not long after the Crystal experience, on a Friday, the bar was nearing max capacity. A witchy, gothic type, that resembled Siouxsie minus the Banshees belted out seventies classics, while the bar's manager, Tracey, served a mixed crowd of bikers, blue collars, and broke college students. Tracey once posed in *Hustler* and had been a hang around with an assortment of eighties and nineties hair bands. I heard it from a middle-aged bouncer, Walt, who wore a mullet and had faded tattoos on his forearms. I overheard others at the bar mention that she'd dated a famous actor for a while. Fame was in her hands for a minute, close enough at least to feel its spell, but she didn't crack its code. Now, she settled as queen of the biker bar. Her long bleached-blonde hair, overly tan skin, and bony figure resembled a weathered Pamela Anderson. I can't say for certain, but pills seemed inevitable in her story. She poured solid drinks, stepping outside every fifteen minutes for a smoke, then tearing each cigarette in half after three long pulls. The young bar-back, a student at a local college, was the son of a famous Hollywood director. He was determined to cut his own path away from his father's shadow, opting for Tracey's abuse instead.

"Andy! Andy! More Millers and Buds, NOW! I shouldn't have to tell you that shit, that's your fucking job, son. Go in back and bring more ice. And grab two more Cuervo Gold!"

Tracey's admirers filled the horseshoe mahogany, grinning as her sailor mouth went to work. On that Friday, Tracey's sass rubbed a patron the wrong way and a full beer breezed dangerously close by her head, shattering a mirror behind the bar. The commotion slowed everything; even Siouxsie paused.

Instinctively, I grabbed the man from behind and put him in a chokehold I'd learned in the military. I pulled him off his stool, taking him to the ground with my right arm around his neck, latched to my left bicep.

"Stay down, asshole! Stay down!" the adrenaline yelled.

I said it again, with the choke in place, though loosening it. Slowly I pulled the man to his feet and walked him outside. He clutched onto my arm and gasped for breath. Patrons looked on expressionless, clearing a path. He raised his hands with palms facing upward and said through broken breath, "I'm sorry, man, I'm sorry. I don't know why I did that. I'm sorry."

My heart beating quickly, beads of sweat trickled down my forehead and converged on my nose and lips. The man and I stood looking at one another, while the fire waned. A flood of empathy and kinship surfaced, though I wasn't sure why.

"I hear you, brother. I hear you. But you can't be throwing shit like that. Especially at women."

"I know," he offered, looking downward at his feet. "I know."

Collections of faces stared from partially tinted windows. The man's eyes fixed on the sidewalk. I peered over at the park, joyful memories of a preschool field trip, crossing the street holding hands. A nursery rhyme about a dog looking for his shoes.

"I'm getting divorced, and she comes here sometimes," the man said.

Almost immediately the saloon doors swung open, and a mass of blonde hair bolted out.

"You motherfucker! You tried to kill me, you son of a bitch! You are done. Do you hear me? You are FINISHED here. You can NEVER come back into my bar; do you understand, you prick? I ought to have my biker boyfriend handle your ass!"

I raised my hands in a sign of peace toward Tracey, standing in between her and the man.

"And who the fuck are you?" she demanded, cocking her head to the side. "I don't know you. You can leave, too, pretty boy asshole who just sits at the bar drinking and moping 'round like a little sad puppy. You both are DONE."

I grinned at her, then laughed. I'd never been called a sad puppy before. Or a pretty boy.

"Okay, but my wallet and keys are on the counter. May I go in and get it?" I pleaded softly.

Tracey stood there fuming at both of us, not speaking for a few seconds. She drew one deep breath and exhaled forcefully.

Initiation

"Fine. Go. This asshole is finished, though. He ain't coming in."

I nodded to the broken man and half smiled. He nodded back, then walked toward a newer full-sized truck parked next to a trove of Harleys.

Walking into the bar, a few people applauded. Even the vixen spoke into the mic, "There he is folks. A round of applause for the sheriff."

A guy in a red-and-black-checkered flannel patted me on the shoulder as I strolled by still wiping sweat from my face. As a kid, I fantasized of these moments; a terrorist takeover at school, only to be foiled by my heroics. The cutest girls beaming in the assembly while the principal affixed a shiny medal to my chest. But something was off here. I grieved for the 86'd man and the thought of his hurting heart. I pictured him getting into bed alone and the shame he must be carrying. There was some unknown connection there, too. A resemblance. Then I thought about a few pictures I saw on the refrigerator at Crystal's, and the man with the distinctive chin.

Standing above the stool I collected my wallet and looked up, my eyes meeting Tracey's.

"You can stay. Didn't mean to call you names, either."

I gave Tracey a partial nod and sat down.

"But no free drinks. You'd need to get stabbed or shot for that. Or save my pretty ass."

That evening a window opened. Previously, my life had the regimented grind of academics. I taught classes to undergrads and worked part-time in a veteran's office. I also did the military reserves on weekends. I scraped by. But this new phase stripped me of those responsibilities. I had a clean slate and time to dwell. In the day I worked out and drove to the coast to write in my journal. The overcast haze cooled me, providing a reassurance that I was in a different type of school, with a curriculum for the soul. I researched doctoral programs, sensing this was necessary for the career I envisioned. I cringed at the lengthy application and never-ending checklist. Most of my peers had gone right into one out of the master's program, but I was burned out. I lost nearly fifteen pounds since leaving Humboldt. Back in the forest. *How long will I be in it? What am I chasing? Why are things so confusing? When will shit get easier?* Yes, the soul curriculum.

Security at the bar was mostly on weekends when the live music and scraps happened. Not long after subduing the bottle thrower, I was approached by a behemoth of a man resembling a real-life version of

Captain Morgan. Dressed all in black, in a long leather trench coat, the man had an almost shiny beard that was neatly maintained. The mystery pirate towered as I looked up from a stool and took his hand. His large bear paw squeezed with enormous strength, cracking a few of my knuckles.

"I'm Big Rob."

"Nick."

"Mind if I sit for a minute?"

I motioned toward a stool next to me, and he sat.

"I run security here. Heard about your little incident the other night."

Rob was a prison guard at San Quentin, or Q, and ran a security company on the side, working a handful of local bars and nightclubs. One of the bouncers I became friendly with told me about him. He was also an accomplished martial artist, I'd heard.

"Interesting line of work, Rob."

"Don't need the money. Do it for the perks, and most of those are in skirts," he chuckled.

There was something about Rob I immediately trusted. He walked slowly and purposefully. When I first saw him inside the bar my eyes went toward him for an unknown reason. My dad often told me growing up that people give off radiance; an invisible energy you can tune into and that either draws you in or pushes you away. Rob rode a newer Harley. He would later share that he had escorted Charles Manson, Richard "Night Stalker" Ramirez, and a few other infamous desperados while working in Q. His speech was steady; his voice calm as it exited his wide mouth and impeccably white teeth.

"It isn't much different than working a prison. You talk to people. Most of us don't think right when we're drunk or high, so you be direct and let 'em know what they're doing won't be tolerated. But you do it professionally. Nothing personal. It's a respect thing. Sometimes you put hands on them, but mostly you talk 'em out of the tree. Get them to put the pieces together and change course."

"Makes sense. Everything happened fast the other night, and the guy threw a bottle. Hands on felt necessary," I said, somewhat defensively.

"No, no, I'm not challenging you," he began, shifting a little on the stool.

"You were right with that. It happens fast, so you make a choice fast, right? Tracey gave you a compliment, and trust me, that's a miracle,

Initiation

bud. She also said you might need some work, so here I am."
"Look, I'm down a guy here and could use the help. Got a club opening, too, if you're interested. Twenty an hour, cash, plus a share of the tips. You cover your own medical. If you drink on the job, show up high, or start shit with people, you're done. You let friends in without paying or score 'em drinks, done. No second chances. Steady work, Thursday through Sunday."

******

An acceptance letter to a lucrative PhD program arrived in my mailbox hours before four Hells Angels and two prospects entered the bar. It wasn't uncommon for them to stop in, but they mostly stayed to themselves in a darkened corner near Tracey. More than once, a patron walked in, scanned the bar, and stared wide-eyed at the cut on the back of their leather. The iconic death-head emblem brought both fear and admiration. They were a tribe of outlaws no doubt, and many tales circulated about what it took to join their elite brotherhood and the kind of work you had to carry out once inside. I asked Rob about it one time, and he shook his head and told me not to ask those questions. One of the Angels had dated Tracey, and they remained on good terms, though she reminded the security more than once to give them a wide berth.

Rob told me my first night, "Any patch holders come in, just leave 'em be. They won't cause trouble. If a fight breaks out and they're in it, don't get involved. If I'm here, I'll handle it."

The senior member of their chapter walked in first and gave me a nod, having seen me before. I returned it and nodded to the others, who didn't acknowledge me. As they filed through, a large KaBar knife in a leather sheath was affixed to the right leg of a prospect. A prospect is exactly that, a prospective member, essentially undergoing an exhaustive evaluation with the club. It's like an outlaw job interview where a person must be available 24-7 to meet the needs of the club or any of its members. Some prospects are intentionally put in situations to test their mettle. Rob told me prospects would be more likely to start shit than the actual members, so I noted that comment and held onto it.

"Hey, brother, I can't let you come in with that knife," I said, placing a hand in the air with my palm facing the prospect. His grayish shark eyes drifted upward, then stopped at mine.

He stood only a few inches shorter than me, probably around six-foot-three, but a solid two hundred and fifty pounds. His head was shaved clean, and a tattoo of a noose around his neck looked like it was done in prison. He didn't blink. I saw unholy things in those eyes.

"I'm not your fucking brother, asshole," he said.

My heartbeat shot up immediately as we faced each other. I could smell his sour breath. A brief scan of his meaty forearms and fists showed more jailhouse ink. I didn't look around, but sensed the bar watching.

I cleared my throat as quietly as possible.

"It's the law. Nothing personal. Tracey will get a big fine," I said, discretely pulling a long breath through my nose.

The patched members turned around. It was a paused moment, dreamy, where I stood outside myself witnessing events from afar. Briefly, I wondered if I would die. I pictured the man quickly pulling the knife from its brown leather sheath and stabbing me with it. A faint voice from my dad's younger brother, an outlaw himself who had underworld ties, bubbled up. He said that guys with two felony strikes on their record often committed murder for their third offense, just so they could have higher status in prison. The mind kept going. Rob would run over, and eventually the paramedics would arrive. Tracey's shriek would keep my brain focused as my soul began its separation. I thought about the phone call to my parents and them trying to piece together how I ended up working in a seedy bar, and how they would inevitably blame themselves in some way. The utopian vision sidetracked by my ego's stranglehold to prove something unprovable. But peace came, too. I believe that our lives follow a destiny, that there is a divine presence that brings circumstances beyond our control in order to teach us. Surrendering in these moments is the only truthful medicine.

As thoughts flooded in, the senior member circled over, then intervened: "Give him the knife, prospect."

The prospect stood rooted to the floor, staring. Those eyes cut right to the chase. All of the tests he probably encountered in prison, and God knows where else, those eyes could see things mine would never see. Slowly, he opened his silver skeleton belt buckle. Then he slid the sheathed weapon and forcefully slapped it into my hands.

"You're responsible for this," he said.

Rob looked on from a stool, expressionless. Mike, who covered the far door, watched intently. I walked to Tracey.

Initiation

"See this knife here?"

"Mm hmm," she nodded.

"Pretend it's a satchel of cash, and put it someplace safe. If you lose it, I will die. With pain."

Tracey chortled.

"You got it, sweetheart," she said as she winked. Then she added with a snort, "I was hoping to see you fight again."

The bikers walked toward Rob and surrounded him. I looked across the room at Mike for direction, but there was nothing. After a moment, sets of eyes turned and looked at me. Then laughter. Rob's infectious snort could penetrate a concert crowd, and the prospect with the neck tattoo shook his hand before the group dispersed to a shadowy corner.

Later that evening, after Tracey returned the knife and they left, Rob walked over and handed me a cold Miller.

"What the fuck, Rob?" I asked, still shaken from the incident, and worried about the walk to my truck.

"Relax, pretty boy. He remembered me from Quentin. I escorted him a couple times. He just wanted to thank me for being respectful to him. Prison is all about respect."

"Why'd you guys all look at me, then?"

Rob looked at the ground and smirked. After a pause, he said, "I told them you were Tracey's new beau. That you were weak and couldn't fight for nothing, but she hired you out of pity, and cuz you're a pretty boy."

At that point, Rob unleashed a belly roar that turned a few patrons' heads.

"Seriously? You really said that?" I asked, embarrassed.

Rob shot a look he often gave before saying, "C'mon." He reflected again, then stated unemotionally, "It's not important what was said. You handled the situation, and nobody got stabbed. That's all that matters. It's not always about you, Nick."

******

The person of noble heart acts spontaneously, and will avoid the Wasteland, the world of "Thou Shalt."[14]

—Joseph Campbell

---

14   Osbon, *Reflections on the Art of Living*.

It takes great courage to step left of the traditional path to pursue your bliss. It takes great courage to not get bogged down by the plans others have for you. But the alternative of not embarking on the hero's journey is to live an inauthentic life. Have you ever been in a situation you didn't want to be in that lingered? A job, or a relationship that you knew wasn't compatible, but you stayed in it for a while because it was convenient, or you told yourself you were happy, or it would get better. Maybe you went through the motions and tried to stick it out, but eventually you couldn't hide what was there. Something deep down confirmed this. Your wiser center spoke to you. This is what Campbell warns. If we build the structure of our life around telling ourselves we are content when we're not, if we acquiesce and just accept that this is our life and it's not changing, we go to sleep. We live in the slumbered existence of the Wasteland. We embrace a hypnotized reality devoid of a substantive life force. Our life becomes burdened with bitterness, resentment, and regret. A myth is a metaphor symbolic of the spiritual powers within us. They come from where the heart is and where the experience is. But we are stubborn creatures, too. And we also have free will. So, what happens when we flat out refuse the Call and choose to not go on the journey? As we have already discussed, sometimes the journey chooses us. The choice is made. However, for those who continually pass up the opportunity to take the adventure, a worse fate awaits them.

When we refuse the Call, we become someone else's servant and life loses its juice. Anxieties build up, and what we would experience positively, through the journey, will subsequently leak out in our lives negatively. For instance, if Daniel flat out told Mr. Miyagi to pound sand and abandoned the path of karate and competing in the All Valley tournament, there would be fallout from his decision. Consequences. The villain in these sacred stories is symbolic of our own shadow patterns. What is a shadow? Think of it as the darker parts of ourselves that are unhealed and that sabotage us in different ways. Our addictions, our excuse making; the subconscious patterns and things we pursue that deep down we know are not helpful to our growth. The text we shoot off around midnight to an ex-girlfriend after we've been drinking in the bar.

If Daniel elected to not go through the journey and do the hard work of transformation, he would in time take on the qualities of those he feared most. In other words, he would become a bully himself. He would become Johnny Lawrence of the Cobra Kai. It might manifest

Initiation

as Daniel becoming an overpowering and pain-in-the-ass boss, or an emotionally empty and cynical husband. Or maybe he would have children and be overly controlling and harsh toward them. His life would be plagued by operating from his shadow rather than from his mature and balanced center. Think about people you know who are like this. Are they enjoying their lives? Are they enjoyable to be around? They carry pain. They have things inside them that need to be healed. And remember, your gender, race, sexual orientation, religion, political party, income level, education, the way you look, etc., doesn't mean a thing. Nobody is exempt from this. It's an equal opportunity truth.

It is also important to emphasize that the stages are not set in stone sequentially. They provide a helpful blueprint and show a natural flow, but real life is seldom so clean in its unfoldment. So, with that said, to reduce this first part to its most basic principle, the Hero senses that something is missing or off in his ordinary life. He is bored, or frustrated, or maybe he is quite successful, but something still feels missing. Then his life shakes up in some profound way and he senses the Call to Adventure. He may reject the Call out of fear, or he may be totally oblivious of what awaits him. That's when a mentor arrives to assist the Hero with answering the Call and subsequently starting a journey in pursuit of a jewel or some treasure. The riches the Hero pursues, or the mission he chases, are symbolic of finding wholeness. And it is through the journey that great transformation unfolds. This next section is a very rich part of the story. The Hero now awake begins the process of leaving the Ordinary World for the Special World. To do this, he must cross the threshold.

Crossing the threshold is a pivotal point in the adventure. In some mystical stories, the Hero might jump down a tree trunk or enter a mysterious cave that transports him to a sacred world. I personally like the visual image of a dark forest. There is often an immediate reaction when the Hero enters the new world, such as the walls behind him close quickly. This is symbolic that the Hero is trapped and that he can only progress forward on his quest. Psychologically, the new territory is very different from the Ordinary World, and anything can happen there, both favorable and unfavorable. The Hero has to begin letting go of his attachments and the things that hold him back. It is in the Special World that the Hero finds power he never knew he possessed. Another point to emphasize is that benign power that follows the Hero. In Star Wars *it's called the Force. There are many ways one can interpret what this presence is: God, the divine, the supernatural, good luck, destiny,* synchronicity, etc. How you choose to define it is up to you. The point here is that the Hero is being guided and to some degree, protected, by an unseen benevolent presence.

Mythologically, Daniel stands outside the forest when he leaves the Cobra Kai dojo with Mr. Miyagi. Think about films or stories where there is a dark forest, and all sorts of scary noises emit from it. Shady characters hang out close by. Who wants to enter that? Bad things happen in there, so fear naturally shows itself. When we give in to fear, what do we feel? It weakens us, yes? Especially when we run from it. But thankfully, we have the presence of a wise elder, Miyagi, who also happens to be a karate master. And something tells me he can read everything going on with Daniel. This is a classic theme in a hero's journey; a mentor who possesses strong intuition and knowingness. Someone who has been around the block and knows the human condition in profound ways. This person has to push the Hero enough to motivate and move him forward, but not so much that he overwhelms him and the Hero cracks. As they leave the Cobra Kai dojo, in the next frame we see them drive to Miyagi's home to formally begin karate training. Daniel has accepted the Call and he's accepted Miyagi as his mentor. The story moves forward, and Daniel enters the unknown.

Driving over the railroad tracks to Miyagi's home is where Daniel crosses the threshold into the Special World. This is the labyrinth for Sarah, or Oz for Dorothy a strange environment with even stranger characters that defy our understanding of reality. The rules of the previous Ordinary World are different or may not apply at all. We may witness superpowers or magic. The teachings we receive may come disguised.

On a more realistic level, the Special World may be a deployment to a combat zone. You complete months of pre-deployment training and say good-bye to your family for the next year. You board the long flight overseas and land in a strange and unforgiving landscape that is barren, hot, and dangerous. Behaving in a humane way during war may become decidedly unclear and ambiguous, as survival becomes the most significant thing. Moral dilemmas arise, but we don't have the same laws and order that govern our behavior and decision-making process like we do in the Ordinary World. Think about the fog of war, or collateral damage. We have a high-value target, a terrorist for instance, responsible for some significant attack, and our intelligence says this person is holed up with his family. Is hitting the compound and killing the terrorist and his family in the process the right decision? If

Initiation

we take out this guy, won't someone just step up and take his place? Or will killing this individual give us tremendous advantage and ultimately save American lives? What happens when the intelligence is flawed, and we end up bombing a school by accident?

As we cross the threshold into this new environment, the landscape changes on many fronts, both externally and internally. When people go to war with their unit, they may experience similar events, but how they navigate and manage them, how they make sense and ascribe meaning to what they're doing is an individual process. And how they grieve or heal also varies.

I was tasked overseas to lead a detail where we loaded dead American bodies onto planes to be sent home. We knew about their deaths before their families and that thought haunted me. I envisioned a proud child talking about their heroic parent to their class, maybe even bringing something military to show and tell. They didn't know what we did. As we lifted the shiny gray caskets, flags were adorned on top and salutes rendered. Horrid smells wafted throughout the flight line. One man had been killed less than twenty-four hours earlier. A small group of us wept together in a circle next to an artificial Christmas tree. It wasn't easier the second time we loaded planes. But over the course of my life, I reminiscence with deep gratitude that I was part of it. I was able to respectfully send them home to their families and offer them prayers for safe passage. It was tragic, yes, but there was also tenderness. There was humanity in it. Remember, the hero's journey is solo. This Special World is where the process of intensively forging the Hero's spirt takes place. You cut your path and deal with whatever comes. You discover new power and layers.

> You enter the forest at the darkest point, where there is no path. Where there is a way or path, it is someone else's path. If you follow someone else's way, you are not going to realize your potential. Opportunities to find deeper powers within ourselves come when life seems most challenging.[15]

---

15 Osbon, *Reflections on the Art of Living*.

Part 2

The Special World

Whatever your fate is, whatever the hell happens, you say, "This is what I need." It may look like a wreck, but go at it as though it were an opportunity, a challenge. If you bring love to that moment and not discouragement, you will find the strength there.[16]

—Joseph Campbell

Chapter 14

The Wasteland

Fall 2017, My New Condo

>Sometimes it is okay if the only thing you did today was breathe.[17]
>
>—Yumi Sakugawa

"Nick, this is one fancy bachelor pad, man. Bring a chick back here and you're set. She ain't leavin' dude, I mean that."

Contractor Larry pointed his brush at me as paint droplets descended from his weathered ladder onto a blue tarp that covered the hardwood floors below.

With a fresh pinch of tobacco centered evenly on his lower lip he continued, "Seriously, man, you got the world by the balls. Good on you, boy. Have a brother about your age and he's nothing but a fuck up."

"He's back in Indiana?" I asked.

Larry tilted his head for a moment and stopped painting.

"Don't think so. He lives somewhere in Methville, I suppose." Then he spit into a plastic pop bottle.

Right around the seven-year mark, thoughts of an escape from the university became distant. I received significant raises, and before I knew it my student loans and other debts were paid off. It didn't take long to develop a routine blowing money on craft beers, eating out, and other bullshit. Packages arrived frequently; even some furniture

---

[17] Y. Sakugawa, Personal Blog: https://www.yumisakugawa.com/post/13759359719, December 4, 2011.

snuck under the curtain. I purchased my first bed. A luxury one with an ornate headboard, down pillows, and sheets with some kind of magical thread count. It was time to be respectable I figured, to grow up and put down roots. I counted one time in my early thirties; I had moved so many times that it had surpassed my age. Visions of a beefy Tacoma with a bed and drawers in the back, parked in some mountain town in Colorado or Humboldt County faded. I wasn't accustomed to the security of staying in one place for long, and it's largely why most of my relationships never lasted. Most commitments, from jobs to love interests, had an unconscious expiration date.

The woman who sold me the condo was beautiful. Her brunette hair hung stylishly over her tan and unblemished face. She wore a skirt and top that showed a figure of someone who took care of herself. I liked D immediately, and even went on extra viewings just so I could spend time with her. She didn't have a ring, and at one point during a showing there was a silent pause between us. My heartbeat accelerated, as I considered kissing her against the faux stone laminate. But I didn't. Instead, we signed documents at the bank together; the Amish builder handed me the keys with a smile that glowed through his scruffy beard. My realtor crush, knowing my bachelor status, gave me a card with some gift certificates to local restaurants. Then a slight hug good-bye. I also owned the house in Iowa that my father and his wife lived in. Now here was home number two, all before age forty. The Tacoma definitely faded.

I moved into the condo days before Thanksgiving in 2017. Setting up my new belongings, pride circulated as I put fresh energy into a space that was all mine. A local veteran who'd discovered woodworking to help his PTSD delivered an exquisite custom bookshelf, which housed an eclectic array of hardcovers and some vintage first-edition paperbacks. Heavy philosopher head statues kept the books tight and upright. The shelf glowed regally as sunshine hovered from the vaulted skylight and descended onto a thin sheen of oil coating. Pictures of family members and old military pals hung above the fireplace, along with expensively framed images of landmarks I'd visited across the globe. I was also away from my neighbor, the professor. We were supposed to spend Thanksgiving together, and I offered to cook. But she drank too much at a friend's house and didn't make it to the store, so I had a protein shake.

The undefined, but sensuous, relationship without a name was officially broken after nearly five years. We would sometimes go weeks

The Wasteland

without talking, only to break our silence with long weekends in bed and Vietnamese take-out. Once we stayed a long weekend together in a drafty cabin in winter watching scary movies. But mostly we didn't leave the county. A lot of wine drunk together. I had my martial arts, and she had her horses. We both read and understood the university circus, and she wisely shared that it was junior high school with money. Neither of us married or had kids. She was intelligent and inquisitive, but losing her father young and some other wounds left complicated scars. Sometimes she picked fights, her southern accent accusing me of being closedminded or racist, a term easily tossed around by folks in her circle.

 The job loss came exactly one week before my fortieth birthday, and just seven months after buying the condo. It was supposed to be my annual evaluation, a typically painless affair that brought praise and a renewed zest that lingered for a moment. I often went out afterward and celebrated with colleagues, acknowledging the gold that came with the fifty-hour weeks, politics, and insomnia. But this time things were different. A couple awkward email exchanges between my boss and me started months earlier and never healed. Then our weekly meetings got canceled, but I chalked it up to our travel schedules. The communication line dropped while I had grown more outspoken with colleagues and campus officials about changes that needed to be made. We were mispresenting ourselves, I felt, and quickly moving into the waters of exploiting our students. There was a whole "wounded veteran" story they wanted pushed, and pushed particularly hard at donors. Embellished stories of broken spirits and hopelessness fueled by emotional rhetoric and sensationalized by the media. There was a student, our only student with a visible disability, and they used him like a prop plastering his image across the website and glossy outreach materials. I pushed these thoughts aside, rationalizing that the meeting would clear the air and allow for amends. Maybe a chance to break new ground together, a fresher and more truthful direction. I was starting two weeks of vacation after the meeting, too.

 Thirty minutes later, I sat in my Honda staring at the drab brick building, dazed. I hated that building. There was a presence in it that immediately dried my mouth and punctuated my breathing. Meetings and presentations, donor and alumni events. Committees. A story line to stick to; litanies of speeches and worn masks adorned with eloquent narrative. My hands stayed on the steering wheel, turning the engine on felt cumbersome. I replayed the conversation, fixating on body language and the sharpness of her words. The seething tone and the way her lips snarled. More glimpses of details. The way she waved me off when I attempted to speak and counter her indictments. Her mind was made up and it had been for a while. The witch hunt had been brewing behind the scenes for months I later learned. This was just a formality.

The distant colleagues and canceled meetings now made sense. She pointed from the circular cream table in the middle of her office and told me a person from human resources was waiting with a pile of papers. They'd explain how unemployment works, she added curtly. The good friend and colleague I'd known for years was also at the table, sitting stone faced and silent. A company man that prioritized keeping appearances in place. A non-boat-rocker. Today he was simply a witness. My throat drier than usual, I took a long sip of water from my stainless Yeti, listening to the ice clinking around inside. *I just bought a condo. I have a dojo here that I love. I have the mortgage in Iowa. How will I explain all this in my next interview?* A litany of thoughts rushed in. I looked upward through the roof of my car to the heavens and shook my head in disappointment.

"It's me. You there?"

Immediately, a familiar voice on the other end.

"How'd it go?"

"Fired."

"Bullshit. You're joking."

"No, Dad. Well, technically they're not renewing my contract. But that's how the university gets rid of people they can't legally fire."

A pause.

"Wow. Wow. Well ..." his words faded.

The line was silent for a couple breaths before he continued.

"Well, how are you feeling right now? In this moment, I mean. You want to do a quick check-in?"

"Processing, I guess. I knew shit was bad, but I didn't see *this*. Things were off between us but ..."

Thoughts of temporary unemployment and the complete loss of a healthy salary stoked more fear. I had a horrible sensation of living at home with my father and stepmother at forty.

"I feel blindsided. Yeah, that's what I feel more than anything. Pissed, too. Really pissed, actually. Carl was in the meeting with us and didn't say a damn thing. He just sat there like a eunuch, staring into the table. Fucking coward. Eight fucking years, Dad. Eight fucking years."

"Mmm hmm. Keep going, Nick."

The Wasteland

"Checking in, I feel shame. I feel like I've failed. She even told me that. She used those words. You know, I've never been fired before, so I'm embarrassed. I'm angry. I'm ..."

Although he didn't say anything, I could feel my father listening to each word.

"Dad, I just bought my condo and spent all this money. I was planning to settle. I really was. What am I going to say to the students? To my staff? I want to sue their asses, Pop, and I want to ..."

I paused. A foreign sensation swept over my whole body. It shot quickly from my feet, up through the crown of my head. There was warmth in it, like a green military blanket I wrapped myself in during a windy evening at the coast. The energetic mist covered me as my throat slowly opened, making it easier to breathe. The tightness in my chest, a tightness that had been present for many years and concerned my doctor, subsided. Perhaps my father sensed it.

"You know what I think?"

"What?"

"I think this is *fantastic* news."

I shifted in my seat excitedly and clutched the phone tighter.

"Say more. So do I, but I need to know why you say that."

He laughed, and there was excitement from the timbre in his voice.

"How many times did you tell me that the best part of Illinois was driving and having it in your rearview mirror? You have money saved. You're single. All those camps in Asia. The kickboxing thing. You can do it now. Go there, my son. Do your martial arts. Go to India and sit by the Ganges. Go to the Himalayas. All the stuff you've talked about. This is God's doing. This is a gift, my beautiful boy. You're free, Nick."

My father's words were like honey and filled my eyes with tears. I briefly thought about my many friends whose parents would be irate, telling them to march right back in the building and beg for their job. But my father understood freedom, and he understood me better than anyone else. An important thing for those on the Search is a cheerleader who shows up when they need it most.

Gregorian chant wafted lightly from the speakers, as more calm circulated. Checking in with myself, I didn't have the balls to quit my job. The sensation occurred over the years, even prompting a typed resignation letter. But the Wasteland is seductive, its grip tight. It fills your head with enough insecurity and doubt that towing the line becomes the only sensible antidote, even when the doctor cautions about your blood pressure, and people mention the bags under your eyes. Inauthenticity becomes normalized along with the costumes. Later that day, I donated all my work clothes to the Goodwill, vowing to never wear a suit again. I pushed the button on the backdoor of the sterile gray rectangular building. An emaciated, rough-looking man in torn jeans and oversized t-shirt that reeked of cigarettes collected the multiple bags. He ran his dirty fingers along a string of ties.

"Real silk, huh? Fancy," he said, retrieving a cigarette tucked on top of his ear.

"All yours, amigo," I said.

I drove back to the condo on less trafficked roads, appreciating the tidy rows of corn and farm smells. They were symbolic of quieter living. I hopped on the computer and sent an email to a Muay Thai camp in Thailand that was saved in a folder called "Dream Time." Then, I ordered a duffel bag and hand wraps. Inside a cavernous space somewhere deep in my belly, I heard the Wild Man laughing. That night, for the first time in a long while, I slept like a baby.

Chapter 15

GUIDES

Fall 2017, A Classroom in the Midwest

When the Hero is in the Special World there are symbols, messengers, and events that surround him, though he may not understand all that is happening. In fact, he probably doesn't understand any of it, at least on a conscious level. But that unseen Force is blowing around him like a gentle wind. It is unknowable whether it is free will or divine will that drives the Hero. I think it is a combination of both, personally. We are guided, but we also have to pay attention and put in the work for things to progress forward. When Daniel is in the Special World it really doesn't look much different from the Ordinary World. Miyagi has him come to his home early in the morning and gives him a list of chores to accomplish. The famous "wax on, wax off" eventually becomes an archetypal slogan, as Daniel tirelessly washes, waxes, sands, and paints. At one point in the training Daniel lashes out and complains he's been taken advantage of. He only sees the process as labor and not the agreed-upon martial instruction he was promised. An exploitation. His emotional body makes him feel like a victim, and he responds accordingly, yelling at Miyagi and being indignant. It is normal and a natural thing to respond from our emotions when we feel unsafe. To name call. To make threats. To even think about violence. When the rug gets pulled out from underneath and we feel exposed, an emotional response is guaranteed. Sensing his breaking point, Miyagi reiterates the movements of the chores slowly. The choreography of it unmasks hidden layers. Miyagi strikes at Daniel in various ways, while Daniel instinctively defends himself using the movements. Astonished, Daniel realizes that the martial teachings were there all along. This is *an excellent example of the Special World operating with its mysterious magic. The lessons are disguised.*

The people that show up in the Special World, the messengers and way-showers, wear many different costumes. It could be a lover from a terribly painful relationship that ends with bitterness, or a generous friend from the gym. It could come from some random conversation with a stranger in a diner, or on the train. It could be a coworker or a boss. Some may appear poor or degenerate, maybe even drunk or criminal, though their words and insights carry power. They penetrate through the armor of the rational Ordinary World and point the Hero toward a direction that he needs for his development. There are no coincidences. The Force sees everything.

Chapter 16

TRIBE OF MISFITS

April 2019, Chiang Mai

> It's only pain, it will not hurt you.[18]
> —Bas Rutten

"Well, it's not fookin' fool proof 'den, if you got nicked."

"Nothin' is foolproof, Paddy. The hustle was solid, wanker!" Neil shot back defensively.

"Nah. Lightweight stuff. You're a lightweight, Neil, and so were your scams."

Paddy arrived two days prior to my arrival and wasted no time peeing on bushes. My first morning stretching on the mat he told me I had a tiny head and big body, resembling a tick.

His banter with Neil ran circularly, not unlike a teacup that dizzyingly spins at an amusement park. After my bar bouncing and before I went on active duty, I taught a little to the incarcerated to make ends meet. I worked three different cellblocks, mostly nonviolent offenders serving less than a year. The heated exchange between Paddy and Neil on the long communal dinner table piqued my interest. The Outlaw archetype; the Wild Man's cousin.

Something about both of them reeked of the underworld, though Paddy felt petty theft. Neil swaggered into the training hall, shoulders upright, ready to engage like a rattlesnake accidentally stepped on. His buggy brown eyes and mouth with a pronounced overbite tensed and

---

18   *12 of the best Bas Rutten quotes for MMA and life. www.budodragon.com* August 26, 2021.

clinched like the meth tweakers back home. Dark circular bags hung under his eyes. But he could fight. The heavy Fairtex bags echoed from thunderous roundhouse kicks, while a guttural sound reverberated throughout the training hall. His sinewy elbows cut through pads like a blade. His audible exhales were purges of some sort. A growl. Getting rid of impacted poison from rough living, perhaps. At just under six feet and a lean buck-sixty, Neil resembled the foster kids I mentored during college summers. Many came from a nearby detention center and possessed a hustling acumen and fierceness that was light-years from my coddled upbringing in the commune.

"You did time, eh?" a voice from the table boldly asked.

"Yeah."

"What for?"

"Which time, bruv?" Neil snickered. A silence hung in the air.

"I'm a hustler, mate. Was a hustler, should say."

"And what does *hustler* mean?" Avi prodded, an air of condescension evident.

"Well, mollies and X for the clubbie kids. And a bit of puff, really. Then something bigger. A proper hustle." Another silence. Another tease.

"You can't leave us hanging, dude," I said.

Raj fingered keys on an invisible piano, a mischievous smile glued to his face. He'd not spent much time around the blue collars, except maybe for the workers who attended to his polo horses. Neil's posture shifted as he leaned closer from the head of the table. His knees bounced from side to side excitedly. My immediate impression was that Neil liked telling his stories. A few outlaw friends and family have done time, and most pretend they don't want to confess their transgressions, but doing time is a badge of honor for some. Like going to war, surviving an incarceration gives stature among certain tribes. Masculine currency. How the reality compares to the myth is unknown, but most men are attracted to danger and those who touch it.

"Okay," Neil began.

"I had a mate who got me into boxing. I'd just moved from Birmingham and was living with a fit bird. She had a posh raising, like Paki here." Neil pointed at Raj, who stopped fingering his invisible piano.

"A bit of money, and a flat, right. So, we shack up. I don't have to work. We party most nights. Good fuckin' thing I got going, yeah."

"After a few months or so, she starts on me; you know, pull my weight kinda stuff. Another mate has been selling stuff on the net, steroids, pain pills, and other gear. He's doing a proper for himself. Loads of cash. Anyway, it gets bigger, and he asks me to come on."

Two others from our clan hovered in and joined the table.

"So, you were buying pills and steroids off the Internet and selling them at gyms?" Toby asked.

"No, bruv. Listen. My mate backpacked 'round Asia, the Middle East, and all these places, yeah. In these countries, you just walk into a pharmacy and it's a drugstore, right. No scripts, no doctor, no bullshit. Boom! You just cash and carry. So, me mate works out a deal with some of these pharmacies to ship gear to the UK. He writes up a catalog and builds a webbie. He goes on bodybuilding forums and different chat rooms droppin' bread that he can hook people up. Word gets round. A few emails here and there. A trickle at first."

The details of Neil's story and casualness of his delivery suggested legitimacy. His body language was animated, though his tone low key.

"How did the money work? Like, how did people pay for it and get it to the pharmacies overseas?"

"So, that's the brilliant part. My mate advertised a price list cheaper than what you pay at home. Say you want some D-bol or test to bulk up, that goes for a hundred and forty quid at your gym. My mate gets it from some Paki—no offense, Raj—at twenty and sells it for seventy-five. You get percs for a fiver and sell 'em for a ten."

A part of me deep down has always rooted for the bad guys in movies, depending on the villain and their cause. Some ascribe to a code that make them heroic in their deviance.

"Were you selling on the dark web, like the Silk Road?" Toby inquired.

"No, no, no. This is years before all that. What we did, is we made a bunk email account that we shared. We logged on and chatted with each other through the drafts. If you write a draft and don't send it, nothin' gets transmitted. There's nothin' goin' out, yeah. So, I put a message in the drafts for me mate, he reads and deletes and answers with a new draft. He puts all the orders for me to fill in the drafts. No phone chatter."

A couple heads bob around the table, taking it in.

"Now, the customers. They'd place an order on the webbie and pay with Western Union. Keep in mind, lads, there's over four hundred Western Union shops in London alone, not includin' the sticks. We walk into one, grab the cash. All you need's an ID, and we had a good source for that."

"What name did you use?" Raj asks.

"Mr. Punjab, like that twat from Annie. Just kiddin'. Pay attention, Raj, and learn somethin' useful.

"So, we go in and grab the lot. Then we heads to a different Western Union and place the order to the pharmacy in whatever country, and wire them the funds at a cheaper rate. We give them the name of the customer and the customer's addy. Nothin' comes to us. We don't touch nothin'. We just pick up the bread and pass the order like proper middlemen."

I was intrigued by Neil's story. Barely into his thirties, it was a sophisticated hustle requiring a certain level of intellect. I mused briefly on the legitimate success he could amass with proper mentoring. A flicker of sadness and wanting pinches, as I think about former students.

"What kind of money was it generating?"

"Loads, mate. Heaps. We made twelve grand our first month, and I got five of that."

"Did you stay with the bird and contribute?" Raj asked, grinning.

"Who?" Neil said, puzzled. "Oh her. Oh no, mate. I moved out and got my own flat. New bird, too."

"But all good things come to an end, yeah? Something must've happened," I asked.

"That's right, Yankee boy. So, we run this hustle for months. I buy a bike; lil' crotch rocket and I'm ahead on me rent. I'm thinkin' of coming to Thailand then, yeah. Only snag is a few times customs grabs a packie."

"What do you mean? Like seized?" I asked.

"Right, exactly. You know, some cunt emails us freaked out he didn't get his gear and he got some nasty letter from the customs man. But no biggie. You don't have nuthin' on you. Cost of doing business on the blackie. But most got the goods."

Neil took a long pull of water and licked his lips. Then he jumped right back into the moment. I thought of Canadian Derek and wondered how life was treating him.

"But my mate. My ex-mate, rather. He started puffin crystal. No biggie at first; weekend club thing. A gentleman's drink. But his brain starts blowin' circuits and he gets real paranoid. He comes over one mornin', just smackin' me door, right. I think it's the bloody coppers, but I open it and he hands me a dozen Western Union slips and tells me to get rid of 'em. He's sweating all over like a pig, shaking a bit, mumbling. Incoherent bastard."

"I don't hear from the cunt for a few weeks and think maybe he's dead, yeah. Maybe just keeled over. Then I heard he was picked up by the coppers. They found him in his car sittin' on top of bills. He had like thousands of pounds and was just sittin' on 'em in his car, like a bloody pyramid of gold and he was the emperor."

Neil shifted again in his chair; a wide grin beamed as his voice grew louder.

"Here's the part, lads. Here's the best part. My mate. My ex-mate. He's just sittin' on a pile in his car and beatin' himself off, yeah. He's in some neighborhood and just having himself a wank. Right there on a work night. And he's got a dildo shoved up his arse! Some neighborhood cunt called in a suspicious car and they roll up on him. Just pullin' away on himself and sniffin' some undies!"

A tear-producing roar washed over the extended table. Two of the trainers circled over and hung around, feeling the energy of our hysterics. The belly growl was reminiscent of sleepovers during puberty before life got complicated. Moments like this tightened the tribe. Neil wiped his eyes several times and shook his head back and forth. A natural storyteller.

"For fuck's sake, an honest tale, lads. They cuff him up and think he's mental. Take 'im to the clinic and he starts hallucinating, running his mouth. Just pourin' rubbish. Right now, they just have him as some rich cunt havin' a wank off his meds. But he starts confessing his sins like he's with the vicar. Just in the confession booth like a bloody parrot squawking. And he drops my name and tells 'em he's got demons in him and wants to repent. Confesses the whole hustle. Just bollocks!"

"How did they actually catch you? It seems like anything said by someone in that state of mind wouldn't be taken seriously," Toby said, thoughtfully.

"So, it was the email after all. My mate, he sends me a draft talking 'bout filling orders and which Western to use. And the coppers ambushed me. I had the pounds in hand. I had priors, so I just take it like a man and cooperate. They sent me to the scrubs for eighteen. Served just under a year. Could've done a nickel, but Her Majesty showed some mercy, yeah."

Silence.

******

A Ronin's Tale

I have been in Thailand less than a week, though my former life is distant. There are fourteen of us at camp, but only a partial turnout at the table. Two oscillating fans sit like bookends as well-fed mosquitos strategically make rounds in the middle. Scanning, we're something like the United Nations. Most hail from England and Australia with smatterings from Canada, Germany, France, Israel, and Scotland. I am the lone American, or Yankee boy, as I am called. It's all male. Local Thais that fight on a regular circuit join us three days a week, and a rehabilitation group trains twice a week. I learn from the welcome binder that the rehab bunch consists mostly of Westerners looking to dry out far from their vices at home. The program, led by a former British special forces soldier named Paul, was designed to exhaust addiction through months of intensive therapy coupled with distance runs, hiking, and Muay Thai.

Opposite Neil, Duncan is the other bookend at the table. He's been at camp the longest and is also in his forties, placing us as elders of the tribe. After Neil, Duncan dominates most of the conversation.

"Yeah, I gets to the flat and there's a note. 'I'm moving to South Africa with this bloke.' No warning sign, no nothin'. Could'a just sent me a fookin' text message all the same. So, I call me dad and tell 'im I'm going to Thailand, for real this time. And that's that."

I think back to the conversation I had with my own father, just as the axe dropped at work.

Duncan's skimpy white shorts reveal meaty quads and tan hairless calves. His stature, with his military crewcut and thick veiny neck, makes him the most intimidating figure at camp.

Avi is twenty-eight and finished five years' service in the Israeli Defense Forces. He fought as an amateur in different European MMA venues, and even instructed at a famed Krav Maga Institute in Jerusalem. His intense eyes move quickly, as does his speech, interrupting most conversations.

Raj is the nobility of the group at twenty-five. A refined speech and polished lexicon don't hide his English boarding-school roots. After checking in, I overheard a bit while walking to my bungalow about his family owning polo horses. Tall, thin, with strikingly attractive features, Raj's Indian mother and British father pushed him toward tennis growing up, but he wouldn't have it. He came to camp with a bit of boxing skills and took an extended holiday from a junior exec job in London.

"Paki here wants to be a fighter, in the octagon. But that face there is too pretty," Duncan chides while squeezing Raj's cheek. Raj pushes his hand away and blushes.

Toby is the baby of the group at twenty-three. A construction designer in Vancouver, Toby builds sets for high-budget Hollywood films looking to save money up north. His artist mother, a costume designer, raised Toby alone, along with homeschooling him. I learn that Toby holds a blue belt in Brazilian Jiu Jitsu, an art I am interested to study at some point. We spend time briefly swapping travel tales, then he preps me of which trainers to avoid while sparring.

"Don't go near Champ or Tong. Champ's got the solid legs and checks kicks like a wall, but Tong will set you up with several jabs, then rock you with a hook. Trust me," he warns.

Walking to my room after check-in, I observed Toby seated upright staring into a nearby field in a meditative, trancelike state. He invites me to join him later for tea. There is a silent quality about him that I like. The Muay Thai workouts consist of ninety-minute sessions, twice a day. We are expected to train every day, though I learn the camp record of anyone actually maintaining that is held by a professional Algerian fighter who endured seventeen days without break. I aim for seven. I am here for a month.

The first morning breakfast is light, mostly oatmeal and fruit. I struggle to get it down, but I'll need fuel for what's to come. The last time I ran distance was in the military, with most of my exercise coming from the weights and dojo. We muster as a group, as collections of instructors hover about. Most are short with stocky legs that bear prominent scars from years of unforgiving training and ring combat. It's not uncommon, I learn, for a fighter to have over two hundred bouts before he's twenty. One of them, Champ, repeatedly rolls a glass soda bottle over his shins while I fill up my Nalgene. He looks like he could kick through a car door with ease. The instructors size me up as a new face and rattle back and forth in quick Thai, laughing. Even among the Westerners, my size is larger than anyone else at camp. The scene transports me years earlier to boot camp where various military cadre loom quietly just before all hell breaks loose. A couple trainers approach and offer a handshake and slight bow. It is neither cold nor friendly. The other Westerners make small talk as they stretch. Small social circles and cliques are visible. Duncan animates a tale of some kind, as a group of four hang on each word. He points to Luk, a heavier-sized trainer.

"Coming for you today. You and I, baby. Pain is in your future, mate. That's right, Luki bear!" Luk smiles and shakes his head.

A Ronin's Tale

Of the approximate twenty of us, most appear in reasonably good shape. Endurance warriors. Duncan and I have the meat, while most have the lean sinewy grain of conditioned fighters. Sets of tourists drop in for a day session and "cultural experience." Most of the four are overweight, which lightens my mood.

"Okay, now!" a trainer belts, blowing a whistle. He takes off briskly as the herd follows.

I focus on breathing through my nose and steadying my heart, but it soon accelerates, and my mouth opens as I struggle for breath. The run hits nine minutes, and a cascade of sweat falls from every pore on my body. The heat is intense, cooking the back of my neck and ears. We pass the fifteen-minute mark.

What the fuck am I doing here? the inner voice demands. Putting people through the paces of vigorous activity reveals their mental strength. You find out early who feels sorry for themselves. Self-pity destroys. My mind continues its dance, wandering back years earlier to Kuwait and stepping off a C5 after midnight. The malicious humidity ironed my uniform into my body. Suffering and sweltering temperatures are somehow part of my karmic path this life.

The run illuminates the specimens and losers among the pack. I'm not quite last, but definitely further in the rear. I don't see the tourists. Thankfully, pudgy Warren absorbs most of the trainers' attention. He runs for a clip before pausing, then walks while holding his side. His ruddy face and bleach-white body animate with anguish. I imagine his inner dialogue. The cultural experiencers catch up and walk with Warren, feigning motivation and encouragement. But it's just a hustle really, as they too are done. The instructors don't chide them much, as they're easy dollars. I personally like having a mob of dead weight behind. I drift to thoughts of cheering antelope when one of their brethren slows before a pride of lionesses. *Sucks for you, mate, but better you than me.*

The run concludes at the main training hall, where we're given five minutes' rest. I slam a small bottle of water, taking mental note to bring a gallon to the afternoon class. The water is mixed with an electrolyte packet, and I chug quickly in front of a commercial fan. A young, baby-faced instructor distributes jump ropes, as the chief instructor blows his whistle.

"HURRY, HURRY, HURRY! Too slow!" he yells.

A painful shriek hits like lightning before it dissipates into the surrounding jungle outside.

"SKIP!"

The first interval consists of ten minutes skipping, followed by twenty push-ups and twenty sit-ups. After two minutes, a burning sensation begins in my bare feet and works its way up my calves before settling in my quads. Warren is struggling, jumping too high and crashing to the ground. I silently cheer. *Keep that up, Warren. Keep the attention on you, baby.* I've not skipped rope in years, but it doesn't take long to get my rhythm.

"One minute! Faster! Faster!" a faceless voice belts.

The quads tighten. I count seven trainers circling in and out of the fog. Like drill instructors, they watch for changes in movement. Hesitations. Weakness. Duncan is in front of me, and I watch in awe as his body effortlessly glides between the rope. His footwork is phenomenal as he changes positions. I hear him laugh a few times, enjoying his alpha crown in the pack.

"Stay motivated, gents! This is why we're here," he calls out.

"Warren, stop jumping so high, mate. Little bursts. Jiggle them titties less."

I finish the first round and hit the deck. I push out the last four push-ups while a puddle of sweat congregates under my nose. We are rewarded with another short break before the whistle shrieks and the same cycle resumes. The run and two bouts of skipping constitute our warm-up, my inner tantrum barely under the lid. With the jump ropes secured, the instructors place us in a giant circle and lead us through a series of stretches that prioritize opening the hips. Generating power from the hips is key to effective fighting. The stretching provides a refreshing respite and stabilizes my breath. Afterward, we wrap hands with the long stretchy cotton and begin drilling basic forms and combinations.

Establishing a foundation of basics is paramount in any fighting art. Although high-flying kicks and exotic punches look cool on film, it is the simple stuff that wins fights in real life. Fighting is raw. You jab to create distance and feel your opponent out. You gauge timing. You jab to set up openings where something brutal, like a hard cross or a slicing elbow, awaits. Different instructors move in correcting form as we progress through endless series of punches, knees, elbows, and kicks. It doesn't take long to sink into the movements, though my karate habits reveal themselves through my wide stance. An instructor moves behind and stays there. It is a shadowy energy, and I have its attention.

"No, no, no, Neek! Not like that. Snap from shoulder! Make

snappy! Pivot back foot! Quick quick like this ... boom boom. You too slow."

I shift into the pattern shown and he grunts, then walks off. Another trainer immediately comes over and stands next to me, looking at my tattoos. He rattles something in Thai and two other trainers surround me.

"Neek, you Hindu?" he asks, pointing at my chest and arms.

Duncan peeks behind.

"Those aren't earned, mate! That's just flash."

I pause for a second, then return fire: "And where did you get that barbed wire on your arm, prison? At least you spelled your name correctly."

Duncan keeps his back to me, then raises his hand and middle finger.

The whistle blows, and we crumble to the ground for push-ups and sit-ups, then grab our bottles and huddle around the fans. Warren takes up prime real estate, his reddened face and arms draped around the stem as if holding onto a raft in whitewater. His bodyweight collapses, and the fan tilts. I assume we must be near the hour mark, then feel a devasting wince as the clock reveals we're barely thirty minutes into it. Not even halfway.

"Eh, Warren, move your fat arse! We're all fookin' dying," Paddy yells. Irish Paddy, with his bright ginger hair, was a natural bully. A few times at dinner he made the *Jaws* sound while moving his fork onto Warren's plate to take food from it.

"Yeah, Warren. You wanna be hot, mate. It'll trim that gut of yours," Duncan adds thoughtfully.

Images of hypersensitive academics from past-life committees waft around, producing needed hysterics. They would be fetal from our antics.

Paddy moves closer.

"Still hanging, eh, Yankee boy? You got any fights to you back home?"

"Nothing professional. I'm an old man, Paddy."

"Bollocks! You're younger than Duncan. I bet he'd tear your head off in that ring." They both laugh and circle closer.

"Yeah, Duncan's pretty tough," I state. "But I'm prettier."

Briefly, I think about prison. Living among such a tribe of misfits. A constant performance of one's masculinity. The game of acquiring masculine currency, mostly through violence.

We cool down as best we can, while the instructors place orange cones in various patterns. Others wheel in gigantic tires like the ones on tractors in Iowa. Kettlebells, barbells, and a sit-up board are positioned deliberately.

"Get in circle and shut mouth!" Champ yells before nodding to Tan.

The youngest instructor in the bunch, Tan, effortlessly runs the circuit. Through broken English and hand gesturing we are told to exercise for one minute and then rotate to the next station. A large tire rests on the ground at one station, a pull-up bar at another, a jump rope, a fifty-pound bar to press above the head, and a collection of other tortures spread across the hall. On the inclined sit-up board, a trainer hovers above waiting to crash large pads down on our stomachs between repetitions.

Michael from England whines, "Fucking hell, intervals! This is bollocks! I thought these were just once a week now. Lying bastards. All of 'em. The whole lot."

"Yeah, bastards they are," Duncan agrees and laughs. "I had a mate who did a bit in Bangkok, not much, like a few months. He told me he'd never step foot in this part of the world ever again. Fucking won't even eat their food anymore." Duncan takes a long pull of a generic Gatorade, then stands next to me.

"Eh, Yankee boy! Get your arse next to mine and I'll show you how it's done. You and me, mate, let's see what you got."

It's my first formal challenge at camp, and on the morning of my first workout no less. I think about gym class; the lone pull-up bar and a circle of forty or fifty of us. The heavier kids clutched to the bar, holding on for dear life, shaking for a solid ten seconds before Mr. Reever gave mercy and called the next victim. I did eight pull-ups. Always eight. Enough to keep the bullies away.

One by one we approach each station. Rather than feel a need to mark territory, I am more relaxed in my forties.

"It's your show, Duncan. You're the alpha around here, brother. Show me how it's done."

"Ah, pussy! So, them tattoos just make you look tough, eh? Alrighty, Neeky Neeky, but stay behind me then. Watch what I do, and then you won't need to memorize the whole circuit, yeah. Warren still fucks up the sequence, but it puts the trainers on him and not us."

"Thanks, mate," I say, sincerely.

"Oi, don't want ya to be a twat your first workout. Otherwise, you'll get branded."

The more seasoned of our clan strategically select their station, swapping and changing out with us newer guys. I stand firm next to Duncan. The gesture is unclear at first until the whistle blows. Certain stations, like pull-ups and jumping vertically onto a tall wooden box, are substantially easier to perform in the beginning of the rotation compared to the end when grossly fatigued.

The whistle blows, and our motley crew descends into a chorus of screaming, growling, and shouting as instructors weave in and out yelling. The atmosphere is primal, as if preparing for war, though full of enough theatrics to keep it light.

"Pain GOOD! Pain FRIEND! Put OUT, put OUT!"

An instructor lurks behind, waiting for a stutter or a cheat move. Little angelic windows occasionally open, just like at boot camp, where the sharks turn their back and I collapse unnoticed for a rest. My thighs cramp as the mountain climbers count past twenty on an incline tire. I wait for the whistle and inspect my hands, which are blackened. More sweat cascades off my forehead and stings my eyes. I continue waiting. Electric shocks followed by a sharp twisting sensation gain momentum. It feels like someone pulling muscle off my quads and calves. I am just a lowly dead animal on the butcher's block, as all the good parts get sliced off. My slight hesitation is noticed.

"NEEK! No, no, no! I kill you today! Today you die. Today I kill you! Push, push, push. NEEK, you not hide from me! Get up! Get up!"

Champ stands above slapping my back as I scramble to finish the last repetitions.

A few guys struggle and stop moving altogether. Avi can no longer press the bar above his head and yells with rage. The cultural experience crew keep running out of the hall for the bathroom, but the instructors don't acknowledge them. It's hard to tell who is legitimately empty or just feigning. I laugh heartily at the absurdity. I am still seeking to be noticed and affirmed. I've flown across the globe and trekked north, putting myself in yet another situation to seek the elusive. My insecurities more easily show themselves when I hit this place of physical surrender.

The whistle, that fucking whistle, blows again, and I move toward the pull-up cone. As my chin struggles above the bar, my arms shake from the overload. More thoughts of peers in committee meetings back home talking about all things offensive wander about. I laugh like a mad man at the hypocrisy. I hear debates of the hidden meanings of certain words on the webpage and brochures. Is it inclusive enough? Are microaggressions present? How about unconscious bias? It was madness. Do we ever really get past junior high school? The prospect of being punched in the face brings peace.

Why does one run ultra-marathons in the desert, or at high altitude? Why does one hurl themselves through vicious CrossFit workouts several days a week, or travel far distances to play in the mud and scale military-inspired obstacles? Why do we venerate those who go to war? There is a hunger most of us feel to test ourselves, to uncover where we bend or outright snap. There is a primordial voice that when balanced, serves as an inner drill instructor that yells at us to escape the mind and leave the emotional body. To get off our ass and put out. The search for the heroic. It's an easy formula: sweat, sweat, sweat. And shut your mouth about your problems and your pain because nobody wants to listen.

I stand in front of the wooden box on the last rotation. Duncan set me up. On wobbly legs, I jump the thirty-six inches required to land on the platform. I step down and repeat two more times. A current pulsates through my body. Self-pity dances, as I hit the platform two more times. A month of this. I take a short pause without notice. I stand on the box and take some shallow breaths, then hear the blissful resonance of the whistle.

"Ten push-up, ten sit-up, two-minute break!"

The break extends past two minutes. Warren is collapsed on the ground like a beached whale, and the others step over him as if he's not there. Luk directs me toward the end of the training hall, and I'm given a pair of blue twelve-ounce gloves. The man who hands me the gloves is called "Uncle," a term of endearment and respect in Thai culture. Uncle appears to be in his mid-sixties, and nods with a small grin that lifts my haggard spirit.

I'm paired with Thom, who stands a bit above six feet and is similar in weight. An anomaly among Thais. During check-in, the scale put me at 227 pounds at about 14 percent body fat. I estimate Thom close to this, with powerfully built legs and shoulders, though a soft midsection. Of all the trainers, Thom smiles the most and speaks excellent English.

"First workout, yes? Good job. Strong. We hit pads now. Real slow. Focus on technique and we build rhythm, like dance. Three rounds for three minutes with push-up and sit-up after, okay?"

Thom holds out a pair of thick leather pads, and we begin with a simple left-handed jab, moving circularly. He shows me how to shallow step toward him and drive powerfully from the hips, exhaling sharply as the jab connects to the mitt. It's a full-body movement but I am stuck throwing from just the shoulders. We repeat it a few times before Thom signals for a right cross. The one-two count for the first round is deliberate and easy. I knock out the push-ups and sit-ups.

"Okay, Neek. Now, only knee and elbow. Nothing else. Understand?"

We start the dance again, but the pace is quicker. I'm more confident of the process, as single knee strikes and elbow combinations crash into the pad. Thom lowers the mitts, then mimics how to twist the hips. I flair too quickly and awkwardly miss the pad; a wincing pain reverberates on the side of my right kneecap. The feedback of improper form is immediate, and I repeat this faux pas several more times. We grit through the second round, and a small purplish knot forms. Push-ups close the round, though I cheat the last of the sit-ups.

The last round is devoted fully to kicking. As the whistle commences, Thom turns his torso sideways and covers himself with both pads. I brace and feel my body stiffen as I feebly raise my right leg and graze the pad. Thom laughs immediately.

"Neek, what the hell? What that?" he asks incredulously.

I exhale forcefully and reset. Thom rubs the pads together, then plants his elbows into his side and braces. The second kick is worse. I scan the training hall looking for eyes. Thom places the pads onto the slippery mat and stands parallel to me. He begins slowly, a shallow step forward with his left foot, a slight pivot, followed by a rising right leg that forcefully twists at the hips and arcs into a circle. He duplicates the movement several times. In spite of his size, his smooth delivery and grace are captivating.

He turns back in front and orders me to kick with my right leg.

"Twist hips. TWIST! Like this," he demands.

As my right leg arcs upward, he captures it. I swim with my arms, sinking into the mat, rooting with my planted foot. We practice more repetitions before Thom directs me to kick the pads twenty times on each leg. I complete the set, then hobble from fatigue and knee pain. Without any acknowledgment of injury, Thom points toward the heavy bag.

The clock shows twenty minutes remaining. I convince myself that half of it will be allotted for cool down and stretching. As I jab on the heavy bag, a strange sensation surges just above my navel. The warmth is separate from the heat and humidity. It's a primal sensation that feels like a reservoir of power.

Muay Thai workouts require sparring. This is intentionally added at the end when exhaustion is highest. I scan the gym, observing how each trainer's ferocity is based on where the student is at in his training. I will learn later that it also depends on who the trainer is. Some love to kick the shit out of students, believing the trial-by-fire custom is the best way to learn. Malcolm, another plump Brit I met at check-in, lucks out with a passive one. Like Warren, he struggled throughout the morning, so his sparring was a mere series of slow basics. In comparison, Duncan and Avi received full-throttle blows.

I stand next to the heavy bag and watch Duncan. Each of his strikes are accented with a raw grunt and focus that land like grenade explosions. I wish we weren't so close in age so I could pass it off as youthful poise and endurance, but I know it's more than that. He was born to do this. I'm a mere spectator. Some men are born to walk this warrior's path, and they take full opportunity to put the work in and pay the dues. Duncan doesn't play tough. His Wild Man is wilier and more uncontained than the rest of us. It leaks out of his interior, creating a radiance around him like a fierce, full-body halo. I lose myself for a moment in the ether of intensive fatigue and jealousy.

"NEEK! Get in ring!"

In the middle of the training hall is a full-sized ring. I fought in makeshift rings throughout my martial journey, but never in a professional ring. The ring exudes a powerful energy, like a temple, full deserving of reverence. I noticed it the previous evening when walking through the empty hall, as I psychologically prepared for camp. Men confessed their fears and shortcomings to it.

I coolly slide under the ropes, feigning that I've done it a million times before. I meet my trainer in the middle. His name is Sagat. He is the most muscular of all the trainers and a former champion who fought in Bangkok's elite stadiums.

"You fight before, yes?" Sagat's black eyes lock on, unblinking.

"Uh …" I hesitate. I pray for the Malcolm treatment.

"I just start Muay Thai. Today first session. I only spar a little," I offer.

Sagat laughs.

The whistle blows and we respectfully touch gloves. *I am here. I am inside a fighting ring in Thailand, about to throw shots and test myself.* I meditated on this moment for hours between meetings and presentations. An earlier memory penetrates past my work life in

Illinois; I'm home from school, sick, and Mom has brought me a video. It's *Kickboxer*. I watch it mesmerized. I watch it two more times before it's returned the following day. There is medicine in that film. Here I am, decades later, getting another dose. Sometimes the little boy needs to play.

We move around, and I gauge Sagat's distance. He comes toward me, and I instinctively jab to push him back. I have a solid reach on him, and I use it to my advantage. He comes in again, and again I jab, though I throw a powerful right that he blocks easily. The pace quickens and we continue stalking each other. I throw a right kick that actually surprises me, though it doesn't inflict damage. I chase him toward the ropes, but he's set a trap and the moment I move forward he kicks my right thigh. It feels like a Charlie-horse from junior high. I sink a bit favoring it, and Sagat smiles. The rounds are three minutes each, and there's no escaping the push-ups and sit-ups at the end. The round is nearly finished, and I punch hard with a right that he immediately counters and responds back with a knee that lands on the exact spot as his last kick. I hobble, my leg numb. The whistle blows, and we touch gloves.

Two other trainers hop on top of the ring and watch. They speak Thai and laugh along with Sagat. I would love to know what they're saying.

"Okay, good. Now faster this round. No more play," Sagat says.

The whistle kicks off our second round and we touch gloves. Sagat comes out fast with a punch and sequence of combinations. I duck and cover. As I protect my face with both forearms, he lands a body shot that makes my ribs scream. Then he kicks me on the right thigh again. *Motherfucker, how does he do that!* I use my reach and weight advantage, and charge like a bull throwing hard, but wildly. He covers and is close to the ropes. He doesn't expend energy in his cover; he's at home. I knee him in the thigh and land a strong left jab on his nose. He smiles. I struggle for air; it feels like I'm breathing through a straw. I anticipate the whistle. I pray for it at first, then demand it. He stalks around the ring, and I wonder if I've hurt him or at least made him a bit scared. The thought is absurd, as he push-kicks me with a *teep* into the stomach and I fall into the ropes. He follows quickly and delivers several more punches in succession—Tap-Tap-Tap. I cover and tense. He doesn't hit full force but lands a shot squarely on my nose. Immediately, the metallic taste of blood drips onto my lips.

"Good," Sagat offers. "You are ready to fight our teenage girls now."

The cultural experience kids begin their stretches and snap pictures with their phones. Warren and Malcolm join them.

I look down at my right thigh and it's a puffed mountain about the size of a silver dollar, turning color. My ribs are sore but nothing serious. There is a burning sensation on my toes, little heat blisters from the mat. I limp slightly to the corner and wipe my nose with a soaked towel.

The last round is slow. Sagat hits lightly and stops me at times to correct my form. We stalk, barely making contact with each other. Certain moments feel as if there is lead in my gloves. I drop my hands to his dismay. He positions my arms upward, tucking my elbows into my sides for defense and we continue. There is a fluidity in the slow movements. With time disappearing he holds his gloves together against his body and barks, "Now, ten kicks right!"

I struggle to lift my leg, feeling the bruise in its entirety. I focus on keeping my toes downward, hitting with the shin. The first five shots have moderate power and the last five barely touch his gloves.

"Ten kicks left, FASTER!" Sagat commands.

"Keep going!" he yells, as I struggle to finish the set.

"Now punch! Left right, left right, left right, KEEP GOING!"

The whistle shrieks longer than normal, as thunderous applause fills the gym marking the close of our morning session. Duncan yells, and his lap dog, Paddy, follows suit. The morning complete, it is the most demanding exercise session I've ever done. I limped out of the ring, steadying myself with the ropes, as a few veteran members pat me on the back. Even Avi is kind.

"They don't hit people the first day," he says.

Toby adds, "Yeah, he gave it to you. Nice job. You'll earn their respect if you keep doing that."

A bit battered, my posture is taller than usual, as we assemble around the fan hydrating. There is an immediate brotherhood. Smiles are visible, and a joyous vibration echoes throughout the hall. The whir of a blender whistles nearby, as a camp employee whips up protein shakes. The banter continues, as we share war stories. One of the trainers stealthily sneaks behind and pulls my shorts down to my ankles, spanking me hard on my right butt cheek. Laughter reverberates, and the mood lifts. Perhaps I will be given a ticket into the club after all. *I just want to be enough, whatever that means.*

I strip off my soggy shorts on the deck of my bungalow, and place it on a bamboo clothesline, along with damp hand wraps. Drops of sweat cascade fervently off the shorts and collect into a pool where ants and other curious creatures congregate. I feel the sun for a moment before I walk inside and turn on the air con, saying hello to my roommates clamoring on the walls. I scan for spiders, and hear birds singing a full chorus outside. My mini fridge is stocked with cold water, and I sit on the edge of my queen bed in a state of stillness, sipping mainly to keep my cracked lips moist. Although this was not jungle training to fight Tong Po, or to confront Johnny at the All Valley, I am pleased with my performance. Mainly, I am pleased that I didn't quit or feel sorry for myself. Sitting on the bed, the reality of fighting takes on new meaning and I have a deeper respect for that rare breed who devote themselves fully to the craft; the intensity and discipline of the workouts, the injuries, the putting it all on the line while broke and hungry. Those are people with stories. Why aren't they teaching the young in the universities? Although only ninety minutes, it was enough time to blow off the accumulated dust and romanticism of what being a fighter means. To be a fighter, and anointed as tough, is a special calling. I am merely an observer, a visitor swimming on the surface of an ocean devoid of sharks and undertows. But I accept this shallow end. The sobriety of the thought makes me a bit sad but clarifies that I have other work to offer. The warrior is indeed inside of me. It's always been there, and I don't see it leaving. But the way I call upon these energies and how I use them will be a curious path. I find peace in the thought, the mystery of it all and the mystery of my future. Then I look at the clock and count the minutes until afternoon training.

Chapter 17

LEG CRAMPS AND LADY-BOYS

May 2019, Chiang Mai

> Man is least himself when he talks in his own person. Give him a mask, and he will tell you the truth.[19]
> —Oscar Wilde

I woke early. Being on a trailhead at first light or watching the sunrise above Giza or Machu Picchu made sleep something I could forfeit. As a working man it was different, though. Each minute of rest was accounted for, the snooze button milked as long as possible. A Monday morning death march to the bathroom with crusted sleep caking the corner of my eyes. On the toilet, fingers moved quickly shooting off emails and filling schedules. Donor meetings, dinners, presentations, politicians, committees, and teaching. Office politics, company folk, and perpetual whiners. Another week overbooked. The fog worse if I partied on Sunday with W, my girlfriend neighbor. Sometimes I sat in the shower pretending it was a waterfall.

In the distance, Thai soldiers belted out their morning cadences. I turned toward the ruckus and clasped my hands together, a Thai symbol of reverence. The jungle nearby was silent with only a smattering of birds and insects buzzing through the calm. Early mornings like this brought stillness and allowed the wiser self to speak undisturbed. I pictured my mom sitting on her screened back porch with tea, doing a crossword puzzle and checking for gators. Dad was likely on the couch

---

19 O. Wilde, *Oscar Wilde's Wit and Wisdom: A Book of Quotations* (Dover Publications, 1998).

reading his books with a bowl of chips close by. I missed them.

The reality that I was officially unemployed brought different moods. I didn't have a family to support, and my only debt was a home that had appreciable equity. Aside from the gypsy existence, I was responsible young, and it was paying off. I could piss off for quite a while if I wanted. But the ego still felt tarnished by a lack of title, a lack of a symbol to be defined by. A few of the trainers at camp asked what I did, and I blurted out without much thought, "semiretired."

"He means, 'semi-retarded,'" Duncan corrected, before breaking into his best down syndrome voice.

"Easy, killer, my nephew participates in the Special Olympics," I warned, truthfully.

It was several hours before the morning session, so I wandered into the training hall. Sweat and dampness permeated throughout, and a clothesline balanced two dozen hand wraps drying from yesterday's session. They looked like dead serpents hanging there. Newer heavy bags hung erect from the ceiling. It's barely six and I'm sweating profusely. As I walk inside, I respectfully bow as if entering a dojo or sacred place. A few trainers snore in the corner. The morning session continues on schedule. It's brutal. They're all brutal. Thom hit me hard in the ear and it's made sleep difficult.

The afternoon workouts begin bouncing on an oversized tractor tire. Footwork and balance, hefty parts of the trade. Although it sounds easy, after ten minutes the thighs and calf muscles smoke. The heat blisters splotched around my feet force deliberate landing. A sickly thin man on a bicycle with a refrigerated box on the rear rides on the dusty road in front of the hall. He rings a bell, and some of the trainers run over. Champ looks to me and waves his popsicle.

"Neek, not for you. You must work! I get to enjoy."

After the tires we move to the jump ropes for our staple rounds. Then we wrap hands and go over the basics. The ninety-minute afternoon session is a little less intense than the morning, and there is no sparring. Trainers jump on our backs and have us run around cones, hooting, and hollering. Some attempt jokes through broken English, though the atmosphere still holds an invisible boundary. Slacking off or cutting corners warrants a smack. Warren continues to take shit, but he looks noticeably leaner since the first time I saw him weeks ago.

To keep things interesting in the afternoon, we occasionally leave the reservation for alternative exercise. Paddy coins them our "parole field trips." Sometimes it's three miles around a lake or countless laps in a nearby pool. One day, just a little before I left, we took an excursion to Wat Phra That Doi Suthep, an ancient Theravada Buddhist temple in the mountains and one of Chiang Mai's most popular attractions. With the exception of short walks to the 7-11, I had not left the camp since arriving. On the way to the temple, Thom and Sak jammed out to LeAnn Rimes's classic ballad, "How Do I Live." The volume high, the trainers passionately belted out the words, occasionally mixing up the lyrics but doing a solid job, nonetheless. Asians and karaoke are a real thing, like Brits dipping their chips in mayonnaise. There were seven students in the van, and we looked at each other in wild astonishment.

"What the fook is THAT?" barked Paddy. "I want my bloody money back. LeAnn fookin' Rimes!"

"Are you lads bent? This isn't music for warriors! C'mon, Thom, you finally coming out, mate?" Duncan added.

Caught in the rebellion, I piped up, too, "Haven't you guys heard of Metallica?"

Like popcorn, we hurled insults, while Sak focused on the road stone faced. Thom turned around; a look of genuine concern clouded him.

"LeAnn no good?"

"NO!" we collectively yelled.

The laughter subsided and Francois hummed a tune that was beautiful, though I couldn't place it. It reminded me of something royal, from one of the shows on *Masterpiece Theater* my parents watched every Sunday. Then Francois looked over.

"Neek. I do not understand your American wee-men."

I turned to Francois and cocked my head.

"I was there a few years ago, mostly New York but then Los Angeles. I see some of the most beautiful wee-men there is to see. But I also see these wee-men, and they are carrying ... um, how you say in English?"

I shrug my shoulders, then shake my head.

"Uh, they are ..." he moves his hand back and forth, swinging.

"I see these beautiful wee-men all around, but they are carrying *poop*. What looks like poop, you know, from a dog. In a bag. And it moves quickly back, and like this, as they walk. The poop does, it, uh, swings in the bag," he says incredulously.

Duncan and Paddy turn to Francois, matched smirks adorned across their ruddy faces.

"I even see a wee-men pick it up with the bag, like this, in her hand.

Just incredible. I am just so confused by it."

I look at the floor of the van, noticing nuts and remnants of other snacks scattered about. Then I turn to Francois, sincerely amused by his seriousness.

"In most places in America, Francois, you do that," I explain. "Men, women, children, doesn't matter. It is expected to pick up after your dog."

"*Peek up?*"

"Yeah. You are expected to clean up your dog's shit so that it doesn't just stay on someone's lawn or on the sidewalk."

"And if you do not peek up the dog shit, what happens?"

"Well, you could get a fine, like fifty Euro or more. They take it pretty seriously. People don't want to walk around in their yard or go to a park and step in it."

"That is insane!" he blurts out. "That is insane. It is a dog, it is expected to poop, no? They are like us. Everything poops, Neek! You Americans, you are too obsessed with things. So crazy."

The history and origin of Doi Suthep varies, but there is consensus the temple was founded in the late fourteenth century. Thousands of pilgrims flock there each year to pay spiritual homage, while fleets of buses, mostly filled with Chinese and European tourists, arrive in droves, milling about for the perfect Facebook selfie. To reach the stupa, one must ascend 309 steps. We are tasked to run it three times; however, the unified assault on Ms. Rimes added a fourth, bonus round.

Cramping from dehydration and nonstop activity, I'm in pain during the last cycle. My body has been in pain since camp began, but certain sensations are more concerning than others. The ringing in my ear from Thom's shot a few weeks ago concerns me. I hobble up the steps and wince as my thigh muscles tighten and contract. I try to land on my heels. The day before, Champ called me over while I was working the heavy bag and told me to sit. He went into the back room and returned with a dirty knife.

"Neek, give me foot."

In a quick motion he picked up each leg, one at a time, then sliced into the heat blisters on my toes. A mixture of pus and blood squirted onto his hands. He wiped his hands on my shorts.

"Back to bag," he said, pointing.

I slow on the steps, and Sak makes eye contact with me from the landing and moves his hand telling me to step it up. As I get to the top, he moves closer.

Leg Cramps and Lady-Boys

"Neek, you want to fight?"

"Fight you?" I joke, as I raise my fists to my ears and throw a slow jab at him.

"No, Neek. Fight in ring. We get you ready for next month."

I pause for a moment, taking in the view for the first time and appreciating the serenity. I'm taken back by the offer, and a warmth fills my body. I've been noticed.

I weigh myself each morning at camp, and I've lost nearly fifteen pounds in twenty-one days. Although punishing, the sessions are less daunting, and I've grown to enjoy them. A young married couple from Boston arrived at one point and stared at my bruised legs and battered toes while shooing mosquitos away from their lunch plates. They signed up for two weeks, but after their first morning session we never saw them again. Toby said he heard a taxi leave quietly while he returned from a bike ride. I recall the sign at check-in: *No Refunds*.

"Tell me more, Sak."

As I listen to Sak, the warmth dissipates, and the inner voice tears apart any authenticity or flattery associated with the offer. Westerners fight in matches all the time here. The camp probably just needs someone my weight for their stable of fighters, and there are much more talented guys among our clan. They are preparing Duncan, and Avi is also getting extra attention. Many of the local fighters push taxis and Tuk Tuks full-time and are just fighting for a bit of extra cash. Like most fight games around the world, a nefarious organization controls the matches. I don't have insurance anymore, and if I get the shit kicked out of me, what then? What is the added value in doing this? But it is a test. A bigger one.

I go further through the inner monologue, and at its root is fear. Other than a few years playing sports in junior high, my competitive drive in athletics is nonexistent. The younger shadows of being seen as "less than" or making a public blunder creep up. And I just never took any of it seriously, either. But in the few times we've done organized sports at camp, I've excelled. More than once I racked up scores and winning goals in the hodgepodge of games they sometimes incorporated into our training. Duncan and I pitted against each other, both captains of a team. I tell myself I am too old and inexperienced, even though Sak assures that I'll be ready. I anticipate nights of interrupted sleep, as I dwell on the fight date moving closer and my hyperactive mind works overtime. The workouts will no longer be fun, but instead take on a tone of somber seriousness. And what about Vietnam? I am jumping right into another camp, and I need to be healthy for that. There's an energy in my stomach as I process; apprehension is mixed with excitement.

"Let me think about it," I mumble.

"Okay. Tonight, we go to ring downtown and watch English Jack fight. We drink beer. Maybe we fight others, too." Sak laughed.

The evening before the stair run, I stretched in my room when a solid thump echoed off my door. Outside on the deck, pairs of shorts and Under Armour shirts flapped in a semi-cool breeze. Canadian Toby stopped by as he sometimes did to talk about Brazilian Jiu Jitsu, or to swap travel tales. He had covered most of Asia and had completed a six-month construction gig in Antarctica. The polar differences of these climates mirrored his personality, as his speech shifted to topics of shamanism, Ayahuasca, and other mind-altering substances to MMA, meditation, and what it means to be heroic. He had even read a bit of Joseph Campbell, and that won points. Though close to half my age, I felt connected. He didn't posture, and I never felt like he was comparing dick sizes. We shared a similar unorthodox upbringing; both exposed to new-age stuff, yet trying to balance it with some masculine grit. He carried himself with a quiet silence but unleashed an unholy beast inside the ring. I was intrigued by this dualism and saw a bit of myself in him, though he was more comfortable in his skin than I was at that age.

At our last chat, a couple evenings prior, Toby divulged that he often snuck away at night and rode into a town about five kilometers away. It wasn't much of a town I recall from driving through it; some shabby food stalls and some sort of congregation hall that played obnoxiously loud techno music. Mostly he enjoyed a few beers, he said, but my intuition sensed there was more.

"So, Vietnam next?"

"Yes," I reply. "I did Cambodia, and a lot of Thailand during other trips, so I'm looking forward to something new."

"I think you'll like it. The north and south are way different from each other, yeah."

"How so?"

"The people in the north are more standoffish and kind of cold. They don't make eye contact as much and sort of stay to themselves. The people down south engage more. The south is relaxed and has the different tourist stuff, like the big War Museum and Cu Chi tunnels. The north has mountains and hill tribes. It has Sapa and Ha Long Bay."

"Any adventures to recommend?"

Leg Cramps and Lady-Boys

A smirk brightens over Toby, his boyishness illuminated. It reminds me of the confession mornings when students I mentored divulged particularly interesting stories about their weekend antics.

"District one is a good time." His grin widens.

"And?" I ask, circling my hands for more.

"Well, it just depends what you're into. They have decent weed, tons of bars and places to drink cheap. Stuff like that, yeah. And women. Not like Bangkok, though. I don't think any place is like that, but there's women for sure in Saigon. For sure."

"Do you have a woman here?" I ask.

Toby pauses, looking at the far corner in the room.

"What makes you think that?"

"I've seen you pedal off at night, and you're usually pretty energized in the morning, so I'd be surprised if you're drinking a lot. So, I asked myself what would make young Toby pedal off after two grueling training sessions to a shit town. And the only thing I can conclude is a woman."

Toby offers a partial laugh but doesn't return eye contact.

"Kinda. It's kind of complicated, actually."

"I imagine a relationship with a foreigner would be. I think English Jack is having a tough time."

"That's not it. It's …" his words trailed.

"I'm not going to judge you for being with a prostitute, Toby. I've been with a few myself in my military days."

My words hang above both of us, as I walk to the mini fridge. With my back turned, Toby confesses.

"Pak is actually a *Kathoey*."

"A what?" I ask, handing him a cold water.

"Uh, it means, lady-boy. You know, it's common here, the lady-boys that is. It's considered a third gender, actually."

"Oh," I respond, a bit taken back.

"Yeah. I'm not gay or anything. Pak has breast implants, and plans to have the rest taken care of, but right now she has a …"

"Got it. Hey, man, if that's your thing, that's your thing."

"Please don't say anything. Duncan and Paddy would …"

"Of course not, brother. I actually have quite a few friends who are gay, and a roommate …"

"I'm not gay!" Toby interrupted, his face crimson. He took several breaths.

"Like I said, it's complicated. Pak was technically born male, but everything about her is a woman. The way she looks, her emotions, the way she carries herself. Everything. She is a woman, but she just happened to be born ... differently."

"We don't even have sex really, well, it's just not like that, it's uh ..."

"All good, Tobias," I say, raising my hand with my palm facing him. "Honestly, man, it's all good. And I wasn't implying you're gay. I was just saying that things like that don't really rattle my cage. I actually have family who are gay and many friends. I love them regardless. I love people for who they are."

Feeling Toby's discomfort, I regress back to different mentoring conversations with students. It feels good to talk with young people about uncomfortable topics, to help them see it doesn't have to be weird or scary. I sensed Toby had been carrying this secret for a while. The researcher in me wondered if not having a father was related to it, but how can any study or theory accurately uncover what's inside someone? Some things are just some things.

"If you care for her, or even if you just like hanging out with her, then fuck it, man, go for it. It's your life to live. This conversation won't leave this room."

The uncomfortable silence hangs in the air a few additional moments as we sip our waters.

"So, anything else on Vietnam?" I ask.

"Stay away from the cyclo pimps," Toby warns.

"Cyclo pimps?"

"They're like the Tuk Tuk savages in Thailand. Total rip-off artists that run motorcycle taxis and pretty much work with cops to set up tourists."

"Got it."

"What about India?"

"India? What do you mean?" I ask.

"You should consider it. Himalayas, too. You could pop over to Nepal, it's like less than four hours from here. Then hit India. I haven't been to either, but soon. You'll get sick in India, but there's something there I think you of all people will like."

"What do you mean?" I ask, curiously.

"Maharishi people. You know, the whole meditation thing. All those Hindu tattoos you have."

"Haven't thought about India, too much. I'm feeling like I should stay on this side of the tracks and prioritize training. I guess I envisioned

Leg Cramps and Lady-Boys

this trip as more of a warrior odyssey, doing the spiritual thing some other time. But to be truthful, I don't know how long I can do camps like this."

"Do it all now. Maybe you won't have another chance, yeah."

"My dad trekked to India. He hitchhiked to New York from California, then took a boat to Europe, and trains and buses through the Middle East. He did that in the late sixties. Even got hepatitis, and nearly died," I state proudly.

"Yeah, that sounds like the kind of dad you would have," Toby says and laughs.

The energy in the room shifts.

I look past Toby. Next to the small refrigerator is a stainless sink surrounded by a plastic laminate countertop. The plaster peels from the humid temperature, leaving bits of paint chips scattered on the tiled floor. A small lizard lurks above twisting his head side to side. I want to ask about Pak, but I feel Toby's reticence.

I've learned throughout my life, and it was mentioned during my training in intelligence work, that most people can't keep secrets. Most people have to let things off their chest by confiding in others. Some need validation that their actions or thoughts don't make them a freak. Rather than press people too deeply, step back and witness them organically, move the conversation to the grittier, more exciting parts.

"Yeah, there's definitely women in Saigon," Toby shares, settling into a metal fold chair and grabbing another water from the fridge. "There's this board I follow. Well, I don't really go on it much, anymore."

"What kind of board?" I ask.

"It's like a chat room, where you read posts from people. Some expat who lives in Asia, though he won't say where, made it. I think he's American, could be English, though. Anyway, it's kind of like a big review, yeah."

"Review?"

"Yeah, like different massage parlors. It's broken down by country and cities. Like, you're going to Saigon, yeah? You click Vietnam, then the Saigon tab. You'll come across a discussion board where guys, and girls even, talk about different spots. Some even have pictures of the girls."

"Really?" I ask, curious if he met Pak this way.

"Usually someone writes up how to get to the place, like how much it costs and whether or not it was worth it. Sometimes they recommend certain girls and tell what the massage and room is like. You know, like if it was clean."

I'm intrigued. When I was just a few years older than Toby, I was a graduate student in the remote outlaw country of Humboldt County. Where the thick fog makes its way from the rugged coast, then saunters for miles above colossal redwoods. During orientation for my sociology program, gray-bearded faculty, some donning ponytails, proudly confided their rebellious histories from the sixties and seventies. One had been on the FBI's most wanted list for a minute, connected to various extremist groups, similar to the Weather Underground. Radical environmentalism and "tree sitting" were badges of honor among the population, making a shorthaired, clean-cut military member like myself suspicious.

Sex work perplexingly came into my life through love. I was serving in the Coast Guard while attending school, and on a flight to Puerto Rico, I met and fell for an officer who was stationed in San Francisco, about five hours south. The flight was half full, yet we were mysteriously seated next to each other and content to stay that way. I was enlisted at the time, and fraternization was a big no-no between enlisted personnel and officers. We went skinny dipping together our first night in Puerto Rico, and a fire was lit that spread quickly. We maintained a long-distance relationship for a while, and even planned to get engaged. She was soon to transfer up to Seattle, and I needed to quickly finish my master's thesis so I could move with her.

I decided to research the sex trade after attending a large-scale symposium on campus. A variety of speakers and organizations provided different perspectives on the complexity of the topic, along with pros and cons surrounding legalization and regulation. A competitive travel grant that financed a month of study in Thailand and Cambodia, admittedly, pushed me to pursue the topic.

There is no question that sex work has many dark facets attached to it. I would even lump the entire porn industry in this. While I won't go into its many complex strands, there is also something to be said about agreements made between consenting adults. I say "consenting" because people who are trafficked, enslaved, and abused are not consenting regardless of their participation in the work. Horrific things happen in this world, and particularly in poor countries like those in Southeast Asia. It is not uncommon for rural families to sell their children. Young girls, and sometimes boys even, are coerced into the trade through phony promises of legitimate work waiting for them in cities. Often, corrupt law enforcement and politicians hover in these circles adding another layer of depravity. But when something is illegal, it is underground and there is no protection or safeguard in place. Moral judgments aside, if sex work is legalized and regulated, such as in the red-light districts of Europe, at least some degree of protection is provided. Ultimately my young twenty-something brain was most concerned about what would keep the women safe, and I needed this information directly from those working in the industry.

My second year in the master's program I sifted through an exhaustive collection of data and locked myself in the library, writing. I strolled into downtown Arcata, sometimes literally walking over growing congregations of homeless camped in tents and makeshift dwellings. Occasionally, syringes and human feces littered the sidewalk. More than occasionally, people walked around naked, sometimes screaming at the top of their lungs, or fighting off invisible demons. Pot was passed openly, heroin and meth shot discretely. I was doing law enforcement in the military, yet living in one of the most bizarre communities in America, juggling uniquely opposite realities. This window of time very much encapsulates the thumbprint of dualism that's plagued my existence.

The motivation to complete my degree early and to wrap up the sex work research was to be with the officer as quickly as possible. We stayed true to each other despite the distance, sharing passionate long weekends, and racking up miles on our cars. Before I could comprehend what was happening, we carved details of our future together. Then she was sent away to attend a four-month training out east. Upon her return, I would graduate, and we would move together to begin a new chapter. The grown-up part of life. The prospect of settling down and starting a family. But my astrology at the time must not have been easy.

Just hours after I defended my thesis, my mother called and told me that my grandfather was losing ground, quickly. I wanted to see him before he passed, but my lease was about to expire. The phone calls with the officer became less frequent. There was a guy she mentioned occasionally when we spoke. Just a friend. A nice confidant to grab the occasional lunch and dinner with, especially with me being so far away. But soon his name came up enough that it stuck in the far recesses that keep you up at night. I'd read her emails obsessively, trying to decipher the cryptic tones of certain words. One evening, not quite asleep but also not awake, I hovered above an unfamiliar room and saw them. I watched them intermingled, inside one another. I heard her breath.

A Ronin's Tale

After meticulously watering the roots for a committed life to bloom, I was now homeless, living in my tent.

Festival-going baby boomers that never left the sixties huddled in decrepit RVs, while transient kids from Seattle and Portland chased the fast and loose rave culture. These were my neighbors on Clam Beach. One couple invited me to the Salton Sea for the winter. The husband added that their marriage was open, too. It was a painful time, and I lost nearly twenty pounds in that rugged fog. The officer and I ended things on the poorest of terms, and I never replied to her lengthy emails that showed up later. And then a couple years, just days before I boarded a C5 to the Middle East, I was on a flight deck in San Diego inventorying our weapons and war supplies. Through a stroke of coincidence, or whatever those mysterious forces are, a friend called. He happened to be standing watch when she was killed in an accident, just a month or two before she would leave the military for good. It was a sobering part of my hero's journey, and a long flight to the desert. But it illuminated a fundamentally significant lesson; to never leave things on bad terms if you can help it. There is medicine in forgiveness as difficult as it is to swallow. And sometimes we just need to cry, too, which I did discretely in the bathroom of a Tijuana brothel, just hours after the officer died.

Chapter 18

THE CABIN

Fall 2017, A Classroom in the Midwest

Joseph Campbell was awarded a fellowship to study at the University of Paris. While in Europe, his interests spanned modern art, Sanskrit and Hinduism, along with Jungian psychology. In his words, "everything was opening up." He made a proposal to his thesis committee about what he wanted to research and write about, but they rejected it. He was at a crossroads. Does he honor his path, or acquiesce to his committee by choosing an approved topic that his heart is not invested in? Keep in mind that this was during the Great Depression, and finishing his degree would likely result in a high-status career with financial security. Campbell chose to go rogue, however, and never completed his doctorate. Instead, he returned to New York and spent five years in a cabin in the woods fervently reading the scores of items that spoke to his heart. He lived on next to nothing and had few material possessions. But he was honoring what his inner world asked of him. This is what he said about that time:

> It's very difficult to find in the outside world, something that matches what the system inside you is yearning for. My feeling now is that I had a perfect life. What I needed came along just when I needed it. What I needed then was a life without a job for five years. It was fundamental.[20]

When the Hero crosses the threshold into the Special World, reality changes. He is away from his environment and may find himself

---
20   Osbon, *Reflections on the Art of Living.*

routinely uncomfortable and in dangerous situations. There is an internal battle taking place. The fear is there for sure, along with self-doubt. Depending on the Hero's spiritual leanings, he may plead with God to show mercy, or ask the universe for guidance. He might engage in rituals like prayer or calling forth spirits or supernatural phenomena to assist him. Maybe he burns sage and makes an offering to the fire or cuts himself so that a scar will remind him of his duty to stay with the path. The characters that show up in the mystical special world include sincere helpers and allies, along with a collection of charlatans and evildoers.

Let's shift over to us, now. Have you ever had a passion, or an idea that you shared with someone, and they immediately shot it down? For example, you tell a friend how excited you are to take a free trial of yoga, or maybe you want to do an outdoor wilderness leadership course, or take a few weeks and backpack somewhere. That person immediately shoots it down as a dumb idea. They talk about it being a waste of time or money. Often times when you have these encounters what you're dealing with is someone else's projection. You are listening to their own regrets and inner wounds. They probably heard, or at least sensed the Call at some point in their life, but they didn't act on it. Most people don't. They didn't take the first step which would have propelled them onto an adventure. If you surround yourself with enough people like this, it's easy to get off track. A mentor, in comparison, sees the bigger picture. The mentor understands the emotions that will arise on the journey, and a big asset of a mentor is to not only encourage, but to motivate. A mentor cannot blow smoke and pretend everything is going to be fine, but he must reassure the Hero that the risk he's taking is a valiant and worthwhile one. Even if death comes out of the journey, it, too, can be righteous. I want you to think about these experiences in your own lives. Have you had the good fortune of experiencing a heroic journey? Have you been inside the special world? And let's remember what Campbell tells us here:

> What will they think of me? Must be put aside for bliss. It takes courage to do what you want. Other people have a lot of plans for you. Nobody wants you to do what you want to do. They want you to go on their trip, but you can do what you want. I did. I went into the woods and read for five years.[21]

---

21   Osbon, *Reflections on the Art of Living.*

Chapter 19

JOURNAL ENTRY, SAIGON

May 18, 2019

This morning I left camp. It was bittersweet. After nearly a month in close quarters, the trainers and fighters are like family, and my body is calloused by the punishing routine. Stepping out of the shower, taking physical inventory, my shins and legs display a mosaic of bruises of different hues and shapes. Some yellow and purplish, others a deep brown and black. My feet don white splotches of dead skin scattered around the toes and heels. I recollect Champ nonchalantly slicing my blisters then pointing me back to the bags. My knuckles have thickened, and I occasionally feel a numbing arthritic sensation in my hands. My ear still hurts, as does my nose.

Jack-the-Englishman, the fighter who trained with us but lived off site with his prostitute girlfriend, left a note on my door.

"Nick, you're a prince. I will miss your humor and wisdom. Enjoy Vietnam. Here is my email. I hope to hear from you time to time. Be sure to get to England. Be sure to see the town where your father was born. The world is ours. You understand this, and so do I. Spread the message. Your mate, Jack"

A week earlier, the entire stable of fighters and trainers cheered Jack on, as he traded blows with a Thai warrior at Thapae Stadium. The first two rounds were even, then the Thai opened up and caught Jack with a vicious cross that dazed him. Knees and elbows pushed Jack into a corner where he proceeded to cover and wait out the storm. There was too much time in the round, though, and a forceful head kick put Jack flat on his back. He rose slowly and dazed, so the ref called it, rightfully so. A sickly lean and nonintimidating figure, Jack was mistreated by his stepfather. Subtle crumbs leaked at the pool when it was just the two of us. He'd lived in Chiang Mai over a year and fought nine matches, winning only two of them. At twenty-six, he carried himself like a much older man beaten down by the world. His posture sagged, and his gait was slow, but it was the emptiness in his eyes that spoke loudest. He once confided at the pool that he'd lost all desire for living, but that fighting and getting hit, specifically, kept him in his body. He found purity in it. A sense of grounding and purpose. How does a soul get to a place like that? My stomach ached when he drove by our table with his girlfriend on the back of his scooter. She barely spoke English, and Jack was a voracious reader and conversationalist. An intellectual you could bump into in an Oxford pub. I suspect like most of us he has something elusive to prove. He turned me on to a hauntingly beautiful song called "Steep Hills of Vicodin Tears" that begins in somber fog before lifting toward a ray of light. I didn't ask him about his connection to it, but I have my suspicions. Each time I listen, I think of him.

Jack had balls, though. More than most. He didn't fight well, but he fought, nonetheless. Jack went into the dark part of the forest and spent the night there. Maybe his entire home was contained inside it after a year in Thailand. I told the trainers I was not interested in extending my time to fight in the ring, feeling some disappointment on both ends. My tendency to keep one foot in whatever I'm doing and another somewhere distant showed itself again. But I am also proud of my performance at camp. I completed my time there, and I'm ready for Vietnam.

True to the rumors, the last week was painful. Each morning the trainers asked how many days I had left. The sparring amped up, and at times, blood was on my towel. I considered not training the morning of my departure, but something within led me to the closet where I instinctively donned a pair of shorts and filled my water bottles. My brain was actually quieter once I stepped into the training hall.

A few days before I left, I was the only person at an afternoon session. I inwardly hoped they would tell me to just run or lift weights, but to my surprise, not one of the seven trainers left the hall. Class was conducted at full strength. After the routine warm-ups and basics, I slogged through the pads and heavy bag. Then they directed me to the ring. Sparring wasn't part of the afternoon, but it was that day, and I didn't question it. The first three-minute round was fast and hard but to my surprise, I was not given a break. Immediately after the round finished, a new trainer hopped in and proceeded to attack aggressively.

Journal Entry, Saigon

This happened for three rounds before the whistle blew and I dragged my weary body to the fan. A few drops of blood slid down my nose onto my lips. The rusted taste penetrated the mouthpiece, bringing upliftment. There was fifteen minutes left in class.

"Neek, not finished! Go to field!" Champ commanded.

At the nearby field there was a tractor tire and a smaller one next to it. Originally thinking they were teasing, I witnessed myself within the storm of panic when they demonstrated the exercise. I was totally spent, and there was no way I could flip the tire ten times and then deadlift the smaller one fifteen times. After the first five flips I didn't think I would finish. The self-pity sank in, then rage. Why was I putting myself through this? What am I trying to prove? I'm in my forties now, hiding from grown-up life. I should be on the first plane home with resume in hand. I've walked away from several things in my life, but I had to finish this workout.

As I deadlifted the final repetition, the trainers nodded unceremoniously and walked away. I sat on the field for a few minutes, as a wave of emotion grabbed me. The tranquility was almost spiritual; similar to things I've occasionally touched during long meditation. The gentle graceful hand of God brushing the hair out of my face. On the field, the eldest trainer, Uncle, walked over. Standing there in his sixties, covered in prison tattoos, his energy was angelic. Duncan once told me at the dinner table that Uncle had lived hard and fought in prison because it was the only way he could eat, not having family to provide money for food. He didn't even know his birth date, only a rough estimate of the year. Uncle walked over to me and smiled. With a shaking hand from his Parkinson's, he tapped me on the chest and said, "Neek. Getting strong. Good. Come back, see us." And then he walked away.

Uncle was illiterate and materially impoverished, yet in this moment he stood above the privileged and overly educated Westerner holding the medicine. I got some treasure finishing the camp. I bowed to Uncle, then quietly rose to my feet to pack my duffel.

Chapter 20

Happy Birthday

Late May 2019, Vietnam

> Don't fight your demons. Your demons are here to teach you lessons. [22]
> —Charles Bukowski

After nearly three years in Iowa, Mom persuaded Dad that we were better off living in California again. She was probably right. There was no money to be made in the Movement other than a small stipend, and our free trailer with pipes that froze in winter. There was no retirement or security, other than promises of raised consciousness. There were many rules to follow, and Mom wanted to wear makeup and enjoy a glass of wine. Our extended family were in California, too. So, Dad got a large U-Haul, and we ventured back through a fierce winter, having to stop several times on Donner's Pass just outside Tahoe. We relocated back to our same neighborhood in Penngrove, and I bought my first Beastie Boys tape and took it to show and tell. Dad commuted from Sonoma County to San Jose for maintenance work, and often stayed on the job site several nights a week. One evening when he was gone, Mom and I waited in the car while Becki and her friend went into a clothing store. Smells of grease and msg from a nearby restaurant wafted through our cracked windows and made my stomach growl. I asked Mom if we could get sweet and sour chicken, then put the Beastie Boys tape into the player. But she didn't say anything. Her eyes fixed intensely

---

[22] C. Bukowski, *34 Life-Changing Lessons to Learn from the Authentic Charles Bukowski* (Purpose Fairy).

Happy Birthday

upward into the store, distracted. When I looked up, a cluster of people zigzagged between stainless clothing racks. Then two frightened faces rushed past our car. One of them smacked the roof as they hurried past, reverberating sounds like frigid hail. Somebody screamed. Mom undid her seatbelt just before a man stormed through the unblemished doors with a black revolver in his hand and a bag in the other. He was slender, in an overly baggy Adidas track suit. He stopped when he saw us, his shins pressed against our bumper. Mom grabbed my hand as I gasped audibly looking into the man's yellow eyes. Then he took off into the shadows. She told me later that he was considering getting into the car with us. A mother's intuition, and a nightmare thought that haunted for years. It was two days before my tenth birthday.

******

The wheels glided smoothly onto the tarmac, as steamy haze fogged the windows of the cramped commuter plane. Gazing through the humidity, I thought about the many young lives abruptly snatched from farms and inner cities. They were told to do their part on a nondescript piece of soil on the other side of the world. What thoughts sprang into their adolescent minds when they arrived in this sweltering paradox? The first Vietnam veteran I remember seeing was on the streets of Berkeley when I was five. He was homeless, in a weathered olive-drab army jacket, rummaging through a trash bin outside a restaurant. It ruined my entire day, even after I persuaded my parents to give him a couple bucks. Decades later while working at the VA as a doctoral student, I heard punishing accounts of lives battered by failed marriages, estranged children, problem drinking, and suicide attempts. Trauma that never healed. One Vietnam veteran wept so loudly each week that I could hear him from two offices away. His sobs were childlike, unrelenting in their release. A stark contrast from his day job as a business exec.

    I intentionally selected Saigon's District Seven to be away from the tourist scene and to focus on training. Unlike Thailand where I lived at the camp, I had a modern studio apartment just a few minutes' walk from the new facility. It boasted itself as Southeast Asia's finest gym, and I think they were right. In the midst of a local neighborhood, far from any tourist site or restaurants, was this first-class gem. Different styles of martial arts and fitness classes were offered, along with contemporary collections of free weights and machines. There was even a sparkling swimming pool and small café with organic protein shakes. The whole scene was spotless, an oasis that contrasted sharply from the piles of rotten trash and feral dogs that roamed the congested streets. Posters of professional fighters who'd trained there covered the walls. Some autographed. I looked over their offerings and signed up for a month of boxing.

There were only five of us in the early morning class. All expat schoolteachers from the U.K., and me, the lone Yankee. We began skipping rope, before a moderate mile-and-a-half run. The first laps were effortless, reinforcing the gains I picked up in Thailand. But a few thoughts flooded in on the run. I am again, nearly two decades ahead of the others. Why am I putting myself through this? After the warm-up we trapezed through a circuit of footwork drills, gliding in between bright orange cones before wrapping our hands for timed rounds on the speed and heavy bags. The Filipino trainers were relaxed and took their time, showing the proper way to throw a jab and uppercut, and later, a four-count combination. They didn't raise their voices much. I concluded with light sparring inside the unblemished ring, feeling both relieved and disappointed by the waned intensity. Duncan would not approve.

The relaxed training regimen allowed time to explore, though. There is delightful mystery uncovering the layers of new surroundings. The senses relish change, even subtle ones, like the tastes and texture of certain foods, or the distinctive patterning of architecture. In a hypnotic spice bazaar in Cairo, pungent tobacco clouds released by lollygagging hookah smokers hovered above swirling mint tea emanating from delicate glass cups. A perfumed otherworld, perfect for sitting in the abyss. Logistical changes become apparent, too, like the honesty of taxis, or whether a bathroom has toilet paper or a water bucket with mosquitos above it. My previous international jaunts were often a month long, and usually centered in one country so I could best absorb its spirit. Yes, countries have spirits. And they vary regionally. It doesn't take long to tune into their frequency to see what's there, if anything. Like a first date, you know within minutes.

I unexpectedly dropped anchor in Cusco after being pulled in. Originally just a three-day stopover on my way to Lake Titicaca, I spent two weeks immersed in the Sacred Valley. Fixated on its mountainous beauty and sharp altitude, unseen forces held me hostage. Then interesting people showed up. A sit down in a cramped café with black beer and an egg floating on top could bring anything. Openings that

Happy Birthday

bring conversation of authentic depth and that penetrate the mundane pleasantries we're conditioned to squawk. Soul connections manifest quickly on the road, even if brief. Honesty comes easier with strangers.

In Cusco, an invitation by motorbike to a holy place north was offered after several pints of a beer resembling motor oil. I found myself in the middle of a shamanic festival, during a full moon, eating fresh goat and sipping pisco sour. All of it communal, and free. A national television crew from Lima interviewed me, perplexed at how the only white person for miles stumbled upon such a place. Its imperative travel itineraries remain loose. In the distant ocean of consciousness, I hear Maharishi's infectious laugher and reminder to live as if the whole world is my family.

Developing a routine, and making wherever I am, home, allows me to glide comfortably through most parts of the earth. The world is equal parts chaos and serenity, similar to our internal rhythms. Some of it dangerous. But most of it the same wherever you are. People mill about doing their duties, longing to wrap it up so they can be with the people they care about. They worry about their children, and they have their tacklebox of hopes and dreams. They save money if they can. Some go out and party to let off steam. Most seek love and intimacy of some kind. There are cultural differences and nuances, but most of it's the same. The human condition is universal. When you travel alone it is easy for others, especially those who haven't traveled much, to romanticize it. A trip to Egypt is in search of the Lost Ark. Fighting in Thailand takes place in the jungle, or under the auspices of enlightened monks. But most forget, or don't venture further enough to understand that wherever you go, you take yourself. You take your internal world with you. It's the first thing you unpack, really. At some point you inevitably end up in some less-than-perfect room, staring at the corpses of oversized bugs smashed into the wall, listening to the clang of a dying fan. You wonder how you got there, as you sniff mildew. You may question it all, worried that it's not going as planned. Whatever that means. But you take the waves as they come, like the mantra. I was taught to never pay attention to my meditations; never to score them as good or bad, but to simply accept them as they show up. Be easy with it. Travel is similar.

On June the third I turned forty-one. Two days before that was a Friday, and I was alone. It was late afternoon, as I cooled down from the six blocks I walked to a chain grocery to get almond milk and fruit for my protein shake. A twenty-something-year-old waitress giggled when

I winked at her at the flashy bistro with the good coffee. She carefully balanced a cup and saucer on the tilted table, then struggled through her English pronunciations. We both laughed, and her mouth revealed a glitzy shine of silver braces. I was disappointed the days she wasn't there. I thought about her while peering out my living room window seven stories high. It wasn't sexual, but more an appreciation of her freshness and the innocent stage of her life. Below, the gym's pool shimmered a turquoise blue. For a moment I considered standing in the deep end, under the cooking sun, but the thought of putting on trunks and crossing the busy street was too laborious. I picked up my Orwell book instead and thumbed through it, quickly placing it back on my desk. I sat on the king-sized bed. There was only one channel in English on the television, a European dart-throwing competition. I stared at the pixeled screen, occasionally belly roaring at the grimacing expressions and protruding beer guts of the throwers. One had horrible acne scars and a butchered military haircut. The other looked like someone from a sex offender registry. Idle time steeps the teabag.

With faint applause oozing through the electric mist of the television, I propped two thick pillows behind my back and journaled, then sent emails home. I had been traveling for two months and was through the honeymoon period. Checking in with others was challenging. I mainly sent group emails, and only about every two weeks. I wasn't sure what to share, knowing that most wouldn't really grasp what I was doing. I started an email to D, then deleted it. Our last correspondence had a coolness from her, and I wondered if she had a man. I was too afraid to ask. A recent email from Thailand sat on top of my inbox. It was from English Jack.

> Hiya mate, hope you're well in Vietnam. I know you have a birthday this month and it's in the early part. I hope you do something enjoyable for yourself. Still managing a headache. I wish you'd seen me when I won the others. Thak said my headache should go away in a week. That was nearly two weeks ago. Thai logic, just like the length of a Thai minute. There are new guys at camp, but it doesn't feel the same. Not really as tight. Toby went back to Canada two days ago. He seemed depressed about something. Raj is heading home, too. Warren is actually skinny now and has a Chinese girlfriend he met online. He

Happy Birthday

says he may leave soon and visit her. Classes are small, but Duncan likes having new blood. Oh yeah, he told me to tell you you're a wanker and to check out Peep Show since you like the Inbetweeners. He's still a dick, but I'd have to agree on Peep Show. It's brilliant at showing the collective autism of being British. Keep in touch, Jack.

I reread English Jack's email, the shadowy energies of loneliness intensifying. I missed the lads at camp. I missed the communal meals. Even the chiding and shit talking from Duncan and Paddy carried reminiscent value. There was satisfaction limping onto my bungalow porch, stripping off my drenched shorts and hand wraps, then ceremoniously placing them on the clothes rack as if it were an altar. The accommodations and routine were posher in Vietnam, but the grit and Spartan structure of Thailand made it more special. I ruminated on various comical scenes and conversations from camp, before returning to a seed that Toby watered.

There are times I purposely omit things because of temptation. For instance, a sexy coworker or an attractive student sends an email with a tone that carries a certain something with it. Delete. No records, or loose ends, as they say in gangster films. I don't want those spirits around, flicking their eyelashes and pointing their come-hither finger during moments of weakness. I often delete my browsing history for the same reason, as if it magically erases the stone grip of certain enticements and deviant thoughts. The late-night stuff that pops up in certain moods, especially when drinking. Those can be dark holes to fall into, especially if they become patterns.

There was a time in the undefined relationship with my neighbor where I was out of state at a conference. After my presentation, an overwhelmingly attractive woman approached, chatting me up for nearly half an hour. She was fit, spunky, and intelligent. My version of crack cocaine. And she'd read my work and liked it. I counted six times she ran her fingers through her hair. Even more than that, she held her gaze. She made it a point to tell me she was staying in the same hotel.

"Well, here's my number. Give me a call if you want to grab a drink or something."

Or something, I thought, as she brushed the small of my back while walking away. I marched directly to my lavish room purchased at the conference rate. There, I stared at her business card with her personal number handwritten on the back. I studied it, though not long enough to memorize anything. I sniffed the card, then ripped it to shreds, watching it zigzag like a kite in the breeze before flushing it into the abyss. I rendered a salute above the toilet. She was gone. The energies were gone. I passed the test. This time, anyway. Then I jerked off onto expensive thread count sheets.

I read English Jack's email one more time. His opening words hovered throughout my meditation, interrupting, and finally overpowering my mantra: *I know you have a birthday this month and it's in the early part. I hope you do something enjoyable for yourself.* Isn't what I'm doing enjoyable? Isn't that what this whole trip is about? I look at my spread-out frame on the bed and count nearly a dozen bruises just on my shins. I crack like a theater popcorn machine in the morning. My back pinches when I touch my toes. In certain moments there is the heavy invisible hand that holds the covers over my whole body, cinching tightly. I slept like this when my pot-growing cousins showed me *Poltergeist* at five. But this suffocation whispers that I am unemployed, spending money without more of it coming in. It tells me I won't be working for a while. That I will have holes in the resume and a lot of shit to explain in my next interview. Thankfully, these moods don't linger. The spirits around me most days are happy ones. I have already read six books and not missed a meditation. My body has been totally clean of substances, even sugar, for months. I can't remember when I last smoked pot. The tusks of the elephants on the big green bottles of Chang didn't touch me in Thailand. So, what is it then? What is that *thing* trying to break through the surface to steal my attention, telling me it brings gifts? That it's my birthday, and I should celebrate.

******

The time is 4:38 pm, local. I nestle the pillows into my lower back to redo my meditation, bothered that the last one was half-assed. The mantra shows up, but it's not the meditation one. It's Jack's opening gambit. I flip the consciousness knob and I'm in my bungalow sitting with Canadian Toby sipping water, tasting the faint sweetness of the electrolytes. There is joy in his voice. A devious, mischievous joy that hovers. I had it, too, once. It's Troy and me dropping the others in our

Happy Birthday

posse off at their homes, giggling as we head to an alley with our loaded pipe hidden in the glovebox. It's the website. The fucking website. The dark, I-shouldn't-be-giving-it-any-energy-because-I-know-better website that Toby told me about. But it's there. It occupies my entire meditation, front and center. The wiser part admits it was there while doing cool-down stretches at the end of training. I tried to block it out with images of offerings inside the incense-fogged Wats, paying respect to Buddha and doing extra meditation. But the seedy brothels and the malefic characters of that underworld are there, too. The cheap, cold beer close by. The tinted black windows where mystery lurks. These archetypal patterns may be held over from lifetimes of piracy and pillaging, and I have to own them. *It's your birthday*, the Wild Man reminds. Well, in two days it is. I'm soon sitting with another pillow underneath my computer, a glowing heat transferring throughout my battered thighs and penis.

I pound the keys with excited precision. It doesn't take long to locate the website. It is vast and professionally done. A Yelp for debauchery. There is a map of different countries, including European ones. I click on a few and scroll. Some postings are mini dissertations, complete with pictures of the establishments and even recommendations for certain women. I hover the arrow above Vietnam. Then refine by city. Saigon is a large place with horrible traffic. Most of the action is in District One where the tourist dollars are. On a Friday night it could easily take over an hour to get there, and that's assuming I survive the motorcycle ride. Someone on the discussion board asks about District Seven. My penis throbs momentarily. The post is less than a month old, and the board moderator, whom I learn is the curator of the website, replies:

> *If you want action, go to D1 where the tourists are. Moto-taxi about five USD each way. Heard a new place opened in D7 but can't vouch for it. Will be pricey on that side. They only cater to foreigners so expect to pay top dollar. They will charge Chinese more because they don't like them. Same goes for Indians and Muslims, they will get hosed, too. Sorry guys. But Aussies, Brits, and Yanks will get best deal. Going rate for full service about $40 in D1, so expect $60–$80 over there. If anyone goes, please post write-up.*

I wade through more postings, intrigued. Several recommend dating apps for meeting nonworking girls who like Americans and Europeans. There is consensus that Asian women like us. Some posters on the board shoot down the app idea, warning it's filled with scammers and fake photos. I don't have a phone, anyway. Someone offers a thoughtful comment on outcalls, where a woman comes to your apartment or hotel. All you do is open the door. As if reading my thoughts, a list of rules for my apartment is plastered on the desk next to Orwell. Rule number seven barks prominently: "No prostitutes allowed!" I pace around the studio and look out the window again. The pool is still radiant. I walk toward the chest of drawers and pull out my trunks. Then I put them away. I'm not enlightened.

******

6:14 pm, local.

"Hello, Mr. Neek. Good boxing today, I hopes," the short man with heavily gelled hair said.

His yellowed pit stains glowed under his tight, weathered white dress shirt. His black tie suspended high above a well-fed belly. There was a faint smell of body odor mixed with cheap deodorant they sold in the market next door.

"Hello, Tan the Man. Yes, it was good boxing. I'm a little tired, though."

"Oh, I see. Now you party?" he smiled. "I call taxi to District One? Be here quick, very cheap."

"Actually, Tan, I would like to stay in District Seven tonight. There is an Irish Pub I read about not far."

I handed Tan the scribbled note written on a complimentary pad with the letterhead of their hotel. The pen from their desk, which was brand new, had to be scraped against the pad several times before producing ink. I cast away thoughts it was an omen.

"Ah, pub. Hold one second, please, Mr. Neek. I get you taken care of. You want car or cyclo?"

"Cyclo."

Tan picked up the office phone and barked fiercely. A couple days earlier on a boat ride to the Cu Chi Tunnels, a pleasant older French

Happy Birthday

woman whispered to me, "I love the country, but it is such a *vulgar* language. It just sounds so angry. So barbaric."

Still smiling, Tan smacked the ancient phone onto its receiver.

"It is all settled, Mr. Neek. Five minutes. Nine thousand, include tip."

My brain calculated the new currency and breathed relief that it was only about three dollars for the ride.

Not long after some innocent banter with Tan, an even shorter man, though much skinnier, walked in and handed me a green helmet. They barked back and forth at each other, and I watched Tan slip him five thousand dong.

The traffic in Asia is some of the most congested and dangerous I've ever experienced. The expats at the gym owned scooters, and recommended I purchase one to bypass the notoriously corrupt cabbies and cyclo riders. But I knew I would be perpetually lost navigating a vast city like Saigon, especially without a phone. I steadied on to the back of the motorcycle, sinking deeply into its battered shocks. The green helmet fit snug, the chin strap hovered above my lips, as if hanging from my nose. A dodgy wooden cart selling rank snails and jungle bugs cooking under the evening humidity turned my head as I steadied onto the skinny man. Then I mentally signed the cross, and whispered, "Om Namah Shiva," as we ventured into the shadowy night with unknown deviance ahead.

We whizzed through collections of neighborhoods at blitzkrieg speed, through intersections without streetlights, while choruses of short beeps and long horns echoed from all directions. Different fragrances, most of them foul, mixed into the exhaust fumes. I held my olive-drab handkerchief, a gift from my outlaw uncle, around my nose and mouth. A couple times we exited the road and weaved onto sidewalks, zigzagging around families on plastic stools and tables that looked like children's furniture. They didn't blink as we brisked by, steam rising from their bowls. Ducks and frogs hung from pieces of rope next to frail chickens and different types of mystery meats.

Twenty minutes into the hazardous ride, we approached an affluent-looking plaza. Regal buildings with unblemished windows and flashing neon lights stood erect, next to expensive eateries with hip decor and comfortable outdoor seating. I stared at the colorfully dyed splashing water erupting from the fountain of the BMW dealership. A thought from the long immigration line at the airport; conversations that Vietnam was becoming the boom town of Asia. The moto man exited right onto a small street where various guesthouses and mid-grade hotels consumed the block. A rectangular gray guesthouse had a sign written in Chinese, the one beside it in Russian. Some showed prices in U.S. dollars. More twists and turns, and then we were parked in front of the pub. Collections of Chinese and Western-looking couples stared as I attempted to disembark gracefully.

I removed the helmet and wiped my face with the handkerchief, then brushed my hair with my hand. As I handed the driver his helmet, his right hand shot forward.

"Tip!" he demanded.

A confused expression washed over. I shook my head.

"No, Mr. Tan told me tip *included*."

"No!" the man demanded. "Tan wrong! Give me money!"

I stared at the man and fiery eyes shot back. They were ice cold, and for the briefest of moments I felt a fierceness that must have been grossly apparent during the American War, as they called it. Despite his scrawny build, the man stood rooted with his chest extended and fists clinched.

The small audience watched from the pub, so I laughed and opened my canvas wallet and handed him approximately two dollars. His eyes slowly shifted away from mine, while he grunted at the bills. Then he kickstarted his bike and whirred like a rocket to his next hustle.

According to the makeshift map I hid in my back pocket, the brothel was just blocks from the pub. Rather than be dropped off where collections of women and goon pimps were likely to circulate and pounce, I strategically set the stage. I would be just another wandering Westerner weaving in and out of random neighborhoods before accidentally stumbling upon said establishment. I could glance at the seediness from across the street, then take internal inventory. I wiped my face again, following my intuition to the left of the pub's entrance. All the street signs were in Vietnamese, and before I knew it, I was back in front of the saloon doors, the same sets of eyes staring. I considered going in for my first beer in over two months, but instead opted for another direction.

It felt wonderful to see activity and affluence after being so isolated. The streets in these parts were much cleaner and devoid of the putrid odors found most everywhere in Asia. Although I often prioritized areas away from tourists, there was something reassuring watching them go about in social fashion, drinking their booze, laughing loudly. Other than brief engagements in training, I was living among the locals,

Happy Birthday

immersed in what I felt was a more authentic Vietnam. A few at the hotel asked perplexed why I wasn't staying in District One, or in the lavish expat enclaves of District Seven. When I told them my intention to be among the natives, they seemed suspicious.

Part of me was detached from going to the brothel. But I had reached a point on the journey where I was beginning to burn out from the disciplined regimen and physical exertion. There is a patterning I carry where fun becomes forfeited if I feel I haven't earned it. For instance, I would postpone watching a favorite movie or sipping a special beer until after something meaningful was handled, like finishing an article I was writing, or closing a big donation. Over time, those pressures grew and eventually the pressure valve had to be pulled. So, a spontaneous evening with a possibility of danger brought fresh breath with it. Plus, it was my damn birthday. Well, close to it, anyway.

It didn't take long to get totally lost. I circled new blocks and looked at the menus written in English posted to the windows. As I walked down a steep set of steps, a moto shot directly at me, hitting its brakes dangerously close. The driver flipped up the tinted visor of his green helmet.

"You go to pub, already?"

"Yes. Didn't like."

"Expensive. Chinese go there. No good! Where you go now?"

"No, I'm okay. I just want to walk."

"Okay. Where you want to go."

I stood in stillness, as my mouth dried. The Wild Man pounded his drum, which reverberated in sync with my heartbeat. I could just hop back to the apartment and pick up some beers. That could be fun, perhaps; getting shitfaced and watching the Euro dart throwers. But it also felt like failure. And lonely. Without thinking I blurted, "I want to go to Red Hornet."

The man's black eyes dove deeper into mine, as his body cocked to the side confused. He stood stone faced.

"*Red Hornet*. What is Red Hornet?" he asked, his eyes not leaving. I thought about detective shows and the way investigators scrutinized suspects in the interrogation room.

I didn't say anything.

"Mmm," he grunted. Quickly, he snatched his phone from a Velcro pocket on his black cargo pants and typed. He grunted again. Then the sharp glow of a map radiated from the tiny screen as he rapidly scrolled. Then laughter, obnoxiously loud laughter.

A Ronin's Tale

"Red Hornet! Yes! Lady! Lady! You want LADY? RED HORNET LADY!"

I nodded, carefully scanning the surroundings, then raised my pointer finger to my mouth.

"Close! Very close! Get on," he demanded holding out his helmet.

"No. I want to walk. Can you show me?"

"Mmm ..." he exhaled.

"Tip! You give me tip!"

Out went the canvas wallet. Another two dollars liberated. With a series of more grunts, his leather gloved hands pointed forward, then left, then right, then left again. I asked him to repeat it two more times. The moto pirate nodded, before kick starting his moto to life and buzzing into the shadows. I looked around as if under surveillance, then walked with my shoulders stooped forward, reminiscing on my tenth birthday and getting a basketball hoop.

Chapter 21

GRITTIER FLAVORS

Fall 2017, A Classroom in the Midwest

As the Hero moves along the Special World and encounters different types of tests and temptations, we need to cover a few things. We need to learn what archetypes are. Though since this is not a psychology class, we won't go into detail. Our purpose is only a basic comprehension so that we understand the hero's journey more efficiently.

We can think of an archetype as a universal pattern that is understood similarly around the world. It is not impacted by time, or culture, or even language barriers. It never dies or goes away. If we dip our toes in psychology, archetypes are inherited symbols that exist in the collective unconscious. These symbols are things we can relate to in our own lives, and they help us to better understand ourselves. We may sense or feel them in certain moments or moods, too. For instance, you might find yourself struck with emotion when you watch Gladiator, or Braveheart. You are watching a movie, which you know is not real, though the emotional response is immensely powerful. You identify with the Hero on the screen, and perhaps you envision yourself in a similar role sacrificing for some honorable cause.

The Hero is a primary archetype that symbolizes couage. When we dismantle the different bits and parts of the Hero, we find things like bravery, service to others, risk-taking, confronting fear, and the like. Most cultures have sacred stories they revere which help us understand the significance of the Hero. Admiration is part of this. In our own culture, law enforcement officers, firefighters, and the military are classic examples of heroic subcultures. We see the people working in these professions as heroes, and we picture the kinds of hazardous duties and risks associated with their work. But aside from them, think about the things people post on Facebook and Instagram. It is common to see pictures of one skydiving, climbing, or rafting a wild river, or shooting a big gun. Some mention they're a cancer survivor, a special needs parent, or a combat veteran. Why is this? There is a fundamental need to be recognized by others; to be affirmed. Being seen as courageous is connected to this need. And again, we can't think of the Hero along gender lines, though the ways that men and women navigate these experiences differs from each other.

 I like to think of archetypes as a specific energy that show themselves in different ways. For instance, when I'm in the gym, I have metal or gangster rap jamming out loud in my earphones. I don't usually listen to this kind of music, but in certain moments it is exactly what I need because it brings out a Warrior archetype. I like to put myself into the mindset that I am preparing for a battle or test. I can literally feel my emotions change as I become fiercer. My posture is erect, and my bounce is strong. It is not just an external thing, there is a storm of energy also taking place inside. There is something primal stirred up. I allow my Warrior archetype to essentially take over and rule the kingdom of my personality for that moment.

 There are many different types of archetypes, and each has their strong and weak side. A Sage can be tremendously wise and benevolent in its highest form, or a closeminded fanatic or cult figure in its lowest expression. A King can be revered by his people or become drunk on power and tyrannical. These polarizing manifestations, which exist in each of us, are important to pay attention to. Part of what I enjoy about The Karate Kid is it portrays these two distinctive sides through Mr. Miyagi and Mr. Kreese. Miyagi is the wise, elderly Okinawan man who not only has remarkable karate skill, but also possesses deep wisdom. There is a silence about him, and he doesn't get worked up that much. He is effective at calming Daniel down, bringing him back to center. And he doesn't showboat his martial skills to impress or intimidate others. Even his karate stems from a natural place, as they practice at the ocean or as Miyagi disguises the training through basic household chores. He reminds Daniel that what he is learning is for self-defense only, and that winning in competition is irrelevant. In comparison, when we inspect the shadow expression of the Warrior through Mr. Kreese, we see a domineering and cold instructor obsessed with brutality. He's loud and brash and expects his students to win at all costs. The Cobra Kai motto, "Strike first, strike hard, no mercy," symbolizes the *ethos of his dojo. Their training is centered on a militaristic discipline. Compliance through fear; running as part of a wolfpack. Consequently, we see the influence the shadow has on his students.*

When the Hero is in the Special World, he encounters different types of archetypes that help him discover the deeper layers that exist inside. These characters the Hero comes across each symbolizes some part of himself, good or bad. As the journey unfolds, the Hero becomes more self-aware of the parts that need to be healed. He starts to understand where he is lying to himself, or cutting corners, or hurting others. He thinks more thoroughly about his behaviors and the consequences of his actions. But this awareness won't occur unless the Hero sees his Shadows. He must.

The Shadows are the darker parts of the unconscious mind that harbor repressed ideas, desires, and our limitations. They're the grittier flavors of the human condition. The Hero must confront these elements that operate from his lower self in order to understand how he is held back. Do you ever get the sense you're not being fully truthful with yourself? Part of the Hero's maturation is awareness that he can no longer hide behind his muscles, sharp intellect, fat bank account, or all the awards on his wall. He needs to reflect on why most of his relationships fail, or why he continually argues with others, or how drugs and alcohol rob him of his life force. Or maybe he needs to understand how his lack of assertiveness allows others to continually take advantage of him. Without understanding the Shadows there is no wholeness. Keep in mind that some schools of spirituality consider these things "sins." For instance, if you have these thoughts, there is something bad inside you and you need to stop having them or ask for forgiveness. In the meditation commune I was raised in, there was an emphasis that dwelling on negative things only created more negativity. Therefore, we were encouraged to not address the darker parts. But is this realistic, to go through life pretending certain things aren't there? Quoting the philosopher Nietzsche, Campbell says, "be careful, lest in casting out your devil, you cast out the best thing that's in you." In other words, instead of trying to run and hide from these shadowy patterns, the hero's journey encourages us to take ownership that they exist and to learn from them. To listen to what they whisper.

The maturation of the Hero means that he takes ownership of his bullshit; the way he manipulates or lies, or does the bare minimum, or drifts through life without a mission or purpose. He understands his patterns, and the changes he needs to make. He accepts that being a victim is unacceptable. And most importantly, he identifies the hard work ahead if he is truly committed to his rebirth. If the Hero abandons the quest, or never begins one in the first place, he will go through life asleep.

Chapter 22

UNDER THE SHEETS

Late May 2019, Vietnam

> The wound is the place where light enters you.[23]
> —Rumi

The brain hemorrhaging wanes as I advance on the Red Hornet. A numbness, a void of some sort, floats about. I consider a beer at the tourist pub, but my stride is led by a mysterious purposefulness like when hiking a mountain. If I slow, thoughts invade. From pulled weapons to large public-speaking venues, I've grown accustomed to adrenaline and the calm that hovers after. I'm in that strange middle space where charging forward is the only viable option. My eight years in Illinois as a working man, something got lost there; something significant. The innocent boy, devious with mischief and curious to throw off the bowlines, forfeited his rope for silk ties and Italian leather shoes. Juiciness dried up.

The last block is long and eerily quiet, but the electricity is there. Half a dozen beautiful women across the street sit in cocktail dresses that look tailored. Most sit with their legs crossed over one another, texting. A couple watchful eyes scan the street. I stay on my side with my hands in my pockets, looking straight ahead. The humid night feels warmer. Eyes perk up from their phones as I inch along the concrete. Heads turn. Prey is spotted. A tall, foreign man in a nation devoutly religious to all things Western and wealthy.

---

23   M. Mafi, *Rumi's Little Book of Wisdom* (Hampton Roads Publishing, 2021).

A Ronin's Tale

"Hey, you, very tall man! Come here, tall man," one of the faces shouts.

I glance to my right, noticing three girls wooing me with their hands. The others stop their sojourn in cyberspace and join the chorus. I slow my gait, then look over and smile. Three men in expensive suits swirl the ice in their glasses. One smokes a cigarette and is wearing sunglasses even though it's night. I walk toward the women.

"Oh, handsome! Hello, Mr. Handsome, where you from?"

"America," I croak.

"Ooh, Ameri-ca. Obama! Oh, Ameri-ca very good. We love America. How long you in Vietnam?"

Two of the women stand and saunter over. One of them, unusually tall even without her heels, reaches for my hand but I politely pull it back and place it in my pocket. She steps closer.

"Not too long. A little while," I say.

The taller woman utters sharply to the other, who immediately turns and walks back to her seat.

"You have girlfriend? You very handsome. I like these, how you say?" Her finger delicately brushes my cheek. It's the first touch I've received since D.

"Those are called *dimples*," I reply.

"Deen-po?"

"Dimples," I repeat.

"Oh, deen-po. Deen po." She repeats it several times, while giggles echo from the tables.

"You big man. Grrrr ... What you do in Ameri-ca? Policeman?" She clasps her hands into a gun and mimics shooting the three Chinese men drinking their cocktails.

"No. I am a teacher," I say, without thinking.

"Teacher? No, no, not teacher. Really, you teacher?" She cocks her head, then turns around and translates for the table. More giggles.

"You teach me English. My English not so good."

"No, it sounds good. Very good," I lie.

"So, Mr. Teacher, you make lots of money?"

I shake my head and make a sad face. She imitates and exaggerates the face, then pretends to wipe invisible tears before laughing again.

"Why you come here?"

"Uh, well, I wanted to see Vietnam ever since ..."

"No, no," she interrupts. "Why you come to Red Hornet?"

She stands close enough that I smell perfume. It differs from the

Under the Sheets

aggressive cheap fragrances that breeze in markets or temples. There are no tattoos or markings on her slender frame. Her muscular calves and shapely thighs rock slightly back and forth as she speaks. Her jet-black hair is long and shiny, hanging down most of her back and stopping just above her thin waist. Her beauty could effortlessly place her on the cover of a Bangkok or Saigon billboard, or one of those magazines they put in business class. But her eyes are stern, as they scan back and forth sharply. She is smiley outside, but all business. Another woman from the table asks a question in broken English and is curtly shushed. The tall woman's Vietnamese is quick, its tone abrasive.

"I'm just out for a walk."

"Where you stay?"

"Far. About twenty minutes by moto. I came here to go to pub over there," I say, pointing in a random direction.

"Oh, English pub. Expensive. You go Vietnamese club with me and buy me drinks. Then we dance. Better there."

The woman laughs and rattles to her consorts.

"No, I am just going for a walk tonight. No dance. Me, old man."

"Not old man. You handsome, Mr. Teacher. And I like deen-po."

I look over at the four-story establishment, and it resembles an expensive hotel, similar to ones I saw in Paris. There is a small fountain with lush plants outside. I notice the sound of the flowing water for the first time. The lighting is dim, and the entrance doors completely tinted. I cannot tell if anyone is watching from inside and the thought makes me anxious. On both sides of the street, green and yellow taxis sit with their engines off. The driver's congregated together, they watch us while chain smoking.

As if reading my inner dialogue, the woman steps closer and whispers, "No, walk. You come inside with me, okay?"

Her fiery eyes soften just slightly, as something innocent pierces through. I stand looking back into her eyes wondering about her past; wondering whether or not she was trafficked and doing this work voluntarily. Other thoughts rush in. Assorted and difficult to decipher. What kind of karma am I creating here? I consider walking away but an image of riding back to my apartment creeps in. I hear the distinctive sound of the key reader before the satisfying click that unlocks my door. I know the smells that will greet me from the kitchen. Then I'll take off my shoes and strip to my underwear, before climbing into bed under the mosquito net. In those quiet moments I will sit with this evening and replay the Red Hornet over, a cloud of dejection hovering overhead.

An inner voice admonishing me for pulling out, especially so close. Although the scene is an unnatural one, the awkward small talk, the forced flirting, and her cutting to the chase, it still feels like the better choice. The schoolboy explorer wants to know what's beyond the black doors. The Wild Man wants whatever it is he wants. My soul, perhaps.

"Okay," I pause. "We go inside."

"Yes?" she asks.

"Yes."

She smiles and takes my hand, clasping it inside hers and we walk toward the unknown.

The black, spotless doors opened into a pristine lobby with slick white tile floors and dark wooden furniture. Clusters of women, some on their phones and others laughing with groups of smartly dressed Chinese men, sit on large purple chairs near a bar. Each of the men holds drinks with bright umbrellas sticking out from the top. I'm escorted to a reception where an elderly woman with a long gold chain and floral top sits counting money earnestly. She says something but doesn't look above her librarian glasses to acknowledge me.

"You pay mama," my date whispers.

"Uh, how much?"

"Depend. You want boom boom, or sucky?"

"Uh," I pause. I'm transported to a childhood sleepover, going out for ice cream. The server asks if I want nuts and whip cream on my hot fudge sundae.

"Sucky."

"You pay dollars or dong?"

"Dollars."

"Forty for sucky. Plus, you give me tip, okay?"

I nod and hand her two crisp bills; Mr. Jackson stares back, witnessing the shenanigans. She reaches over the counter and places the bills inside a light-colored wicker basket. The mama-san hands her a key without raising her head off the stack of cash. As we walk toward the elevator, in nearly perfect English, someone yells, "Have fun, USA!"

Another memory floods in. I'm young, at the boardwalk in Santa Cruz. My father and sister eat cotton candy far below, while Mom and I ascend in a mysterious contraption, climbing high on a track. Sounds of a chain reverberate, as the capsule we're in rattles toward the top. Rickety rattling, side to side. There was foreboding anticipation; fear mixed with excitement, and something else. Something dangerous told me I was being tested. It's an internal sensation that words can't describe, though the feeling is palpable. It led to a pierced left ear in fourth grade.

Prostitutes were never my thing, more just to have the experience and to be a good wingman. A jaunt on the train to Tijuana, despite the narco wars getting ridiculously violent, we hit the El Revolucion district. Our plane landed in San Diego after nearly a year deployed. My comrade, a short Texan with wrestler's ears, convinced me to skip the homecoming to get a jumpstart to the border. He was nearing sixty and had a wife whom he'd married at sixteen, a mandatory choice he confessed, after she got pregnant. He once told me he played the lottery each week so that he could one day cash her out and buy his freedom. That comment pained me.

The stainless elevator doors open, as smells of bleach permeate the confined space. The woman lets go of my hand and pulls out her phone. Her manicured nails text quickly, and I look at myself in the reflective mirror. The room is small and dark with a massage table next to a queen-sized bed. The white sheets smell fresh from the laundry and are without wrinkles. In the corner, a knee-high purple table has two bottles of water and a real rose in a crystal flute. Although barren, even among American standards it is a clean set-up. The woman puts away her phone and tells me to shower and climb under the sheets. Then she leaves.

I squat low under the showerhead, as lukewarm water mists over my tattooed chest and arms. I think about the time difference, wondering what people are doing back home. They were soon to begin their day. Did the people in my old life think about me? When my name came up, were kind things said? Then poisoned arrows from scorned lovers drifted by. God, if they only knew what I was doing. I towel off and slide under the top sheet on the table, naked. A few minutes later a crack of light enters the naughty cavernous space, and a figure dressed in red negligée walks over. I recognize the perfume.

"What's your name?" she whispers softly, kissing the top of my ear and biting it lightly.

"Nick," I say.

"Neeeeeek," she breathes.

A squirting sound punctuates the silence, as my breathing wanes. Moments later, a pair of oiled hands move up and down my shoulders and neck, progressively sinking deeper into my skin. I close my eyes and drift back to my last massage. It seems long ago, but it wasn't. D comes into focus with her radiant glow. Warmth covers me. The agent who sold me my condo, then captured my heart. The one who reminded me of all the tan-skinned, athletic girls I longed for in high school. Fit, sharp, with a smile that kidnapped entire rooms, her beauty amplified by her devout faith and principled ways. We closed the real estate deal platonically, though I thought of her often. Months later a few text messages went back and forth, and then an email from her asking if I could teach her to shoot a gun. Of course I would.

I lost my job a couple weeks before our first date. The sand would eventually run out of the hourglass, and we were on rationed time, we knew, but she blindsided me. It happened so quickly, sleeping in the same bed most nights, cooking meals together. She rubbed my shoulders and back every evening, after destroying me in board games. Next to her Bible, collections of success manuals were neatly stacked. We spent ten days at an all-inclusive in Mexico, making love every night and most mornings. Then we hid from a swinging couple from New York who stalked us. Eating the worm at the bottom of the mescal our first evening there, the booze gave me its euphoric assurance that everything would work out. There would be a plan. There had to be. Sinking further into the massage table, I ruminate on D's trademark smile before the channel switches, and I see us crying on her couch. The same couch we made love on our first time. I was packing my belongings and preparing to leave for good. The night before, she still rubbed my shoulders.

Hands move lower to the mid and small of my back. The squirting echoes softly again, before I'm lost in another dream. I whispered something to D under my breath. Something about being so truly sorry for the hurt I caused. Something about it being the healthiest relationship I ever had, and that it scared me to allow that kind of love in. I inspected artifacts in her home, familiar pictures and décor imprinted as if my soul were there visiting.

I take a few more breaths. I reposition my face in the tiny hole in the middle of the table with the towels pressed into my cheeks and forehead. I wiggle my toes, hearing an audible crack. Then, my old neighbor, my other love, comes in. I hear her vintage leather boots land forcefully on the wooden floor of my bedroom. Her entrance, a storm. I feel her long blonde hair gently breeze across my back and hear her loud southern cackle. And her sneeze. My God, her sneeze. The chancellor once stopped talking in the middle of his speech when she did it. It took her several minutes to remove her jewelry, the silver bracelet with the colorful stones and strange names. Then the rings. All the rings. Piled together like a pirate's booty on top of the antique table with the drawer where I kept a loaded revolver. We were drunk. Drunker than usual. Wine bottles clanged against the bed, as we rhythmically moved in and out of each other. Her breath fresh with toothpaste, her lips purple from the cabernet. She grabbed the back of my head forcefully and stared. Just stared deeply, as if there was a soul she was coaxing out. That gaze penetrated somewhere beyond. I'd look away and come back moments later, her eyes in the same place. I remember how skinny she got when I had another woman in my apartment. Before the cruelty, I washed dishes from above, watching her graceful moves as she loaded a saddle into her cramped black Civic with shit strewn about inside. Greg Dulli belted his own sorrow, as she peeled out too quickly through the narrow drive. I can't listen or look at Stevie Nicks and not think of her.

    A year after I moved into the Brooklyn Building, I taped a note to her door. A year spent peeking through curtains, I needed to know her. I told her to call some time, then rushed down and grabbed it as the beer buzz waned. Eventually other plans summoned; the forces of attraction took their place above the earthly realms and orchestrated our meeting in the laundry. Memorial Weekend, and a couple days before my thirty-fifth birthday. But I treated that woman in a miserable way. The things I wish I could undo.

    The massage loosens something. Blocked energies open, and for the briefest second it places me in the womb again. A tiny boy, afraid to come into the world of noise, artificial lighting, and chaos. It was the warmth of a lover I wanted for my birthday, but instead I find myself chilled under the fan, burrowed under the sheets. The woman's hands are on the back of my legs and then up around my butt cheeks. Her slippery fingers penetrate deeply under the skin, digging, prompting me to wince aloud in pain. It was in this place, this shadowy ethereal dimension, that the last of my true loves came in.

    She was the first woman I ever loved, and the only woman I lived with. I met her when I was bouncing in the bars. Early into our relationship, we were eating at a restaurant, and I came back from the bathroom and noticed that a man next to us had slipped his business card to her. It happened more than once. Random strangers stopped me in bars and coffee shops, shaking my hand, patting me on the back. Sometimes I just stared at her in the morning while she slept, enamored by her beauty. The way her nose looked. She was a northern California girl through and through; sea salt in her marrow with blonde hair and perky personality. Not an intellectual, but just a kind heart and generous mother. Her young son, I loved, and taught to swim. But I was in my mid-twenties, in bumper-to-bumper traffic on the 101 each morning, headed into the city on edge with the others. I looked out across the Golden Gate and cracked my window feeling the fog and its ominous breeze. Alcatraz was out there, but my prison was that condo. A domestic routine I wasn't ready for. I thought of my mountain of student loan debt and wondered if I would ever be free again. We wanted different things, in different places. A decade age difference part of the issue. I pulled back and retreated to my quiet world. It was those nights that I'd lie on the edge of the bed and feel her arms pull me tightly toward her. A part of me had already left. And then one morning I told her I was moving out, just like that. It haunted me for years the way I handled it. It haunted me when her son asked when I was coming back, and I just smiled and didn't say anything. I sent him a birthday card with cash each year until he turned eighteen, telling myself that somehow made up for it. About a month after I moved out, I volunteered and was selected for a unit headed to the Middle East for a year. Those were my three loves. My holy trinity. Each the victim of my uninitiated selfishness, collateral damage in a war of emotional imbalance and a fear of being loved. That's what I thought about when this Vietnamese prostitute asked me to turn over so she could place my penis in her mouth, then collect her tip.

******

I walk past the British Pub, the same eyes on me. A conversation with a convict I once worked with looms.

"I hate that feeling walking down the street, right after getting out. It's like everyone knows where I've been. They smell it on me. It's dirty, dirty. I'm dirty. Not free at all, man."

I follow familiar music, eventually finding myself in a smoke-clouded bar. Pictures of icons grace the wall, though the clientele is exclusively Vietnamese. There are Clark Gable and Brando black and whites next to Marilyn and Janis. The eras scattered, but it feels good to see them. I glide through the plume and park on a comfortable stool, scanning the beer list. It's been just over two months. Ten weeks to be exact. I naively told myself I would go the entire time without a drink.

Under the Sheets

Bullshit and justification of one shade or another somehow veto my promises. I order a Saigon bucket of triplets, and they come quickly on ice. The first sip sends ripples down my throat and burns a little in the nose. I take another long pull and the beer is three-quarters empty. I briefly think of the numerous members of my lineage, living and no longer, who struggled with the drink. It's in me, too. As if feeling their presence at the bar, I raise the bottle and drain the last of it. My love-hate history with booze, but tonight I'm a gushing schoolgirl.

"What are we celebrating?" a voice from behind asks. It sounds American, and I clutch.

I turn, and a plump younger man with a round boyish face and messy sand hair looks back.

"Oh, uh, nothing. Just having a beer is all."

"Fair enough. Where you from?"

"Wisconsin, mostly."

"Me too!" he says excitedly. "Went to school in Madison. 'Mostly' huh. That's kind of a strange way to answer. You live here now or just visiting? Where in Wisconsin? Mind if I sit down?"

I don't know if it's the beer, which I'm already feeling, but his inquisition is bothersome. I just want to enjoy my post-orgasmic confusion of the past hour and sit in solitude while catching a nice buzz. Maybe drink enough that I feel sorry for myself, despite living a life of total freedom and pleasure. There is a silver lining, though. I don't have a phone on me, so I won't be texting any exes.

"Just passing through. From a small town, near La Crosse."

"Oh really. I live here. Teaching English."

"That's interesting."

"Well, it's going on two years. Time just flies. Real nice people, but there's a lot of dishonesty, too. I'm not too good at negotiating stuff, so I end up paying a lot more for things. I bought a scooter, but you know how the driving is around here. Can't get dairy here either, and us being Wisconsin boys, well, that's a sacrilege."

"Mm hm." I nod.

"You don't have a Wisconsin accent." He shrugs, then leans closer. "Where'd you say you're from again? And you traveling alone? Where you headed off to next?"

"No, my fiancé is with me. She and a girlfriend were seeing some sites in District One. I should get going soon. Supposed to meet them for dinner."

"Oh really. Where'd they'd go in D One? Where you gettin' your grub?"

I open the second beer while he rattles an exhaustive list of tourist attractions. Within seconds, it's finished.

"Wow, you got to be celebrating something."

"Just thirsty is all."

The chatty stranger slides onto the stool next to me. He is a bit overweight, though not obese. His undersized white polo barely covers his gut, and there are miscellaneous food stains on the front. Above his khaki shorts is a blue fanny pack with an oversized silver zipper. Across the bar, a striking cocktail waitress looks over and smiles. The beer, although weak, settles quickly, as a peaceful sheen covers like a warm blanket. I drift back to a pile of hot laundry when I was younger, and Mom letting me sleep under it. Truthfully, I missed the drink.

"What kind of work you do?"

"I am retired, actually," I say, sitting up tall.

"I won a dance scholarship in high school, and that paid for college out east. Economics, and a minor in finance."

"A dancer?" he asked, squinting his eyes. "No offense, but you don't look like a dancer at all. And those tattoos, is that like one of those Hindu gods on your arm?"

"Yeah. I was part of a troupe that performed this tribal dance. A pretty big thing in Africa, actually."

"Really?" he says, cocking his head, leaning in.

"Yeah. When young men are initiated into manhood, they go through this rigorous rite-of-passage, and then finish the ceremony dancing in front of the elders and the whole tribe. Then they get circumcised. I was one of only four white men they ever taught the dance to."

At this point the beer glows, and I fondly embrace that I am out of fucks for the evening.

"Holy cow!"

"Yeah. But you can't make much money dancing unless you get on with the Chippendales or something. So, after college I worked a few firms, then hit it big with crypto when it surged. Now just traveling. My fiancé and I were in Europe in the winter, then decided to do Asia, you know, someplace warm. Probably do some sailing in the Caribbean after."

I feel like an insane parrot squawking pure rubbish at another equally insane parrot. All the fucking meetings and strangers that showed up to my office wanting to talk. The listening. The Wild Man loves it, too. He tells me to order several more buckets, and to toss

Under the Sheets

magic toward the cute waitress. Maybe even go back to the hornet ranch for some boom boom.

"Get out of here! Whoa, nelly. I read about a few of those 'bitcoin millionaires,' but never actually met one. Holy cow. I still kick myself for not getting in on Netflix. Facebook, too, even though they steal your data. But Netflix. I watch a lot of movies, so ..."

He cut himself off mid-sentence while I opened the last beer and the attractive cocktail waitress shot over.

"Hell-o, boys. More drinks, yeah?" she asked in fairly good English.

"Yeah!" my companion exclaimed, unzipping his fanny pack, and pulling his wallet, its Velcro sound penetrating through a Tom Petty riff.

"I'll take a bucket of Saigon, like my friend here."

"I'm okay, love," I say.

"Oh, come on. You just downed three beers in like five minutes, at least have one more with me."

I scan his ruddy face, awash in compassion. I wonder what his P.E. classes were like. The chin-up bar in the middle and his sleepless nights beforehand.

"Sure. But put your wallet away, cowboy. I got this." I smile.

I wink at the waitress and add, "Another bucket for me, and I'll have a shot of whisky. That local stuff, with the scorpion in it."

He beamed and took off his glasses to wipe his forehead. His face was pockmarked with acne scars. He hadn't shaved in a few days and most of the stubble was congregated around his large chin, though he still looked like a teenage paperboy.

The drinks were promptly on the table, and I slid the equivalent of fifteen dollars to the waitress, which included a generous tip.

"So, what brought you to teach English in Vietnam?" I ask, genuinely curious.

"Well, I just thought I needed to do something before I settle down. I'm nearly twenty-five, and most everyone in my family is married with kids. Well, my younger brother just got separated."

He takes a sip of his beer and continues, "My parents were high school sweethearts. Well, technically, they met at church, but they went to the same high school, too. So they pretty much tell everyone they meet that they're high school sweethearts, so ..."

"Um huh." I nod, looking at the waitress. Another waitress assembles close to her and then looks toward us. She laughs before walking away to a table.

"Well, I don't really get out that much. I do a lot of gaming, and there's a pretty good game store in D One. And I like the food for the most part, but I miss pizza and you can't really find any decent Western food unless you're prepared to spend a lot. But I guess for a big shot like you, that wouldn't be a problem. I guess I do miss some things in America, but not our asshole president. That's for sure. Hope that's not offensive."

I throw up my hands, "Don't really follow politics. Just busy living life."

"Oh Lord, he's a piece of work, that one. My parents love him, but I just think he's a total arrogant bastard. I was a global studies major, and I'll tell you, it just opened my eyes."

"Mmm hmm. Hey, is there a head around here?"

"A what?"

"Uh, a toilet. I gotta piss."

"Oh yeah, yeah. They're upstairs. You see that James Dean picture, well, go around that corner and you'll see the steps near John Wayne. Just go up and it'll be close by."

I nod and tap him lightly on the shoulder as I push in my stool. Then I steady myself. The alcohol worked quickly, and the quiet numbness I sought on stressful weeknights return like an ex-girlfriend. I nod to Mr. Dean as I turn the corner, and then another one for the Duke. Immediately, I scan for an exit. On the lower level is the primary entrance, but I'll be caught if I scurry out. I slowly ascend the steps, enjoying the hodgepodge of Americana. An aura of patriotism and pride swells internally. As I get to the top of the stairwell, the waitress from below follows behind. I stop and smile.

"Are you okay?" she asks.

"Yes, ma'am, fine and dandy," I say. A confused look springs across her face.

"What?"

"Oh, never mind. Yeah, I'm okay."

"You friend with Charlie?"

"Who? Oh, no. Just met him. Actually, I need to sneak out of your bar."

"Sneak out?"

"Um, I need to escape. Leave. I need to leave this bar without Charlie seeing me. Do you understand?"

She laughs loudly.

"Yes, you want to leave bar and Charlie cannot know."

Under the Sheets

She laughs some more.

"Exactly."

"He has bad breath," she states matter of fact.

"Oh. Okay."

For a moment I am self-conscious of my own breath, though I had a mint just minutes earlier.

"Why leave? Just tell Charlie go away and you don't want him sit with you."

"Yeah. Well, that is not considered polite. Do you know what polite means?"

"Yes. You Americans are too concerned about polite. Vietnamese, you just tell people, go away. I don't like you. You bother me, so leave now."

"Yeah. Anyway, is there another door I can leave from?"

As I speak, the alcohol drums. Some parts of my life bring about natural confidence, while other parts bring an uncanny shyness. Women have always been in the latter camp. But a few sips of booze changes things. Indeed, there is some truth in wine, though she also whispers our wounds. I follow closely, through a labyrinth of doors and descend down another stairwell, this one hidden from the customers. As we approach the exit door, I turn to thank her. It's an odd kind of charged moment, where our eyes steady. I consider kissing her, but just as quickly as the moment arose, it passes and approaching her seems awkward and clumsy. A tinge of dejection overshadows with sobering thoughts that those days of randomly kissing women in the bathroom line of a random bar are over. Maybe this whole thing is a midlife crisis, after all. Just arriving prematurely. Maybe I should've just stayed in my room and watched the European dart throwers.

Then a shimmer of light.

"Come back and see me. Charlie does not come on Tuesdays or Thursdays."

I nod and wink, walking backward until I'm through the doors and surrounded by darkness. A hint of guilt for ditching Charlie lingers. The street is without a light source, other than a fuller moon. Collections of rats rummage through a pile of trash. They are the largest rats I've ever seen, and they make an eerie squeak as they scurry. Then I think about fourth grade. We're seated on a carpet in a circle, talking about different countries around the world. Mrs. Chalmers calls on me, and I proudly stand.

"Vietnam. That's the country I want to visit. There was a war there, and Steven's dad fought in it. They like mysterious foods like noodles with soy sauce, and some eat dogs and cats. And they have big rats, and they wear strange hats when they plant rice. I think I will go there one day. I think I will travel around the world and have a lot of adventures."

Chapter 23

FATHER'S DAY EMAIL

June 16, 2019, Nha Trang, Vietnam

Hey, Dad, I didn't sleep much last night, only a few hours. I wonder if the moon is full or near full, as I usually feel something around that time. There are a lot of barking dogs here, too. I'm in Nha Trang, despite several unfavorable things I read, it's actually my favorite part of Vietnam so far. It is a coastal town, and there is a seedy vibe here, but also a sweetness along with beaches and mountains. There are Chinese and Russian tourists here, but I have not met or seen one American, Canadian, or European, which is nice.

I went to Thap Ba Hot Springs and had a serene mud bath followed by a mineral bath up in this secluded mountainous spa. It was private and cost about $43 for several hours, and it poured with rain as I soaked and ate fresh fruit. Becki would love it. After the bath, there was a private section and swimming pool for only a few guests who had paid more money, like I had. There were a handful of Russians, and one guy doing karate, which I enjoyed watching. Nice and relaxing day that felt cleansing. I couldn't help but wish a woman were with me, though.

The following day I went to Ba Ho Waterfall and hiked all three waterfalls. It was an enjoyable climb, and I like bouldering. When I get home, I want to spend more time in Colorado. Remember those camping trips we went on to RMNP? Remember that sweet lady at the diner in Estes Park who gave us a bunch of free food because she thought we were homeless? Those were special times. I also got a few sparring sessions in at Hoang Gia gym. I hit this Israeli guy pretty hard, and it pissed him off, but other than that things are peaceful. I am down about fifteen pounds! All the bruises are healed, too.

Today, loneliness is showing itself. I don't know why, as I am very much at peace with my own company, but today I wish I had a family, or at least a committed mate. I am sort of beyond the waiting game and all the astrology predictions. I miss D. She sent a short email on my birthday, but its temperature was cool. I thought about emailing her and sharing some things, but something stopped me from sending it. This trip has been sobering, as I have time without distraction to sit with the changes I need to make. I have done a good overhaul in terms of looking at my patterns and the shit I need to take out of my backpack.

I am now 41 years of age. I lost my job, and I am wandering without any clear sense of what the future holds, yet I also feel a deep sense of peace and liberation with it. More often than not, this journey teaches gratitude. I see a lot of impoverished people who are living hard existences, and it sobers me. It is ironic how I taught the hero's journey for years and talked all about faith and devotion to my students, yet I was pulling in six figures and living a cushy academic life. Now here I am, fully in the Now, with an uncertain future, and few worldly belongings. How often do people get to just wander like this, especially at my age? There is something behind it all, but I am not spending too much time trying to analyze or figure it out. That can come later. One tourist I met joked that my midlife crisis came a decade early. I laughed, but that's not it. I know all of this is happening for a reason, and I am grateful for that. I know that I am being guided.

I am off to Hanoi tomorrow, and I am ready to leave Vietnam soon. I encounter many nice people, and share many sweet exchanges daily, but there is an intensity here and a rip-off-the-tourist factor that gets draining. Egypt was worse, though. I don't feel fully connected here like I do in Thailand, but I appreciate it, nonetheless. When I head to Halong Bay I will be on a boat for several nights, and then up to the mountains in Sapa to climb Mt. Fansipan. I will be complete to move on to Laos afterward, and will probably email you when I get there. Anyway, I mainly reached out to say hi and to wish you a happy Father's Day, yet I made this email all about me! You know we're tight. You know how much I value you as both my father, but also as my spiritual guide. It is immeasurable what you've given me, and thank you for keeping me steady, especially as different sized waves hit my board. I look forward to our morning drives with coffee when I get home, but I still have not figured out when that will be. I originally said four or five months, but I am feeling I will be extending it. I have been thinking about India, too. I hope all is well, and I know that it is. If you see Troy, give him my best. Your loving ronin son, Nick.

Chapter 24

ISLAND MESSENGERS

August 2019, Sanur, Bali

The plane taxied the runway in Denpasar a little before midnight, then idled with the seatbelt sign on. A noxious chemical aroma flooded the cabin, as vehicles with flashing lights surrounded us. I was seated in the front and had to pee. Looking back to the faraway toilet, I noticed the family who'd made a racket for the past four hours. The mother brushed their daughter's long blonde hair, while the father earnestly pounded keys on his laptop. She went on about the villa in Ubud, the yoga classes, and the Montessori school the young girl would attend. After fifteen minutes the captain came on, and without explanation for the delay, directed the flight crew to dismiss us.

It's difficult to connect to a new country when fatigued and it's dark outside. It's an inward time; not a time to try and figure out what you're feeling. I was awake for over thirty hours when I landed in Cairo. Unable to find a vacant hotel at three in the morning, I roamed the streets for hours in the sweltering heat and dust. I took respite in a dingy petrol station of sorts, sipping mint tea and smoking from a hookah while seated on a yellow milk crate. I wondered what the hell I was doing.

As the taxi weaved through the narrow and moderately trafficked roads, even at one in the morning, I thought about Troy's trip to Bali years earlier. He was visiting family in Guam and took a short jaunt to surf, but was badly injured when a rogue wave wiped him out and the fin on his board slashed his wrist. He shared the ordeal, closing off a gaping wound while keeping his composure to get medical help. In a third world country, no less. But Troy was good in those types of situations. He kept it together when others collapsed. Eventually he found an English-speaking doctor who treated him. Afterward, the doctor followed him into the hallway, and whispered, "By the way. Be sure to try the mushroom milkshakes. They're amazing."

Mushrooms are semi-legal, or at least tolerated in Indonesia, though I tried to forget that as we made our way to Sanur. "Snore," as it's called by those seeking a break from the party scene in Kuta, felt like the right place to launch the next adventure. The forty-dollar villa overlooked the beach, and had complimentary mineral water and fresh fruit waiting for me upon check-in. I took two gulps of water, then stripped off my shorts and Under Armour t-shirt and collapsed into the plush king-sized bed.

I try not to analyze dreams that much. Maharishi allegedly said they are simply a part of the body's nervous system releasing stress, and that we shouldn't attach ourselves to them or look for meaning. In comparison though, the shamans I sat with in South America said otherwise. They were bold in their assertions that the dream state is just as real as our waking one and that the symbols and images of our dreams should never be discounted. They contain a wellspring of hidden knowledge.

That first evening in Bali, a dark presence hovered above my bed. It was a grayish, translucent figure that was short and thin, with a weathered expressionless face. It had thick black hair distinctively combed forward. The figure reminded me of those images of man's evolution, progressing from an ape-like specimen to a Homo sapien. His flat nose and fierce eyes looked down on me, and he held a beautifully decorated shield with vibrant hues of blue and emerald. I didn't see a weapon, but sensed he had a spear or sword close to him. Despite getting out of bed and turning on all the lights, then checking each room and closet, I was more fascinated by the marvel than scared. I chalked it up as jet lag, or a possible island spirit checking me out.

The camps in Thailand and Vietnam were the only things formally planned, but I sensed that Bali might be added for trekking and relaxation. I envisioned runs on the beach, ocean swims, and platters of exotic fruits while watching picturesque sunsets. And maybe hike some volcanoes. The first three days in Sanur were relaxing but I quickly became bored. I did some runs and swam, then sat in a cabana lounge chair reading Bukowski. The sea was calm most mornings with a gentle breeze that created miniature waves. About a hundred yards away, a middle-aged man performed a slow and exquisite pattern of karate kata. I recognized the kata and walked closer. The man was lean and muscular, and from his movements he'd clearly studied his craft for some time. His head was shaved, with light freckled skin moving dangerously close to pink from Bali's abundant sun. As the man finished the pattern and returned to *yoi*, he looked over. Without hesitation, he walked toward me.

"Hello, I'm Vlad from the Ukraine," he said, extending his hand.

"Nick. From America."

"Ah, America. Trump. Very good. Are you a *karateka*?"

"Sorta. I've been doing Shotokan for a few years, but dabble in other things."

"Very good. How long in Bali?"

"Just got here a few days ago. Here for a month, and then off to Sumatra for about three weeks."

"Alone?"

"Yes."

"Ah. Very good."

"You?"

"I'm here with my wife and two children, but they are shopping, so I train. Would you like to train?"

"Now?" I asked, a bit surprised.

"Yes. Now is always the best time."

I rose from the chair and bowed to Vlad. He smiled and executed a formal bow in return. I followed his lead, mimicking his patterns and graciously accepting his critiques. The movements felt awkward since I'd not trained karate for months, but my body soon adjusted. We did a series of *kihon*, assorted basic kicks, punches, and stances. It was difficult to slide smoothly on the sandy surface. Pebbles scraped the soles of my feet, tickling at times and occasionally stinging.

"Ah, very good, Nick."

After fifteen minutes of basics, we paired off and went through *bunkai*, where we applied different techniques to various coordinated attacks and scenarios. He made an exaggerated push followed by a right haymaker punch. I slipped inward toward his torso with my arms raised, wrapping his right arm, and locking it under my coiled left. Then I swept his leg back, shifting him off balance and executed an armbar. He grinned as he tapped.

"Very good. That is a top move for a man your size."

I was impressed by the fluidity and grace of Vlad's movements and by his tremendous power in spite of being seven or eight inches shorter and thirty pounds lighter. When it was my turn to attack, he lightly slapped my groin causing me to bend forward, then effortlessly slipped behind and kicked the back of my knee while placing a tight choke, cutting off my airway. As we returned to yoi after performing *Heian Nidan*, we grabbed our water bottles and took a few gulps in the shade. Although we only trained for thirty or forty minutes, immediately a comforting presence, like an elegant wind, blew through me. It felt like the warrior spirits of Bali were appeased that I was continuing to sharpen my sword, even if the workout was rudimentary. Simply going through the basics and taking turns throwing each other into the sand affirmed that I will do this for the rest of my life. Vlad personified an archetype of a wise elder not slowed by age; a man who walked the martial path and ensured that his life made time for his passion. In the brief moment we were together, I thought of my father's talks about radiance and confirmed that Vlad was a dangerous man. Kind, but dangerous.

"You look like you've done this for a while," I said.

Vlad smiled and nodded.

"Yes, a while."

"Do you train every day?"

"Mostly, yes. It is rare for me not to train. I do not feel right when I miss."

"I was in Nha Trang a few weeks ago, in Vietnam," I began, adding idle talk.

"Yes, yes," Vlad interrupted. "Many Russians there. I like Bali. Are you going to the Gili's?"

"Gili's?"

"Yes, Gili's. Near Lombok. You take boat, and there are three islands. One for party, one for lovers, and one for, I don't know how to say, but it is like middle. Maybe that's the one you go to. It is not party, but not for lovers."

"What's it called?" I asked.

"Gili Air."

"Air?" I asked.

"Like air we breathe."

"Gili Air," I repeated. "And how do I get there?"

There was only vast sea where he pointed.

"Easy. You buy ticket from hotel. They will arrange taxi and boat. Whole thing, maybe fifty dollars. Cheap."

"What about Ubud?" I asked.

Vlad laughed and shook his head.

"Ah, not so good. Many tourists. Eat, pray, whatever, made it very busy there. Much better in the past. Now, not so good."

"Yeah, I heard that book turned it into a mecca of sorts," I added.

"What?"

"Uh, it became a popular spot with tourists because that book, *Eat, Pray, Love*, has a part there."

"Yes, yes. That is what I just said," he stated. "It is filled with many beautiful women, though. Yoga women. And skinny men with long hair and some in a, how do you say, a *bun*. I do not like that. I do not like bun. A man should not have a bun or look like a woman."

I laughed heartily, and nodded, though Vlad just stared stone faced at the clear blue water.

"Are there any dangers in Bali, like crime or people to avoid?" I asked.

"Yes. Do not go to Kuta and you will be okay. Very dirty. Not good place."

I was tempted to ask Vlad about the mushrooms but sensed this would spoil our connection and decided to look at the sea instead. After a couple minutes sitting in silence, Vlad pointed toward an amazingly attractive woman with two teenage children next to her. They were walking on the sidewalk carrying bags in both arms.

"That is my family. I go now. Good-bye, Nick."

Vlad rose from his chair and firmly shook my hand, before putting on a white t-shirt with a Balinese tribal design. Then he walked toward his smiling wife.

A pang of joy and sadness penetrated the martial glow at the sight of Vlad's family. I wondered if I would one day have the same; if we would vacation to exotic places and walk on the beach or in the mountains. Would I do martial arts with my children? Would I meet young travelers and offer the wisdom of an elder? Vlad's intensity also kickstarted a need to test myself in Bali, though not in the physical way I had been doing in Thailand and Vietnam. The testing felt spiritually rooted, and in that moment, I decided to fast the rest of the day and try to stay up for at least the next twenty-four hours.

Chapter 25

BOYHOOD MAGIC

August 2019, Ubud, Bali

> Hold the hand of the child within you. For this child, nothing is impossible.[24]
>
> —Paulo Coelho

The *Indiana Jones* films are worthy of being on my altar, seated next to the other sacred objects. I saw all of them in the theater. When they ended, I sat silently during the credits ruminating on the adventurous path. Are some of us just wired this way? Is there a choice to domesticate at some point, or is being rudderless part of the curse? Most of the yoga goddesses walking around Ubud were hitched to the man-bun princes, or sometimes to other goddesses, which brought a thicker layer of loneliness. It ebbed in certain moments, usually sitting at a café or restaurant alone, seeing couples that were clearly in love. They radiated it. There is without question a frequency that emits when people are in love, especially in the juicy beginning. I passed the four-month mark in Ubud and decided that I had only scratched the surface of where I needed to go. There was no set destination or fixed length of time I would be away. I simply knew that I would understand when it was time to return home. One evening on a walk, after hiking Mount Batur to watch the sunset, I came upon an old building that turned out to be a movie theater. I looked over the movie list, a collection of foreign films, documentaries, and some classics from the eighties and nineties.

---

[24] Paulo Coelho quote as shared by Sheryl Silbaugh on Lemonade Makers blog: https://lemonademakers.org/, June 10, 2020.

Boyhood Magic

Scrolling my finger down the list I stopped on the date, jubilant that *Indiana Jones and the Temple of Doom* was starting in less than an hour. The inside of the theater was filled with various teak furniture and long, colorful futons. Plush pillows with interesting tribal designs sprung atop the comfortable daybeds, and the place was impeccably clean. Tall potted plants were scattered throughout, creating a jungle atmosphere. From the ceiling, giant fans quietly rained down tepid air. I ordered a plate of hummus, pita, and Indonesian-flavored tofu with a sparkling water with lemon. Perhaps the man-bun town was rubbing off. About fifteen minutes before the film started, a handful of people cycled in. Most were Western-looking tourists along with a couple of locals. I counted fewer than fifteen people in a room that could comfortably accommodate three times that. As I placed a violet pillow with a pink, floral design behind my back, I surmised that thirty years had passed since I'd seen Indiana Jones. He was one of my favorite archetypes; a dapper, educated professor who womanized a bit, but knew right from wrong. He often found himself in the midst of chaotic danger, but still found humor while taking on Nazis and sword-wielding sheiks.

Another lone wolf came in and asked if the futon beside me was taken, and I smiled and waved my hand that it was his.

As the man settled, he muttered as if speaking to himself, "I can't believe I'm doing this." Then he looked over toward me.

"American?"

I nodded.

"So am I. I'm Keith, from Denver," he said, offering his hand.

I shook it.

"I was just thinking the same thing before you got here. This was one of my favorite movies as a kid and it's probably been thirty years since I've seen it."

"Me too. I'm nearly fifty, but I've been looking forward to this all week. My wife is doing a yoga retreat, so most of my evenings are free."

"Nice."

"You alone?" he asked.

"Yeah. Been gone for about four months now."

Keith's eyes widened, and he shook his head side to side.

"Wow. I wish I could take off like that. Where you coming from?"

"I was in Thailand, Vietnam, and Laos before I arrived here. Just came from Sanur a few days ago. Will be in Bali about a month, and then Sumatra for a few weeks."

"Living the dream, man. What do you do back home?"

I hesitated momentarily.

"I actually lost my job. Kind of unexpectedly, so I just decided it was time to wander around without an itinerary. So that's what I'm doing. Pretty much just doing whatever I feel like doing—martial arts, trekking, spending time in the ocean, mountains … I got to admit, it's pretty damn good."

Keith laughed, then raised his water glass with lemon floating in the middle.

"I'll say. I can't imagine having that kind of time off and being able to just do what I want. I don't know if I could do that, you know, by myself. It seems like that would be hard. You ever get lonely?"

I paused, the natural inclination to feign questions that implied weakness. But candidness comes more easily with strangers. There is no history, nor expectation to impress.

"Sometimes. It's funny you ask that. I mean, certain moods come and go on the road, with loneliness being one of them. But I've been on the road a few months now, and there is something uniquely charming about this place and that makes it hard. Like it's being squandered by not being shared."

"What do you mean?" Keith asked.

"Well, I'm not into all the hipster bullshit that's here, but there is definitely something that makes me wish I had a woman by my side. Someone I really love. This is a town meant to be shared."

A bit embarrassed, I added, "It probably sounds a little weak, but …"

Keith leaned back into his large cushion and nodded delicately.

"I wouldn't call that weakness. It sounds honest, really. I imagine spending that much time alone would put a person through some tests, with loneliness being one of them. And I agree with you about the town. It is romantic … but also filled with a lot of hipster bullshit, as you say."

Keith and I laughed together.

"And what the hell is a *'vegan gastro pub'* anyway?" I asked.

"Yeah, right. Stay out of Denver, they're all over now. Not as bad as Boulder, though. I actually told Meghan, my wife, this is the last year I'm doing it. It was great ten years ago, but now …"

"Have you been to the Gili Islands?"

"Oh, yeah, all three of them."

"Worth checking out?" I asked.

"Definitely worth visiting. You could probably bypass Gili T, though."

"I'm headed to Air after here. Some guy I met in Sanur said it was probably the best for a solo traveler."

"That's the best one, but definitely if you're flying solo," he said, as the lights dimmed.

The conversation quickly waned, with Keith and I complete. As the curtain opened, Dr. Jones appeared on the big screen in a dapper white tuxedo, a bunch of hoodlums seated around a table in Shanghai. The shit was about to hit the fan for him, but the warmth of childhood nostalgia, and a full belief in my hero archetype produced a wide grin. Inside the Source is a reservoir of innocence; an energy that reminds us of the importance to play. To take a rest from roles and rigidities so passions are ignited. Playground recess. I giggled like a schoolboy throughout the film. Keith did the same. The loneliness dissipated. The world was my family.

Chapter 26

MOVING TOWARD CENTER

Fall 2017, A Classroom in the Midwest

Each stage of the hero's journey is significant. In The Karate Kid, *the steps are cleaner and easier to pinpoint than they are in real life. Art is an effective medium for reflecting the human condition. We watch Daniel go about his life in the Ordinary World, but he is just as easily depicting our own lives in some way. He meets Miyagi, his mentor. Events transpire that push him into the Special World, where his life takes on a new arc. For instance, he begins to train, and he gets a girlfriend. The stages move him toward the climactic battle at the All Valley tournament, which is ultimately his final test. Think of the steps like a videogame. If you clear one level, you continue to a more challenging one, right? The hero's journey is similar. You have to acquire the skills and knowledge that will allow you to be successful as things amp up along the road ahead. Daniel couldn't just show up at the All Valley and expect to succeed. He has to forge himself first, through his experiences. And a big part of this is maturing psychologically, developing mental toughness, and letting go of certain things. When the Hero crosses the threshold, Campbell tells us that*

> What this represents psychologically is the trip from the realm of conscious, rational intentions into the zone of those energies of the body that are moving from another center: the center with which you are trying to get in touch. As you now go towards the center, there will come more aids, as well as increasingly difficult trials. You have to give up more and more of what you're hanging on to.[25]

---
25   Osbon, *Reflections on the Art of Living.*

Moving Toward Center

The Hero, in other words, is steeped in the belly of the journey in the Special World, and something is driving him while there. He senses that something is out of sorts, and his goal is to find it to become whole. Yes, there are helpers and allies there. But the trials and tribulations are also present, and they are expected to intensify. If the steps are skipped, the Hero won't have the juice or mental capacity to survive. A lot of what is taking place is inside the Hero. It is his emotions, his shadows, his poisons, his addictions, his fears, his patterns, his attachments ... it's all of it. Pouring out. The pot begins to boil over, and the Hero starts to see what's inside, in need of healing. As I've mentioned several times already, the journey is just as much, if not more, an inward transformation. It is the recognition of the stuff that holds us back; the extra weight in our backpacks we want to take out. The patterns that limit us or that create suffering in our lives. According to Campbell, the further the Hero goes, the deeper he descends to the parts of himself that are repressed. It's that repression system that the Hero has to pass through.

Chapter 27

SMALL DOORS, BIG DOORS

August 2019, Gili Air

> If you get the message, hang up the phone. For psychedelic drugs are simply instruments.[26]
> —Alan Watts

I've been on many boats in my lifetime, though ironically few were in the Coast Guard. The fast boat to the Gili Islands was cramped as it chopped along rogue waves in spite of a windless blue sky. I closed my eyes and breathed in rhythm to the hull, as it smashed forcefully into the crisp idyllic waters. A couple to my right held hands. She closed her eyes and pushed further into her man's chest. He kissed the top of her head and whispered something soothing; a contented smile washed over and warmed the atmosphere. Another lone guy rested his head on the hard plastic seat in front of him, looking down. He opened and closed his fingers as if counting prayers on a mala. Whispers of sickness circulated, as different groups exited the hatch for sea spray. The young intrepid, with unpleasantly fragrant dreadlocks and thick hemp bracelets and cheap jewelry, giggled on the roof under the cooking sun. Some said the ride was only an hour, others said twice that.

"Gili T, Gili T, Gili T," one of the crew yelled throughout the cabin.

A mob of scurried movements unfolded; blurs of sundresses, tie-dyed yoga pants, and a few man-buns filled with anticipation and glee flooded about, collecting backpacks. What was a docile scene moments

---

26   A. Watts, *The Joyous Cosmology: Adventures in the Chemistry of Consciousness* (New World Library, 2013).

Small Doors, Big Doors

earlier was soon injected with the magical life force that trekking and destination arrival bring. Most of the clan were in their twenties, with a couple of stragglers much older than that. The elders were weathered vagabonds; wrinkled skin, shoddy faded tattoos, and long hair that hadn't been washed or brushed in a while. The Keith Richards archetypes committed to the pirate code that it's better to burn out than fade away. Though most looked pretty faded.

The three islands are close to one another. Gili Trawangan, or Gili T, was the first stop and where three-fourths of our tribe disembarked. Whistles and yelling echoed from the pier, as an uncreative playlist of Bob Marley beats penetrated through massive speakers on the beach nearby. Clusters of the young embraced, reunited with their brethren. It was a festive scene, even for a lone wolf watching from afar. Rascally looking figures, shirtless and muscularly lean in pitch-black sunglasses, hovered among the new recruits literally fresh off the boat. With toothy grins, various wares and services were pushed. Some handed out small flyers. A café had a hand-painted sign with a giant rainbow-colored mushroom on it. The tone pulsated a drumbeat of a rave, as the searchers earnestly prepared for exploration. Indeed, the drugs were plentiful here. A lagging, undeveloped part, the part not fully cooked to maturity, still looked on lustfully. Soaking in the landscape, the vessel fired its rickety engine as gray smoke and hydraulic fumes smothered the remaining party poopers and lovers. Three sets of couples, exuding the stable bliss and confidence of honeymoon, snuggled closely during the brief voyage to Gili Meno. They left quietly, the remaining six of us alone on the last leg. It was less than ten minutes to Gili Air. A striking woman, a little younger, looked behind as she picked up her North Face backpack with the distinctive red-and-white divers patch sewn onto the sleeping bag compartment. She smiled warmly. Her hair was blonde, her skin tan and freckled. Effortlessly, she slung the pack on her toned shoulders as if having done it many times already. She picked up another smaller bag and I followed behind, fixated on the durable curvature of her triceps and diamond calves.

The dock was crowded with at least a hundred people milling about. Some waited for their boat back to the mainland, while others hung out taking it all in. Packs of predators pounced on the new arrivals. One bee-lined toward me.

"Hey, brotha, what's up, man? Nice tattoos, G. Where you going? Where you stay, I'll get you there. Hey, G, come here ..."

I walked through as if he wasn't there, and he soon lost interest.

A Ronin's Tale

Horses with buggies collected handfuls of weary passengers. One woman quickly pulled her camera and leaned into her beau as they sunk into the green bench, grinning. I read somewhere that the animals were mistreated on the islands, and I opted to avoid their services. I picked a random direction to escape the bum rush and hurried away. A large white rugged sign with a "You are Here" marker showed the various guesthouses strewn across the island. There were only three directions I could take, and eventually I would run into water regardless. I scanned for my new home unsuccessfully, then ambled down the main road trusting I'd eventually find what I'm supposed to.

The first few blocks were primarily shanty drinking and eating joints. A handful of locals sat on mismatched tables watching. They were gaunt with sunken eyes. The burned-out kind worn by perpetual users. I nodded, and they looked away. On both sides of the road handmade signs with different styles of lettering and colors pointed in various directions. There were at least a dozen guesthouses camped throughout the labyrinth of side alleyways. I intuited to walk straight, but the duffel and smaller backpack were burdensome.

A place on the left of the path looked like one of the last establishments before an unkempt jungle began. It had an open area with sturdy-looking light-colored picnic tables and a giant swing that hung between two trees. Overgrowth, lush and darkly green, surrounded everything and produced cooling tones that made the space wily and inviting. A couple tables had people laughing, some texting, though a mostly sparse affair. Then I saw her. The beauty from the boat. Her back was to me, and she was drinking some fruit-looking shake in a tall glass, reading. I couldn't see the title, but she was a reader. I approached cautiously, smiling at the grinning man behind the bar and pointed to a table in the shade. He nodded, and I sat down and stowed my gear underneath, then rubbed my shoulders and temples. I watched her discretely, behind sunglasses. I scanned toward the bathroom to see if anyone was there, a lover perhaps. Both doors were cracked open and unoccupied. Her radiance glowed.

A random local handed me a map when I arrived at the pier. I placed it inside my journal to avoid looking like a tourist. The pleasant man behind the counter came over.

"You are new here, yes?"

I nodded.

"Ah, excellent. Welcome to Gili Air. My, what beautiful tattoos," he said, pointing to my arms.

Small Doors, Big Doors

As he spoke about the various organic dishes and freshly pressed drinks, the woman's eyes didn't shy from her book.

I held the menu high, peeking over the top with alligator eyes.

"And where are you staying?"

I pulled out a scribbled piece of paper from my journal and handed it to the man. He had a grayish goatee that contrasted dapperly against his very dark skin and beaming brown eyes.

"Oh, yes, that is a nice guesthouse. About ten minutes' walk from here, back in that direction," he laughed, pointing where I'd just come from.

"If it is helpful, my son will walk you after you eat. Please take your time, and just raise your hand when you are ready to order."

The prominent muscles of her back left my gaze, as I briefly scanned the menu. I ordered three skewers of chicken satay, cooked with Indonesian spices and coconut rice. Then I took a big swig of water from my Nalgene and thumbed through the map. But the map was just a collection of mere squiggles and words. Nothing coherent. A golden light shone around her, like a halo, or an aura. I thought of Pablo Amaringo's sacred artwork. That's where my attention was. I often met women when I traveled. Not just in intimate ways, but in many different settings and circumstances. Solo travelers hold an immediate kinship, as if sharing a secret. Something was different with her, though. It wasn't sexual energy. Well, not fully. A feeling to not approach or pursue conversation rose from the pit of my stomach. The message said to simply observe. For now, anyway.

The guesthouse was a traditional Balinese concept that sought to integrate nature with the living space. Sitting about a hundred yards from the beach, vibrant flowers of different varietal graced the perimeter of the structure. After ascending several steps, I entered the A-frame which was a mix of coconut wood, teak, and bamboo. Tiny lizards climbed the walls, and I did a cursory check for spiders. Staged along different parts of the dark hardwood floor were tall green plants reminiscent of the jungle. The interior gave a feeling of being outside. In the middle of the room, a king-sized bed, palatial and clean, rested under a large white mosquito net.

I stripped to my underwear and climbed under the net for a brief meditation. My waist was noticeably leaner, the cord of my pants and shorts continually cinched tighter. I made peace beforehand that I would lose weight and likely get sick. It was part of the surrender, though. Part of the commitment. I meditated on what I was learning, all of it coming from direct experience. The Warrior archetype was still there when I climbed Mount Batur a week prior, but a two-day fast and staying up all night in Sanur symbolized that new teachings were ahead. A quieter, more introspective tone, reminiscent of a monk or a king in isolation, was opening.

Gili Air was sparse and quiet. It took less than forty minutes to circumnavigate on foot at a leisurely pace. Different paths snaked through the jungle, taking me back to the Utopia Park days with the electric buzz of a quest. With my bright redhead New Zealand friend, Mitra, his father paid us a quarter each to walk half a mile to collect the daily paper. A mission. Boys and men need them. It was common practice once settled in a new place to grab a handful of business cards from the guesthouse, then wander freely. Inevitably I would be lost, necessity forcing me to flag down a stranger, or a cabbie, or a rickshaw. No phone or computer. No map app or questions for Siri. Just walking with full presence, absorbed in the fragrant glow of uncertainty.

A section of Gili Air had a radiance noticeably darker than the other parts. Situated on the beach, a shabby bar-like establishment with firepit sat abandoned. Its lone skeletal presence like an eerie remnant from an apocalyptic event. It was just before entering a dense part of jungle that meandered toward a civilized part of the island where affluent baby boomers danced to Jimmy Buffet grooves. After some days of walking, I cut through the jungle to avoid this shady section. But then one afternoon I descended further into its nest, eventually stumbling upon a hut with a mushroom sign.

When asked about drugs, Maharishi once said, "They open small doors, but close big ones."

In other words, one could experience crumbs of the holy realms through various substances, though it was not a lasting path. It wouldn't take the seeker to the true palace of wisdom in the same way as meditation and a disciplined routine. Maharishi was adamant about lifestyle and routines that shied away from negativity and toxins. The way this was interpreted varied among the community in Fairfield. There was an irony, too. Several meditators confided in hushed tones that their use of LSD and other mind-altering substances in the sixties served as the catalyst that brought them to TM. The mystique of the numinous landscapes, and of the Far East wisdom traditions somehow felt tied to or sprung from the psychedelic waters. But there was consensus too, that drugs of any kind, except those prescribed by a doctor, were to be avoided. People who used drugs emitted a frequency that sucked the life force from others. At least, this is what we were told in so many words.

One of my favorite teachers lost his son shortly before we moved to Fairfield in 1984. His boy became disoriented after taking acid, dehydrating in a cornfield. His body was found some weeks later by a farmer. As we grew into our early teens at MSAE, sex and drugs naturally showed up as they do. A faculty member giving a guest lecture told us that having sex with someone created seven years of attached karma. In other words, if you did the deed, a karmic attachment or exchange of energies lingered for at least seven years afterward. Everyone in my class was a virgin, but the artistic and expressive culture of the school brought a Dionysian flair that radiated the erotic.

My drug history isn't too exciting. A bit of drinking, and a little pot in high school, followed by long bouts of nothing. But altering consciousness is seductive. It's seductive to journey into the realms where the senses shift and one's perception of reality cracks into something different. When Troy and I did our alley missions in high school, the universe opened up and revealed all the grand adventures ahead. We were at a playful age, under the spell of youthful exuberance, but without question there was something divine in it. Marijuana was a sacrament that held a certain mysterious knowledge, and on occasion, it would take us through the garden on the serpent's back. Later on, the magic wore off and it became a crutch to escape work stress or to simply get some sleep. The big doors were closing.

The first time I tried a hallucinogen was the evening I graduated from college in North Carolina. Troy drove out from Iowa, and I bought the fungus from a professor who had introduced me to the works of Aldous Huxley, and who later became a close friend. Troy and I stood in the kitchen drinking carbonated mineral water, laughing hysterically as the bubbles rippled through our bodies. Years later, I tried peyote during a sweat lodge ceremony with Shankara. A stern paternal presence lingered weeks after, as if I were being observed by a watchful father. Eventually, I participated in an Ayahuasca circle. I was intrigued by its mysterious history and the alleged miraculous nature of its properties. Reports of telepathy, astral travel, and other mind-blowing accounts circulated the bruja's brew. Then one evening I had a vivid dream where a beautiful woman with strawberry hair and pink skin and a mermaid's body visited me. She danced and flirted. She sang a harrowing song that made me weep, as the notes of her flute visibly descended around me. When the notes touched, they tickled, causing me to giggle uncontrollably. A palpable lightness rose like a new dawn. I heard the wind whisper to let go and that I was too attached. To everything. The world wasn't a scary place, but I was making it so. I woke up laughing, convinced a message had been delivered. Two days later, an elderly friend I met through circuitous events called and left a message.

Pulling into the cool foggy parking lot of Peet's Coffee about twelve miles north of the Golden Gate Bridge, the man sat at the main window in a dapper tweed sports coat. A white silk scarf wrapped around his thin neck. In spite of the pick taped to his hand, he rose from his stool, and we embraced. He had been an early student of some renown shamans. A retired architect, in his eighties, he was terminally ill but laughed more than anyone else I ever met. He had twin boys that were grown. One an interior designer and gay, the other, a homicide detective and Catholic. Because of the vast medications he was taking, Ayahuasca was too dangerous. But he had a longtime student who'd just begun leading retreats, so he wondered if I was interested.

"Hell yeah, Dudley!" I shouted exuberantly.

I told him about my dream, and he confirmed it was, indeed, a message. That I was ready. He discretely slipped me a piece of paper, then told me to wait a few days before calling. I nodded, and gave him a hug that lingered, sensing it could be the last one. He died two weeks later.

******

The old Victorian was palatial and sat prominently above the newer and more chic designs of the gentrified San Francisco neighborhood. A hip coffee shop on the corner was closed, which made sense for a Sunday evening. Obsessively worried about parking in the city, I breathed deep relief at the ample vacancies on the block. My mummy bag was crammed into my duffel, making a lump on top like a camel's hump. It was seated above a change of clothes and several pairs of underwear. There were eight of us going under that evening, with another five who would serve as helpers. The five had already journeyed before and would not be taking the medicine. They were doing a payback service to Mama. This is how it was explained, anyway, when I sat on a comfy leather recliner in a room filled with crystals and Peruvian paintings.

Small Doors, Big Doors

Dudley's student, Jan, went over the basic ground rules and emphasized the significance of secrecy. She emailed me from three different accounts to set up our meeting, then changed it last minute to a friend's home on the Marin coast. She was a full-figured "earth mama" as my mother would say, with short spiky black hair just beginning to gray. She welcomed me with a sturdy hug and offered a glass of water with a generous chunk of lemon floating on top.

"It is such a joy to finally meet you, Dudley speaks so highly ..." she began, her voice quivering.

I nodded, looking down at a beautiful cat that sauntered into the room, moving closer, though still keeping distance. Saying Dudley's name brought a noticeable heaviness. His book had closed for the last time just days earlier.

"I'm so sorry," she waved, as small tears formed in the corner of her blue eyes. She pulled a tissue from her pocket and dabbed.

"He is just such a good man. I mean, he *was* such a good man. So tenderhearted and wise. Just a brilliant, brilliant mind. And he was in so much pain there in the end, but you would've never known. I know it's a relief. I know he's laughing, even now. One of his spirit animals visited me, but ..."

I nodded and smiled.

"Let's try this again," Jan said, taking a deep breath.

"Dudley said that you're a man who can be trusted and that you've been walking an interesting path since you were young, is that fair to say?"

I nodded.

"Good. It's important that a person has done some degree of work on themselves. It makes the medicine, or *Mama* as we call her, easier to work with. The medicine is for everyone, but those with impacted or unaddressed trauma can be overwhelmed by it. Does that make sense?"

"It does," I began, taking a small sip of water, and tasting the subtle lemon accent.

"I read somewhere that one ceremony was like completing ten thousand hours of intensive therapy."

Jan laughed heartily.

"I know that book, and, yes, there is some truth in that. There is no one way that Mama works, though. She may be gentle and kind to some, and stricter with others. But even her strictness is sourced in love. There is nothing malicious; nothing to be afraid of. Tell me, what has sparked this interest? Dudley told me you look like a grown high school quarterback or, forgive me, the-boy-next-door type, and I laughed when you got out of your car."

I giggled with Jan, and the room's energy lightened.

"Yeah, well, wait until you see me throw a football, that will squash that theory."

We laughed together, before I said, "Dudley once told me that if he combined his sons into one person, he thinks I would be pretty close. I think it was a compliment, but you know Dudley."

"Oh, yes. It most certainly was. And, a military background, too? Something to do with law enforcement and intelligence?" she asked, cocking her head.

A heaviness returned.

"Yes. But that was only a part of what I did," I corrected.

"You see, this is how Mama works. She doesn't work with just one type of person. But before you share more about your intention, your law enforcement is something, well, I want to speak further about that. It's something we should …" She paused as her words trailed off.

I shifted in the chair, feeling the waves. My face slightly flushed, as heat pulsated around my forehead.

"This medicine, as you know, is illegal. It is used throughout certain parts of the Amazon with great reverence, as a healer. However, it's not recognized in our culture, at least not yet, though I am hopeful that will change. But as it is written in the law now, even having it in my possession could send me to prison."

Jan looked out the window, as the silence took over. Then began again.

"Do you understand how important it is that you not share this information with others? Even a harmless email or referencing Aya on a phone call or text is unwise."

Jan's eyes moved from the window to mine, and she held her gaze. There was intensity there. Yes, there was genuine warmth around her, but her apprenticeship deep in the Amazon jungle with strict diets and intensive purges produced other qualities, too. Above everything, there was firm strength. I'd been in the presence of several medicine men and shamans throughout my life, and Jan was no exception. No lightweight. She was not some Marin County new ager, living in a multimillion-dollar home and driving a Prius, doing this as a hobby.

"I understand, Jan. And I promise that I will keep this strictly confidential."

Jan smiled, and then walked over to a small desk in the corner of

Small Doors, Big Doors

the room. A cat brushed up against my leg, and I delicately stroked its head. It was the same one that sniffed my shoes after we moved into the living room.

"Oh, look, Lady has a new friend. How rare she came over like that. She usually doesn't interact with people. Hmm." She smiled.

Jan handed me a white sheet of paper, as Lady scurried to another room.

"This is a list of things you need to bring with you: A sleeping bag, change of clothes. We need to be responsible explorers. And I recommend a few extra pairs of underwear. Everyone spends the night, and there is no exception to that. You will also need to bring a power object."

"Power object?" I asked.

"Dudley told me you have an altar, correct?"

I nodded.

"Bring something important or sacred to you, as we will create an altar as part of the ceremony. But nothing too large or heavy. Some people bring their entire altar, or precious family heirlooms, and we only need one small item. Something simple."

"Okay," I said. "I think I know what I will bring already."

"Then there's the diet. You've probably come across this in your readings, yes?"

Each book I read mentioned the criticality of not eating certain foods or drinking alcohol several days before ingesting Ayahuasca. Another book emphasized abstinence for at least one week before, and one week following a ceremony. Women on their moon cycles were also forbidden to be anywhere near the ceremony.

Almost as if reading my thoughts, Jan stated, "The diet, or *la dieta* as they call it in the Amazon, is not to be feared. However, some precaution is necessary. Mainly, don't eat red meat or pork, and cut out salt at least three days before. If you drink alcohol, best to take a break for a week. Dairy should be avoided, too, but if you cream your coffee a little, that shouldn't be a problem."

As I scanned the sheet, my heart began to accelerate. I replayed the bits and pieces I read online. I could stomach the bitter concoction that some compared to drinking pond water mixed with molasses. I was adept at doing self-improvement work and wasn't too concerned about what Mama would teach me, knowing it would be insightful. But throwing up in a bucket for several hours, or for some lucky space travelers, a dual-cool release that shot out both ends, that alone curbed any thoughts that this would be recreational fun.

"Do you have any questions for me, Nick?"

"Two, actually. Is there a charge for the ceremony?" I asked.

"Only a love donation. If you wish to make a contribution you may, but this is simply about spreading Mama's work. There is no expectation for that. And I understand that you're a student."

"How many times have you taken the medicine, Jan?" I asked.

Jan, sitting with her hands folded on her lap, looked down as if counting. Then she raised her head and held her gaze.

"Over four hundred," she said, matter of fact. "And each time something new is revealed. And in case you're wondering what *la purga* is like, it is quite cleansing. You will feel lighter afterward, as long as you can let go."

"Let go?"

"Yes. You have to put down any walls you have. You have to step aside from allowing your intellect to try and figure out what is going on. The more a person resists and tries to analyze their experience, the more difficult it is for Mama to work with them."

"That makes sense," I said.

"You need to come prepared to let it all hang out, spiritually and literally," she laughed. "There are two communal bathrooms, and they will be well used. Now, please tell me your reason for doing this."

I took another sip of water and shared with Jan about my dream. She confirmed, as I expected, that Mama had already begun working with me. Like Dudley, she said the dream was a vision and that it shouldn't be taken lightly. I didn't have a clear understanding of my motivation, aside from curiosity, but I knew such a response wouldn't go well with Jan. Or Mama.

"I lost a woman I cared for. We were in a relationship, briefly, but it was intense, and she died just days before I went over to the Middle East with the military. We left things on bad terms, and ..." I paused, before continuing. "I don't think I properly grieved it. That was about eighteen months ago."

"I see. Did you experience anything over there that you're still carrying?"

I reflected on the Angel Flights I was on, loading the dead bodies of U.S. servicemembers for their transport home, but that didn't really bother me. Even at the time, I saw it as a tremendous honor to serve in that capacity. It was painful in part, but the memory is something I cherish as being put in a place of deep reverence by the divine. Years

Small Doors, Big Doors

later while working at the university, one of my students had various dates tattooed on his forearm. When I asked about it, he told me they were the dates of the Angel Flights he worked on.

"No, not really. My tour wasn't traumatic. It was just a lot of different energies and personality types to navigate for nearly a year. You know, being in close quarters all the time, off my routine. Not having solitude or time for my spiritual practice. What I'm carrying is more along the lines of feeling isolated, like I could possibly die alone having never married. It's a thought I'm okay with in certain moments and haunted by in others."

Jan sat upright in her chair, and leaned in.

"Please, tell me more about that."

"Well, I'm almost thirty, and I feel like it's becoming time to settle down, and I would like to meet someone and begin that portion of life."

"I sense some sadness inside you," she said.

"I don't know if I consider it sadness, or if I'm finally allowing pieces that have been guarded and suppressed to come up to the surface. I see them now. And I know that some of it needs to be healed. I know that changes need to be made, like the way I go through life. The vagabonding. Not owning a bed. I can be totally self-absorbed and selfish, sometimes. The way I shut people out. How easily I walk away from friendships. The women I've hurt. I just, um …"

Jan took it all in, seated with her eyes closed.

"Yes. Maybe that's what I'm picking up from you. I'm not saying you're a sad person, like you're depressed, it's more of a somber feeling. Many light beings, and star seeds, carry things like that. Some of its theirs, but some of it is what others have put on them, what they've taken on from others."

I sat with Jan's comment for a moment as Lady entered the room and stared. I snapped my fingers, but she rooted into the floor, listening.

"Yeah. I feel like it's easy to feel smothered, especially in relationships. I seem to do best traveling with a lighter backpack. Anyway, I guess I am open more to what Mama feels I need to know. I would also like to know what my work is in this life, like my dharmic path. My contribution. What am I really here to do?"

Jan listened to each word carefully and when I finished, we sat in silence for several minutes. The cat returned and hopped onto my lap purring.

"Well, I would say that is a good omen. Thank you for sharing what you just said. You're a fascinating man, and not even thirty! I understand why you and Dudley connected."

A Ronin's Tale

Rising from the antique Victorian chair with red velvet cushion, Jan took my glass of water from the small coffee table. I rose and walked with her toward the front door to collect my shoes that were stored with a mishmash of other pairs on an Oriental rug.

"I will need to speak with the others, about your participation, which I feel strongly is possible. I will reach out within a month and provide more information. In the meantime, continue to read about Mama. Meditate on what you want her to show you. I feel you have a better sense than you realize in terms of your motivation for doing this work."

Jan's last comment hung in the air, as I gave her a firm hug and patted Lady on her white head, feeling her whiskers scrape against my fingers. Then I walked down the long steps, past a black cast-iron cauldron, and waded through the thick coastal fog to my car. A feeling of wizards and witches dancing around, watching it all, saturated the air. Three weeks later, an email surfaced in my inbox. It had a San Francisco address, along with a date and time to arrive. Nothing else. I retrieved a power object from my altar.

Chapter 28

The Purge

Fall 2017, A Classroom in the Midwest

At some point, the Hero cracks up. He has to crack up in order to crack open. In the midst of his karate training in the Special World, Daniel is also formulating a romantic relationship with Ali. So, in addition to all the pressure of preparing for the All Valley, he's also confronting things like shame because she comes from a wealthy family and eats at the country club. She runs around with friends that drive convertibles, and she is part of a different tribe. Daniel therefore sees himself as an outsider, not good enough for her. At one point he even says as much, "I'm from Reseda, and you're from the Hills." These pieces symbolize how the Hero is stretched uncomfortably in the Special World, confronting the buried parts of himself that feel inadequate and unhealed. They rise to the surface because he must confront these toxins and release them. Yes, Daniel is focused on his training and being prepared for the tournament, but his internal world is equally getting a shakeup.

What I call "the purge" is more precisely known as the Approach to the Inmost Cave. The Hero has adjusted to the Special World, but setbacks continue to plague him. He continues to doubt himself and the purpose of his quest. The angst, the rage, the frustration, the fear ... all of it shows up, in an even scarier form. The floodgates open and it comes out like hot lava from a place inside the soul that's reaching its breaking point. This is where the Hero learns humility. He begins to sense his heart, which he'll need if he is to survive the Ordeal that is quickly approaching.

Can we relate to a purge? The person we love cheats or no longer loves us. We feel we never measured up to a parent. We get picked on for being fat, skinny, gay, wearing the wrong clothes, being into Dungeons and Dragons, listening to the wrong music, driving the wrong car. Do we see how easy it is to get to that point? Unfortunately, we see elements of this all over YouTube as people post videos of someone having an awfully bad day. We watch a Karen have a complete meltdown inside the grocery store, or a Ken in a seething road rage. The video goes viral, and we see a person in the midst of a purge. This is a horrible part of our culture, the public humiliation of someone clearly going through it. But it also speaks to a larger immaturity and lack of initiation in the Ordinary World. The purge of others, which is ultimately their suffering, becomes our entertainment. It's because it is easier to watch others in this place and to feel better about ourselves than it is to inspect more deeply what we need to change.

One of the most poignant pieces of The Karate Kid is watching the mentor, a coveted archetype, also reveal an emotional purge. Toward the end, we see Miyagi in a drunken state. He reads a telegram he received in the army and it reveals that his wife and infant son died during childbirth. We learn that he received the Medal of Honor during the war, and it's assumed that he must have experienced war trauma, too. The mentor is no longer the always-perfect and enlightened wise man. He, too, is carrying rocks in his backpack. He becomes humanized.

When I was in South America studying shamanism, I met several teachers who use Ayahuasca: a very potent hallucinogen from the Amazon. If you read Carlos Castaneda's work, he studied with a Yaqui medicine man, and part of his apprenticeship included the use of peyote. I don't think a person needs to use anything like this to open up, though I recognize the appeal and attraction of altering consciousness, and I have done it myself a handful of times.

I will tell you a personal story of a very visible and unfortunate purge I witnessed. A purge of highest extreme, actually. Not too long after I moved here and began working at the university, a good friend from the military called. I had just picked up my dry cleaning and put it in my car. When I answered the phone, my friend Andrew said: "Can you believe that about Dorner? This is nuts."

I don't have a television, and I hadn't been on the Internet that morning, so I was dumbfounded. I drove to a nearby café and pulled out my laptop and there on every major news network was my friend from deployment, Chris Dorner. Chris was this hulking black guy who was gentle and very much like a teddy bear. He joined us overseas for several months, and he and I worked together regularly on a twelve-

The Purge

hour watch. Sometimes it was just the two of us. He was a reservist in the navy, recently called up to serve overseas. As a civilian, he'd just finished the rigorous police academy for the Los Angeles Police Department and had begun his probationary period. He told me all about the police academy while on watch, and how excited he was to be a cop in LA. Chris was a physical guy who loved to jump on peoples laps and clown around. There was a noticeable affection to him, again, that was like a big teddy bear. And he was a massive man. Just a beast of muscle and power. I was exactly one year and one day older than him. So, I'm in this café here in town, and I learn that my friend Chris has just killed a few people, and there's a huge manhunt going on. I am watching all of this in real time, trying to comprehend how Chris got to this place. He eventually gets spotted in Big Bear Lake, and there's a standoff with local law enforcement. There are gunshots, and then a fire. And eventually Chris shoots himself. Now, I don't want to reach so far to imply that every person has it in them to do what Chris did when they explode. But it's important to understand that even a distinguished military officer and police officer, two professions we hold in high regard in our culture, could snap like that.

The purge is where all the unhealed pieces inside us come flooding out. The fragments symbolize our toxins. They symbolize our wounds and unfinished parts; the wellspring that produces our limiting thoughts and the lower expressions of ourselves. The Hero, which again is simply a mirror of each of us, has to be in a constant state of self-awareness to see what afflicts him. He has to be diligent and purposefully aware of all the shit inside, so that he can figure out how to heal what needs to be healed. To not do this work of transformation, and to allow these poisons to accumulate, robs us of our bliss and our ability to navigate the world in our most powerful way. And eventually, they will force their way out in one manner or another.

Chapter 29

Dark Microscope

August 2019, Gili Air

> The soul's medicine is found in the embrace of nature, and the spirits that dwell within it.[27]
> —Anonymous

If you hit your forties and have never married, people wonder. At first, your sexual orientation is called onto the carpet for inspection. Once that mystery is sussed out, other hypotheses go on the table. I once dated a woman a solid decade older, in the same club. She was a working professional, educated, had her own interests and routine, and staunchly independent. When you live that way long enough, and there are no children, you become accustomed to a certain degree of selfishness. The freedom is addictive, too. The freedom of weekends and evenings all to yourself. But there is a distinctive flavor of freedom that most men chase in general, whether they're single or hitched. The freedom to pursue the "wonder if" adventures that bring seductive thrill. The rhythmic beat of the Wild Man's drum.

I know a few people who met online and are happily married. I even attended two weddings. I also know wedded people who have profiles on dating sites because they like the attention it brings. One wedded guy in my unit made a profile just to pass time overseas. A woman sent her soiled underwear in care packages. He sniffed them when he jerked off, he said. She thought he was getting shot at every day.

---

[27] This quote was spoken to me in Bali by a stranger I met at the beach. I could not locate a source or origin for this quote.

Dark Microscope

Profiles are addictive. I tried it a couple times and was glued to my phone. The anticipation of new faces being added. The build up after sending a wink or dropping a flirtatious note. Wonder if. The curiosity of placement on the desirability scale. Will they swipe right for me? The inner voice coaxing and urging challenges. *Wonder if I can net her? Wonder if she'll kiss on the first date? Something more?* The challenge of conquest accompanies the wonder. Entire fantasies birth this way, and they bring a lot of bullshit and drama, not to mention pain. Even colleagues in the ivory tower confide that most of their social media contacts are people they find hot. When you sit in the ether of those quiet, darker moments, free and alone, eventually the wonder ifs get acted on. I have gay friends who have literally screwed thousands of men, yet they're depressed. My coupled-up friends tell me I got it made. That I am free to be selfish and available to chase all of my dirty thoughts. But even the ones that balk at their arrangements, or scoff at their perceived loss of freedom, they get into bed at night with someone they love. They get held. They get someone to ask how their day was. Deep down, that's what most of us want. To be loved, and to share that love. Wonder if it will come?

Two guys sit at the shabby counter across from me. It's three in the afternoon and the skinny one has piercings through his septum and along the tops of his ears. His baby face doesn't hide well behind the uneven stubble above his lips and chin. He stares blankly into a drink of some kind, lost. His companion is heavier set with shoulder length blond hair that falls freely under a gray Quiksilver cap. He's clean shaven, with a dimple on the left side of his cheek. He says something to his friend, and I detect an Australian accent. Without breaking gaze from his glass, the skinny one fetches a cigarette and hands it to him. A very dark-skinned man behind the bar congregates with two other equally dark men. They laugh and slap hands. Trance music booms from large subwoofers, rattling the bamboo countertop at times. It's too loud for this scene. I look around and contemplate leaving. Maybe pick up some chicken skewers and rice and read Bukowski in my bungalow. Maybe another night swim under the stars. A quiet evening. But my eyes don't wander long, as they fix on the rainbow mushroom. Wonder if. The local barman lends a final nod to his friends, then moves toward me.

"Hello, brudher, what can I do for you?"

Without saying anything, I point to the mushroom. He laughs. Then, I laugh.

"Ah, okay, okay. You want to try?"

"Maybe," I say.

"It's good, brudher. Comes just from over there, in Lombok. Picked fresh. Good for sunset."

I turn to where the man pointed, though it's all jungle. The sunsets from the Gilis are epic, and I've witnessed evenings where clusters of mostly young people zone out on the dissipating sun. Some giggle, though most are silent, even reverent in their gaze.

"Good mushrooms from Lombok, eh?" I ask.

The man laughs again, and nods.

"Yeah, brudher. Best in Bali. Better than Kuta. And the good ones on Kuta come from Lombok, so here you get from source."

"How much?"

"Do you want light, medium, or heavy?"

"Maybe in the middle of medium and heavy," I say.

His grin produces an impeccable array of white teeth, mostly straight. He nods.

"Ten U.S., and I'll make you a pineapple shake. It will be good, and I guarantee."

I pay the man the ten dollars and pull out another three singles.

"This is for you, friend."

"Thank you, brudher."

Through the thumping bass, the man walks toward the thatched home connected to the bar and a young pregnant girl, still in her teens with an infant wrapped in a sarong next to her chest, stands close to him. I watch her nod and disappear. It could be his wife, or maybe his daughter. Moments later she returns with a brown paper bag; a lunch sack as the Townies called them. The man fetches through the bag and pulls out an assortment of mushrooms. He places them on the counter next to a large industrial blender and a pack of cigarettes. They look like dead sea creatures.

The heavier Aussie perks up.

"Eh, good on ya, mate," he says, raising his sweating beer in toast. I hold my hand up as if holding something and nod back.

"Care for a smoke?" he asks, walking over. He pulls out a high stool a few feet from me and sits.

"John."

"Nick."

"Fellow countryman?" he asks.

"No, American."

Dark Microscope

"Ah, I hear it now. You look Aussie. Where in the states?"

"All over. Mostly California," I say.

"Ca-li-forn-ia," he says, pronouncing each syllable deliberately. "Surfing?"

"Nah. Just taking a break. Walking around Southeast Asia for a bit."

"Good on ya, mate. That's the spirit," he says, patting me on the back. "Had a shake here before?"

"My first."

"Did you go light or hard?"

"In the middle, closer to hard," I say.

He laughs heartily and slaps my back again. I can smell the tobacco from his breath mixed with the lager.

"Don't miss the sunset. Fuckin' spectacular. Best in Bali, eh. I come here from Melbourne about once a year, but Kuta's just so noisy and cramped. I like the Gilis, not Gili T so much, but I like it here on Air."

"Me too. I was only going to be here for about five days, and that was over a week ago."

As I said it, I realized I didn't know what day of the week it was.

"It does that, yeah. Just grabs you under the undies and before you know it you've pissed a good bit away, but so what. You find a place you like and there's no reason to leave. Fuck all that 'experience the culture' stuff. I experience most of it inebriated anyway, and it suits me fine."

"Is that your mate?" I ask, pointing to the skinny pierced thing, still lost in his glass.

"Yeah. He had a light-medium."

"No shit?" I ask, somewhat startled.

"Yeah, but he's a skinny cunt. You'll be fine. We was supposed to dive earlier, and he got tanked this morning, so I decided to have a few beers. That's the day on Air. Pissed away. And you, you alone?"

"I am. I was just in Thailand, Vietnam, and then Laos, and then back to Thailand. Decided a month in Bali sounded cool."

"Oh, mate," he began. "You're just gettin' fuckin' stinky, aren't you? Just a dirty little devil, yeah? I lose my mind in Thailand. I really do, mate. I usually hit the Nanny in Bangkok for a couple. You been?"

"Yeah, right next to the Muslim community. I've been there."

"That's right, mate. You get your good hummus and then you get a good blowie. I may live in Thailand one day. Just love it."

A Ronin's Tale

The man behind the counter brings the shake over and smiles as he places it on a coaster. It resembles a tourist beverage from a ritzy resort in Mexico. I wander back to Cancun, just a few months before the condo sold and I left for good. I'm on the beach with D. We make love in the morning and hold potions with umbrellas just after lunch. A stout man walks the beach late afternoon touting his coconut drink, "Cocooooooooooo!!!"

We snicker, and she makes a recording on her phone. I yell it out after an orgasm, and we embrace laughing. It seems so long ago. What is she doing in this moment? What does she feel when she gets into bed at night? Is there someone next to her? A tinge of pain surrounds my heart and throat.

The first sip is sweet, but not overpowering. Small bits of mushrooms resembling soft sand or soggy grape nuts crunch in my mouth. I take another long sip before the man returns.

"Drink slowly, brudher. Give about an hour, then you will know."

"Well, I'll let you enjoy your adventure, mate. I'm goin' to grab the cunt and take him for some food. Seafood is killah here."

"Is it safe to wander around at night alone? I mean, high on mushrooms?"

"Oh, yeah, mate. Big fella like you, no one's gonna mess. People are cool here. They start rolling the tourists, people stop coming. They cut their own throats, yeah. Safe as a kitten."

I shake John's overly large hand and giggle as he whispers something into his friend's ear. His friend waves him off and returns to his trance. John lifts him off the stool and attempts to throw him over his shoulder before the man comes to. The man behind the counter laughs with me.

"I hope you can carry me like that," I say to him.

"I got you covered, mate, just give a holla."

I rose to pee and was directed toward a dingy broom closet on the side of the connected house. The open hole in the ground reeked and had brown and yellow stains all around it. On the wall, a cheap velvet poster with bright psychedelic mushrooms stared back. The corners on the poster curled upward. A friend had the same one in high school. Troy and I marveled at it, stoned.

It hadn't kicked in yet when she walked by. She looked over and I smiled, and she paused. Her gaze was on the mushroom sign. Then she sauntered over and sat down, close to where the Aussies were.

"Well, this is a funky place," she said. She was American, and younger than I thought.

"I seem to gravitate to these types of scenes," I replied.

Her smile ignited her entire face.

"I'm Brooke."

"Hi, Brooke. Nick."

I hesitated to speak too much. I still had a window until the fireworks began, but I didn't want to introduce her to fourteen-year-old Nick. Not yet anyway.

"What is that you're drinking? It looks good."

I smirked and pointed to the sign.

"First one. In many, many years."

She dropped her chin and raised her sunglasses, like a mother admonishing her child.

"Seriously? You're having a 'shroom shake?" she asked ecstatically.

"Yes. But honest, I've not done this in years," I pleaded.

"Uh huh. I'm sure if I ask that man, he'll tell me you're a regular. Bet he already knows your entire life story, too."

Her eyes pierced through, softened by a sultry grin.

"No, honest. I just walked through this side of the island today. About an hour ago, actually. You just missed some Aussies who sat right there," I said, pointing to the empty stools beside her.

"Change of subject, huh?" she laughed.

I laughed with her, and our eyes locked for a few breaths.

"And where are you coming from?"

"I was in Sanur, then Ubud ..."

"No, I mean where back home?" she clarified.

"Oh, um, California mostly. But I was just in the Midwest for about eight years working. How about you?"

"Denver, but I'm originally from New England. Connecticut."

"First time in Bali?" I asked.

"Oh, no. Been here bunches."

"Bunches?"

She laughed again, and I shook my head.

"That must be New England speak."

"So, what do you do back home?"

It was my turn to laugh.

"You're about to get my life story if you open that can," I cautioned.

"Like the bartender here, huh? That's okay. Tell me your life story."

"Well, I worked at a university. Ran into some drama. Was shown the door. Sold all my belongings, well, most of them anyway. Then

A Ronin's Tale

decided to come out here, hoping to meet a woman from New England that I could charm with my 'shroom-induced wit." I winked at her, though she broke eye contact.

I first noticed how energy functions on dates in my mid-twenties while living in the Bay Area in the military. I dated a lot; most of it online and a self-imposed challenge to grapple with a type of confidence that was lacking. Although only a handful of those dates resulted in other ones, I learned to pay attention. I refined what it meant to be present in conversation, to pick up subtle cues, and ultimately tune in to radiance. Women are naturally more intuitive and secretive than men, making them harder to read. Brooke glowed, but she also recognized her ability to stoke a powerful flame in others. And with little effort. She wielded the Goddess, and expected a man. My boyish charms would only carry me so far.

"Really? Like that seriously just happened to you?"

I nodded, feeling the energy shift.

"Wow. That's kind of intense, actually. Were you like a professor?"

"I had a faculty appointment, but primarily an administrator. First in student affairs, then later with veterans. Student veterans, I mean. I taught a course on the hero's journey, too."

"He was that myth guy, right? The 'follow your bliss' thing?"

"Yep, that's the one. And good on you for knowing who he is. Most people don't."

"Yeah, I have a friend who has his books, or maybe just one of his books. It was the myth one, I think."

"*The Power of Myth*. Are you traveling around?"

"I am."

"And what do you do?"

"I run my own advertising firm and I also teach yoga, but that's mainly just because I enjoy it. I just did a retreat in Ubud."

"Ah, Ubud. Yes, home of the yoga queens with hairy armpits and man-bun warriors."

She didn't laugh or respond, and I immediately regretted my comment.

"I saw you on the boat. About a week ago, or whenever we arrived. I was on it, too."

"Yeah, I know. I liked your tattoos," she said.

"Can I buy you something to drink? I hear the mushroom shakes are fabulous, but I can't really vouch for them just yet."

"Are you really drinking one?" she asked.

Dark Microscope

"Uh huh. I feel like they are here for a reason, and it's moments like this in traveling that you just have to seize them and not overanalyze. Just jump in. Otherwise, I will be laying in my bed many years from now thinking I missed out."

"I don't know. That's like saying there's crack in the ghetto, so one should smoke it." She must've seen my puzzled look. "Totally kidding. But tell me more about the myth stuff. Is that what you studied, like is there a program for that kind of thing?"

"I think there is, but I took a traditional approach. I actually specialized in higher ed administration and policy, student affairs, and masculinity. But I became most known for working with veterans and ended up creating a transition course that used a lot of mythology and work from Joseph Campbell. It got picked up by other schools ... blah blah blah." Admittedly, I put it on thicker than usual.

"Masculinity? Hmm. That's not something you hear every day. Interesting."

"Yeah. It's not really a topic that is approached within the larger gender framework. Or when it is, it is typically not in favorable ways."
"What do you mean?"

"I don't think you want to open this can. Inevitably, I will stand on my soapbox and once the mushrooms kick in, there is no telling where I will go. I could end up naked, standing on this very countertop quoting Campbell and other wise thinkers. Could be dangerous."

"Try me. And standing on a soapbox isn't always a bad thing. But keep your clothes on. This is still a conservative country," she said.

"Okay, but I warned you."

"Noted."

"Well, it is fair to say that most colleges have some type of gender program, but the truth is that it's disproportionately for women, and when men and masculinity are brought into that setting, it is usually spoken of as 'toxic' or destructive or being used in some hurtful or misogynistic way."

"Well, I think it can be."

"Yeah, but so can femininity," I replied, feeling a bit defensive. Then I added, "Can you imagine if groups of male academics coined the term 'toxic femininity' and the fallout that would bring? When you put things in a power-focused way, you inevitably create division rather than a mutual respect for how things are different."

"That's interesting," she commented, then paused. "I'm listening."

"Well, for example, and let me speak generally for a minute. If there is consensus among some in our culture that men are predators and destructive, and that masculinity is essentially poison, it's not hard to find examples to support that. For instance, you can easily find a video on YouTube of a guy losing his mind, or you can cite domestic violence statistics. But the truth is that most men will go through their entire lives without laying a hand on a woman, or even another man. The vast majority, in fact. Most men are not violent or predatorial. But if you only keep the direction focused along those lines, along the lines of an agenda, then you create a damning picture, and you ultimately push away a lot of young men from being involved in a very important and needed conversation."

"What do you mean? I think I follow, but say more."

"What I mean is that most of the so-called gender programs are disproportionately led and attended by women. And that is true across the board, both nationally and internationally. If the bulk of these programs are without men, how can a balanced conversation even happen? And more to my point, what kind of guy would enroll in a class or program where his gender is essentially being scrutinized and on display? That's a real problem, because men grapple with masculinity in many ways, yet there is no real framework for them to explore it, let alone talk about it without feeling shame or being embarrassed."

Brooke looked down at the counter, then nodded slightly.

"That's interesting. I guess I never thought of it that way."

"I've concluded that higher education really only talks about masculinity in one way. Destructively. In comparison, it provides a much more complete discussion for women that is both sympathetic and reaffirming. It's out of balance, and it doesn't provide tools to men. Not to mention that it creates a conflict model that ultimately serves no one."

"Wow. It sounds like you do have a lot to say on this. Are you on your soapbox, yet?"

"I am. I could go on about male suicide, or porn addiction, or the terrible pattern of texting exes when we're shitfaced and lonely, but … I'm actually starting to feel it. My fungus friends, I mean."

She smiled warmly.

"Sure you don't want something?" I asked.

"Actually, I will have something. A beer, maybe."

I waved to the man behind the bar and ordered a beer, indicating to put it on my bill.

A warmth flooded in that spread over my body. I looked to the jungle to see if any shapes or faces appeared in the foliage, but nothing yet.

"Would you totally disregard male privilege?" Brooke asked.

"I think that's a really complicated topic. Generally speaking, I think it exists, but I also believe that men and women are privileged and rewarded differently. Men and women have different gifts. But this crusade to equalize *everything* doesn't work, and it creates a lot of inauthenticity."

"Interesting. And what about things like pay inequity, men earning substantially more than women for the same work?"

"I have a better idea. It's starting to ramp up, and I am going to start giggling soon. Let's talk about our favorite TV shows. I'll go first. I really like *Saved by the Bell* and *Beverly Hills 90210*. And I think it's bullshit they've recreated both of those classics."

Brooked rolled her eyes, then laughed.

"I'm not saying that privilege is a myth, I just think it's not nearly as clear cut as it's taught. For instance, men disproportionately seek out careers that pay higher salaries. I could also argue that men are institutionally discriminated against in the courts with child custody."

"What do you mean?"

"Well, it is much more likely that a woman will win custody of the children following a divorce. It is assumed that women are more nurturing than men, and therefore, better equipped for custody. But I don't like doing tit for tat on all that. It goes back to that whole power and conflict model I just mentioned. I think that many men feel beaten down in our culture. Just emotionally spent. And all of the political correctness and shots against them just make them retreat to their man caves. Or to a bar. Do you know how many grown men play videogames?"

"Shots?"

"If you turn on the television, which I don't watch often, so many men are portrayed as buffoons now. They're almost childlike, without any sort of fire or honor. It's like you can't show a grown man looking out and being kind to a young woman without putting some spin on it to make him a pervert, or to have an ulterior motive. It's common to see men displayed like this, as women beaters and rapists. We put so much sensitivity into not offending in our culture, so much that wokeism has become a religion of sorts, yet we continue to stereotype men in such hurtful ways. How on earth can a man give the world his deepest gifts from a place like that?"

"And you don't think that women also deal with stereotypes and societal pressures?"

"I didn't say that. I am simply speaking from my observations and the research I've done with men. I think the entire human species grapples with their internal worlds, but ..."

"And what are some of your conclusions?"

I glanced again toward the jungle, and a witch apparition stared. Then an island goblin.

"That we're pursuing the wrong conversation. That we're moving toward a victimization crusade that serves absolutely no one."

"What does that mean?"

"When men are weakened and they suffer, women receive their poison and wrath, right? And vice versa. We don't put enough emphasis in how to become the best version of ourselves. It's definitely not taught in school. We don't teach about confronting the deeper layers inside that hold us back. Our shadows and wounds, and how these contain tremendous knowledge. We've become a complacent society of uninitiated, whiny, and overweight clowns, frankly. And that creates a shame and acting out which makes it easier to blame others. I would say that America is in a deep state of blame, and it detracts us from doing the necessary and hard work that leads to real transformation."

Another glance into the jungle revealed that a legion of archetypal figures had congregated and were listening.

"We're not designed to be unkind to each other like this."

"And how are we designed?" Brooke asked, her eyes shimmering brightly.

I thought about it for a moment, as delicate pangs of vulnerability pulsed. After breathing a few times, I broke eye contact.

"We are designed to operate from love. I know, I know, pretty cliché, right? But really. It's the source, and we've moved away from it. But something wiser inside senses our need to return to it."

I realize I've not had much conversation with others in nearly two weeks, and perhaps I am spewing too much. However, there is liberation when these moments arise; a cleansed sensation that follows a verbal purge. I shifted my gaze back to Brooke but couldn't read her expression. She sipped her beer, occasionally nodding as if sorting through her own conversation.

"That's really interesting. I don't meet too many men who think about these things. You seem passionate. And it sounds like you are advocating for both men and women to become mutually powerful and supportive of one another. That's honorable."

I tune further into the trees, and more faces materialize. The trees look like African warriors. The sturdy wind from the sea moves their leaves, as the warriors shake their shields and perform some kind of ritual dance.

"Well, Brooke, I got fired for running my mouth, and for not accepting the institutional crusade to create victims among our students. So, maybe barber college is where the gods really want me.

"I'm just trying to figure it out like everyone else, really. And that's why I'm walking. Around the earth, I mean."

"No, no, no. I don't think that's what the gods have in store for you."

"Anyway, thank you for hearing me dump. Sometimes ..."

"No, I get it. And I know what you mean about the political correctness. It's out of hand."

"Yeah?"

"Oh, yeah. I'm in advertising, c'mon. It's like most accounts we do now have to follow a script, or there's this fear of backlash and bad PR. It's definitely affected creativity. And most of our interns are fresh, right-out-of-college millennials."

"Interesting. I personally think we need more mullets in ads. Old muscle cars, too. Mullet pimps standing next to their prized possession on four wheels, like a Trans Am or old Camaro. 'Merica!"

I looked at Brooke and rolled my eyes, laughing.

"My God. You just covered like fifteen levels in five minutes."

"Fifteen levels?"

"First you started off as this articulate academic type, then you moved into this saintly, 'I'm on a crusade to better the world,' now you're onto mullets and gold chains."

"I'm a shaman, Brooke." I winked.

"Guess so, or maybe just schizophrenic." She smiled.

"Another beer?" I asked.

"Oh, I wish. I actually have to run. I'm teaching a yoga class in a little bit."

"Whoa, whoa, what? You just had a beer before teaching *yoga*?" I asked, incredulously.

"Says the man drinking a hallucinogenic shake."

"Fair play, girl. Fair play. I'll stop talking now. Well ..." I began.

"Well, Nick, uh, how long are you on Air for?"

"Don't know, but at least another few days."
"Well, then, maybe we'll run into each other."
"I hope so. That would be nice."
"It would. Okay, bye for now."

A warmth overshadowed any pieces of isolation that could have come once Brooke left. I stared into the packet of cigarettes nearby, watching the color hues and tracers that hovered around it like an aura. Its energy malefic, though. But any malevolent forces around me were quickly dissipated by the early rumblings of love energy, or at least the excitement of its possibility. Were the soothsayers right? Was I finally in the window of meeting my life partner? Convinced that I'd just met a significant person, I thanked the barkeep and rose from the stool to trek deeper into the jungle path.

Tiny goosebumps popped around my body. Different pastel colors fluttered around the fiery circle, as the sun made its departure for the evening. I slogged to an isolated piece of beach close to where I snorkeled earlier that morning. The pastel expanded around the entire island, and the clouds shape shifted into animal figures. I intuited they were animal spirits of the islands and clasped my hands in prayer. I asked reverently that they show what is still unhealed.

The sun descended into blackness, and an array of bright stars pockmarked the Indonesian sky. They were brighter than usual, maybe the brightest I'd seen. People in the distance snapped selfies. Two lone fishermen in dingy rowboats caught waves and returned with their half-filled nets. I was under the axis mundi. The center. I was in the birth canal and could hear my mom's screams as she pushed. It was warm and dark. I was comfortable. Then a frenzied chaos of light and noises broke through. A hand pulled forcefully, as laughter inside the cavernous space echoed.

You will enjoy it all, a voice said, as I descended into the swirling light. I was clutched by my mother, and I knew her love was supreme. It covered like a halo, around the crown chakra, then draped downward like a blanket. The light spun clockwise. My father was in the room, and I felt his joy. The voice from the cave was in the room, too.

She will show you the third dimension. She will prepare you for that world. He will be your guide and teach you the higher work. Learn from both of them. You need both. You've known them for many lifetimes. You have been given more than most.

I looked up again, at the stars, and clasped my hands thanking my mother and father, reminding myself to email more often. I had not

Dark Microscope

spoken to anyone on the phone for nearly six months. More figures, this time from the celestial plane, danced in the sky. They swirled and twirled, showing off. I laughed heartily at the grand display. A voice bubbled up as a thought, *Stop dwelling so much. Go enjoy. Get up and walk, dear child.*

I rose from the tip of the beach and skipped a rock along the glassy water. The ripples frolicked circularly, creating miniature waves. Then I looked over at a dark entrance; the path that led into the jungle.

Go confront the dark. Feel the intensity there, the voice directed. *The energies are a union. Pairs. You can't have light without the other.*

I entered the path, which was completely black. My eyes needed several minutes to adjust, but the sensation that I was no longer on two feet distracted. The movement of my body was irregular. Slowly I sank into the foreignness. I was a large jungle cat, a jaguar. My back and neck muscles stretched and contracted. I recognized the devastating power I could inflict. I once knocked a guy out as a bouncer with one punch. He fell to the concrete, and I immediately regretted it. There was no fear in the forest. A strong breeze swept through the trees, as the African warriors danced again, shaking their rattles and shields. I nodded to them.

"I understand. Thank you."

They blessed me for paying attention to them. Then the serpent's energy showed up, and alarm took over. I recalled a trip to Malaysia, long ago, stumbling upon an enormous python. It stopped moving as I got less than four feet from it.

I scanned the unkempt path, worried about stepping on a poisonous snake. The trepidation was fleeting, though, so I took off my flip-flops to feel the earth crunch between my toes. After a quarter mile, perhaps, I recognized that I was on the edge of the deserted bar. The abandoned, apocalyptic one. But life emanated from it this time. I moved closer, cautiously popping out of the thick foliage. A large fire, a couple yards from the water, had six or seven people staring into it. Trance music thumped, as green and brown objects descended from the speakers. The music produced an eerily visible chaos of shapes and hues. I watched each note float by until they dissipated. They felt acidic. A hippie girl in a shabby yellow sundress danced seductively like an ancient courtesan. There were two men behind the thatched-hut bar. They had very dark skin, and one had horribly stained, crooked teeth that glowed from a torch nearby. He wore his hair in a ponytail. They were the messengers I was to visit.

A malevolent wind blew around both of them. It swirled throughout their camp, but the fire on the beach provided some type of protection from it. I moved closer, the six or seven people were vacant. They were off journeying somewhere far, far away, and only their shells stayed behind. Two young children, no older than five or six, sat close by making sandcastles. A boiling rage that parents would be so irresponsible churned from my stomach and brought sweat to my forehead. I was still a jaguar, and I could kill every motherfucker on the island if I chose to. I stared into the glowing embers for strength.

"Brudher, welcome," said the man with bad teeth.

A luminous comet tail followed his hand movements. His onyx eyes stared intently into mine, and there was not a lot of life force inside. His companion stood close by, but he was just a phantom. There was no soul in that one.

"Hello," I whispered. Each letter, laborious.

"Hello, brudher," he said, again.

I felt his gaze; it shifted up and down with a palpable heat.

"You want some X? Just came from Australia. You want to chill with us?"

From Brooke to here. The light, and now the dark. I found the mirror.

My entire existence I find these places, or perhaps they find me. A sense of bravery and accomplishment venturing into the lower realms to be tested in some manner. The walks through dangerous neighborhoods in Oakland at night. Buying weed in foreign slums. Red light districts and their hoodlum pirates. Knocking on doors in the early hours, in a drunken fade, a loose woman on the other side waiting.

I wanted the X. Maybe dance with the concubine on the beach in her sundress. Maybe other things later. The half-melted candles breathed ominously.

Feel it. Feel what you are drawn to. Smell it. Taste it. It's all here inside you, spoke the voice from the ether.

Watch. Watch. Watch. Learn. Learn. Learn.

The shadowy figure moved closer, inspecting me with an unknown intention. His light force dim, he was barely existing. He was taking from me, like a vampire. I could only make out that he was wearing a tank top. Light seeped out of my body, going into his. Confused thoughts, impulsive behaviors, addictions, and bad deeds spiraled out frantically next to the musical tones. They purged rapidly, as I steadied myself on a wobbly stool. The bass reverberated throughout, as nausea

Dark Microscope

overcame me. These were the watchmen of a sinister chamber, where unfinished karma existed. They were symbols, the diabolic messengers of my own shadows. I knew their existence was always there, but here they literally stood in front. I called to my protective allies to please come. Then to my guides and guardian angels. But I am easily seduced, and something ambiguous told me I was on my own.

Further, further. Nearly there.

"No X, brother," I said, reluctantly.

"Are you sure? C'mon, brudher, have a time with us. I can see you want to." As he smiled, his teeth were more horrid than I realized, and his breath was equally ominous.

"No, no, thank you. You have mushrooms, though?"

For a second, I thought back to Costa Rica, and the dark Caribbean side where I met a real reptilian. David Icke wasn't kidding.

"Of course, brudher. Of course. You want a shake?"

"No. I eat raw," I said.

"Ha, ha, okay, okay."

He said something to the other, then disappeared behind a black curtain. I turned around and stared into the fire.

"Grandfather Fire, keep me safe. Keep me grounded. Bless me," I prayed.

I felt the fire's presence, as its glow intensified from afar. Words of certain writers, psychedelic conquistadors, echoed from the abyss.

"Take your heroic dose, Nick. You can go further. Quit playing it safe. The other side is near. Let go of the line. Let go of the line. Let go ..."

A shaman in South America once told me about his work retrieving souls. I was in no place to ingest more mushrooms, or anything for that matter, but my soul was still intact, at least. The phantom returned with a dirty paper towel bundled in his hand. He laid it open on the counter, and the long-stem mushrooms vibrated eerily like some off-planet creature. I worried a moment they could be cursed. The figure ran in circles. Smugglers. Maybe child traffickers, even. There was violence attached to those realms. Was I contributing to all that darkness buying this? Surely, I had to be. Would the teachings no longer be gentle, but instead show the knife's edge? I was in no place to analyze, still peaking from the earlier shake.

"I want all of them," I said.

"*All* of them, brudher?"

I nodded, pulling the equivalent of twenty dollars from my wallet.

The bulk of my cash was hidden in my bungalow, in case I got rolled.

"No, no, brudher. It is more than that. You give me ten more," he demanded.

"This is all I have. Give me enough for this." I waved the bills and placed them on the counter next to his overgrown fingernails.

"Okay, okay, no problem. We will do, we will do," he whispered. His eyes returned and stared into mine. The hollowed cavernous space was completely vacant.

I counted seven mushrooms total. It was a little more than what I saw go into my shake earlier. That was so long ago. It was such a lighter scene then. The Aussies. The comical drivel. And Brooke was there. Brooke! Oh goodness, Brooke! My God, a mere thought of her washed over, bringing cotton with it.

I popped a third of the mushrooms in my mouth and chewed sharply. They didn't taste too badly but the texture reminded me of gritty worms fresh from the soil. Before the last bit was swallowed, I devoured the rest.

"Easy, easy, brudher. You want to chill with us? I can make you a place over there," he said, pointing into a black mass.

"Thank you, brother," I said, extending my hand.

"But, I have to go now."

He clasped my hand and held it. Shockwaves of energy jolted, as a childlike innocence emanated into me. He had lived so rough, from such an early age. Never really given a fair chance. An unfathomable compassion descended. It washed over, lightening the poltergeists and sinister creatures around us. I had no place to judge this man. After all, he was me, and I was him. I put my other hand on top of his and looked into his eyes reverently.

With the new medicine in the system, I got lost on the numerous paths that snaked back to my bungalow. I staggered off trail at times, eventually arriving at the port where it all began, what seemed lifetimes ago. From there it was a familiar stroll through the labyrinth of alleyways. Once inside my sanctuary, I lit a candle and propped myself onto the comfy bed. I sat in full lotus, underneath the mosquito net, my back pressed firmly in the hard wood of the frame. The headphones in my ears played a long playlist of sacred chants. The Vedic sounds immediately washed away the darkness. The angelic teachers came into the bungalow, while the African warriors went back to being trees again. Shakti radiated up my spine. I was creating my reality, as I knew I could do. I had touched the inner demonic realm and become

Dark Microscope

reacquainted with its grasp. The misdeeds and bad behaviors; I watched as they floated like kites from this obscure reservoir of energy. But I was still a jaguar, too. The meditations, the healthy diet, the making time for center had pulled me through. I would always prevail if I stayed balanced and clean. I had to maintain a routine. I could still do immersions to the swampy parts every now and then, but even those would need to be forgotten in time. It was not a path. Not a true one, anyway. Maharishi was right. I sunk further into the familiar prayers, chanting my own mantra softly. Then the voice, which had been silent for several hours, breathed.

The mountains! You will go to the mountains! The great Himalayas. Go there. And then to India.

I stayed upright and unmoved, occasionally nodding into a dreamless dimension of sleep. Then the elixir left, as a residual fog lingered. Rising out from underneath the mosquito net, I cut up a small pineapple, its sweetness producing an immediate smile. Then I swam into the lukewarm sea to float on my back until the sun rose.

******

"You look exhausted. Rough night?"

I looked up from my book, where admittedly I was rereading the same paragraph for the past fifteen minutes. It was Scott, my new friend from the café. I'd seen him several days earlier when he randomly approached and asked if I was a martial artist. Impressed by that, we chatted for a while. He was originally from Canada but living in Southern California. About ten years older, I was equally impressed by his collegiate wrestling background and how he still took care of himself. He stood in a tank top, broad shouldered and muscular.

"A little bit. I didn't sleep too well, maybe from the full moon," I lied.

"Ever try CBD? I have some in my gear bag if you need any."

"No, thank you. I should be fine. Was just planning to relax today and read. Are you diving?"

"You betcha," he said excitedly.

"Feel free to sit," I offered. I wasn't wanting company, but it felt like the polite thing to do. Scott grabbed his tiny espresso glass and a larger cup of water.

"Joseph Campbell, eh? That's a bit cerebral for the tropics. I've got the *Power of Myth* on my shelf back home. Should probably crack it open."

"Yeah, I sort of just carry his work with me. Almost like a shield."

"How so?"

"Well, it doesn't really matter where I'm at in his work. I can just open to a random page and find something I need to hear."

"Need to hear?"

"You know, I start to think more clearly, less emotionally. His work balances me. He was tuned into something profound."

"Interesting. I'll definitely check it out when I'm home. Reading Clancy right now. Fun reading. Mindless, but fun."

I nodded.

"A few days ago, you mentioned the *hero's journey* when I told you about my move to LA."

I nodded again.

"How does that apply to relationships?" Scott asked.

"Well, that depends. Do you mean like can a relationship be a hero's journey?"

It was Scott's turn to nod.

"Of course, definitely. I mean, one could think of their entire life as a big hero's journey with many mini journeys that pop up in between. For instance, my year overseas with the military was like that, or even my time as a bouncer. But relationships can definitely bring out a different kind of flavor. Each journey has its own theme, like its own curriculum," I mused.

"Flavor?"

"Yeah. Flavor."

"Like, what do you mean?" Scott asked.

"I'm going to project here, so this just might be my own thing. But the few serious relationships I've had, the women were all so different from one another, yet each one of them taught me something."

"Different how?"

"Like one ran a good bit of masculine energy. She was an avid runner. Did the whole CrossFit, mud-racing thing. Her life was fitness, and she was vivacious, but she didn't really have any sort of spiritual path. I'm not saying a person needs to believe what I believe, but she didn't think along those lines at all. It's like she just wasn't wired that way. But she made me realize I needed to revisit and consider my own masculine energy. I was much too academic while with her, neglecting certain things I needed to be balanced."

Scott took a long sip from his water, then leaned closer.

"At first, I was intimidated by it, but then I saw it had nothing to do with her. She was simply showing me things that needed to get charged up again. Like I had lost my way, and I was living a much lazier existence."

"I can relate to that. But the relationship didn't work, huh?" Scott asked.

"No, but I got a helpful message from it. She was the teacher for that lesson."

Scott chewed on that briefly.

"What about now?"

"What do you mean?"

"You don't have a woman?" Scott asked.

The question produced an unexpected twinge of pain.

"I actually was in a relationship not too long ago. Just before I went on the road."

Scott nodded but didn't probe further.

"She ran a successful real estate firm. Went to church regularly, a devout Christian. Even though I'm not a Christian, I respected how committed she was, and how her faith helped her. She was career driven and independent. But also feminine in what we would consider a more traditional way."

"Traditional how?"

"Like she cooked meals. She would bring me a beer and rub my back when we were in bed. Little things like that, which seem to be much rarer nowadays."

"You can say that again. Why the hell did you let that one get away?" Scott asked.

"Too long and complicated of a story. And truthfully, too painful for me to go there, but the short version is I couldn't stay living in the same area. She was rooted there." I sighed.

Scott took a sip of espresso and ruminated.

"My point is that every relationship I've had has taught me something, and I like to think has made me a better man for it. Those early beginnings, when love or intense passion show up, it's like being propped down into the Special World. But tests come, too. That's inevitable. Eventually the honeymoon wears off, and you have to see if there is something substantive to keep it going. But both people have to do the work; they have to really want to grow and to be able to understand where they're limited, and the patterns that are holding them back, and how they create friction in their own relationship."

"I guess I'm on a hero's journey then, with my new girl, I mean. We've been together about six months, yeah, but live in different states. She's very independent. Actually, she sounds like a mix of what you just described. Like the alpha personality that is masculine, but then this other feminine side, too."

"Does she make you a better man?" I asked.

"Oh, for sure, for sure. She is, uh, outspoken, but not critical. First thing she did was get me to drink less. Said I needed to grow up. I still enjoy a beer, but not every day, and not six at a time."

"She sounds quality. If she is teaching you, are you also teaching her?" I asked.

"It's funny you ask that. I get the feeling like she is teaching me more than I'm teaching her."

"And why do you think that?"

"I dunno, she tells me that I'm 'fun,' but ..." Scott made quotes with his fingers.

"Have you asked her about it, like what 'fun' means?"

"Nah. Not really, but it bothers me some when she says it, yeah."

"Then I would start there. Communication, Scott. It can be a great thing in a relationship." I laughed then added, "There's a school of thought, that whoever comes into our life is essentially a mirror for something we don't see inside ourselves. They can also represent some aspect, like our shadow."

"Wait a minute, wait a minute, that's important. That shadow thing. Hold that thought, I gotta piss, but I want to come back to that."

Scott rose from the table and placed his empty glass on the counter. Then he ordered a dessert made with some local fruits.

"Nick, anything? My treat."

"No, I'm okay. Thank you."

Scott paid the cashier, then disappeared to the restroom. I looked at the main path outside and listened to the clickety-clack, as horses galloped by. A new crop of tourists arrived, bright eyed with full backpacks. Others said their farewells to the magic of Gili Air. Impermanence. As I opened my book, I thought of a passage for Scott. I scrolled earnestly through the many marked pages, then felt a presence hovering nearby.

"So, you survived the mushroom adventures," the presence said.

I looked up and nearly jumped out of my chair. It was Brooke.

Goddess Brooke. She was wearing tight gray yoga pants that displayed a perfect figure, and a black tank top that accentuated those toned arms of hers. Immediately, heat flashed through my body, and I began to perspire.

"Hey," I squeaked. "Yeah, it was insightful."

"*Insightful*, huh? That's a safe word," she said as she laughed.

"Yeah, not too intense, but I didn't really sleep. Kind of a vision quest, but gentler."

"Interesting. Funnily, you popped into my mind sort of intensely."

"Really?"

"Really. It was around three this morning. I was having this dream, which I don't really remember. But I remember you were somehow connected to it. Mind if I sit for a few?"

"No, please. I'd love to hear more about it. I'm actually with someone right now, though, but I think he's leaving soon. Please join me, I would like that."

Moments later the bathroom door opened, and Brooke's eyes darted intensely toward it.

She shifted her posture in her chair quickly, though her eyes didn't move from the bathroom.

"Hey, babe," Scott said.

"Uh, hey. You're not diving?" she asked, a different inflection in her voice.

Scott walked over with his dessert, and two forks, then handed one to Brooke.

"Bad vis this morning. Should clear up later, yeah. Try some of this, babe, it's killer."

I began to breathe more heavily. A bead of sweat collected on the corner of my forehead, then cascaded toward my brow.

"You all will have to excuse me," I said.

I walked into the broom closet bathroom, as a grand finale of fireworks shot off in all directions.

What the hell, man! No way! Noooo wayyy! You've got to be kidding me! I looked up through the cracked cinder roof that had specks of dust and paint chips dangling from it. I pierced through it, right into Heaven.

This is not fair, you guys. This is not fair. I know you're laughing, and I'm sure I will too, eventually, but this is not cool.

The water was tepid, but I splashed it over my face and dried it with my green handkerchief. The sweat disappeared momentarily, then returned. There was no mirror, but I leaned over the faucet and breathed deliberately, counting each inhale to five one-thousand, before exhaling slowly. I repeated, my heartbeat slowly beginning to normalize. After wiping my forehead again, I looked up and shook my head.

Scott was sitting close to Brooke with his arm around her. She didn't make eye contact as I approached.

"That's crazy, Nick. Brooke told me she met some interesting guy and it's you! What are the odds?"

"Yeah, crazy."

"Anyway, Nick and I were talking a little about the hero's journey and relationships. I told him you often tell me I'm fun, and I was curious what you mean by it."

Scott looked into Brooke's eyes, which were turned away, watching outside.

At different times during the week, I envisioned meeting Brooke. I envisioned that there was some karmic connection. Our circuitous meeting less than twenty-four hours prior was a clear omen. At least I took it that way. I mean, there are many restaurants and shacks on this island, even though it's small. But she found me, and it was just the two of us there. Even in the midst of my hallucinations and brain chatter, she continued to enter my consciousness. Then she tells me about her dream. And to make matters worse, Scott is a gem.

"I hate to do it, guys, but I'm feeling a bit under. I didn't really sleep that well, and …"

"Yeah, you're sweating," Scott said. "That came on fast. I got something in my bag."

"No, I'm good," I said, as I pulled the olive-drab cloth from my pocket and dabbed my face.

"Please forgive my abrupt departure. But, uh …"

"Oh no, totally. Go get well, man. How many more days you here?"

"Another three or four," I said. "Don't worry, we'll see each other again."

As I walked briskly toward the sliding door, I lightly tapped the back of Brooke's chair and said, "Nice to see you again."

She didn't turn around, but quietly uttered, "Mmm hmm."

That was the last I saw of Brooke and Scott.

Journal Entry—Gili Air

August 27, 2019

Nature told me it is time to uncover the true dharmic work. The job loss was necessary, or I would have missed what's ahead. I've meditated here on Gili Air a good bit on relationship and my patterning and afflictions are becoming clearer. To experience the Divine through a relationship is part of God's path. It is a spiritual dimension in and of itself, but an expression of God, nonetheless. I don't know why Brooke showed up, but I can feel subtle voices saying, "This is what a woman of significance looks like. This is the type of woman who won't stand for little boys, or half-assed attempts." I am thankful our paths crossed, and I am humbled by the power she revealed. And as always, the divine wasted no time showing their sense of humor.

Chapter 30

ELIXIR THEFT

Fall 2017, A Classroom in the Midwest

Some of you asked about what happens to the Hero if he doesn't finish his journey, or if he gets lost down in the Special World. These are great questions. The Hero is trying to find his character, his true center, or this higher self we've already talked about. If he doesn't finish the adventure, he won't complete the journey. He could still return to the Ordinary World, but he won't be changed in any meaningful way, and he will regress into his old patterns. The reason that completing the journey is so important is because the Hero is in search of a treasure of some kind. Now, in a film or story, it may be a classic hunt for fortune and fame that spurs the Hero forward, like we see in Indiana Jones. But the treasure is more succinctly a symbol of an elixir. I don't want to spend too much time on this, as we will cover it later, but an elixir is a magical potion. It has special properties, and it is coveted. The elixir is also a metaphor for something that is lacking in the world. The Hero went in search for something lacking inside him, but this missing piece is also absent in the larger world. The true fulfillment of the hero's journey is the return with the elixir, to bring a sacred gift back into the Ordinary World so that others can benefit from it. Although it seems self-centered, the journey is actually a selfless phenomenon.

If the Hero skips the steps or cuts corners, the elixir won't be available to him. An example that Campbell talks about is the "Elixir Theft," where the Hero steals the elixir rather than engage in the hard work to obtain it legitimately. Campbell uses an example of the 1960s and the widespread use of LSD to raise consciousness. Through these substances a person can have all sorts of fantastic and transformative *experiences. And they may even serve as a bridge to connect them to things like meditation. But drugs are not a true path by themselves. Simply taking them will not complete the work or produce the pearls of deep wisdom that stick around. Therefore, the Hero will attempt to return to the Ordinary World as quickly as possible after a profound experience, but he won't have an elixir to share because he did not appease the powers. In some cases, with members of my own family for example, the continual chasing of wisdom through ongoing psychedelic use can cause what Campbell calls a "schizophrenic crack up," where the Hero subsequently remains in the Special World, lost. There are no shortcuts. You either do the work, or the work does you. And when it comes time to sit in the fire, you do that part alone.*

Chapter 31
FAMILIAR GIANTS

September 2019, Sumatra

It was an uneventful, just under three-hour flight to Medan. A different circus from the boat ride Troy and I endured from Malaysia nearly twenty years earlier. After checking our passports, we were herded into a windowless, concrete chamber. Little brown bags rested atop the faded yellow seats that were still available. The seats soon filled to capacity, as a long line continued to snake downward. I thought the bags had snacks inside. About half of the two hundred voyagers opened them, as the seas roughened. Within minutes, the sickly smell of vomit and penance wafted freely inside the miserable bunker. A larger-sized lady with several missing teeth brushed against my leg and offered food. Her luggage, nothing more than a heavily taped cardboard box, contained various plastic baggies of treats. They looked like the cinnamon squares I had in my cereal as a kid, but turned out to be a fisheye inside a cracker coating. It was chewy, and the fishy saltiness lingered despite an onslaught of cinnamon gum. Salty eyeballs and seasickness; those were my first memories of Sumatra. But in retrospect, they were worthwhile dues paid for Lake Toba's priceless admission.

  An unknown we ventured on a whim, Toba became a highlight of our month abroad. I'd thought of that oasis over the years; its opulent shimmering blue waters nestled below vibrantly green mountains. I floated there some nights while living with my first love, as the walls closed in. I went there on Sunday evening walks, as a busy university week loomed. Going back, but alone this time, made sense. There were spirits I tuned into but didn't have a chance to communicate with. Carved totems depicting ancestral roots of the Batak people spread

Familiar Giants

throughout the earthy landscape, along with an assortment of churches. Remnants of its Christian ties.

Done are the days of breathing the acrid sick of others or being crammed into an oversold minibus. While in Bali, I made arrangements for a driver to take me from the airport to Samosir Island. The driver said it would take just under five hours, and we negotiated the price to fifty U.S. It's important to see the surrounding parts of a country, to witness its citizens going about in daily life. The congested tourist areas are often nothing more than *a façade*, shielding the pulse of a nation's heartbeat. You have to get tangled in weeds and sticks to uncover the treasure. Rest easy, Bourdain.

The car whisked through patches of fertile land and jungle and occasionally through smaller towns. Women in burkas walked a few paces behind their male counterparts, who were also in formal dress. Periodically, a call to prayer crackled through a town's speakers. We passed a university of some kind, watching clusters of young people in uniforms and funny square-shaped hats laugh with their peers. It's a gift to see people happy. When it's bothersome, it means there are wounds still to be healed. Seeing their bright ties, I thought of MSAE, and a calm presence filled the car. Home didn't feel as far.

It's mysterious how a handful of hours in one's life can remain imprinted like a tattoo. Trauma is an example, but good things do it too. There was a Halloween party we had at MSAE when I was thirteen. It was close to the time I had my first real kiss. Dad and I called in sick on a Friday and drove to Iowa City for Chinese food and to see a movie. We did that every now and then. I bought a mask and plastic knife at the Halloween store at the mall, preparing for the dance. There were two girls in my class that liked me, and a warmth of anticipation and nerves hovered on our drive back to Fairfield. I shared it all with Dad, and he smiled. He told me I had an exciting life ahead. The boys and girls stayed on their respective side of the hall. Then one brave couple formed. We made fun of the brave, knowing truthfully their confidence exceeded ours. Later on, two girls ran over and said they were dared to kiss me. I kissed each of them on the lips before they dashed away giggling. One of our chaperone's, a French-Canadian who taught art, told me I'd be married young.

Our car switch-backed several times as it descended the steep hill. Then the lake appeared. It was just as shimmering and blue, though larger than I remembered. Monkeys gathered on the side of the road, preening one another, looking for scraps. Small, dilapidated huts sold water and other sundries nearby. The inner voice confirmed that returning here was the right thing. I considered Hong Kong and the Philippines. It went to a coin toss. Then Hong Kong got pitted against Toba. Perhaps I still had knowledge to uncover here; unfinished business to figure out. We eventually reached the bottom of the hill and pulled onto a small port. My driver spoke to a guy wearing a blue vest, smoking a cigarette near gallons of petrol. He nodded and pointed.

"Okay. We are here. Go to that building and buy ticket. Boat to Toba. Maybe twenty minutes it comes."

I collected my duffel and backpack. After thirty minutes on the creaky pier, I was still the only person, except for the man in the blue vest, who smoked another cigarette. The shantytown was dusty, most of the buildings built from cinderblocks. Trash of various kind blew across its streets, and I worried it would blow into the water. A tiny restaurant that would never pass a health inspection back home had a small sign in English. I purchased tea. The smiley lady had a crucifix necklace and told me the boat would arrive in another hour. Time is elusive in the nonindustrialized world. I ordered another tea.

I splurged on a room with a balcony overlooking the lake. A Swiss man who married a local owned it. It was the low season and empty, so he gave me a good rate. There was a chessboard set up on a small table in the lobby and we talked about playing a game, though I never saw him again. As customary to my routine, I dropped my bags in my room, then wandered with only the assurance of intuition. There were few activities on the island, and even fewer touts, which made it easy to relax. There were hot springs an hour away by scooter. A local girl I met on my first trip took me there, before taking me to her one-room home, where I had lunch with her entire family. The grandmother had kind eyes and offered me the largest fish on the plate. The water came from a well. Scanning the room, each person had their little area sectioned off with a thin sleeping mat and handful of modest belongings. I wasn't sure of the etiquette, but offering a bit of money felt appropriate. When I touched my wallet, the girl immediately pushed my hand away. It was just pure hospitality. Nobody, including the girl, spoke English, so the afternoon was a collection of pantomime gestures and giggles. That's a tattoo memory.

August 27, 2019—last day in Bali—email from Troy, two days before Sumatra

I've been going through my belongings discarding nonessentials. The one box I'm having trouble with is all my papers, exams, notes, etc. from college. As a scholar, I want to hear how you regard these items. I think I should have a fire and burn them ceremonially.

This week I leave for SoCal sun and surf. I love tapping into the intensity and excitement there.

Hope you're well, amigo. I'm constantly thinking about how you're experiencing this pilgrimage. I think it's fucking fantastic. Troy

August 29, 2019—email back to Troy

I burned it all, amigo—the papers, the notes, even my military stuff. I have a box with all my degrees and awards that my dad holds onto, but I'd just as soon it go up in smoke, too. I'd have no regrets parting ways with it. Several years ago, I asked people to not call me "Dr. Osborne," but only Nick. I never liked the rank-and-file rigidity of the military, or the power trip egos of higher education. But I needed to step into those circles to truly understand them; to see their illusions and take greater ownership of who I am. Those circles can be places where people hide. There are wonderful people there of course, but some are so heavily attached to their titles. It's like it is the only thing that defines them. Right now, I prefer the path of the anonymous Wanderer.

This pilgrimage is a culminating test of sorts, as I do think a more domestic life is eventually coming. I need to get certain things out of my system in order to accept what the future brings, and part of that is confronting these deeper layers. A maturing is happening. But I need to get dirty, too, to keep it balanced. With the different kinds of tests that show up, there is indeed a destiny to all of it. It's not vacation. Not at all.

Going to SoCal is exactly what your spirit needs, hombre. These things re-calibrate the soul and provide balance. In 48 hours, I will be in Lake Toba! BTW- I am having dinner with a middle-aged Aussie expat tonight. He's a former lawyer, or so he says, and now he directs porn films starring lady boys. He is also married to one. I met her last night. Such a strange scene, dude. He's my neighbor here in Kuta, and all this came out while I was just reading on the porch. It's amazing what one beer can bring. The shits and giggles of the Search. But the show must go on. Love you brother, and live bravely. Fullness to fullness, Nick

Chapter 32
The Surgery

September 2019, Sumatra

> Almost everything will work again, if you unplug it for a few minutes, including you.[28]
> —Anne Lamott

An elderly mystic in Bolivia sauntered over and sat on the rickety bench beside me. His intricately carved cane had a brass bird's head for a handle. A golden light from the sun glistened off it. I watched him earlier, singing faintly in Quechua on the banks of Lake Titicaca, about a hundred yards in front of us. On the side of his hat, which was similar to a fedora, though different, was a long feather. I watched the feather bend side to side from the cool wind. Then he spoke his first words.

"Do you live for you, or others?"

Being a new doctoral student, I was accustomed to speaking on my feet. I sifted quickly through my active intellect trying to pinpoint an articulate response for my mysterious companion.

"Well, it's important to be of service, and when you devote yourself to others ..." I began.

"No, no, no ..." the man interrupted, waving his hands.

"Think. You did not think before you spoke. Those are *empty* words," he admonished.

---

28   ted.com/talks/anne_lamott_12_truths_i_learned_from_life_and_writing?autoplay=true&muted=true"Anne Lamott: 12 truths I learned from life and writing | TED Talk, April 2017.&muted=true"Anne Lamott: 12 truths I learned from life and writing | TED Talk, April 2017.

The Surgery

I sat silently, deliberating, before he continued.

"If you do not live for *you*, what can you offer others that benefits them? How can you serve God when your attention and time are given away?"

I processed his words. Memories of going the extra mile for friends and coworkers, only to feel taken advantage of and drained. He proceeded to explain that it's easy to overfill a day, cramming it with engagements that others expect, along with saying "yes" to things out of guilt or obligation. He confided that Americans and Europeans are the worst offenders, finding it challenging to just be.

"The contented man can sit on a bench in complete fulfillment. He needs nothing, as every moment is full. Fullness to fullness," the man said.

Then he rose from the bench and walked away.

******

After four days on Toba, a lack of things to do and absence of tourists made me restless. The vibrant mountainous scenery continued to dazzle, as I ate breakfast and sipped well-made coffee just feet from the water's edge. But there was no substantive human connection, other than innocent flirts with the younger staff who didn't speak English. The isolation and alone time prompted generous doses of reflection.

Writing freely in my journal, an obscure pattern revealed itself. As a kid, I was out of the house early on weekends, honing survivalist skills in the woods, or playing war with other neighborhood soldiers. I fantasized heroic adventures, as I climbed trees with scraped knees to find my sniper position. Later as an adult, I carved out time for private karate sessions, or shooting at the range. The down time, it seemed, was more often than not filled with a subconscious arrangement. A structure. And then a sensation came through in meditation.

It began as a collection of incoherent thoughts before a ball of energy formed in my stomach and solar plexus. The feeling was like a foot going to sleep, only this tingle went upward into my throat. A soft voice penetrated through and asked what I was preparing for. I went deeper with the question, soon realizing that much of my life had been training of some form or another. Even as a prepubescent warrior, or throwing eggs at the security guard, there was a prominent theme of preparedness. The vigorous exercise, the recent interest in martial arts, and all the guns were mysteriously tied to it.

Coincidentally, this theme seemed to hover within the collective subconscious, too. Books, films, and even reality TV shows sprung up en masse, centering on apocalyptic events, followed by a scramble for survival. Lengthy mud runs with military-inspired obstacle courses became popular forms of recreation, paracord bracelets were in fashion. When Donald J. Trump assumed the presidency in 2016, my university town became noticeably on edge. Radical leftist speakers visited the community; coffee shop chatter and bulletin boards called for resistance and revolution. On the other end, at the gun club I belonged to, members rumbled on about ammunition shortages and various shit-hit-the-fan scenarios. A sense of something to come loomed within the collective. The Shift. Was I ready?

******

About a mile from the Swiss guesthouse, I stumbled upon a path that led up a steep hill. As I ascended the muddy trail, a local woman gathered wood as a dozen cows grazed and chickens pecked. The lake was behind and sparkled like a jewel amid the rich greenery. I climbed higher, astounded at how breathtaking and remote the area was. The path finally leveled onto a vast rolling field that provided a 360-degree view of Toba. Small burial sites were clustered in unusual parts, with white crucifixes protruding from the dark soil. I walked for a while, enjoying the silence, as storm clouds formed overhead. Mountains are brilliant at changing weather. I sat within a cleared space close to a crucifix and closed my eyes, delicately thinking my mantra. Then, I switched directions toward a lone tree that resembled an oversized bonsai. As I got closer, a gray face stared. There was a delay with my eyesight, but when things focused, I froze. The stare was fierce. A large horned bull dipped below the ground in a vat of mud breathed forcefully through his nose, watching. He covered himself in the grayish sludge, as his breath accelerated. I was less than fifteen feet away, and immediately raised my hands in prayer. The breath shifted into a snort, as I backed away slowly. Then he dropped his gaze and returned to the mud.

Droplets of rain bounced off my scalp and shoulders. They were sporadic at first, then grew larger and more frequent. I descended the

The Surgery

trail before the big bang hit and the rain showered. A quick descent soon put me on the hard-surfaced road, just as the rain unleashed with full fury. Nearby was a home that doubled as a restaurant. A homemade sign and hodgepodge of plastic chairs and tables, none of it matching, spread around the warped porch. A reeking petrol pump was a few yards from the tables. I counted nine people under the tin roof watching the downpour.

 I walked the steps to the porch, as a woman brought over a battered wicker chair and motioned to sit. Her husband had long black hair and tattoos over most of his body. His sinewy frame had story-worthy scars scattered throughout his torso. A cigarette dangled from a mouth of missing teeth. Three or four children wandered around, eyeing me suspiciously. Two puppies ran over and played, taking turns jumping onto my lap and nipping my ankles. I asked the woman if she had food and she smiled and said, "Soup." I added a cup of strong Indonesian coffee. To my left, two old women with creased faces sat on a shabby mattress and stared blankly into a field ahead. One of them had a timeless face. She could've been six hundred years old, and her bland affect revealed little emotion. She yelled at the puppies, and they obeyed.

 The storm intensified. Symphonic sounds filled the valley, as water smacked firmly against the tin roof and thunder roared. Aside from a minefield of rusty nails protruding on the porch, and animals walking freely, the vegetables were straight from the garden. They were served in an off-white crockery that was slightly chipped. The broth was a curry, and there were noodles in it. It was the best soup I've ever eaten. The coffee was black, strong, and sweetened with sugar and goat's milk from a pail. After serving me, the family sat together a few feet away to eat their lunch. The puppies dozed on my feet, as chickens sauntered onto the porch. In the field the old women stared into, monkeys wandered. I sat with this family for nearly two hours while it stormed. Other than a handful of smiles, nothing was spoken. Fullness to fullness.

 I walked back on the main road toward my guesthouse as a light mist fell. Separate groups of families sat under cover, watching. Some waved, others stared suspiciously. As I neared the hill just a hundred yards from my place, a sturdy-sized woman motioned me over. I saw her every day, as she never left the porch. Occasionally we spoke, though her English was limited. She asked if I were alone, and I told her yes. She asked if I had a wife, and I said no. Then she asked if I was gay. When I walked up the stairs to her home, there were four others smoking cigarettes, talking. She brought a cup of fragrant tea and offered a seat. She said something to the others, and they left promptly, leaving just the two of us.

"You want mushroom?" she asked.

I laughed.

"No, I am okay. No mushroom."

"You *need* mushroom," she demanded.

"Need?" I asked, curiously. "Why you say that?"

Without asking, the large woman took hold of my hand and looked into my eyes. It was a bold gesture for a woman in that culture, so I sensed its significance.

"Mushroom told me."

"Mushroom told you?" I asked, furrowing my brow.

"Yes," she nodded.

"And what did it say?"

"It said you need to have. And that's all it said. I told my son to collect, and now we have."

A litany of thoughts rushed in. After Gili, I didn't feel it necessary to venture into another psychedelic adventure. Enough had been revealed to process for a long while. But I was curious by her approach. I've traveled enough to spot scams, though some are so elaborate and clever that clarity comes only after the fact, and once wrapped in its tentacles. The off-season lack of tourism dollars was no doubt impacting Toba, and perhaps this family affair was her hustle.

As if listening to this inward monologue, and still holding onto my hand, she said, "I give you free."

The storm clouds moved on, leaving a crisp blue sky behind. A commuter ferry with protective tires on its side carefully bumped onto the pier, as three locals jumped off.

"Do I take now?"

The woman laughed heartily.

"No, no, no," she replied.

"Must wait, not now. Cannot eat. Two days, only water. Then, I give to you. When finished, go to lake."

"Lake?" I asked, pointing behind. "You mean, into water?"

The woman smiled. "Yes. To get clean."

A test! Another damn test! If I were watching a film, I would shake my head at the stupidity of the character. He is obviously being set up; he will be given a strong dose of something that will knock him unconscious, then he'll wake up in a bathtub on ice, maybe with his

The Surgery

organs missing, or his wallet pilfered, if he's lucky. Briefly, I wondered if some sinister appendage had followed me from Gili. Something passed by the phantom twins, perhaps. I'd read accounts of poltergeists and other malevolent forces following people home from ghost tours. The woman let go of my hands, then touched my dimple and laughed.

"I like," she beamed.

I was introduced to fasting in my twenties by my father. It was a helpful reset for giving the body a break, but it did other things, too, I'd later learn. Much of the shamanism writings I came across emphasized fasting for going into altered states of consciousness, which subsequently enhanced the medicine being ingested. We Americans have strong attachments to food. Aside from "foodie culture" becoming a status symbol of sorts, most of us eat too much, too often, and too poorly. I often suppress this truth while bingeing on chicken wings, sweet potato fries, and multiple pints of craft IPA.

The first day was the hardest. Stomach pangs rumbled after my morning swim, thinking about freshly cut fruit and sticky rice with coconut. I cheated a little with coffee but stayed disciplined for the rest of the day. The second one was easier. I woke up full, contented that I was more than halfway there. The fasting brought lightheadedness and cracked openings for old wounds to enter. I dwelled on the porch conversation. I replayed the meeting multiple times, unable to pinpoint a hustle. If I had my tarot deck with me, I would have done a reading, but those were hiding in a box somewhere at Dad's house. During meditation, I didn't sense danger. The woman had a saintly face, her energy clear. I learned to trust the universe and its inexplicable mysteries through my quests. But perhaps those would be the words inscribed on my tombstone.

As instructed, I made the short walk toward her home. Three boys, probably in their mid-teenage years, spoke hastily to one another.

I shyly walked up the stairs, and smiled at the woman, then nodded to the others. There was an uncomfortable number of people in the enclosed space, and I worried that I would be on display.

"They want to know if you are wrestler, like on Smack Down?" the woman asked.

I chuckled and shook my head.

"You are big for American, too, yes?" a different woman asked.

I nodded.

"Big is good," she said, before breaking into another laugh.

"This is my sister. Her son picked mushroom with my son." She pointed to a male in his twenties, who looked away.

She held her gaze, then asked if I had eaten.

"No," I said, truthfully.

Her stare lingered momentarily, perhaps truth-checking.

"Good. I will make you omelet, and mushroom will be in it."

"Um, before we start, I need to ask you a few things, okay?"

She nodded.

"Why did you choose me to have mushroom? Have you done this before, like with other tourists?"

A confused expression spread across her face. Her sister said something, but the woman waved her off.

"I did not choose. Mushroom did. I tell you this already. I just dreamed and saw you. Then you showed up off boat, and I knew. I knew it was you."

"And this hasn't happened before?"

"No."

"I'm a little nervous," I confessed.

The woman spoke to no one in particular, but several on the porch laughed. The youngest one said something to her, and she laughed heartily.

"You have big muscles. My nephew not understand why you scared. He has taken before."

"No," I began, feeling a bit defensive. "I've taken mushroom before. Several times. I just always paid for them. I never had someone tell me to take them, and that it was from their dream. Do you understand? Strange, yes?"

"I understand," she said emphatically. "But not strange."

Her son rose from his chair, then motioned me to sit. Immediately, half the people on the porch went inside, including the lady. The lack of audience brought my breath closer to normal. A scrawny cat with sores around its eyes wandered around the porch, then disappeared. The others sat among themselves talking as if I weren't there. About ten minutes later, the son reappeared with a small portable table and a knife and fork. He smiled as he handed it to me, and a warmth flooded over, lessening the tension.

Not long after, the woman appeared with a plate and an aromatic omelet. It smelled delicious, though slightly strange. I touched the top of her right hand as she placed it on the table.

"Thank you, auntie," I said.

"Yes. Eat all," she commanded.

The Surgery

"Do I need to stay here, or ..."

"No," she said and waved. "Not necessary. You can leave, but don't go in water until finished. And do not ride moto. Maybe best not to go far."

The rational part of my brain tried to process that I was looking at a psilocybin omelet, served by a complete stranger who told me about a dream she had. I also tried to block out that the Batak people had a history of cannibalism and that the nearest hospital was hours away. I ruminated on all of it briefly, then placed an open napkin on my lap. The first bite tasted like a regular omelet. Even better, perhaps. It had onions, peppers, and various Indonesian spices with a tiny amount of cream. I could see specks of what I assumed were mushrooms but didn't taste their earthy flavor. With my habit of eating much too quickly, the omelet was finished in just a couple minutes.

The wait game of anticipation after taking a substance is both nerve racking and exhilarating. The clock was now started. I was tempted to ask her how many mushrooms were in the omelet, though it seemed that questions of that order would be distasteful. Admittedly, my ego wanted to know whether or not an even greater "heroic dose" had been consumed. I recalled the mushrooms from twenty years earlier on Toba. They were the strongest, and best, I'd ever had. They were the benchmark against the other entheogens, and they continued to hold the belt.

After fifteen minutes, my stomach gurgled, and I felt the pressing urge to fart. I thanked the kind woman for this very strange and mystical encounter, and considered hiking back to where the bull was mudding itself. But a stern feeling swept in, similar to the island's storms, and it directed me back to my room. It's strength overpowering, it left no space for negotiation. I knew then that it would not be an evening of recreational fun. Throughout the various seven hours I was under, I made entries into my journal, knowing it would be nearly impossible to accurately capture this experience later.

******

A Ronin's Tale

Lake Toba's Magic Mushroom Ride

Finally coherent enough to write, and I should do this before I peak. I am going to write stream of consciousness so that all these ideas are unpacked. If I try to make it too concise, or stop to edit, I will miss things. So, here goes. We are collectively standing on the precipice of a divine transition leading us toward a Great Awakening. This is simply our time. That time when we see our attachment to the lower dimensional realms that bind us to our emotional body. Something big is coming, on the collective. Insatiable desires, feelings of being wronged or duped, being enough, being victims, and the preoccupations with our shadows. The obsessive and destructive tendencies that produce fear, tribalism, and that divert us from love and the Law of One. We're ready to be free of these chains, now. The time is upon us where the fog dissipates, and we see through the illusions that separate us from the Source. What is the Source? It's that infinite, and unified field of all possibilities. It's the cavernous silence where our own God-Self lives. We're ready to live from this place. But a big Storm is about to hit.

Break.

I am now three hours or so into it. I felt a bit sick at first, and thought I would throw up, but then it went away. I've been in my room the entire time. I'm not leaving. Only white walls, and the mosquito net are here, so I won't get preoccupied and distracted by visuals. Then I opened my sprawling window and went onto the balcony. The sun hit, and shimmered a holy light off the lake. Tears immediately fell from the splendor. Oh, holy blessings to all living things. What a sight before me. What a magical, glorious world this is. How can anyone not believe in God? What a sad thought.

The faces I remember are still here; the colossal mountain gods. Both strong and playful. I grin and wave, these old friends I've missed. I confess what transpired in my life since I saw them twenty years ago. The trees continue to shake their war shields and spears. There are little tree families clustered together; different sets of relations. The flowers sing high pitched notes, off key. I laugh hysterically. Large birds continue to fly overhead in formation, next to the shifting clouds that look like dripping wax on the side of a candle. I think about the direction they should fly, then they crow and immediately go to it. Amazed at this marvel, I mentally change directions and they follow. Tiny flickers of pink and purple trail their wings. I whispered that they are "showoffs" and a symphony of cackling sounds erupted. I've never

The Surgery

laughed so hard. We're just playing with each other. It's elementary recess; schoolyard magic, and I can't run from my desk fast enough. My throat is wide open, my body has waves of light pulsating up and down. The waves move in sync to my heartbeat.

Break.

Six hours since the porch and omelet. The mushrooms on Gili were more inward, while Sumatra is *showing* the magic. I've never seen such vibrant colors before. A pastel sky, the greenest leaves, and this holy lake. After musing on the balcony for some time, I got on top of the bed under the mosquito net. Looking up at its cone-like awning, I stared into the white without blinking. Then I saw movement. Something scurrying around. I held my gaze.

The less I blinked, the more quickly I ascended. I am in a spacecraft of some kind; it's an advanced craft that uses technology not yet available. I am no longer on my bed, but instead, on a gurney about to undergo surgery. I can read their thoughts. Communication is passed without words. There are three primary doctors, and a support staff. One of them is a woman, and she reminds me to stop thinking, or trying to rationalize what's happening. She tells me they are going to change my DNA; she tells me there is a war taking place on earth for our DNA. She assures I won't feel pain. A slight jab of a needle penetrates into my chest, and I exhale. They have large buggy eyes, but they're gentle. Thoughts continue to flow like waves, but it seems like they are inputting messages this way.

You must make your vessel as clean as possible. Your diet. Your health. What you watch and listen to. It must be disciplined. You must stop making excuses. What is it that you want? Tell us what you want. We are listening.

Tides of emotions lodge into my throat; my eyes tear. The tears grow larger and slide down my cheeks. I have never been good at crying. A stiff wall shoots up and my mind tries to override what's happening. My fists clinch; I am simply on mushrooms. This will pass. This will pass. This will pass.

The female presence places her hands tenderly onto my chest, and a blanket of love overcomes me. It's a warm, liquid sensation that reminds me of the mud bath in Vietnam. My fists soften, as my palms face upward toward the medical staff. I breathe deeply, while she soothingly rubs around my heart in a mandala-like pattern. Then she asks again; to tell them what I want. I tell them I want love, that I am tired of waiting to meet my wife. That I am tired of moving all the time and being without a stable home. That I want permanence. Stability. I share secrets; things I envision from the dreamscape. Holiday rituals and celebrations. I picture myself in the mountains, maybe with a son, telling him a story about my travels as I teach him to light a fire. The emotions are mixed with longing and bitterness, but her hands continue, cupping first then dissipating the fiery edge. Soon after, as if turning a large knob, a venomous bitterness toward the university and the people who wronged me floods in. A dark color enters the room. It runs up and down the walls of the guesthouse, across the ceiling, painting it in a sea of gloomy red. It looks like a slaughterhouse.

I process memories. Faces of colleagues appear, and I ask why they won't help me; how they could betray me. I want to know why. I want to know how they could do such a thing. I contemplate the corruption I witnessed, and the absurdity of their aggressive woke culture. A rigid stiffness envelops my whole body. Then the knob changes, and a mosaic of women's faces, faces I recognize, faces from different intimacies vibrate faintly before disappearing altogether. A sickly feeling rumbles in my stomach and moves upward to my throat where it stays lodged. I consider going into the bathroom to vomit, but it subsides.

The hands continue, penetrating deeply into the skin. Something is moved around. The red slowly fades to a lighter shade, before a cooling light blue mist fills the room.

Close your eyes. Pay attention.

I do as instructed. I'm on a stage, seated on a stool. It feels like I'm auditioning for something. There is no audience, though a presence of many people watching. An announcer I can't see tells me to remain seated and that it will all begin shortly. It has the tone of a game show, though not as casual. A name of a woman is announced. I recognize it immediately. It's my old boss. She walks across the stage toward me, smiling, and I feel love emanate off her like a wellspring. She opens her arms and walks toward me crying, and we embrace. We hold each other. Her tears turn to laughter, and I laugh with her. The voice I cannot see introduces her, and tells the story of how we made this sacred pact to teach one another. That we've known each other, and volunteered to serve this role. A lightness floods over, and she holds her smile before she vanishes. The announcer says another name. I recognize that one, too. It's my first true love, Aimee. She glides onto the stage, we hug affectionately as the moderator recounts the different lifetimes we spent together. Different images of our time, in other lives and this one, flash quickly. I see her son standing in front, smiling. I tower behind

The Surgery

him in my military uniform with my hands proudly on his shoulders. I whisper, "I love you, Jake," and his smile widens. Tides of blissful warmth assure me he knows it. She stops on the stage and looks into my eyes. She tells me we finished our karma, but that we still needed a short amount of time together. She tells me that we're always connected by love and that she doesn't harbor any ill feelings toward me.

I feel the presence of D enter the room; the same feeling when we spooned in bed each evening swirls above. A serene peace. Occasionally I woke in the middle of the night, conflicted about whether I should just stay and forfeit the adventure altogether. Just dive in and make it work as a realtor. My mind twirls around the layers of love she showed me. Layers I'd never known. She was the only woman I ever trusted without reservation. Thoughts of a man in her life descended, prompting me to change the thought pattern.

More faces saunter across stage, and our infinite histories are revealed. My parents, my sister, Troy ... I understand the teaching behind my nephew's condition. I understand the way he's brought our family to unbounded thresholds of compassion, as a teacher. One at a time, I hear each story; the profundity of how we serve one another in a sacred circle. There are no mistakes in the universe. The interconnectedness is real.

Slowly, the doctors and staff disappeared into a swirling light, one by one. With my eyes still closed, I clasped my hands in prayer, gradually returning to waking reality. The visuals calmed considerably, as the mosquito net returned to focus. I took a couple deep breaths, twisting onto my side and holding different stretches. Then, I raised my arms, and listened to my fingers and wrists crack. As my eyes opened, things felt blessed. Radiant light emanated from the windows. The room had been consecrated as an altar.

I grabbed a pen and piece of lined paper next to the bed, and wrote the following:

> *The wisdom traditions, each in their own way, guide us toward the Source. The Source has many names—the I AM, the higher self, mother nature, God. It is what we're crying out for; all of us. People in prison, people in the universities, people reading self-help books, the new age vegans driving to yoga, the meat eating hunters seated*

in a blind, the people purging in the Ayahuasca circles. We collectively FEEL the old patterns dissolving. Our instincts guide us toward wholeness. We blame each other because we're scared. But new structures are coming. New ways of being. My time in the red light districts, bars, gritty characters, tasting danger; it all allowed me to feel the deepest levels of the lower realms. The afflictions that are so strong on the planet right now. Our collective addictions from the dark reservoir that exists in each of us. I am ready to let this go now. I am ready for my rebirth.

The sun began to set, cooling the room and prompting me to secure the windows. The task took some effort. My legs wobbled as I inched slowly toward the bed. But I wasn't finished yet. The ceremony still needed to close appropriately. I put on my swim trunks, the ones with a blue floral pattern, and grabbed a small white towel from the bathroom. The lake would take all of it. That was the instruction, anyway. To leave it there, perhaps as an offering, or perhaps because it was generous enough to absorb my poison. As I balanced against the banister and descended the three flights of creaky stairs, the smiley man behind the counter cocked his caterpillar eyebrows.

"Mr. Neekolas, it is cold. Are you sure you want to swim *now*?"

I grinned. Then I asked him to prepare a fresh pineapple for my return and slid a few bills onto the table. Goosebumps spread across my body as I descended into the frigid water. I shook, and exhaled through my mouth, as my teeth clinched. A residual face hung on the mountain, watching, holding accountability. Then I prepared to dip. Without further thought, I plunged fully, embracing the sharp cold as it enveloped my crown. My entire system sprung to life, as I made my way through the birth canal. Was this the culminating test? Had I fulfilled my part of the hero's journey? Was it time to go home after a half year away? As I broke the surface gasping, the familiar voice from an hour earlier whispered. It said two words. *Himalayas. India.*

Chapter 33

THE ORDEAL

Fall 2017, A Classroom in the Midwest

The Ordeal is the significant and poignant part of the journey where the Hero fully applies his skills. It's the big daddy, and a culminating test. For Daniel, it is the coveted All Valley Karate Tournament. For most of the film, Daniel is emotional and fearful. It even carries over into his first match at the tournament. Then shortly after scoring a few points, he turns a corner and comes to life. The music starts, and our Hero becomes confident, as he operates from his center. The poise we see is Daniel accessing for the first time the tools he's acquired through his journey. He quickly clinches some victories and climbs up the winner's bracket. Much of his preparation in the Special World was learning martial arts. It makes sense, right? You are competing in a karate tournament, well, you better know some karate then. But it's more than that. His time in the Special World was about changing his character more than it was learning to fight. It was about becoming a new man; self-assured and composed. The martial arts were only a vehicle to help him let go so that he could metaphorically die. In other words, karate was only a piece of a much larger initiation.

    Another interesting point in this phase is that the Hero shows more independence. We witness Miyagi right there with Daniel from the vicious beating at the Halloween dance and through the tournament. Miyagi is without question his mentor, and a dedicated one at that. But Daniel begins to stand on his own more solidly during the Ordeal. When one of the Cobra Kai hits Daniel with an illegal shot, the test thickens. Daniel is rushed to the locker room and the doctor declares that he cannot continue. This is a pivotal scene, for many reasons. As

A Ronin's Tale

Daniel lays there feeling defeated, Miyagi tells him that there is no reason to continue. He proved himself; he showed up and fought well. The end. But Daniel doesn't accept that. He respectfully tells his mentor that the Cobra Kai cheated; that every time they see him at school, they will know they got the best of him. And because of this, and this is where Daniel's newfound wisdom shines, he tells Miyagi that he will never have balance, not with himself and not with Ali. This is a new Daniel. Acknowledging this, Miyagi famously smacks his hands together and rubs them vigorously to heal Daniel, so that he can fight in the final match and ultimately win the tournament.

Chapter 34

SHIVA'S PLAYGROUND

Late September 2019, Nepal

Being rudderless is not the same thing as being reckless. The morning after release from the UFO craft in Sumatra, I plugged in my laptop and researched trekking outfits in Nepal. I sat with my feet dangling over the pier, while my toes comfortably numbed in Toba's cool waters. I dreamt about the Himalayas, maybe as far back as the womb. In high school, an autobiography of a famous Swami who traveled the area visiting mystics and holy ones enraptured me. Several of the sages lived in caves in complete isolation. I loaned it to Troy afterward, and he was mesmerized, too. Maharishi occasionally dropped bits about his time in the great mountains. The Himalayas are Lord Shiva's playground, he said.

Brief sleuthing on a series of articles and blogs suggested that most trekkers opted for the notorious Everest Base Camp route. Only a paltry 10 percent went further onto the laborious Three Passes, that were less populated. I made some inquiries with different companies that had high marks, then sent an email. I didn't have proper gear for the mountains but was assured I could rent some in Kathmandu. That part didn't worry me as much as finding a decent pair of boots, size thirteen and a half, in a nation where most citizens stood just a hair over five feet.

As customary in the underdeveloped world, seven lines of passengers stood sleepy-eyed, under the mercy of two customs officials. After languidly stamping half a dozen passports, one of the officials disappeared for a smoke. When he returned, the other one vanished. With the wisdom of the mushrooms still fresh, I made a concerted effort to work on patience. As I sunk into the stillness of the moment, a fellow

A Ronin's Tale

trekker with a Norwegian flag affixed to his pack stood a few paces ahead bellowing Bob Seger.

Sharks strategically positioned themselves outside and waited. Us newly stamped visa holders meandered the dusty landscape with heavy luggage, weaving in and out from their crosshairs. The monsoon had two weeks left, so this was an opportune time for beating the crowds. The downside of a lingering monsoon was a possibility of dangerous ice and snow on the mountain. Some of the touts shot their hustle arrows at me, but I knew they weren't the right ones. I told the email guy to look for a very tall American with tattoos. Compared to my peers, I was a lone vanilla wafer in a box of Oreos. Wading through the crowd, the activity thinned. Then I saw two short men, standing shoulder to shoulder with beautiful full-mouthed smiles. Our eyes locked and held. Their faces beamed something authentically kind, and one extended a flower garland, like the ones on Hindu altars.

"Mr. Neekolas? Mr. Neekolas? You must be him," the one without the garland said.

I walked over and clasped my hands in prayer, bowing slightly.

"Namaste," I said.

They greeted back, placing the colorful and fragrant offering around my neck.

"Namaste, namaste," they repeated.

The garland handler, now with both hands free, picked up my duffel which was more than half his size, and effortlessly slung it over his shoulder. He walked ahead at a brisk clip, his steps short and hurried. He steadied the bag with one arm and fished for his car keys with the other. From the front, he had a pronounced receding hairline, though the back revealed long hair draped to his shoulders. It was jet black. His nose was prominently pointed, giving an appearance of an indigenous figure. He was not someone of this time. Then a mental flash popped, disclosing something familiar, as if perhaps I'd seen him during one of my hallucinogenic escapades from long ago. There was without question something I recognized. The other one hung back with me.

"I am Bibek, company owner. That is my employee, Kitar. If we are so humbly honored to take you to mountain, Kitar will guide. I, unfortunately, take Chinese couple to Annapurna circuit. I do not like Chinese, but I need their money."

Kitar opened the passenger's side of the small hatchback and waved me to sit. Immediately, the car rushed at breakneck speed into a frenzied traffic of dark smoke, honking horns, and swerves that would

Shiva's Playground

take your license back home. Every conceivable light, from needing an oil change to check engine, beamed off the dash.

The main road took us into a congested city center where hordes of people sat idly, some talking, others just staring blankly. On some blocks, hundreds of people hung around. The sweet aroma from a plume of beedi cigarettes breezed through my half-opened window. Trash blew around the dusty streets and congregated into makeshift piles, as cows and people rummaged. A shirtless man sat in a dilapidated reclining chair next to the road, as another shirtless man on a stool shaved his face with a straight razor. Women in soiled dresses held babies, while sifting through mounds of rubbish with broom handles. Young children with snotty noses ran wildly, kicking at a deflated soccer ball. The exotic architecture and signs with Sanskrit script produced an otherworldly feeling that I was indeed far down the rabbit hole. It didn't have the glitz of Bangkok or Saigon. Instead, it felt like a nation on the fringe. Tourist dollars the blood meal.

We traversed the urban jungle for thirty minutes, as sensory overload and a jerky steering wheel on a couple hours' sleep produced nausea. Truth sunk in that in a few short days I would be high up in the colossal mountains, with a moderate pack on my shoulders, slugging thin air. The glory and excitement this radiated in Sumatra's oasis was different in the hatchback. But the reality check of travel is painfully different from the romanticized vision of the homesteader, or office stiff punching keyboards. The exotic path is a deceptive teacher. Most places I've dwelled are oppressively filthy and diseased, lacking infrastructure and comforts. You worry about finding clean water and food, so you're not sentenced to a squat toilet peeing out your ass for several days. You miss meals and shed pounds from an unforgiving climate. You make a daily scramble through crowds of hustlers, all eyeing you as a walking wallet, while trying to maintain assertiveness and compassion.

Kathmandu overflows. People and livestock, both with horrific skin conditions and deformities, saunter near elaborate shrines and altars. It's these microlayers that take a wanderer deeper into dignity. To try and understand how others make sense or even find peace with the plight of their existence can only open the heart. We, of course, suffer in the west, too. And part of our suffering is rooted in our overly active minds and tech addictions. But it's different on the far end of the globe. It's a slower burn.

As I walked with Kitar and Bibek for some local nourishment, I surrendered that Nepal was going to be a gut check, and possibly my

Ordeal. After less than an hour of sandals on the mucky ground, I was already inclined to lie down for a rest. Yes, the mountain would test me, but so would the rampant suffering. It would be a different part of the curriculum, and a prerequisite for maintaining center in India, which was just a month away.

"Mr. Neek, have you had *momo* before?" Bibek asked.

I shook my head.

"Ah, good. You will like. And *paratha*, we will get, also."

Bibek spoke to an elderly woman who handed me a weathered plate with small cracks on it. Her wrinkled face and the colorful wrap around her forehead resembled a *National Geographic* cover I saw in second grade. She pointed upward, and a younger man, maybe a son, escorted us three flights of stairs to a barren room. The kitchen was on the first floor, on the street, while a living space occupied the second floor. Dining was on top, and the large screenless window invited all sorts of mosquitoes and flying pests. A stainless container with communal utensils sat in the middle of the table. One of the forks had dried bits of food around it. After ascending the stairs, I tried to hide my breath as it lapsed noticeably from my chest and mouth. Kitar witnessing this, laughed.

"It will be harder up there," he grinned, pointing through the window, upward.

I wandered off watching the activity below through the big window. Hypnotic music with flutes and sitars boomed obnoxiously, as cars beeped. Bicycles and carts canvassed the narrow streets, kicking up more dust that rose into the dirty air. The woman below entered the room with three large bottles balanced in her hands. I watched her breath, which was normal. Bibek popped the caps with a lighter, then poured them into the spotted glasses. The thick foamy head looked like a pencil eraser. My eyes were heavy.

"Everest beer. Good for going to mountain. Keep spirits happy. A toast to Mr. Neek, and welcome to Nepal," Bibek said.

We clinked our glasses, and I took a long pull. The suds punched through my nostrils, kicking an immediate glow. It had been a while. A long while. I took another pull and drained the glass. They laughed heartily, as Kitar promptly filled it.

Nine beers and two whiskies. Could be a country song, maybe. But that was the tally so far since landing in Bangkok six months earlier. The whisky; one in Vietnam and another in Laos, with the full scorpion and snake head at the bottom of the bottle. A passerby at the night market in Laos whispered it was like natural Viagra. But it only burned my throat and kept me up most of the night.

Everest beer is Nepal's signature ale, brewed locally in Kathmandu. On its label, a lone mountaineer stands confidently atop the world's highest point with snow axe in hand. I stared at the label and scratched at it with my fingernail until a corner peeled. Then I tore it off and rolled it in my fingers, before dropping it down the bottleneck. It's a ritual I do sometimes while drinking alone. The ale went to work, and an optimistic rejuvenation of the coming weeks raised my eyelids. Kitar and Bibek excused themselves to run across the street to retrieve the trekking information from their office. The alone time and replenished bottles brought on the wheel; a chance to sit with the multitude of costumes and masks worn by the ancient ones.

Alcohol breeds introspection, so I took inventory to make sense of some of it. A fitting topic for the solo drinker: the friendships and women of our lives. I've had a good amount of both, but none of them sticking around long. There has always been fluidity in the company I keep, save a select few. This is where the archetypes revealed so much. Certain men I know are Warriors; whether it shows itself through martial arts, military service, the gun club, or the hours they grind in the gym. It is not so much what they do, though, as much as who they are at their core. Their personality, the way they carry themselves, their interests. When I'm around these guys, those energies in myself become primed. But I can't live in that space exclusively all the time. My gay friends allow me to play in my feminine; to enjoy the Artist archetype. Extended café time. A rich glass of wine, while talking literature. Amusement at their outrageously candid and seemingly endless sex-capades; details of dick sizes and the full-time work of online hook-ups. Brave tales; listening to their courageous stories of how they eventually owned and made peace with who they are. My new-age friends bring out the layers of the Shaman, or Monk. The ethereal realms where the mystics play. Sometimes nature brings the Outlaw along my path, an interesting character at the bar or bus terminal. A gritty story that floats underneath his leather jacket, next to his knife. I've met some killers in my life. One of my uncle's shot pool with Charles Manson. It goes on and on, the people who serve as guides. Each illuminating a piece of me.

The women archetypes, like the men, run a diverse spectrum, too. The athletic, blonde Valley Girl is my sexual crack addiction. God bless Jenny McCarthy. The bubbly, lighthearted type whose shine fills a room. That was my first love, Aimee. But I fall to my knees for the

A Ronin's Tale

sharp intellect; the independent thinker who muses in the cerebral and philosophical worlds. Quietly strong. More subtle with her power. The Wise Teacher, not so much under the bright light of the chandelier, but ruminating quietly in the corner, watching it all. Taking notes. My shadow urges seem to invite a lot of Vixens and Witches, though. They bring the intense fire, along with their tarot decks and crystals. Their passionate heat burns in so many directions, not all of it positive, though. My neighbor, I was under her spell. Her punk background and pre-academic life in a record shop. Her leather and jewels. Her sturdiness and ability to tame a horse. But it's the Queen I long for. The one that occupies the still moments. The one who wears pieces of all of the above, and she wears them well with the added gift of cooling. The one who brings me back to center, never letting go of the lifeline. The one that understands my need for solitude, and the rituals that empower me to give her and the world my deepest gifts. She is the one that holds me accountable; to operate from my inner King, and to live as a better man. She's the one I ask about when sitting before the soothsayers and their crystal balls.

I polish off another bottle of Everest and relish the unabashed serum. Kathmandu's chaos buzzes along below. I delve further, looking at how the pieces fit together, and the divine symmetry behind it. How it is playing out. It began in Thailand, the Warrior archetype. That's who I flew over with. He followed to Vietnam. Those first months were nothing more than physical exertion. Hard workouts, disciplined routines. Traditional masculinity tests with bravado. After twelve weeks, I needed a break from the pace. By the time I arrived in Hanoi, I was training intermittently. The Warrior let his bruises heal, as the Explorer hopped out of the closet. Laos brought recuperation, and that allowed the Monk to come through. Rising before the sun, getting lost in extended meditations. I dropped a clip of weight from the vegetarian diet and the lengthy hikes into the mountains. Several hours spent silently adrift in the temples each day, lighting oversized incense and praying for my family, and especially my nephew. Copious amounts of green tea consumed on top of Mount Phou Si. And I filled the bowls of beggars each day, careful that no one was excluded. Then an attractive woman at the night market who spoke excellent English appeared, and I watched how easily I veered off course. I cheated with a few beers and a whisky. The following day, she hired a boat down the Mekong, a spot on a secluded island where we collected rocks for her garden. A sultry fantasy took over on the boat, but quickly dissipated after I hauled the

Shiva's Playground

heavy load ashore and up a steep set of stairs. She smiled and offered her hand for a shake, then drove away. Looking back, she just needed a laborer. The Monk rolled his eyes at my foolishness.

Bali and Sumatra brought the soul purges; a chance to bucket the impacted poisons. The Magician, or Shaman as some call him, held court for most of it. Jungle and mountain treks, and some ocean time, too. Island spirits with the ferocious energy of the territory's violent heritage. But Indonesia was mostly about diving into the internal abyss and taking stock there. Layers revealed wounds, which revealed soul fragments. The pieces that needed to come back together for wholeness. The forgiveness that was missing. Now, I was back in an environment where the Warrior was needed again. He rose excitedly at the prospect of the Himalayas. I trusted him fully and knew him the longest.

Six empty bottles stood in a circle, like elders outside a sweat lodge, when the food arrived. Moments later Bibek and Kitar returned with a white binder, like the kind I had in junior high. They looked at the bottles and laughed.

"Mr. Neek, please eat. Momo is *boof.*"

Bibek placed a steamed dumpling on my plate, and two paratha, which resembled naan.

"Boof?" I asked.

"Water booffalo," Bibek clarified.

Aside from being dry with the booze, my other intention was to go vegetarian in Nepal. Strike two.

"Oh, okay," I said, attempting to block images of livestock with their ribs showing, rummaging through garbage heaps.

Kitar inhaled, looking intently at the bounty.

"And please have some with me," I said, motioning to it.

Kitar looked at Bibek in a way that an employee does when seeking guidance from the boss.

"Oh, no, no. This is for you, Mr. Neek," Bibek said.

"No, please. It is better to share. Plus, I am paying for it, so it is American custom that you have with me."

Bibek cocked his eyebrows.

"You are paying? No, no. This is our special meal, and you are guest."

Kitar continued to stare at the food.

"Well, if you pay for this, I will have to hire another trekking company, then." I laughed.

Bibek spoke his local language to Kitar, who wasted no time

rushing downstairs to retrieve two plates.

Just as fast as he vanished, he reappeared and handed them to me. I divvied up the bounty in three equal parts.

"I don't think we have enough food here, guys," I said. "Bibek, can you please order two more boof and three orders of paratha?"

Bibek barked at Kitar, who leapt from the table quicker than before.

We finished another round of beers. Most of the time I couldn't follow what was said, but was moved more from the gold of the moment. Kitar's dark cheeks rosied, and he repeatedly held his hand up for a high five. I had no idea what I was doing; if I was being ripped off, or if these were the right hands in which to place my life and safety. A couple clouds floated by asking if I was hiding, and if it were time to return home. Save the money. Get the suit out of the closet. But that is the growth of this path. To understand the significance of faith, and to embrace that a numinous timeline exists, where doors open on their own accord.

"Okay, Bibek, we talk business now," I said, in a semi-serious tone.

Bibek said something to Kitar, and they chuckled hysterically.

"Okay, okay, Mr. Neek. Yes. Business, business."

I sat upright in my chair and folded my hands, as images of past meetings whizzed by.

"I know from looking on the Internet how much this should cost. And I want you and Kitar to also make money for your family. I don't want to be ripped off, but I don't want you and Kitar to be ripped off either. Do you understand?"

Bibek translated, as Kitar leaned closer. The laughter ceased, and I had their attention.

"I know I will need to rent gear, too. I know that you will get a commission if I rent gear from the bazaar you recommend. I am okay with that, but again, I don't want to be ripped off. Understand?"

Bibek stared, puzzled.

"Rip. Off. What is that?" he asked.

"I don't want to pay too much. Uh, don't make too expensive, okay? Fair price."

"Yes, yes. Fair price, I understand."

"Okay. So, if you give me fair price, and if Kitar takes care of me as guide, I will give you both good tip at end. But I am only going to pay twelve hundred U.S. for the trek, and sixty to rent the gear."

Bibek and Kitar spoke quickly back and forth. It lasted less than thirty seconds, until they nodded. Kitar sipped the last drops from the remaining bottles.

"Mr. Neek, you are happy man. You are smiley, and you make me laugh. I understand but cannot do twelve. Cannot make money. How about eighteen U.S.?"

From the research I gathered, a competitive rate for the twenty-one-day trek with everything included, except tip, hovered around fourteen to sixteen hundred U.S. That was with a reputable company. It could be done cheaper, but that required hiring an independent guide in Lukla, which was a crap shoot, along with having to negotiate many moving parts on the mountain. A moderate number of horror stories, alcoholic and unreliable guides, flooded the various discussion boards I sifted through. Some also cautioned about bunk houses that inflated their prices to weary trekkers who had few options available. Who wants to deal with that kind of drama, or risk having a once in a lifetime experience spoiled on account of a couple bucks?

"Okay, okay," I began. "Eighteen is no good, though. Too much. Can we do cheaper than eighteen?"

Immediately, Bibek shot back.

"How much you pay?"

"So, the most I can do is fifteen hundred for the trek. I will rent gear from the place you take me to, but no more than sixty I pay. You will give me a tour of Kathmandu before we leave, and when we return from mountain. I will give each of you good tip in U.S. dollars when finished. Also, I don't pay extra for insurance. You include that in price."

Bibek and Kitar spoke a little longer, before Kitar nodded. The energy in the room lightened, as Bibek laughed again.

"One more thing," I said. "You help me find good boots for my big feet. And, we have three more beers now to celebrate."

******

The following morning, Bibek and Kitar waited in the lobby of my guesthouse. When I walked downstairs, a kettle of masala chai filled the room. The guesthouse owner wore a traditional red hat and handed me a steaming mug. He tried to broker a trekking deal just minutes after I checked in. When I told him that I was already committed to another outfit, he immediately asked how much I paid. Then he asked what I did for work, and what my salary was.

A Ronin's Tale

Thamel is the tourist backpacker ghetto of Kathmandu. Clusters of trekking companies, guesthouses, and gear stores hawk their wares there, while shadowy figures whisper the market price of hash. The labyrinth streets snake around in dizzying fashion, all looking the same. Most of the shops are identical from the front, too. It's sinful to stop, even for a second, as hordes of jive-talking salesmen stand at the ready. Knife stores push iconic Gurkha weaponry next to depots with prayer flags and bronzed statues of gods and holy figurines. Most everything quoted in U.S. dollars.

Bibek took a sip of chai, then unzipped a duffel that revealed quality gear inside. He told me I could use it for free. The morning began on a high note. He did mention getting some beers at just past eight, though.

"Maybe later," I said, regretting my actions the previous afternoon.

I only spent thirty dollars for the remaining kit; a down sleeping bag, trekking poles, gloves, and an assortment of long-sleeved thermals. The air and heat were uncomfortably sticky, making it difficult to shop for cold weather gear. The first bazaar they took me to was owned by a family that greeted us with a cup of tea. The old man, slightly hunched and under five feet tall, sat me on a regal-looking chair that resembled a throne, while he and his brood disappeared behind an orange curtain. They took turns, wandering through the curtain with stacks of colors and sizes, as we began an exotic fashion show. Most of the shirts would have fit fine when I was ten. We shared laughs as I slinked into them, sometimes my pale belly showing midriff. The old man's wife stood close by, revealing how the top of her head stopped at my navel.

The gear was solid, but the big issue was the boots. Kitar and Bibek assured that quality footwear could be had in Thamel, but we would have to distinguish it from the abundant counterfeits that circulated the bazaar. The first four shops we visited only ran to size eleven. As I struggled and strained, the shop owner jubilantly smiled and exclaimed, "Yes, yes. Fits good."

Around noon, we found a beautiful pair of La Sportiva boots, that were the real deal. But knowing the plight of my situation, the owner demanded three hundred fifty, and stood firm. I was close to pulling my wallet, but Bibek pushed my hand back. Of all the gear needed, boots were most essential. Without adequate footwear, the trek would be highly difficult to complete, not to mention dangerous. Feeling impatient, we scurried across Thamel to one last place. Bibek sent Kitar to retrieve our plane tickets for our early morning flight to Lukla, then confided that the store we were going to was owned by a woman he had history with. The context of their relationship was unclear, though. When we arrived, he spoke to the woman, who disappeared behind a curtain. Minutes later she emerged with the exact pair of La Sportiva boots we'd seen in the previous shop.

Bibek rattled back and forth with the woman. Her body language couldn't be deciphered, though several times she looked at me with sad eyes. Her bland affect, perhaps just a strategic poker face, arose pangs of guilt that Bibek was possibly hustling her. Before I got too lost with this, he turned to share a mischievous grin.

"It has been in store for two years. She wants gone. The best she go is one hundred seven-five. Can you do?"

"Will she make money on that?" I asked, earnestly.

"Oh, yes," Bibek assured.

Knowing these run over two hundred back home, I opened my wallet while silently cheering. On the way out, I slipped Bibek a ten.

We went back to their office to store the gear, and the distinctive sound of a dial-up Internet connection whined as Bibek turned on his computer. On the screen, a beautiful family beamed with truthful smiles. I stared into the image.

"This is my wife and my children. Three girl, one boy."

The boy was the youngest of the bunch and resembled his father. A tinge of pain and envy spiked as I admired the picture.

"Okay, we break in boot now. We go six kilometer to Monkey Temple, and up big step. You see all Kathmandu from Monkey. Then, we walk back and have momo and beer. And tonight, you meet my family and have dinner with us, okay?"

I looked at my watch and realized I spent nearly five hours with Bibek. I was hoping we were finished after the boots so I could return to my hotel to rest and meditate.

"We walk *today*?"

"Yes, must break boots in. Important. We walk now," he said, rising from his chair.

I met Bibek at his office later that evening. My feet felt surprisingly comfortable in spite of walking close to seven miles earlier. The long steps up Monkey Temple ascended through clouds of incense with collections of devotees, mystics, and beggars hanging about. Monkeys walked around undisturbed. At the top, a full view of Kathmandu expanded for miles. It was the first moment on the trip that I felt an absence of time and space. I was simply existing. Much like the clouds, floating freely through consciousness, without worry or thought.

A Ronin's Tale

Bibek was buzzed when I arrived. I could smell the beer, though it was the way his eyes fluttered that gave it away. With the detailed handwritten notes I jotted earlier in his office, I wandered for twenty minutes from my guesthouse until I reached a muddy patch of cinderblock homes with trash strewn everywhere. Bibek stood on top of a roof of a three-story building that he later mentioned had seven families living there. Low electric lines drooped dangerously close to my head, as I slouched underneath. A communal squat toilet that stank horrendously was on the first floor where I met Bibek. He nervously sighed as we passed by. We ascended the stairs, his young son close behind. He was smiley with dimples, and said something to his father, who laughed. I thought about my nephew.

"He likes your tattoos," Bibek said.

I turned to the boy and made a funny face, then smiled.

Bibek's residence consisted of two separate rooms. His four children shared one, while the kitchen and a cramped bed for he and his wife occupied the other. Two of his daughters were on their beds as we walked by, both on their phones. He introduced them briefly and they quickly returned to their texts. As we entered the other room, his wife swept away dust particles and debris with part of a cardboard box. I clasped my hands in prayer and greeted her. I wished I had brought flowers.

"Namaste." She smiled as she greeted me.

Bibek offered a cushion, then went outside and returned with a cold bottle of Everest. It was another big bottle, about two full beers' worth.

"Oh, no, no, thank you. We have to get up early for flight tomorrow," I protested.

"No, no, Neek. It is okay. It is okay. Just one bottle. One bottle each," he snickered.

His wife quickly turned her back to us, then lit the stove. She said something that made their son disappear.

"Can you please tell your wife that I am honored to eat in your home?"

Bibek rattled something, though she responded without turning around. He slurred his words, or maybe it was the language barrier.

"Come, come, to roof. We leave now and go upstairs," Bibek said.

I cautiously ducked under more power lines, as we climbed a battered ladder onto the rooftop. From above, the surrounding buildings appeared to be built over a rubbish dump.

"You are a lucky man, Bibek. You have a nice family."

Shiva's Playground

Bibek drained the last of his beer, then looked out toward the dump. "No, no, Neek. You are lucky one. You live in America."

Bibek flipped a white plastic painter's bucket upside down and waved me to sit.

Peering across the rooftops, sets of eyes descended upon us from the miscellaneous dwellings nearby. I don't like the feeling of being watched, though I sensed the eyes were just curious. There is not a lot of privacy in the underdeveloped world, especially among the poor. Bibek shared through limited English that he was from a mountain town, about a six-hour jeep ride away. His extended family was still there, but he lived in Kathmandu near his younger brother, who recently married. The trekking wages provided enough to stay afloat, while a house of their own was built back home. He proudly scrolled through an album on his phone, showing off the nearly finished flat.

"Fifteen hundred U.S. more, then finished," he said.

The temperature cooled, as the moon took over. The area quieted down, aside from a few kids that kicked at a soccer ball along the hilly dump. It didn't matter that the weather was clear in the moment, as it could all be different by five in the morning, when we were scheduled to fly to the mountain. Lukla, allegedly holding record as the most dangerous airport in the world, beckoned us. I'd read horror stories online, and even sat through a couple YouTube videos, though it didn't faze me much. It was the fastest and most efficient way to begin the trek, and to die in such a holy place wouldn't be so bad.

Bibek's son climbed up the ladder and walked over, smiling. He held a small Spiderman flashlight and waved it at my eyes, laughing, as I made faces at him. I rose from the bucket and motioned for him to sit, while I stretched my legs and looked over the edge. Not long after, more noises rumbled. Through the shadows, Kitar, and a handsome companion who looked to still be in his teens came under the light. Kitar, with his ancient indigenous face, looked over. His eyes were strange under the moon's light.

"Good evening, boss," he said.

"This is my brother, Sejun," Bibek said.

I smiled at Sejun and offered my hand, which he shook delicately.

"Congratulations on your recent marriage," I said.

Sejun looked at Bibek confused, and Bibek said something that made him smile.

"Yes, married," Sejun said.

"How old is Sejun?" I asked.

Bibek counted on his fingers, then said, "Uh, sixteen plus three. And he have two children."

Alcohol emanated from Kitar, an even stronger aroma than the one floating beside Bibek. He slid the backpack off his shoulder, as glass bottles clinked inside. Sejun moved a weathered table in the middle, as Kitar placed six large Everest bottles on top.

Different internal whispers and body sensations danced. I was raised, and further attuned through travel, to accept most things offered as a form of etiquette and respect. A part of me, the part that wanted to believe, anyway, was that they simply sought to bond, and alcohol was their chosen medium. It can be a miracle elixir for language barriers, and uncomfortable moments, like work socials with unfamiliar colleagues. It allows one to drop guard a bit, to connect more authentically or playfully, even if the juice is driving the linkage. But what I learned from alcohol and pot, and even things like coffee and sugar, is that a little can serve as medicine, while too much, poison. I'd seen what the poison could do personally, and to those I cared for. Other voices waved flags about the coming three weeks. Would this be a nightly custom? Were the stellar reviews of their company bullshit? Filled in by friends and relatives, perhaps. I had to trust the path, the will of the divine, but also recognize that freewill existed for a reason.

"Thank you for the kind gift, Kitar," I said, as I popped the caps off with a lighter and distributed the beers.

Kitar wasted no time with a lengthy gulp. I pointed to a beer, but Sejun shook his head.

"No drink," he said.

Then I turned to Bibek.

"We will enjoy tonight, okay. But once we are in the mountain, I do not want to disrespect the spirits by drinking alcohol. Do you understand?"

Bibek nervously giggled, then grinned. My intuition, and his wife's earlier reaction, suggested he more than likely began his celebration hours earlier.

I walked closer to Bibek and placed my right hand on his shoulder, giving a slight massage.

"Bibek, it is important we do not drink in mountain. It would not be right," I whispered.

His eyes cascaded the same flickering flame I'd seen among the club patrons, during that volatile hour before last call. A look that could go many ways.

"No, no, Neek. No drink. Sejun not drink, and Kitar will not drink, too."

"Sejun?" I asked perplexed. "I thought Kitar was guide. Just Kitar and me on mountain, yes?"

More thoughts of a last-minute audible swirled in, bringing frustration with it.

"Oh, yes, yes. Kitar will be guide. Sejun is apprentice. Don't worry, no money. No charge for Sejun. He is learning to guide but does not know trail above Namche. So Kitar will teach."

"No pay Sejun then, huh?" I asked, somewhat defensively.

"No, no, no. We already made deal. You pay nothing extra. But you can tip, if like."

******

I awoke at three the next morning with a dry mouth and slight headache. Sipping from a big bottle of water, I stared at the dingy bathroom and grimy tub from the edge of the tiny bed. Half asleep with a mild hangover, I passed on the shave and shower. These would be absent for the next three weeks anyway, so what was another day? Bibek arrived promptly at three-thirty. Walking toward the hatchback, Sejun wiped sleep from his eyes, and moved into the backseat next to a sound asleep Kitar. We flowed quickly through an uncongested road, arriving to the airport in less than twenty minutes. Then, we said our good-byes to Bibek. The security was ultra-lax, consisting of nothing more than a cursory pat down and hand wand over our luggage. The battered wand beeped multiple times, but our gear was collected regardless and tossed next to an expanse of other bulging bags. Thin men in blue outfits efficiently moved them outside to the flight line.

Inside the terminal, about a hundred tourists meandered, sipping tea, and checking their phones. I ordered a chai, and stood next to a large window, looking out toward the expansive range. I couldn't believe I was here. I was about to check off a sizable item from my boyhood bucket list. There were no flights the day before on account of weather. We initially planned to leave then, but Bibek's brother-in-law, who worked at the airport, told us to wait a day, and subsequently added our name to the first plane going out. He demanded a surcharge of ten dollars. The transport was nothing more than a battered troupe of old Soviet prop planes that held about nineteen passengers each. The planes didn't have bathrooms, and I wasn't expecting any complimentary beverages or nuts on the thirty-minute flight through the mountains. I mentally accepted that a ruggedness phase had begun.

At five-thirty, an unrecognizable voice cackled through the speakers. Kitar explained that our flight was postponed for an hour due to ominous clouds, though waved his hand when I asked if that was a concern. About ninety minutes after, the same voice returned with a new anticipated departure of ten o'clock. Impatient energy flooded throughout the filthy terminal, as clusters of mostly English-speaking voices chided their guides. One woman, with a German accent, berated her guide, who gently reminded his group that he could not control the weather. As I listened to the intrepid voyagers in the midst of their emotional bucketing, my stomach began to gurgle and twist. I thought of the chai. But, before the thought even finished, I dropped my backpack to Sejun and as casually as possible, sprinted to the bathroom, bouncing off my toes like a ballerina.

Too much in a hurry to grab my emergency stash of double-ply luxury toilet paper, I hovered above the putrid hole, staring at a sinister metal pail with dark water inside. An equally evil-looking plastic cup floated in the middle. I barely had my trekking pants to my ankles when an unholy waterfall of warmth shot out furiously. I stayed squatting, fearful of rogue drops hitting the back of my pants, as reinforcement bursts continued to rain down. After four good purges, my stomach stopped its symphonic rage. I repositioned my feet for stability, as beads of sweat cascaded down my forehead.

It was the first diarrhea of the odyssey, and it hit right before going into the mountains. I knew I was overdue for such a bout, but the timing couldn't have been worse. I prayed to the ancients, then begrudgingly steadied myself and reached for the pail. Walking back into the terminal, my ass was on fire. Razor blades soaked in lava pinched and prodded. An uncomfortable feeling that all sets of eyes knew what had just occurred loomed as I delicately slid into my seat.

"Neek, everything okay?" Kitar asked.

"Uh, it is now. I had to go ... poop. Stomach not so good," I whispered, pantomiming that I was holding in my guts.

Kitar said something to Sejun, who straightaway unzipped his backpack. He fumbled inside briefly, then handed me two pills.

"Very common, Neek. Take," Sejun said.

I downed the pills and finished the bottle of water just as a shrieking army of voices penetrated from the speakers. Commotion ensued in all directions, as guides barked orders to their frenzied flock.

"Neek, we go!" Kitar barked.

"Follow me, boss. Stay close!" he yelled, as we dashed toward the flight line.

I looked at my watch and it was only nine-fifteen. I shadowed Kitar and Sejun, as more men in blue outfits rushed us feverishly to one of three planes idling on the runway. We were on the first plane, leading the pack. A kind-looking woman in her thirties met us with a clipboard, then promptly directed us to board immediately. My name, along with my companions, were the first ones read. God bless the bribery codes of the third world, I thought. As I slid my still raw ass into the claustrophobic bench seat, passengers nervously filled the plane. Barely with time to buckle my seatbelt, the plane darted down the tarmac and ascended, almost vertically.

A small line of tourists stood single file, as we walked down the short ladder onto hard ground. In the distance, a whirring sound echoed and grew louder, as two additional planes drew near, following us. Lukla airport is just above nine thousand feet. My stomach gurgled faintly, as I collected my internal-framed pack and moved into the terminal. It was much cooler. Then my stomach sloshed again.

"Coming from Kat?" a tall Norwegian-looking man asked, as I moved urgently to find a bathroom.

"Yeah, just landed," I said, not stopping.

"Lucky you. They just closed the airport. Storms all week."

Chapter 35

Embrace the Suffering

October 2019, Himalayas, Nepal

My hands ached as pin-needle jabs of electric currents pulsated up and down my arms. Even with down gloves extended past the elbows, the pain forced me to regrip my Black Diamond walking sticks often. The knockoff North Face balaclava I picked up in Thamel for five bucks clung to my face, giving an appearance of a battered ninja. It was damp with condensation, as I sucked feverishly in and out trying to catch a breath near 18,000 feet.

"Neek, no stop here. Avalanche zone."

Like Sejun, Raju was not part of the original contract we toasted over Everest beers, what seemed like lifetimes ago. It was over those same beers that Bibek confided, matter of fact, that anything under five thousand meters, or about sixteen thousand feet, is considered a "hill" in this part of the world. Once a person ascended past that point, they were considered in the mountains. Before we technically got to the mountains, however, a litany of tests popped up announced.

We departed Lukla airport with heavy packs cinched tightly, reminding me of road marches and the old ghosts of my military past. Approximately one hundred tourists remained stranded, with another couple hundred grounded in Kathmandu. I was one of fewer than sixty people to land safely, before a rogue storm shut down both airports for a week. With the trails and guesthouses empty, and literally having Everest Base Camp to ourselves, my guide with over twenty years' experience confided this was an extreme anomaly. He said several times that I should consider myself blessed. But all good things have their price tag, and the Piper expects to be paid one way or another.

Embrace the Suffering

As we waded through a small trove of touts and a disheveled-looking group looking for guide work, the belly gurgling continued its wrath, prompting emergency stops for explosive dumps. Eventually, a local Pepto and some prayers got my stomach in check. A minor hiccup, despite that one of the squats was without a bucket of water. We continued onward, and less than an hour off the plane I stumbled upon a long black snake on a rocky path. Seeing its proximity, Sejun hurriedly placed a hand in front of my chest, warning that it was both rare and poisonous. Being in a superstitious land, Kitar surmised that the sighting was mainly a positive omen, though we would need to take extra precaution, nonetheless.

Places of reverence have a knack for testing their initiates. They want to know about commitment. I knew "something" would begin on the trek, to affirm this divine mystery. A pop quiz. As we descended downward to our first place of rest in Phakding, not long after crossing a swaying suspension bridge high above a fast-moving current, Kitar began to cough violently. As I moved closer, he was sweating profusely, with a horrid expression on his face. I thought about the snake.

"Not feeling so good, boss," he said. "But I will be okay. I have finished every trek," he added proudly.

But he wasn't okay. His condition worsened over the evening, and during the night I lay in my cold room listening to an aggressive stream of projectile vomit shoot into a bucket. The room filled with a sickly odor that felt like the presence of death. I put on my headlamp and assembled a few packets of medicine I picked up in Thamel from a pharmacy. With tears welling in his eyes, Kitar accepted them, while looking at the floor.

"I have failed you, boss. I cannot continue. Something is very wrong with me."

The immediate thoughts were all selfish. I wondered if I would finish the trek. I fluttered at the thought of walking back to Lukla to find a suitable guide, who would no doubt capitalize on the plight of my situation and the storm. I contemplated whether Bibek would refund my money, at least in part. Then I thought about just packing up and heading to India early, forgetting that I was stranded. But these thoughts didn't hang around long. Although probably still in his forties, Kitar looked like a small child on the bed, holding his side. His face revealed authentic misery, as he shook and shivered. All I could do was connect fully to the Source vibration within the moment. In truth, I wanted to hold him. What my active mind focused on was insignificant. I sat on the side of the bed and rubbed his back, whispering that we would figure something out. The presence of death lightened, but his condition was grim.

A few minutes later, the guesthouse manager came into our room and squinted his eyes.

"Smell very bad," he said, plugging his nose.

In his other hand was a satellite phone, that he passed to Sejun. I hadn't seen one since the military. A familiar voice brought relief, as a rapid-talking Bibek dominated the conversation. Sejun adopted a posture worn by both younger brothers and subordinate employees. After several minutes, he handed the phone over.

"Neek, hello, boss! Not to worry! We make plan!"

Before I could say hello, Bibek continued at breakneck speed.

"Kitar will go to Lukla hospital. His village is close, family will see him. I call them next. Sejun knows walk to Namche. See, good thing Sejun joined you. You are blessed, boss. You get to Namche guesthouse, and I call owner, who is friend. He find new guide. Simple, simple."

"What about getting Kitar to Lukla? I don't know if he can walk, and he shouldn't go alone. Sejun and I can walk him, and then backtrack. It's not an issue."

Hearing this, Kitar whispered feebly, "I'm okay, boss. I will walk. Just need little rest."

"No! Phakding guide taking Kitar," Bibek shouted.

"Guesthouse owner will arrange. You just walk with Sejun to Namche for two days' rest. Must acclimatize before mountain. Important."

As if reading my earlier dialogue, Bibek added, "Everything paid for. You not pay more. Same same. Enjoy trek, Neek. Have fun, boss!"

The sat phone went silent, and I handed it back to the guesthouse manager, who said something to Sejun before leaving quickly. Kitar continued to heave into the plastic, yellow bucket as the smell of sick overpowered the room. For the next two hours, I lay in bed stroking the quick-growing scruff on my chin. The altitude was low, but a stream of thoughts and anxiety prevented any meaningful slumber from happening. Kitar threw up three more times, then curled onto his side before snoring faintly. Around four, commotion began downstairs, as the guesthouse sprung to life with the few lucky trekkers who had a spot on the plane.

The highlight of my morning was a solid dump without stomach chatter. When I returned to the room to finish packing, Kitar looked at me with pleading, yellow eyes. Tears flowed down his pale cheeks.

"So sorry, boss. I failed you."

I went to the bed and sat next to Kitar and placed an arm around his small frame and pulled him in. I could feel his bones.

"No worries, brother. You did not fail me. You get sick, you get sick. Most important thing is you get healthy. We trek together another time. Maybe Mera, or Lobuche, like we discussed."

Kitar wiped his cheeks but stared into the warped floor. Not long after, the guide who would escort him to the hospital stood solemnly in the hallway.

I nodded and handed the escort a kit of medicine for the nearly six-mile walk. Unfortunately, most of it would be uphill for them. Then I pulled a fifty-dollar bill from my wallet and discretely passed it to Kitar, who proceeded to sniffle. After a warm breakfast of noodles and eggs, we filled our Nalgene bottles with boiling water. Stepping outside, a cutting cool wind struck, as the sound of the fast current echoed near the suspension bridge. I cinched the pack tight against my torso. We would walk upward to Namche. We would walk upward all of the days. I turned on my headlamp and extended my trekking poles, feeling gratitude that the teachers of grit were with me. Thank God for the Warrior.

******

We picked up a new guide, Raju, in Namche, where we rested. Days later, Raju walked point as we inched our way across a relatively flat clearing that resembled a hilly soccer field. A Namche local, Raju came of age in the land of thin air like midwestern kids mature around cornfields and Busch Light. His short agile frame glided smoothly as I struggled awkwardly to keep pace; my size thirteen and a half boots leaving gigantic craters behind. We'd made great time to Everest Base Camp (EBC), shaving two days off the average itinerary. I crouched under the rock with the colorful prayer flags away from the fierce wind, indifferent that it wasn't an overly taxing accomplishment. The next morning, we made way to the highest point of the trek, Kala Patthar (18,514 ft.), and watched the sun rise over Everest. It was a more challenging endeavor, especially on four hours sleep, though not the

A Ronin's Tale

test I'd hoped for.

We found out later from another phone call with Bibek, that Kitar had typhoid, and would remain hospitalized for a while. I briefly thought of my close contact with him, then brushed off those fears, accepting that I was protected. The mountains affirm faith, and I've left many purifications on them.

The Passes were isolated, and Sejun and Raju walked paces ahead, leaving most of each day in silence. The monsoon was ending, but the altitude we were at turned the rain into beautiful thick snowflakes. It reminded me of Iowa, and the first time I saw snow at Utopia Park. My stride, long and confident at sea level, was short and punctuated by frequent breath stops. Leaning on my poles, the scene pulled me into the dreamscape.

Most evenings I got in bed at seven with Jon Krakauer's masterpiece, *Into Thin Air*. The frigid wind howled outside, occasionally shaking the thin wooden veneer walls of the icy room. My breath visible, I burrowed under my mummy bag, fully clothed with hat and gloves. A newfound respect arose for those brave ones who possessed the fortitude to ascend beyond the safe tourist trails. I wondered, while slowly roasting in the mummy bag, if the summit and I would one day meet. In the morning, I put on my boots and slogged outside to the outhouse. Squatting in the dark, I took a deep breath before dipping my hand in the chilled water; feeling the unforgiving droplets slide down the crack of my ass and hang from my balls. Although the Passes were considered relatively safe, hazards of all kind hovered close by.

Two days before we reached the EBC, a lone Frenchman in his mid-twenties wandered in, disoriented. He was ill, with what we believed was altitude sickness, and had to subsequently backtrack from Gorakshep, missing the EBC by mere hours. I went through my pack to give him some medicine, then realized in the absentminded fog of treating Kitar, that I had given it all away. The Frenchman's condition worsened in the evening, and he was eventually airlifted by chopper to Lukla, where he died. Raju confided unemotionally that tourists die every year on the great mountain, but that decision was handled by the mountain spirits.

The lack of tourists and English spoken by Sejun and Raju made the three weeks an inward time. I typically rose at three to meditate, and to be ready for the trails by four, walking through the black as various-sized snowflakes descended. Each day was a slog. All of it uphill, with thin air. Switchbacks only led to steeper ones. At times, the goal was a

Embrace the Suffering

mere twenty yards, then a rest. My body smelled. My trekking pants had to be cinched tighter each morning, as weight disappeared. Toward the end, I was in a dilapidated room with mold all over the walls. A cracked mirror hung next to the bed, and I stripped naked to feel the cold. My broad shoulders and arms were still visible, but everything else had shrunken considerably in the nearly seven months I'd been away. My scruffy beard was partially gray. I looked aged; tired and ragged. The walk was a penance of sorts. Each step imprinting something to ponder. The striking landscapes often went unnoticed, as thoughts of lunch and a discrete place to take a shit prevailed. But the spirit relished all of it. Each evening ended on a high, as the sword continued to be forged.

    Our last evening in Lukla, I sat in an empty restaurant, watching new crops of planes and tourists arrive. They were clean shaven and giggly; their gear pristine. The bubbly exuberance steamed off them, as they hiked in large groups with cameras at the ready. I felt like I had finished a tour of duty, watching the replacement troops as I sat in the corner with a kettle of steaming chai, running my hand through my thick beard. I was so far from America. I was so far from a title, or a care about publications, or even a reputation. Hell, I didn't even know what day of the week it was most times. Those seductive illusions, crafty at how they work, can become a drug if unchecked. But now I was living life. I was going through it on my terms, defining my own success. Peace resonated as I blew on the steaming cup. Forgiveness, too. And for the briefest of moments, I knew that love, real love, the kind of love that goes far into the marrow, would soon find me somehow. I sensed that I would be called to work again, in time. The perfection of the universe, real. So was its magic. I watched the last planes arrive, one after the other. I had finished another test, at least a physical one. It was on to India next, to officially die.

Chapter 36

The Sweetness of Death

October 2019, Varanasi, India

At nine, we went as a family to the Health and Harmony Festival in Santa Rosa, about an hour north of San Francisco. Hundreds of tiny booths and cubicles made out of chairs and bedsheets spread across the vast fairgrounds. They pushed meditation classes, tarot readings, reverse osmosis water filters, and stainless juicers. One woman, with flowing salt-and-pepper hair and long white fingernails, looked like a witch. She sold my mom elaborate quartz crystals that spun from windowsills and cast specks of rainbow light. Beside her, a dark-skinned sturdily built figure with tidy black beard and saffron robe placed frankincense bits on top of a square charcoal. He wafted the sweet-smelling fragrance in a circle, as sitar music played in the background. Dad said something about the smell, recalling trains he rode through Pakistan and India. But I didn't pay much attention, as I was too distracted by the jolts of energy that ran through me.

Later that evening, the mysterious bearded man visited again. As he smiled, a blinding light emanated from his eyes, growing brighter. Eventually I could no longer see him, but a golden framed picture stood in his place. Inside the picture was a bluish figure, but he didn't look fully human. He had unkempt dreadlocks with a crescent moon in the middle and a cobra wrapped around his throat like a necklace. There was a trident in his left hand, and as he sat in full lotus, smaller cobras were near him. The picture felt eerily familiar. When I awoke, the strength of his presence filled my room, then lingered for a couple hours. It wasn't until a few years later, in Iowa, that the blue man appeared again while I helped my father clean carpets. Dad and I did it every Saturday

The Sweetness of Death

to supplement his paltry teaching wage from the Movement. One of our clients had the same golden picture sitting on top of an altar in her bedroom. She saw me stare at it while I vacuumed, then told me it was Lord Shiva, one of the most powerful and respected manifestations of God in Hinduism. The woman explained that Shiva was a destroyer and was considered a supreme warrior of the spiritual realms. She said that he often spent time in the Himalayas meditating, though he also had a wife and family. I repeated his name silently, as another current spiked upward through my spine.

******

It was a short evening flight on Buddha Air from Kat to Varanasi. With over seven months logged on the road, and the recent weeks burrowed in the snowcapped Himalayas, a sixty-dollar-a-night hotel room felt befitting for my entrée into India. It was without fail described as not an easy place to venture; intrinsically filthy, hot, and crammed with chaotic frenzy. Although I'd never been to India, growing up in the commune with so many Hindu influences around, it felt intimately familiar. It was supposed to have been my inaugural trip abroad during my early twenties, but other life circumstances arose. In retrospect, India would be a tough loss of travel virginity for even the most intrepid soul. It's another planet, really.

India was like walking into a timeless rock concert that had been playing for thousands of years. Not a slice of empty space or quiet. Tiny cars zipped haphazardly, beeping horns without purpose, as black smoke leaked from any open crevice. Bodies flowed along a dusty, uneven path of trash, peppered with the acrid smells of urine, body odor, incense, and curry. Excrement from diseased animals strolling freely littered the ground, while ear-piercing ballads from cracked speakers merged with the hypnotic chants of Sadhus smoking clay chillums. On half a block, legions of rickshaws pedaled through scores of vendors hawking counterfeit Levi's, colorful fabrics, chapatis, and even greasy auto parts. One skinny man pushed a broken wooden cart, balancing a mound of used toothbrushes stacked like a pyramid. Royal-looking women in elaborate saris with gold nose piercings and henna script on their hands glided past beggars with horrific skin deformities. I dabbed my forehead, then my nose, as it leaked stringy gray snot.

A Ronin's Tale

You couldn't see the sun through the putrid air, but everything cooked under its unforgiving scorch. It was as if every thought, emotion, color, and archetype contained within was given free rein to run wildly, uncontained in its rawness. India is a psychedelic.

Varanasi, also known as Banaras, or Kashi, is considered India's most sacred city. Indians and devotees around the globe flock there for pilgrimage, bathing in the consecrated Ganges, and worshiping in its many temples. Maharishi's teacher spent time there, even holding a spiritual post of great significance. Through the surreal carnival streets, clusters of men walk with bodies wrapped in brightly orange and golden hues raised above their shoulders. The men sing songs and mantras, as they near the fire. Nearly three hundred bodies are cremated each day at the burning ghats. Their ashes donated to the river under the belief that the soul's attachment to the birth-death-rebirth cycle is broken should one exit the world this way.

Death is a fitting symbol of Varanasi. And death's unmistakable force greeted me my first morning. As I strolled along the muddled, crowded streets, a decrepit-looking dog with open sores and flies buzzing around its tail, staggered toward me, before falling at my feet. It flopped for a moment, breathing strangely through its snout, shaking. Then it died. A Sadhu with thick dreadlocks wrapped above his head like a crown, watched from across the road, then looked with piercing eyes and laughed. He nodded affirmingly; a lesson of some sort had been imparted.

I followed the busy street for several blocks, as hordes of women with babies approached, holding out their hands, then motioning to their mouths.

"Food, sir. Please, food for baby," they begged.

The women wore soiled saris and were barefoot. The tops of their feet, black. The bustling street had a handful of signs written in English, and one had an arrow that pointed to the Kashi Vishwanath, a sacred temple erected for Lord Shiva. As I walked toward the temple, touts rushed from all directions. I breezed through the sea of madness undisturbed, before approaching another line of beggars. Some lay on the street whimpering in pain. Many had infections of different sorts and little brass bowls in front of them. More legions of half-naked Sadhus roamed by in loincloths, their entire earthly possessions wrapped in small bundles that dangled from the edge of a stick.

I gazed at the psychedelic splendor, watching as a spectator. Then something, a mysterious lifeline, anchored me back to level ground.

"Ah, Shiva is pleased you are finally here," a faceless voice announced.

The voice spoke English; accented, though exceptionally clear. I scanned through the masses and dizzying activity, then locked onto a pair of eyes that shimmered.

"Did you just say something?" I asked.

The figure looked young, perhaps mid-twenties at most. He was dressed in crisp blue jeans and a smooth green button-down shirt. His skin was darker than the others, and his teeth were white and immaculately straight. But when he smiled, his regal beauty shifted back to his eyes. Everything sprung from there.

The figure motioned toward me. A fabric shop, behind him.

"Shiva has waited. And now you are here," he beamed.

"This is the road to Shiva's temple, friend," I said, dismissively.

He laughed heartily, moving closer.

"Yes, it is. But this road travels to many places. Just like you."

I looked at the ground and shook my head, mildly impressed. Several of my hardcore travel brethren had been to India, and not one forgot to mention the scams, bullshitters, hustlers, and sophisticated antics that were all designed to extract rupees from the wallets of unsuspecting tourists. Even among the most holy of holy temples, I was warned, scores of priests, and other anointed ones, stood at the ready with open hands. Thinking back to my dear Kitar, just moments before he slogged toward the hospital with typhoid, his words reverberated with unabashed honesty:

"Be careful in India, boss. The Indians are very clever."

"I'm not interested, bud," I said sternly, raising my right hand, with palm facing toward him.

The figure was tall, just a little over six feet.

"Not interested? Not interested in *what*?" he asked.

"Whatever it is you're offering—a rickshaw ride, a tour, a special deal in that fabric store behind you, a magic crystal or necklace ..."

I continued toward the beggars, then glanced to my left, perplexed the man was no longer there. I scanned the crowds of people in all directions, expecting to see his green shirt. Then all of a sudden, he just appeared again, a few feet in front. Seeing the puzzled look on my face, he shook his head.

"I am not selling anything. And I do not want money. I just thought you should know about Kashi. It is over seven thousand years old."

I looked around again, dismissing what just occurred as fatigue.

"What, you want to be like a tour guide? I told you, I don't want a guide. I'm okay."

The man walked into my invaded space, just two or three feet in front. The top of his head, inches below my chest. He must have been standing on something a second ago. He was now half a foot shorter.

"My, you are quite tall," he said, touching my heart, where ironically, a tattoo of Lord Shiva hid under my Under Armour shirt. When he touched me, that inexplicable jolt fluttered up my spine, creating a spasm. The young man's eyes pierced. I'd never witnessed such clarity before.

"I don't mean to be rude, but I just got stopped by dozens of people on my way from the hotel. Every one of them was trying to sell something, or they were begging. My heart really goes out to every one of them, but …" my words wandered.

"They are just living out their karma. Just as you are doing," he said.

"What do you mean?"

The man laughed.

"The universe is perfect. Come, shall we walk together?"

In nearly every situation similar to this one, I would've kept walking through the maze, leaving the hustler to scramble for new blood. However, it was the sensation that rumbled internally that piqued my interest. The eyes. The trickery. I was willing to pay a little to watch more of the show. I walked behind the mysterious figure as he glided effortlessly through the sea of people.

"I'm Nick. From America."

"Nice to meet you, Nick. And India is happy you are home," he said, not turning around.

"Okay, before we get started, I need to establish some things. If you are going to give me a tour, I fully expect you will ask me for money. So …"

The man stopped walking and turned around. Then he raised his hand, showing me his palm.

"I said already, there is no money I expect."

We waded through the crowds, eventually reaching the ghats, a confusing labyrinth of alleyways that snaked in all directions, ultimately ending at the Ganges. We walked in silence for most of it. The horrific sights of the poor and desperate were heart wrenching. As if listening, Rishi looked over.

"That is just their karma. Everything is perfect, Nick."

The Sweetness of Death

We descended a pair of steep steps and crisscrossed the crumbling concrete path. Ahead, the milk chocolate river flowed. I had seen images of the sacred Ganges in countless spiritual books and nature shows. But in person, like most landmarks I've seen, its potency was less dramatic. Clusters of Indians held onto a rope and dipped into the filthy water, cleansing their souls. Some washed clothes. A handful of fishermen sat idle in their tattered boats, the water too low for their services.

"Would you like to get in?" Rishi asked.

I read in an online discussion board that Varanasi was among one of the dirtiest sections of the Ganges. One commentor divulged the parasitic illness he inherited, and the months of antibiotic treatment he endured upon returning home. Aside from the occasional dead body or cow that flowed downstream, some parts were mixed with raw sewage.

"No, not today. Maybe later," I said.

"Would you like to see the burning ghat?" Rishi asked.

We ascended the stairs, and I struggled to keep pace with Rishi, as we meandered through the labyrinth. Little cubby holes that sold glass bottled Coca-Cola, fried samosas, and bright garlands of flowers occupied the shadowy space. A sweaty boot smith polished brass buckles and the tips of shoes. Scents of different varietal, ranging from the most pleasant to rank, filled the grimy air. After nearly twenty minutes, we approached a clearing of land where half a dozen cows grazed. Shabby, partially demolished dwellings sat on top of a rubbish wasteland that resembled Bibek's home. Dark smoke billowed in the distance. Chanting and fast-talking chatter echoed.

Chapter 37

GOOD-BYE, HERO

Fall 2017, A Classroom in the Midwest

Death is an interesting thing in our culture, isn't it? For the most part, it is somber and dark. Even tragic, in certain ways. When we contrast our views of death with say, the Samurai, who approach each day as if it's their last, and who find honor through death, it really shows how unique our world is. The Hindus and Buddhists, for example, believe in reincarnation, so death is simply a dropping out of one lifetime and shell, before progressing onward to another. Among Christians, the question of whether or not a person will be allowed into Heaven, or destined for Hell, is paramount. Even atheists have their views on this complex and ambiguous phenomenon. None of us knows for sure what the next chapter entails, but death is a universal collector who eventually comes for each of us. Considering this, think about the billions of dollars spent in the U.S. and Europe on plastic surgery. By and large, aging is symbolic of death. As we get older, we get closer to the final act, right? Maybe these surgeries are a subconscious way to delay or hide from death. If this is true, even in part, what does that say about our relationship to death?

The Hero understands the significance of death. The journey is a symbolic death, because the way the Hero lived previously wasn't enough for him. He was caught up in all the emotional swings and enticements that many of us are attached to. But something from somewhere deep inside him hinted that there was more to this reality than he realized. His journey, as we know well by this point, is about his search for wholeness. If it were easy, or if he could do it half-assed, an authentic shift would not occur. Campbell reminds us that for a

Good-bye, Hero

hero's journey to truly provide transformation, a threat of death must be there. Now, that doesn't mean that a person must risk their life or live irresponsibly in dangerous fashion. But he must be willing to accept that his old self no longer serves him. He must be willing to let go of the raft, where his ego is so very much clutching on for dear life. The Allies and Wayshowers continue to pop in and out of the Hero's path. They are messengers. They provide the necessary wisdom that pushes the Hero along. And they wear many costumes.

Chapter 38

LET GO OF THE RAFT

October 2019, Varanasi, India

The bodies didn't smell. The only aroma was of burnt wood, mixed with tall grass and hay. I observed with Rishi from a small hill about fifty yards away, as groups of shirtless men passed logs of varying size to one another. The logs congregated on top of a raised concrete platform. Smoke and heat rose above it, integrating into the already humid breeze. About a dozen kids dammed up a section of the river below, moving their homemade nets circularly. Rishi explained they were searching for gold teeth and other jewels discarded from the dead. Nothing wasted.

"Would you like to see the bodies?" Rishi asked.

"Yes, if that is okay."

"It is okay. But you cannot film."

We walked down the sloping hill, where a hundred men stared. Some spoke to Rishi, who waved them off. Although young, there was an apparent heir of authority around him. A lighter-skinned man with discolored spots on his hands and face said something to Rishi.

"He would like to explain the burning ghat to you. Do not give him money, though."

The man with the strange pigment took my hand and clasped it inside his. We walked together up a broken wooden ladder to the concrete platform, where ten bodies burned. I said a silent prayer, blessing each one, then stared reverently into the mystical scene. The wood was passed efficiently, and an older man in a soiled blackened tank top stoked the fires with a long stick that resembled a curtain dowel. One of the bodies still bore the colorful orange and golden cloth

Let Go of the Raft

wrapping. I watched, as the Firestarter strategically placed materials underneath. Then, with a glowing ember, a cluster of straw sprung to life. He blew on the small flames, then fanned them until they spread. The cloth quickly dissolved, revealing a thin face that looked deep in sleep.

"How do the bodies get here?" I whispered to my guide.

"Family bring to Kashi. Some stay in Kashi many weeks, until dead. Then, some men pick up, bring to ghat."

"So, these bodies come from all over India, not just from Varanasi?"

"Body die in Kashi. But people come before they die. From many places."

Below the platform, a small circle of elderly men dipped into the river. One plugged his nose, while others poured water from large brass containers that cascaded over their heads.

"There are only men here. Do women assist?" I asked.

"No. They will weep and cry, and it keeps soul attached to body. Only men can do."

The bony man with the stick stoked a fire next to us. He mumbled something to my guide, but my guide did not respond. Then the man looked at me.

"Rupee," he said, extending his hand.

I fumbled through my pockets and handed him a small amount, before he grunted and attended to another body.

"Can Westerners, like me, be burned here?" I asked.

"Depend," he began. "If Hindu, and how die."

"What do you mean?" I asked.

"Pregnant woman, child, and bit by snake cannot."

"They have to be cremated differently?" I clarified.

"Yes. No more talking. We go."

The guide grabbed my hand, then led me down the rickety ladder. I scanned the crowd, but Rishi was nowhere to be seen. Immediately on the ground, the guide and several other men surrounded me.

"You give us money now," the guide demanded.

"What? I was told this was free," I protested.

The guide translated to his companions, who shot back quickly.

"No, not free! Must help. Some family cannot pay for wood. All workers do for free. You gave fire man rupee. Must donate to me!"

I looked again for Rishi.

"No. My guide told me not to pay," I said, trying not to raise my voice.

A Ronin's Tale

The man's eyes grew fierce, and his friends continued to speak rapidly, moving closer. Tension burned along with the fires.

Briefly, I wondered if this was Rishi's hustle. The young guide could be a brother, or a cousin, or a friend of some kind. They probably concocted the scheme, with Rishi playing the good cop who spoke excellent English. Here I was in the middle of their web as it spun.

"No! He is wrong! You must donate! Give me fifty U.S.!" he demanded.

I fumbled through another pocket and handed over a small bill, the equivalent of three dollars. It was the same amount I gave the fire man, who watched the unfolding scene from above.

"No! Need more."

"I do not have any more money. At hotel," I lied, padding the sides of my pockets.

"We go to ATM. Close to here!" he shot back.

I stared into the man's eyes, then shifted my gaze to the others. The situation teetered delicately. I often make it a habit to donate small amounts of money to organizations and even to individuals I come across in my travels. But few things piss me off more than people that demand it, or feel entitled, especially if they use a charity or spiritual front as cover.

Staring into the eyes of my guide I said, "I want you to translate to your friends here, do you understand?"

The man nodded.

I pulled up the sleeve of my shirt, showing an elaborate tattoo of Lord Shiva, similar to the one from my dream years ago. Then I pulled the top of my shirt down, depicting Lord Shiva in his famous Nataraja pose, which was tattooed over my heart.

I took a couple breaths to gain composure, then stared firmly into the guide's eyes.

"I am not a tourist. And I will not pay you. Lord Shiva is watching. He is watching all of us. If you continue to ask for money, you and your friends here, and your entire families, will be cursed. Do you *understand*? Do you understand what I am saying to you, and the seriousness of what you're doing?"

The man's eyes fluttered quickly, as he translated in haste. His brood conversed fervently among themselves. By this point, a larger audience had formed. Part of me was enraged that they would pull such a stunt on this sacred ground, using the dead as pawns in their scheme. Though, the other part softened, understanding it was part of their

Let Go of the Raft

lifestyle, a third world reality I would never fully comprehend. Immediately, the man's posture relaxed. He nodded up and down and stepped backward.

"My friend, my friend, you are *Shivaite*?" he asked, surprised.

I nodded.

"You worship Shiva? You are Shivaite, Shivaite?" he repeated.

"Mmm," I grunted.

The different voices that surrounded us, mumbled, as the scene became electrically charged.

"Yes. I am here on spiritual retreat. I will be fasting and doing *puja* in a couple days. I am here in Kashi to honor Shiva; he is my *Ishta Devata*. I will go to Haridwar soon, and bathe in Mother Ganga."

Some of the faces in the crowd moved closer, gently pulling on the sleeve of my shirt to inspect the tattoo. I heard a voice yell out, "Jai Shiva!" as collections of frenzied conversations continued.

"I am so sorry, sir. So sorry. I did not know. Your tattoos are very beautiful, my friend. I am so sorry. I did not mean …"

My heartbeat waned, as I felt my jaw soften. Then I smiled at the man.

"I want to thank you for telling me about the ghats. This is honorable work, and you will receive many blessings for it. *Om Namah Shiva*," I said, clasping my hands together.

Without interruption, the entire group clasped their hands, then returned to their rumblings.

I ascended the hill rapidly. As I returned to the broken dwellings atop of the trash dump, next to the malnourished cows, Rishi appeared.

"And how was your tour, Nick?" he beamed, the twinkle in his eyes still luminous.

"Did you see what happened?" I asked, somewhat angrily.

"No. Come, we get chai now. And you tell me what happened."

******

Rishi provided a comprehensive tour that took me to several temples and an elaborate mosque. Each place we visited, he was greeted as a royal. He also picked up the tab for the chai and paratha, despite my protests. He didn't speak much, though sometimes infused the sightseeing with stories from the Bhagavad Gita and other sacred texts.

A Ronin's Tale

He explained the intricate carvings on the side of temples and translated the mantras a Sadhu chanted as he poured Ganges's water over his head. Occasionally, Rishi asked questions about my profession, and motivation for coming to India, but I sensed he already knew most of the answers. I couldn't pinpoint the root of this feeling at the time, other than it sprung from my intuition. After spending hours together, I relaxed my guard that he was not out to hustle. At the end of our day, I pulled the equivalent of twenty U.S. dollars from my wallet and handed it to him. Rishi refused at first, but I persisted, until he finally smiled and acquiesced. As I departed from the front of the same fabric store where we originally met, we made plans for the following day. By the time I reached the end of the busy block, I heard his voice come through in a faint whisper, prompting me to turn around. Through the sea of faces, I witnessed Rishi place the money I gave him into the bowl of a beggar. A blind man with many sores and a tattered hospital cloth wrapped around his head. Rishi walked off nonchalantly. The scene sent a pulsing sensation through my heart and produced a subtle tear that I shielded under my counterfeit Oakley's. The next day, I stopped at a market near my hotel and purchased ten dollars' worth of bananas and powdered baby formula. I walked the hectic road with the items secured in a canvas satchel, then proceeded to give it away to various beggars and mothers. I made it a ritual, for the next two weeks in Varanasi, feeling a surge of warmth as the satchel lightened and the faces brightened. I knew I would not put any meaningful dent in India's horrific poverty, though that was not the point. There was no point for any of it, really, other than to connect on the human level. Something Rishi embodied in fullness. *Vasudaiva Kutumbakam.*

******

Rishi stood in front of the fabric store, impeccably dressed in dark slacks and turquoise polo shirt. He nodded toward the empty satchel.

"What is that?" he asked.

"Oh, this? Uh, I decided to buy some things and donate them to the poor," I said, shyly.

"I want to know more about your old job, Nick."

"Yes?" I asked, surprised.

"First, we meet someone. There is a very wise man I know. You

Let Go of the Raft

will enjoy meeting. Come," he said.

I did my best to keep pace, as his gait sliced through a series of crowds. The heat was worse than the previous days. I dabbed at my forehead and neck, smearing specks of dust into the cascading wetness. The beggar he gave the money to was still there, mumbling to himself, as if pleading to God to end his suffering. A group of Sadhus smiled, and one flexed his arms at me, laughing. I laughed, too, as did Rishi. As we neared the steps toward the ghat, Rishi led us into a new section of the maze. It was cooler in the shaded labyrinth. Different vendors selling bulk sacks of rice and lentils acknowledged Rishi as we moved past. I felt a similar wave when I accompanied admirals and generals in the military. But Rishi's energy was more grounded.

"Just a little ways, over here," he said, pointing ahead.

We walked into the open space. It reminded me of a garage with metal doors, pulled by a chain. Inside, a large, wide man in a white dhoti with several colorful inscriptions on his forehead sat staring. His full face gazed blankly, not depicting emotion. He looked me up and down, then said something to Rishi. After a brief interlude, Rishi turned to me.

"This is Guru-ji. He is a famous teacher and wise man. He is an astrologer and has worked with many famous people. I am going to leave for a little while but will return later."

I turned around, watching Rishi exit the space and retrace the path in which we'd come. I briefly thought about the ghat but trusted that Rishi organized this for a reason. Or more accurately, "they" organized it. The ancients.

"Oh, turn around and come here, foolish boy," Guru-ji said.

A bit taken back, I chalked his words up as a cultural difference.

"Come, come. Sit on that cushion, while I make us chai," he said, motioning to a dilapidated velvet cushion that rested on the filthy concrete floor. Pictures of regal-looking men who were likely relatives graced the walls, along with a calendar with a sparkly Ganesh on it. The calendar was from 2005. The year I moved in with my first love and her son.

"I have worked with many people, and I can see you are not well," he said.

I adjusted myself onto the cushion, attempting to cross my legs.

"Not well?" I asked, surprised. "What do you mean?"

"Tell me, yes or no, is what I said true?"

"I, uh ..."

A Ronin's Tale

"Yes or no!" he barked.

"No," I began. "I feel, um ..."

"Give me your hand," he demanded.

Guru-ji sat cross-legged on a much-grander and equally decrepit cushion. Then he grabbed my right hand and forcefully pushed his fingers into my wrist. I had my pulse read by an Ayurvedic doctor thirty years earlier in Iowa.

"Yes, yes, yes," Guru-ji said. He opened his eyes, then released my wrist.

"You have had a most unfortunate event happen to you recently. yes or no?" he asked.

"Uh, well, I lost my career. And I lost my home. And I lost my girlfriend, so maybe that is what you are feeling. But I also ..."

Guru-ji quickly interrupted. "Yes! I was right, you silly boy. I have read the charts of many famous people and even a famous American actress. Nobody can fool me!"

His words resembled the generic horoscopes I sometimes glanced at in the Sunday paper. They were broad and ambiguous, enough to ascribe all sorts of meaning. A hesitation in my stomach began to boil as more sweat ran down the back of my neck.

"That's interesting. Can you tell me more about why I am not well?" I asked.

"Yes, yes. But wait here."

Guru-ji rose from his purple cushion, appearing even larger. He must have stood at least six foot three and weighed close to three hundred pounds. His dirty bare feet hurriedly crunched up a set of stairs, my intuition screaming to get up and leave. But another part of me was curious to see where the path led. Rishi possessed a certain truthfulness; an energy of someone in a higher state of consciousness. It wouldn't make sense for him to set me up. He vouched for Guru-ji, and that meant something. I heard a door open; the hulking swami descended with a box in his arms. Little sprinkles of concrete debris exploded like bombs around his feet.

"Here, here, look here," he said, passing a tattered Polaroid. As he repositioned himself, another plume of dust rose above his cushion.

I inspected the picture carefully, noticing the beautiful figure immediately.

"That's Goldie Hawn," I said, smiling.

Guru-ji nodded proudly.

"Yes, yes, yes. And here," he said, retrieving another one.

Let Go of the Raft

The Polaroids were old and looked authentic; however, they only showed Goldie. As if reading my thoughts, Guru-ji fished further into the box.

"Here I am with Goldie. I remember this day. It was special."

I scrutinized the picture carefully. Indeed, there were several Indian men seated around Goldie, and one of the figures was large. I stared into the fuzzy bulky man, then shifted my gaze to Guru-ji. Judging from Goldie's looks, the picture was at least thirty years old.

"Very nice, Guru-ji," I said, handing it back. Guru-ji nodded and let out an audible grunt, satisfied he'd made his point.

"Now, Rishi tells me that you are a follower of Maharishi-ji and his meditation, yes? And he tells me you have had your astrology chart read many times, yes?"

Vedic astrology first entered my life in Iowa. Rumblings in the trailer park and at school dropped bits and pieces of it, but it wasn't until my mid-teens that I had my chart officially read. It was from a renown astrologer from India who passed through town. The electric buzz radiated throughout the campus. Most meditators often spoke in annoyingly soft inflections, but weeks after the astrologer left our community, all that went to the wayside. Boastful parents confided loudly at the Saturday commissary, or in line at the health-food store, about how little Billy just had his chart read and was most likely the Second Coming. It was part of the shadow patterning in the commune; ego-driven spirituality, and too much praise bestowed upon the young. But as I grew up, I continued to work with different astrologers, usually having my horoscope looked at every couple years. Some were better than others, and a handful were profound.

Vedic astrology, or *Jyotisha*, is a complex predictive system that uses a person's birth date, time of birth, and the exact location of their birth to generate an individually specific horoscope. The horoscope is a symbolic representation of the Earth, planets, and stars at the exact moment one is born. As explained to me, the elaborate science uses different celestial and planetary positions to forecast a person's life, as well as the circumstances that show up in specific time periods. Jyotisha has been purportedly used for thousands of years and continues to be widely integrated into the lives of most Indians, dictating things like the profession they pursue, the spouse they marry, and other significant life decisions. Without going into a confusing explanation of its process, which is beyond my understanding, a professional astrologer offers much more than the gimmicky, ineffective predictions found online or in a newspaper.

In simple terms, Jyotisha assumes that each of us is born with a specific destiny, a hero's journey to fulfill. One can think of their lifetime as being in school, with a curriculum customized just for them. The planets serve as teachers, bringing a multitude of diverse experiences that guide our soul's evolution. Even tragic, and what we consider negative occurrences, are necessary parts of our journey. For instance, a parent with a special needs child may learn compassion and patience in profound ways that never would have been achieved had their child been born without these differences. A workaholic husband may be called away from his executive job to dutifully care for his terminally ill wife, finding deep humility and selflessness through caretaking. What appear on the surface as heartbreaking circumstances are actually teachable offerings from the divine. Many of us know people who experienced supremely challenging events, only to remark that it's one of the best things that ever happened to them. It woke them from a slumber. These wise souls speak of the underlying and often disguised magic of their curriculum.

In its essence, astrology is merely a tool to stimulate intuition, self-understanding, and growth. Although Jyotisha provides a big picture of a person's life, nothing is set in stone, and freewill dances in step with divine will. I often explain Jyotisha to others as if we're taking a road trip, and there's an interplay of both fate and free will. If we wanted to drive from California to New York, for instance, Jyotisha can show us the direct routes (fate). However, our free will may prompt us to take certain back roads, or we may put the wrong kind of gas in the car, or we could meet someone and decide to ride down their road for a while. A person should never base their life on any predictive system, as they forfeit their own relationship to the divine. A wise person will use this information to exercise their free will; to optimize the good while offsetting the not so good. And most solid astrologers simply affirm what our intuition and inner voice already whisper to us.

In early 2006, I was living with my love and her son, though feeling trapped. She was ten years older than me, and I was struggling to make ends meet given the high cost of living just outside San Francisco. I had an hour-long phone call with an astrologer I worked with for many years, and who eighteen months earlier predicted I would soon be involved in a significant relationship, possibly leading to marriage. I sat in my car on my lunch break, in my military uniform, underneath the Bay Bridge, surrounded by thick fog. Without knowing details of

Let Go of the Raft

my current life circumstances, our phone call went like this.

"Nick, I sense you've been dating and playing a lot since we last spoke," he giggled as he spoke.

He explained the different planetary configurations that prompted his comment.

I confessed about my work in the bar and nightclub, and how I was living very much in the moment, enjoying adventures and sexual escapades. I then told him that I felt stuck in my life, though I didn't disclose my girlfriend or living situation. I harped on my student loan debt and my desire to travel, to buy a property, and to eventually return to school to earn a doctorate.

"Are you living with someone?" he asked.

"Yes," I confessed.

"And is she older?"

"Yes."

"Ah, I see. She is wonderful, both beautiful and kind, yes? She very much has the attributes of a wonderful mate for you."

Having enjoyed several readings from Mark over the years, I wasn't surprised by his accuracy, though I could sense an ominous cloud approaching our conversation.

"I feel a *but* coming, Mark."

"Well, you obviously have some karma to share together, but what the planets show is that this really isn't the time for you to entertain marriage. As you know, your chart shows that you could have more than one marriage throughout your life, especially if you marry before thirty-six, which is many years from now. I definitely do not advise you to break up with her, but my indication from your chart, especially Saturn, is that you will soon be going overseas for a while. Saturn is with Mars in the twelfth house, so I suspect this could be with the military and related to war."

"Overseas?" I asked, confused and a bit excited.

"Yes, overseas. It is connected to your work. I see some separation coming in your relationship, or time apart at least. It doesn't mean a breakup, but there will be a period where you'll be away from each other. Your relationship will be tested."

"Okay, and do you have a time frame when this will happen?" I asked.

"Most likely spring, but I see you going overseas in the fall. Because of Saturn's influence here, it will be a faraway place and it could be for over a year."

A Ronin's Tale

At the present time, I was working in the Coast Guard, in the Bay Area. My law enforcement job was like a traditional nine-to-five. I then asked Mark about money and finances.

"Yes, I can see that you are feeling a large weight around you because of your student loans. Interestingly, I don't think you will have this debt too long."

"Really?" I asked, surprised.

"In fact, with the position of the Saturn transit from your Moon, going into the eleventh house, it seems likely that over the next year or so, most of this debt will be paid off. It also seems likely you could purchase a property within eighteen months. Prosperity is coming."

In that moment, a spike of rage shot through me. There was no way that was possible unless I won the lottery. I was barely paying bills, and the cost of a starter home in our zip code hovered just under a million dollars.

"I just don't see it," I lamented. "I don't sense how I am going to get myself out of debt so quickly, let alone buy a home."

A few months after the phone call with Mark, things degraded between my love and I, and I eventually moved out. It still pains me, in part, the way I handled the situation. Ironically, it was shortly after I moved out that I was randomly approached by a senior military leader. He told me about an expeditionary warfare unit that was to begin training in spring for a nearly yearlong deployment to the Middle East. He thought I should apply for selection, and I took him up on his offer and tested for it. In early May, I relocated to San Diego and trained for nearly five months, before deploying overseas. Because of the money I was earning, and most of it tax free being in a combat zone, I paid off my student loans and purchased the home in Iowa that my father and his wife were renting. At the end of the deployment, I also received an acceptance letter for a lucrative doctoral program. This all happened within the eighteen-month timeline.

******

Goldie's shine radiated off the other Polaroids Guru-ji fetched from his magic box.

"You see, you see. Goldie was also not well, when she met me."

"What do you mean?" I asked.

Let Go of the Raft

"She had a nervous mind, like you. Health, not so good. Very bad. I start her promptly on herbs and Ayurveda, and ..." he snapped his fingers, "Just like that, full recovery. You understand Ayurveda, yes?" I nodded.

"Very, very important you have this done. Or you will get very sick."

Before I landed in India, I prepared myself for shyster mystics, employing fear and fated tragedy in their hustle. Numerous astrologers I knew cautioned this, explaining that a common ploy was to look at someone's chart and exclusively harp on terror, or to conversely blow smoke up their ass with only talk of fame and fortune.

"It just so happens the most well-known Ayurvedic doctor in all of Varanasi is a friend of mine. He is never available, always traveling and treating many famous people. He is probably in Delhi as we speak, but I call him now. Hold on," Guruji said, pulling out a flip phone.

I could hear a voice on the other end, as Guru-ji spoke excitedly into the phone. His voice loud, he arced his hands in large circles, and laughed. Then he grinned widely.

"This is unbelievable! Unbelievable! I just spoke to the famous doctor, and he's agreed to see you *today*. What good fortune this is, my foolish boy!"

"Yes, how interesting," I said, staring into Guru-ji's eyes. "And how much does this good doctor charge for his treatment, Guru-ji?"

"And that is more good news, silly boy! Since you are a follower of Maharishi-ji, you will receive a most significant discount."

"Mmm hmm," I said.

"I will need to look at your chart. I can tell you will need certain remedies. I have a very good friend who will do that. And then you will need at least a week of Ayurveda treatment. I believe I can make all this happen for a mere two thousand," he said, beaming.

"Rupees?"

"No, no, silly boy! Dollars! Two thousand dollars. U.S."

"I see. That seems quite expensive."

"It is for your health, you foolish boy! How on earth can it be too expensive. Very cheap. Treatment of this kind in your country, ten thousand easily," he barked, waving his hand downward.

I glanced at the outdated calendar, wondering what Ganesh thought.

"I'm sorry, Guru-ji, but that is just too much money. I cannot do that."

"Well, then perhaps I can make you an even more special deal.

Since Rishi spoke so kindly of you, and I can see you are destined for fame, I will make you a most special offer. I am willing to organize all of your treatment, plus my astrological services and remedies for the low, low price of only one thousand, four hundred."

"And that's rupees, right?" I said stone faced, though laughing hysterically inside.

"No! No! DOLLARS, NOT RUPEES!"

Remedies are a legitimate part of Hindu culture and Jyotisha. The rationale is that a malefic or unfavorable aspect in the horoscope needs to be addressed by an offering or sacrifice. For example, a person may enter a period in their life where they are susceptible to serious illness or an auto accident. Therefore, the various deities are contacted by a Brahmin priest who is specially trained to lead the ritual, essentially asking for their assistance. These ceremonies range from simple to elaborate and are also used to appease specific planets through chanting, incense, flowers, and other *prasad*. I had actually contacted a priest in Varanasi upon returning from the Himalayas and scheduled a ceremony to honor Lord Shiva. The Brahmin was referred by a trusted friend.

"I'm sorry, Guru-ji, but I will not pay you any money. I appreciate your insights, however," I said, hiding my annoyance.

"It is very foolish to not do! You will not live much longer!"

"I understand, but that seems like an enormous amount of money. And I believe that Lord Shiva will take me when my work is finished."

An uncomfortable silence hung between us, and I silently prayed for Rishi to return, though I was beginning to feel irritated toward him, too. Guru-ji shifted back and forth on his cushion, then asked in an almost whisper, "Well, how much you pay, then?"

I looked away from Guru-ji, relieved to see Rishi walk into the space. He said something to Guru-ji, which resulted in a fiery exchange that lasted several minutes. It was unclear what was said, as simple conversational speak in India can appear emotionally charged. After a moment, I turned to Rishi.

"It is time to go," I said.

We returned to the same dingy tea spot that we went to after the burning ghat. I sat in a tilted chair, three stories above the flowing Ganges, and looked out with a sense of peace. I was finally in India. The real India; absorbing all its craziness and fury, yet finding doses of humor in it, too. A paradox of illusion. There are two Indias. One, the realm of abject poverty and filth. A wasteland of chaos and diseased suffering. The other, a holy realm, taking tea with all things sacred in

Let Go of the Raft

the most vibrant and fragrant garden. Sensing my enjoyment of this duality, Rishi's sparkling eyes stared into mine.

"You are much more Hindu than most Indians your age," he said.

"Maybe my tattoos fooled you." I laughed.

"No. You are a seeker."

"Rishi, can you tell me a little more about yourself. Like, are you married, do you have children, how did you learn to speak English so well?"

He took a meaningful sip from his steaming cup of chai. His pause was genuine, unlike the many new-age folks I've met over the years who take deeply exaggerated breaths through their nose before speaking. Most of it mood making.

"I do not have a wife or children," said Rishi. "I've lived in Kashi my entire life. Now, I want to know more about your job. Your *university* job."

"Why do you ask?"

Rishi smiled.

"You know, I'm not really comfortable talking about it. I mean, I lost my job. But, so what, right? It just seems so insignificant now, especially as I walk around here and see people who are suffering. Really suffering. I mean, like that line of lepers with their begging bowls. Those are the ones who have something to complain about. I've been a bit of a child lately."

Rishi continued his gaze.

"Okay. The short version, Rishi, is that I felt like the place I worked was trying so hard to create victims among the students. It was part of the culture, and I wasn't okay with it. So I pushed back, making some enemies. Don't get me wrong, I made mistakes too. But I believe something is very wrong with American education, and it is creating a lot of confusion among young people. I brought in money for the university, but I felt like I wasn't telling the truth to the people who gave us that money. Anyway, it was humiliating in some ways, how it unfolded, but liberating more than anything else."

"Liberating?" Rishi asked.

"Yeah, like, I'm free now. I never bought into the culture there, and when I lost my job, I was relieved. I was too attached to the money I was making and the ego of awards and notoriety in my field. I met with politicians, powerful people. I saw how a certain type of game is played and then found myself playing it."

I watched a fisherman glide slowly with a half-broken oar.

A Ronin's Tale

"You know, the day I was let go was the first time in years that I actually slept."

Rishi nodded, then took a breath.

"It was not your dharma, was it?"

I shook my head.

"It was okay for a certain moment, but then it was no longer okay, yes? And your lifestyle. It became toxic, yes?"

Slide images of empty wine bottles, naked bodies, and sleepless nights clicked by. Then images of frivolous spending. The pictures flowed from Rishi's eyes. I stood at the window of my kitchen, exhaling a plume of marijuana smoke.

"Alright, Rishi, how do you know all this? I mean seriously, man, I literally just got reeled in as you stood in front of a fabric store. My first thought was you were a total fraud, and then I changed my mind. But now after Guru-ji and all that nonsense, I'm not sure what's going on."

Rishi shifted in his chair and refilled my cup with the aromatic brew.

"Your mind is rarely quiet, even in meditation," he began. "The few American and European people I meet come to India for peace. They search for it, yes?"

I nodded.

"They've learned that they can chase their desires endlessly. But then only more desires show up. So they chase, and they chase, never satisfied."

Rishi's insights conjured images of *Fight Club* and of the comment about how what we own eventually owns us.

"Everything is inside, Nick. You have to establish the peace of God in your own heart. And Guru-ji is a wise man. He told you something. Something you needed to hear."

"Yeah, like to give him two grand. I bet if I gave him ten thousand, he would guarantee me enlightenment." I snickered, rolling my eyes.

"What did he tell you?" Rishi asked.

I picked up Rishi's cup and poured the last of the chai.

"Well, he started by telling me that he was an astrologer to many famous people. Then he basically told me I am sick and will die soon unless I have some elaborate *yajna* performed, and some Ayurvedic treatment."

"You told me yesterday you are having a yajna performed for Lord Shiva, so maybe he sensed that. And the Ayurveda ..." Rishi began, closing his eyes, before laughing. "Yes, yes, that was the message."

Let Go of the Raft

"That I am supposed to have Ayurveda?" I asked, frustrated.

"Yes. But you are not that sick. Your mind could be more quiet is all, so maybe just a small treatment. It will help your heart, too, which is a little sore."

I stared out the window, as more fleets of fishermen rowed toward the current. A fresh pot of chai soon arrived at our table, and the woman smiled tenderly at Rishi, before saying something.

"Do you know her?" I asked.

"No. Well, not really. I helped her a little bit, but that is all."

Rishi rose from his seat and pushed in his chair, then looked at me.

"I need to return to my shop now. The chai is paid for. I recommend you not eat for the next two days. When did you last have meat and alcohol?"

"I have not had alcohol or meat for nearly two weeks. I will not have either while in India," I said truthfully.

"Very good. Be sure to tell Lord Shiva all your heart's desires. Americans and Europeans, and more Indian people too, believe they are lonely because they are without spouse. It is not the truth. It is the compassionate heart that unites with the love of God. That is the most important spouse one can have. When one does not understand, the wrong person will continue to come into their life. But you know this already."

Chapter 39
NEXT TO THE FIRE

Fall 2017, A Classroom in the Midwest

We already know a little about ritual. Most of us think about it in a religious or spiritual way but consider mundane things and their power. We humans are a complicated bunch, and part of what balances us is the engagement of ritual. A quiet cup of tea on a Sunday morning when the world is still, and the house quiet, can be a powerful ritual. It gives time to think, to sit with our thoughts, and take a breath away from the chaos. The guy who goes into his garage at night to woodwork, or tinker with his tools, feels it. Even the electric energy of a dojo, or a close-knit gym, can be a ritual, too. It produces a community around a passion. I don't like to define what a ritual is, other than it is a way we connect to something that makes us feel better, so we make it a habit. Dare I say this in a public university, but a ritual grounds us, and it can bring us closer to something divine within. This is an example, in part, of what Campbell means when he urges us to live mythologically. We are to make time for ritual.

    Thinking through our everyday lives through a mythological lens, consider tattoos, for instance. When I asked all of you inked students to raise your hand, it was nearly three-fourths of the entire room. Okay, we know that tattoos are more mainstream today, but is there something deeper beyond that? For many, a tattoo is a symbol of a secret. It tells a part of their story. It reveals things, and some people get them after a challenging event. I had a friend who was a powerful executive. Definitely not what you would consider the tattooed type, as she got out of her BMW in a designer suit. But she had her mother's signature tattooed on her lower back, you know, like when her mother signed

Next to the Fire

checks and things. Her mother died of cancer, so she and her sister decided to commemorate her this way. They also had a recording of their mother's voice that they listened to every Mother's Day and on her birthday.

Now, let's return to the Hero, since he's nearly finished with his journey. As we know already, the tests and tribulations in the Special World bring the Hero to his knees in reverence. It is this place of humility that his ego gets the kick in the ass it needs. He metaphorically sits near the fire, feeling the heat of his emotions and meditating on his toxins. He is face to face with his patterns, ready to purge and relinquish them so that he is never again afflicted by them. This is a ritual cleansing; preparation for his rebirth. The Hero will soon begin his return to the Ordinary World, but he must ensure that his baggage goes to the flames.

Chapter 40

PRASAD

October 2019, Varanasi, India

> Within you is a stillness and a sanctuary to which you can retreat to anytime and be yourself.[29]
> —Herman Hesse

I swatted at the well-fed mosquitoes to no avail. The cheaper hotel was a step down from the opulent, sixty-dollar-a-night palace just four blocks away. The tiny lumpy bed in my new abode ached my back, and the air con only worked when it wanted to. The back of my legs bore strange welts, too. Plus, there were six flights of stairs and no lift. Four blocks was another world entirely. Gupta said in the email to meet him in the lobby at seven sharp, and here I was swatting mosquitoes at a quarter to eight. Through the foggy glass, I looked across the pitiful road to the park where just days earlier I led an impromptu karate class with a dozen street kids and a few hash-smoking Sadhus. One of the kids approached while I was in the middle of *Heian Nidan*, my favorite kata. He didn't speak English, so I showed him a couple moves, then class began. Afterward, the misfit gang and I walked to Chandra Ghat and lit firecrackers. One of them lit some hash and passed it my way, but I shook my head, opting to buy several pots of chai and samosas for our brood instead. I'm sure Rishi was watching.

"My dear boy, my dear boy, I am so sorry. Come, come, the car is out front!" a tall, sweaty figure shouted.

I clutched my satchel with the items from the market and followed

---
[29] H. Hesse, *Siddhartha: A Novel* (Bantam Books, 1982).

the brisk figure into the punishing heat. Gupta provided explicit instructions on what I needed to purchase and where to obtain them. The ceremony was fifty dollars; a deal considering it would run three hours, and cost nearly ten times that at home.

"Come, come, dear boy. Sit here with your long legs," he said, opening the passenger side of a newer Mercedes.

He barked at his driver, then upped the air-con dial.

"What a joyous occasion it must be, to honor Lord Shiva in this most holy city, yes?"

Gupta's smiling face beamed truthfully through the mirror on the visor. His forehead cast the prominent markings of a Brahmin, different colored squiggles of red, yellow, and white. I was curious of their meaning.

"I am most blessed, Pundit Gupta."

"And the bag, was there difficulty with the items?"

"No, Pundit Gupta. Your instructions were very clear and easy." It was a total lie. The contents took an entire afternoon to assemble, not to mention the requisite haggling. Nothing is easy in India.

"Most excellent," he said.

"Thank you for organizing this. I am excited and honored to participate."

"Oh, yes, yes, kind boy," he began. "I will not lead the ceremony, however, but my most trusted colleague will do so. He oversees temple. There will be two other priests, also. You will be in most good hands."

"The temples here are wonderful. I've enjoyed walking through them," I said.

"Oh, yes. We are driving to a most holy temple here in Kashi, and Mother Ganga is just steps from it. We will use her milk while we speak to the gods."

After ten minutes traversing a confusing zigzag of alleys and side roads, I was grateful for the free chauffer service. India's circus unfolded forcefully outside the arctic Benz, as legions of rickshaws and heavily polluting cars and scooters beeped in all directions. More dead bodies, wrapped in bright colors and held above the sturdy shoulders of chanting escorts, marched between sacred cows and malignant dogs. For a short moment, I contemplated. Will my chapter conclude in the vibrant cloth? If I remain a lifelong bachelor, will my last days be spent here before the big voyage? Equal parts of peace and sadness filled me. In the distance, a prominent picture of a smiling Maharishi looked back. I knew that picture. My fifth birthday.

"Pundit Gupta, that is Maharishi," I said, pointing at the billboard.
"Oh, yes, yes. I understand you follow Maharishi-ji, yes?"

He said the words so quickly that it sounded like "Marshi-gee."

"I have been meditating since I was five."

"Oh, most excellent! It is said, to be born into a spiritual family is the greatest blessing from God. A blessing far greater than riches."

I thought of my parents, and a warm sensation filled the cab.

"Is Maharishi well known in India? I mean, is his success from bringing TM to different parts of the world well known among Indians?"

I was reluctant to ask, having heard an assortment of tales and rumors over the years. Like Bruce Lee taking flack for teaching his martial art to non-Chinese, stories circulated that meditation was not for Westerners. Some also alleged that TM was a big money-making enterprise and that the technique was essentially created for overly eager spiritual adepts, riding high on the magic bus of the sixties. I recalled rumblings in Fairfield; disenchanted ex-meditators claiming that Maharishi's extended kin were among the richest in India. Although a good bit of research verified the positive effects of meditation, it wasn't without its critics. I was curious how Indians perceived the export.

"He is most honored. Oh, yes, yes."

"Do most Indians approve of something rooted in Hinduism and the Veda to be shared with outsiders, like people in America?"

Pundit Gupta took several breaths and nodded. Briefly, I wondered if my candidness and questions were rude, but before I dwelled too long, he continued.

"It is an important question. Please do not take offense, my dear boy, but I will begin by saying this. America is a most wonderful country. A place many Indians would live, if given the chance. But, in spite of its grand riches, it is spiritually sick."

My eyes continued to look through the visor mirror, our gaze held. Kindness emanated throughout his face.

"I agree with you, Pundit Gupta, and I do not take offense."

"Yes, yes. America is like the father of the world. And India is the mother. When you have a family without a father or mother, it is very bad for the children, yes? And the mother helps the father, just as the father helps the mother. It must be balanced to be harmonious."

I nodded.

"Maharishi-ji must've recognized that his meditation must go to the great America, because it will be used to do good things for the entire world. It is much better for the most powerful nation to use the spiritual teachings of Mother India. It serves as a model for the whole world that way."

"Do you think meditation should be free, instead of making people pay for it?"

Pundit Gupta paused again and breathed deeply.

"I once heard a story, that Maharishi-ji spoke with a council before he left India. He had to ask permission to teach his meditation. The council agreed, but there would need to be some benefit to India."

"Benefit?" I asked.

"Yes. We are a poor nation, as you see. Many people do not have access to clean water, nourishing food, or medicine. It was agreed that some money must return to India to assist. But I do not know if the story is true. It is only what I heard."

"My last question, Pundit Gupta, and I hope it is okay I am asking all this, but is it possible to do too much meditation? Can a person meditate too much?" I asked.

I thought of Fairfield, and the strikingly high percentage of meditators I knew who seemed socially awkward, or perhaps with mental health issues.

Pundit Gupta let out a hearty laugh that filled the cab.

"Oh, my dear boy, please ask all your questions. I can practice my English." He chuckled as he answered.

"In terms of too much, yes. It is like most things in nature. A little bit can be very good, but one must have other pursuits. Too much of anything is not good."

"But what about the Sadhus, don't many of them meditate for hours each day?"

"Yes, yes, but they are rare. To live as a Sadhu, even among Indians, is a most deliberate calling. These men out here, not all are real Sadhu. Some are tricksters, who do not work but smoke hashish all day in the park. Not good, not good. The real ones do not ask for money, and they live simple lives in isolation. In the forest, up in the Himalaya. They have the physiology to meditate for long hours, but most people's karma is to be engaged in life, living fully. I am married, and I enjoy all the headaches of a family man." He laughed again.

It was helpful to hear a perspective from someone like Pundit Gupta. Fairfield, over the years after Maharishi's death in 2008, began an interesting transition. The town continued to attract eclectic groups of spiritual seekers, though they weren't exclusively followers of TM. As the anointed interpreters of Maharishi's guidance to establish a society based on Natural Law, the senior Movement echelon continued to disregard other spiritual practices, while doubling down on all things Vedic. Neighborhoods, and even a town called Vedic City, were established. Rather than just a technique to alleviate stress, some within the Movement turned it into a full-blown lifestyle. It worked for a few, but disenchantment also grew. People who had meditated for decades at this point, and diligently followed the rules, were skeptical that nobody had levitated yet. Some grew bitter, with the financial strain of low wages and fanaticism dissolving many families.

I visited my father in Fairfield regularly. There was the proverbial sweetness as we drove with our contraband coffees through the campus, reminiscing on the golden years when the Movement was in its zenith. The beautiful domes were freshly painted, and the campus grass was still unkempt and wily. But long faces were there, too. While seated on my cushion watching the old guard enter the dome, the gaunt, khaki-clad diehards walked more hunched and slowly, as the Movement loyalists aged. The dome numbers, which peaked in the thousands in the glory days, barely had a hundred. I was the youngest person there, by several decades. Beater vehicles caked in rust and dents still lined the parking lot. I wondered if they were truly living Natural Law.

I followed the clapping beat of Pundit Gupta's sandals. He picked up the flowing slack of his dhoti, as he briskly covered the muddy ground. The temple was twenty yards ahead, perched on a gentle hill. Beggars lined the path, some with horrific skin conditions. Pundit Gupta did not acknowledge them, as he walked confidently up the steps. A mere stone's throw away, the Ganges flowed. Half a dozen younger priests immediately went outside and greeted us. Pundit Gupta spoke quickly, and they scattered to their tasks.

The temple resembled an egg-shaped dome, similar to a Shiva *lingam*. Two rectangular chambers had an open breezeway, with blackened firepits dug in the ground. The sound of the Ganges and fragrant smoke temporarily transported me somewhere. I had not eaten for over fifty hours.

"My dear boy, this is Pundit Sharma. He maintains this temple, and he will lead the ceremony. I understand from your email we will also make offerings to help you find a suitable spouse for marriage."

A bit embarrassed by his comment, I nodded approvingly.

I handed Pundit Gupta the money, which he placed in his pocket without counting.

"Pundit Gupta, should I tip the priests when this is finished?" I asked.

"It is not necessary, my dear boy. You make small donation if you like, but remember in India, all spirituality is free. Do not pay for God, my son."

A tinge of sadness hovered, as Pundit Gupta descended the steps and disappeared in the white Mercedes. He radiated an energy of someone who had uncovered many secrets. His approach to spirituality and God were genuine and playful. For a brief second, I clutched to a fantasy of staying in Varanasi under his tutelage. But the thought dissolved just as quickly as it came. I passed my satchel to Pundit Sharma, a small, thin man with a gentle face. His bald head and wrinkles made his age cloudy, though I placed him somewhere in his fifties.

"Come, come," he waved, as he interlocked his hand with mine and led me to a firepit.

A teenage priest, an apprentice most likely, unfolded a dusty, decrepit rug and nodded for me to sit. Then he emptied the satchel, reverently placing the items at various points next to the long, square pit. He hummed mantras silently. There was fresh fruit, a coconut and several individual bananas brought from another room. He continued his song, as he pulled sandalwood powder, betel nut, different types of grains, and two large sacks of basmati rice that he stacked like a pyramid. Then, he dove deeper into the satchel, producing camphor, candles, a jar of ghee, and packets of incense. Another apprentice centered a three-foot golden cobra statue in the middle of the pit, along with an egg-shaped lingam placed on top of a *yoni*. On the drive, Pundit Gupta confided that real cobras often visited the temple and occasionally wrapped themselves around the altar; a most auspicious omen he explained, that affirmed the power of the consecrated space. As I scanned the ground uneasy about the possibility of venomous visitors, Pundit Sharma passed two brass bowls, then pointed to the Ganges.

"Water," he said.

I descended the steps toward the water, as two beggars looked up from the ground and raised their hands. One of them had the saddest eyes I'd ever seen. Rishi's words that the universe was in perfect harmony reverberated within, though I whispered a prayer regardless: *Lord Shiva, please help these dear souls. Please help alleviate their suffering. May they find grace and peace.* I waded into the murky water, to my knees, chanting *Om Namah Shiva*, as I filled the bowls with the pungent liquid. An empty chip bag, soiled towels, and other rubbish brushed against my ankles. Ten yards ahead, a bloated dog carcass with a partially visible skull floated by.

I handed the bowls to Pundit Sharma, then sat on the carpet. He tied a strip of red and yellow string around my right wrist. Then he turned two of his fingers into a pair of scissors, pantomiming that I should not cut the strings. I recalled from a previous ceremony, years earlier, that the *kalawa* should stay on until it naturally fell off. It might take weeks, or months even, but it would leave on its own time.

Pundit Sharma walked into an adjacent room, where a dozen pundits sat with crossed legs. He spoke deliberately, "Neek-o-las Osborne." They repeated it until Pundit Sharma seemed satisfied.

"Okay," he said, as he took a seat beside me.

The ceremony began as Pundit Sharma chanted mantras. At different intervals, the other two priests joined in, producing a deep baritone that echoed throughout the chamber. I closed my eyes, feeling a beautiful cool breeze. The camphor and incense swirled above, as the Ganges flowed below. I was in the middle of a holy web, immediately transported out of my body. For a brief second, I felt completely weightless, hovering somewhere beyond the Earth. A priest lit a ghee lamp, then circularly moved it around the cobra and lingam. The buttery smell reminded me of popcorn at the theater. I sat still with closed eyes, until Pundit Sharma motioned me to take a pinch of rice and throw it into the fire saying, *svaha*. We repeated it numerous times, as the Sanskrit names of the planets were called. One of the pundits in the other room chanted my name. A surge of kundalini energy shot up my spine, making me gyrate like a cobra. I knew this sensation from Indonesia and from deep meditations in the dome. It felt like those shock paddles that doctors use, but there was no pain. The exhilarating strike ran like a current. In different moments, my eyes opened, and the lingam was decorated with sandalwood paste and patterns of white, yellow, and red. A priest leaned over the fire, then marked my forehead with his fingers.

Pundit Sharma handed a bowl of milk, then smiled for me to pour it over the lingam. Then he handed one of the water bowls to me and smiled again. As the water cascaded over the lingam, images of high school Townies that wrestled and bow hunted, hovered, along with pictures of hardened military men I knew. A belly roar of glee purged out as I considered their inner dialogue of such a sight. I relished in the humor of the divine, growing up in such a bizarre way. The emaciated and effeminate spiritual warriors of Fairfield. My hardwired obsession to constantly test and prove my masculinity. It was all just nonsense.

Pure illusion, that somehow made sense, too. I thought of the planets and how they brought such unique teachings to my life. Hearing my purificatory laughter, the pundits giggled along. A hysterical sensation bubbled. *This is God, Nick! It doesn't have to be uptight all the time! Let go, man!* Then a quieter mood moved in. The power of my mantra reverberated in sync with the melodic hymns of the priests. I repeated it delicately, as thoughts dissolved. I was somewhere on the bottom of the ocean. Stillness. It was dark, but not negative. There was no voice, but a wavy tingle of light.

> *Lord Shiva, please bless my family. Please take care of them and keep us vital in our health. Please protect my mother and father and their spouses. Please protect my sister and her husband. Please provide extra protection and love around my nephew. Let the world be kind to him. Let him know how much he is loved. Please bring a remedy for autism in our lifetime. Please let my heart forgive those who I feel crossed me. Please allow me to let it go. Please bring forgiveness to anyone I've wronged. Please bless me in living from my inner king.*

I repeated the names of my three loves. Tender moments lying in bed late on a Sunday, sipping coffee after making love, brought warmth and longing. The profound energy love brings to the mundane swirled in. The flames flickered as more rice and fragrant mysteries were tossed into it. "Svaha ..."

> *Please bring me love. Please bring me love of the highest order. A true soul mate, who is awake, and who can teach me. Please bring me a career where my heart is fully invested. A dharma. Let me be a conduit to spread whatever messages and teachings you want circulated. Let me help alleviate suffering in this world. In your most wonderful name, I sit here with an open heart, Jai Shiva, Jai Shiva, Jai Shiva ... Om Shanti, Shanti, Shanti.*

I don't know for certain how long I stayed under. Not asleep but wandering somewhere. Pundit Sharma gently brushed his elbow against my arm. The other priests were seated with their eyes closed, whispering mantras. I felt lighter, like the morning after the Ayahuasca ceremony, though cleaner. Something significant was dropped. Certain poisons and baggage thrown to the fire. Appetite surged, as my brain processed pangs of hunger. The pundits in the other room continued chanting, as Pundit Sharma assembled the various fruits and sweets that rested on the altar.

"*Prasad*," he said, motioning his hand to his mouth. "Eat."

Slowly integrating back into waking reality, my active brain fired on intense cylinders. It sifted through the memory of Ganges water sprinkled over the holy bounty, just moments earlier. I ruminated on the dead dog. Internet warnings of raw sewage and parasites. Even a few drops could hospitalize. Was this what Guru-ji sensed in his pulse diagnosis, which seemed so ludicrous at the time? I considered the beggars out front, strategizing the best way to donate my prasad to them, but Pundit Sharma intercepted my thoughts.

"Cannot give away. Must eat."

I held the offerings in my hands like a newborn, then moved them circularly around the fire, paying homage to the deities. I put a handful of sweets in my mouth and relished the penetrating sugar rush that ensued, before peeling a banana and cracking the coconut. Its juices dribbled off my chin, dripping onto my bony midriff. If sickness showed itself, so be it. I was in the hands of the sacred, now.

******

A residual bliss carried over from the ceremony, as I touched the red and yellow string on my wrist. The colored markings on my forehead smeared from the sweat, but several Sadhus stopped me on the street anyway and asked about them. When I said, "Jai Shiva," their toothless grins widened. God is a universal glue.

My second week in Varanasi waned, prompting consideration of the next destination. Originally, the sun-drenched beaches of Goa crowned the itinerary, especially as I traversed snow in the Himalayas. Dad went there on his journey, and he said it was worth checking out. But a few minutes scanning different chat boards and online travel logs suggested it was nothing more than a rave now. I was forty, well, forty-one to be precise, and had no business rolling on ecstasy, or perving on the young. Rishikesh was the other plan, though like Ubud, it was an alleged yoga and man-bun paradise. People from all over the world converged there, specifically to study yoga among the well known. An influx of international vegans and man-buns worried me, though everything online suggested Rishikesh was the spot. Maharishi spent a good bit of time there, and his famous ashram where he hosted the Beatles was there. I made a note to look into Ayurvedic retreats in Rishikesh when I returned to my hotel.

The following day, I was scheduled to visit an ancient Durga temple about an hour from town. After that, I would meander around Sarnath, where the Buddha gave his first sermon. With my days in Varanasi winding down, the spiritual asceticism brought boredom and longing for visceral experience. An adventure beckoned. Like the brothel in Vietnam, I tried to erase the Internet trolls who cheered emphatically of the famous Blue Lassi shop; the delicious homemade yogurt served in intricate clay bowls. Legend had it that subtle moves and gestures could result in a highly potent *bhang* being added for nominal cost. I had not had marijuana in nearly a year; I think it was with the swingers that tried to accost D and I in Cancun. My intention to be totally clean on the journey was largely intact, but the lower Self and its conniving charms convinced that coloring outside the lines was a necessary part of the illusory dance. I soon found myself inside the dizzying maze of Varanasi's labyrinth, walking the steps of an excited explorer. A mission.

Nondescript signs, like illumined breadcrumbs, eventually led to the Blue Lassi. It was a tiny, open-breeze shop, just a hair larger than a restaurant kitchen. Shallow steps ascended to a concrete floor where an unmatched and threadbare set of chairs and couches were dispersed. The walls were adorned with passport pictures, some in color and others black and white. The black-and-white ones resembled mugshots, but I squashed those energies as best I could.

A man of unknowable age with deep creases across his forehead, wearing a tattered white kurta, sat on the cool concrete floor staring into a stainless bowl. The wooden dowel spun efficiently, as fresh ingredients were tossed into it. From the big bowl, the man swiftly transferred the nectar into intricate clay pots. A handsome teen with wavy jet-black hair collected the bowls and with equal competence delivered them to the exclusively Indian clientele.

"Hello, sir. Where are you from?"
"Hello. America."

The handsome boy smiled and stood proudly, as if rising to sing the national anthem. Up close, his Western dress was impeccably tidy, something that bewildered given my perpetually sweaty and sloven look.

"Oh, yes, very good, very good. Welcome to our shop. We are the oldest lassi in Kashi, and one of the oldest in India. People come from all over the world for our famous lassi. We've served prime ministers, many celebrities."

The extensive menu was written in Hindi with misspelled English words next to colorful pictures of fruits and other treats. The choices were endless: chocolate, coconut and almond butter; mango, papaya, cinnamon, and turmeric. A small team of police officers turned the corner and dawdled near the man spinning the pot. Their arsenal dangled from shiny black belts, revealing tattered batons and sad-looking revolvers. The man with the creased face nodded after one of the officers spoke to him. A different officer stared in my direction, then diverted his eyes as I smiled. The other two lit cigarettes.

"Sir, what would you like?"

"I need a little longer to decide. Your menu is most impressive."

The boy nodded approvingly, then disappeared to a group that beckoned him from the platform above. Every seat was occupied, with another dozen people sitting on the ground.

The officers soon collected their wares, before disappearing down the narrow, snakelike path that led to the Ganga.

I took a few breaths, then held my gaze on the boy until we eventually linked.

"Yes, yes, sir, and what have you decided?" he asked, running toward me.

I cursorily scanned the room, holding the menu an inch from my nose.

"Um, do you have other things, or just what is on the menu?" I whispered.

The boy grimaced, then shook his head.

"I am sorry, sir, I do not ..."

I interrupted.

"Uh, what I mean is ..."

Images of Troy and I in the backseat of the Tuk Tuk scoring weed in Thailand flashed through. Pangs of nostalgia and amusement with them. Twenty years later, in holy India, and I'm still pulling the same shit.

"Uh, do you have Lord Shiva's ... um," I began.

The boy's hair shook side to side, and his brows furrowed.

"Um. Cannabis? Can you put some cannabis or *bhang*, I think, into my, uh, my lassi?"

The boy's confused affect expeditiously shifted to an eerie glow. He beamed, as arcs of light entered the cavernous space, then reflected off his shiny hair like a crown.

"Bhang? Bhang? You want bhang in lassi?"

I nodded sheepishly, the menu covering my forehead.

"Yes, yes, no problem. No problem. It is five American dollars."

"Mm hmm," I squeaked.

The boy, even quicker than before, hopped down the same path as the officers. Briefly, I considered getting up and walking away, perhaps to the nearest temple to beg forgiveness. But the Wild Man would have none of that. Less than a minute later, two men in Western dress, perhaps a year or two older, accompanied my friend.

"What's up, G," the older of the two said, extending a closed fist.

I awkwardly fist pumped him and handed over the equivalent of five dollars with another two dollars.

They walked toward the elder and handed him a brown bag. The old man did not raise his head but continued to stare into the spinning bowl. I scanned the shop, relieved my charades had gone unnoticed.

******

It was half a mile to the fabric store if I didn't get lost. India's rock concert continued at full volume, the congestion overwhelmingly intensified as I left the musty labyrinth. Touts and rickshaws swarmed at an intersection, though I didn't acknowledge them. I needed to see Rishi. I had questions. At our last encounter, he spoke of the demon of egotism, and its vise grip on the Western world. He emphasized the importance of solitude and of maintaining a disciplined practice to expand the inner life. He confided the Western poisons were spreading to India, and I thought of the fist-bump kid with the bag of weed and Eminem t-shirt. I didn't want to see Rishi in an altered state, as most Hindus consider drugs to be a lower path. But my time in Varanasi was quickly ending. I foolishly wondered if being stoned would help me digest Rishi's wisdom more easily, or perhaps give a definitive answer of whether or not he was a crafty fraud. Crossing the hectic road on wobbly feet, I summoned Joseph Campbell to keep me steady.

A Ronin's Tale

Perhaps some of us have to go through dark and devious ways before we can find the river of peace, or the highroad to the soul's destination.

The fabric store where Rishi often stood was within eyesight, but while crossing the frenzied mess, a street kid ambushed.

"Sir, sir, my uncle is a most famous astrologer, and he told me to speak with you."

"Uh huh," I said.

"Please, sir, please stop for just one moment. Let me tell you. My uncle is a wise man, and he's seen you wear the markings of a Shivaite. He has read charts of many famous people, including Americans. He is most willing to read your horoscope for free."

"Is that right?"

"Yes, please stop, sir."

"Free, huh?" I asked.

"Yes. And he also sells many beautiful necklaces that you will be given a most generous discount for. Please come visit my uncle's shop. We will make some chai, and ..."

"Thank you, my friend, but I am actually going to meet someone."

"Oh, just one minute, sir. The shop is very close. Here, here, look at this picture."

The young man handed over a Polaroid, and I stopped walking. I lifted my sunglasses onto the crown of my head and inspected carefully, then laughed heartily. Goldie smiled back.

"Is your uncle the famous astrologer that worked with this actress? Is he this man right here?" I asked, pointing at the picture.

"Yes, yes, that is him! He is the most famous astrologer in Kashi!"

"I tell you what, I need to meet my friend, but we can walk to his store now for just a minute."

The street kid took hold of my hand, as we waded through the brisk traffic, catty-corner from the fabric shop. Outside the store, a short, thin man with a black mustache and gold chain stood smiling. His overly polished shoes pointed upward on the tip, and he wore white slacks that looked professionally tailored.

"Ah, hello, my friend. Please come into my shop. I will give you a most perfect price," he began.

The boy spoke quickly to the man, then turned to me.

"This is the great astrologer I told you about, sir. He also owns this shop."

I scrutinized the man, who appeared a solid decade younger than me.

"I see, and you are the great astrologer who worked with Goldie?"

"Indeed, sir. One of my best clients." The man grinned as he spoke.

The boy and hustler continued to converse, as I waded into the traffic. The surrounding colors brightened intensely, as each step became a laborious pull from quicksand. A giggling sensation, similar to what Troy and I felt in our alley missions, sprung to life. The genie was coming out of the bottle. Once across the street, I sauntered past the beggars, looking for Rishi. Then I stopped, locking eyes with a Sadhu. He sat half-naked in a loincloth, holding a flute-like object. His long unkempt dreadlocks and beard flowed like a lion's mane, as did the multiple sets of rudraksha beads draped around his thin neck. Next to him were two large baskets. A small brass trident was perched on top of one. I pulled some rupees from my pocket.

"Sit, sit," he said.

I squatted, as the Sadhu lifted his trident and removed the top from the baskets. Then he gently slapped his hand down. Within seconds, a black hood shot upright and swayed side to side in unison to his flute. Beggars and street kids ran over, surrounding us, as the Sadhu moved his cobras into a trance. I stared into the magnificent creatures, feeling a similar sway. Electric colors pulsed from all directions, as did a chorus of elation. Wealthier spectators retrieved phones and snapped pictures. The Sadhu moved his instrument for several minutes before putting it down. Then he effortlessly picked up one of the snakes. I placed my hands in front.

"Oh, no, no ..." I protested. "Please, no ..."

The Sadhu cackled like a madman, showing a mouth devoid of teeth. Instantly, the cobra slithered onto my wrist and inched up my arm. I extended it as far as possible, while the holy man fixed the other on the left side. The bhang's medicine turned each thought and image into a slowed, observable artifact. Bumps on my skin rose as they slithered in unison, then wrapped around my armpits and postured above my shoulders. Their opened hoods, inches from my face, swayed like flowers in a soft breeze.

"Shiva! Shiva!" the man clapped.

"Shiva! Jai Shiva," the crowd repeated.

Some unseen faces called out mantras I faintly recognized.

"Yes, yes, Shiva," I said.

"Please take."

He remained in his ecstasy, exhaling dreamy clouds from his nose. He passed the clay chillum to a man with open sores, holding a broken match. I cautiously waved my arms.

One of the cobras stubbornly remained on my right arm, then hissed as the man attempted to retrieve it. I stretched outward as far as I could. The Sadhu, with some effort, uncoiled its tail and tossed it into its basket. I dropped more rupees onto the ground as beads of sweat slid from my cheeks.

Rishi was not in front of the fabric store. I contemplated if he was part of the witnesses, but there must have been a thousand people within the block, meandering from all directions. I walked up the steps, looking side to side, as the scene evolved into a kaleidoscope of mandala patterns. The vibrancy of each color had a corresponding sound attached to it. Beggars with scarred hands and empty bowls moved closer. Nausea and dehydration warned it was time to retreat to safety and sanctuary. But I summoned what coherence was left, committed to see Rishi and absorb the last of his knowledge.

"Good day, sir, please come in. I have the most beautiful fabrics in all of Kashi, and I will give you a most generous price."

I looked up, trying to decipher if there was indeed someone standing there.

"Actually, sir, I am looking for someone. He works in your shop."

"What do you mean?" the figure asked, cocking his head.

The man shooed away the onslaught of street kids and women with infants who pulled at my shirtsleeve. I placed my hand onto a pole, leaning into it.

"Friend … name Rishi. Work here. Available?" I whispered.

A jumbled mess of gelatinous words barely strung together. I descended rapidly, as illogical swirls from each sense poked and overpowered.

The man's face contorted into a scowl, as he conversed with a teenage boy behind him.

"Oh no," the man began. "That is not possible. I am the owner of this shop, and only my sons work here. No one else. Please, please, come in. I will make us chai."

"No, siiirrrrr … Need to find friend. Man. Stands here. Each day. Nice dress."

The owner stood motionless, awash in blank expression.

"Many people walk past my shop each day. But I would know of such a man who stood out front. There is no such man. Please come, I will show something beautiful for your wife or mother."

Had I gone to the wrong place? Admittedly, the blocks were overwhelming. The entire town was. The heat and pandemonium. A vegetarian diet of low calories. Cobras dangling from my arms. The lassi. It all must've affected me. My mind wasn't processing things efficiently. That had to be it. I eventually returned to my room after considerable effort, sitting under the fan, peaking and teetering on a total loss of reality. Mother India was humbling. Only two weeks on her soil, and she punched harder than the fists in Thailand, but dried my tears and sung lullabies too. Eventually, my soul was coaxed back, and I steadied my laptop on a shallow pillow affixed to my belly. I looked at Ayurvedic clinics in Rishikesh and sent emails. Then I looked up Goldie. Several pictures of her, beautifully adorned in traditional Hindu attire. Some near the holy Ganga. Indeed, she'd been here. Then I read about her beloved teacher and astrologer. He died in 2008.

Chapter 41

THE REWARD

Fall 2017, A Classroom in the Midwest

Our Hero did it. He successfully took out Johnny Lawrence with the iconic crane kick, stunning the crowd and silencing the Cobra Kai. Even Daniel's girlfriend, Ali, stormed the mat and fell into his arms, while Johnny handed the trophy over and congratulated him. Does it get any better than this? This is a golden story that depicts how the mythological world plays out in what we call real life. Of course, it doesn't happen so cleanly for most of us, but it gives us a sense of the stages and a map in which we can consider our own lives.

What is the reward for Daniel? He has his golden trophy, and his name in the winner's bracket, but those are merely symbols. What is he really rewarded with? Newfound confidence? Self-worth? A deeper understanding of his inner patterning and limitations? The reward is a beautiful combination of internal and external boons. What I mean is that the Hero is given the gold of a rebirth, along with some tangible treasure, too. His character is stronger. His soul, tempered. For Daniel, he is also recognized within the martial art community and his high school with respect. Throughout his entire life, the Hero can call upon the memories of his journey for inspiration and to access the fire inside him.

We need to remember that Daniel accomplished his journey in a matter of months. As we've discussed, our entire lifetime is one extended hero's journey. Though many mini journeys will occur in between. For some reason, it's easy to mistakenly believe that transformation must take an enormous amount of time. It doesn't. We can begin the process of becoming our best version of ourselves at any moment.

The Reward

What I personally feel is the most magnificent part of this dance, the true crown of the reward, is recognition that no matter what life throws at me—the most ugly and sinister things it can think of—I will be okay. I will get through it. Sure, it will suck at the time. It might even bring me to my knees in absolute misery and humility. And it will leave scars. But I'll get through it. I will manage the beautiful pendulum that inevitably swings for each of us. This to me is faith. Faith of the highest order, not just in something divine, but of that pure divinity that runs through each of us.

Chapter 42

Ayurveda

October 2019, Rishikesh, India

> What you seek is seeking you.[30]
> —Rumi

I negotiated ten days of Ayurvedic treatment after several back-and-forth emails with the owner. We settled on fifty a day, including room and board. About 10 percent of what it would cost at home. Ayurveda was offered through a ritzy clinic in Fairfield that even attracted celebrities. Rumors of who was staying just north of town buzzed throughout the coffee shops. Sometimes, actual spottings occurred. I once shared conversation with a famous Brit comic, not having any idea who he was. But the price tag for India's holiest medicine was far beyond the reach of my working-class lineage.

In truth, I wasn't fixated on Guru-ji's fear skit. I believe in the merits of Ayurveda, and getting purified at the source made sense. The entire trip had evolved into a purification of sorts, mainly for the soul. But stuff in the body also needed flushing. My driver dropped me off late in the evening after an hour slog from Dehradun. It was dark, but in the distance, Mother Ganga continued her flow. She was much cleaner here, having just run down the cool mountains. Dr. Patesh stood erect in the lobby of the regal cement building, dressed in a clean white dhoti. From the center of the cathedral ceiling, a dapper chandelier illuminated the spotless tiled floor. He remarked early in our conversation that he

---

30 Mafi, *Rumi's Little Book of Wisdom.*

was approaching sixty, and admittedly, he looked much younger. After a brief overview of the facility and his medical credentials, he passed me a lukewarm cup of tea. The smell triggered memories of early years.

"Mr. Neekolas, I am so happy you will be spending time with us. However, I must warn you that a group of young yoga students are here, and they are most noisy. It is a rather large group, but they leave shortly. I assure you that peace will be restored promptly."

I sipped the fennel-tinted broth musing if attractive women were in residence.

"My, what beautiful tattoos."

Dr. Patesh lifted my right sleeve, then turned my arm, inspecting closely.

"My goodness, this is Lord Shiva," he exclaimed.

"Yes," I said, shyly.

Outside the temples in Thailand, signs written in different languages explicitly chastised tattoos of the Buddha. They were considered offensive. I sought a more modest dress in India to avoid this faux pas, but it was just too damn stifling.

"Are you Hindu?" he asked.

"That's kinda tricky to answer. Lord Shiva is my ishta devata. But I also do the rosary and pray to Jesus."

Dr. Patesh cocked his head.

"That is quite uncommon, yes? I mean, for an American," he commented.

I paused reflectively.

"Just as Mother Ganga flows through many towns here, she is still one river."

His cocked head centered, as a broad smile revealed perfectly white teeth.

"Ah, fabulous. Yes, God is one. And to portray God on the temple of your body is most wonderful. Now, from your email, you are also interested in astrology, yes?"

"I am interested, though I would like to know more. I met a few frauds in Varanasi, so …"

"Oh, yes, yes. There are many tricksters in Kashi. But I assure you that our Swami-ji is a most honest person who only speaks the truth. I will invite him for tea later this week. Then you decide."

A taller man with a red dot on his forehead stood close by observing, but he didn't speak. After our brief interlude, Dr. Patesh motioned toward my duffel bag, which the man promptly retrieved.

A Ronin's Tale

The room was small, but clean. The single bed had a thin mattress and two layers of lean bedding. A modern fan hovered from the ceiling. In the corner, a wooden desk sat with an unmatching chair. There was no Internet access of any kind, nor any television on the premises. I did have my own bathroom and a Western toilet. I sat on the edge of the bed, as a warm feeling buzzed on Rishikesh. Maharishi spent time here. The Beatles visited here. Many mystics I came across over the years mentioned the magical paradise, that like Varanasi, did not serve any meat or alcohol. In fact, there was actually an ordinance on the books that forbade it. I would have two treatments of different sort each day, with a basti on Wednesday, and another on Friday.

On primary roads in India, it is not uncommon to see people pulled off the side, squatting. The bashful and prepared set up makeshift enclosures, like a draped sheet, while the others just let it all hang out. In the states, it's one of those taboos we just don't give energy to, at least on the outward stage. But we all do it, just as we breathe. I reassured my students before a public-speaking exercise to rest easy on the thought that every person in the audience has had explosive diarrhea at some point. Wealth and credentials don't matter, there are moments when the only true God is a clean toilet and a handful of fluffy cotton. There are moments that inevitably come along when the trousers and *chonies* are barely to the ankles when all hell breaks loose. Travelers to the far side of the earth understand it better than most. Long bus rides and trains without facilities; a sour stomach that wails sinister songs. These thoughts can haunt a soul. Harmony and contentment on the rugged trails of international wandering are largely tied to one's bowels.

Thankfully, my first morning belly rumble was gentle and on schedule. Seated upright on the porcelain throne twenty minutes before yoga, something below captured my eye. Just inches from my feet, the small circular rug flickered. I wiped away crusted sleep and adjusted my focus. I stared into the rug, anticipating. Sure enough, another movement. It was subtle, but the shaggy fluff stirred as if a moderate breeze blew through. I finished my business, then stepped cautiously over the carpet to wash my hands, never shifting my gaze. The brief movement to the sink spurred more activity underneath the fibrous shag. I said a silent prayer it wasn't a spider, then rapidly picked the rug up with my thumb and tip of my pointer finger, holding it cockeyed like someone else's underpants. Not far from my big toes, a three-inch menace with red tail stood motionless. My entire body fluttered with a jolt of energy. Sensing this, it wasted no time readying its stinger and

Ayurveda

pinchers like a boxer. I didn't blink, and neither did it.
Damn, a red scorpion, my inner voice shrieked. I thought briefly of the satisfying sound of a hard crunch. The only thing nearby were my flip-flops, and they were in the other room under the bed. It would have time to scurry and hide, ruining all rejuvenation for the week. A forceful whack would do it, though. It would be quick and painless, and I'd hit it more than once. A small hand towel hung from a stainless ring, but no blunt objects of any kind were close. And what about the karma? I was on some of the holiest soil now, about to further my fasting and devotional rites. Surely, killing one of God's creatures, even a poisonous one, would be a setback. Then, I peered underneath the sink at the metal trash can. Something mysterious confided it was the better option. The little guy held his ground in our standoff. As smoothly as I could, I tiptoed closer to the bin and flipped it upside down. The can had a waffle like patterning, and almost immediately the scorpion climbed its wall. I flipped the can upright, then watched as it ran circularly; angrily. It attempted to climb again, forcing me to spin the can and continually adjust my hands. I placed the bin on a table, as I threw on a pair of shorts without a shirt. Descending the three flights briskly, several Chinese patients stared suspiciously. I meandered the last steps, past the lobby when the man with the red dot who carried my duffel the previous evening called out.

"Mr. Neek, good morning, sir. Everything okay?"

"Yes, hello, Vipak. I am taking this scorpion outside," I said distracted.

Vipak inched closer, peering into the can.

"Oh, goodness. And where did you find this naughty creature?"

"In my bathroom, under the rug. I nearly stepped on him," I said.

"Oh, good heavens," Vipak sighed. "That would make you most ill. It is quite peculiar he was on the third floor. That has never happened before."

I pressed past the communal living room where a cluster of non-yoga goers sat sipping tea and staring out a large window into the dense jungle. Not long after reaching the grass, I tipped the bin over and said farewell to my friend. Another cryptic test completed.

After an intensive yoga hour, Dr. Patesh and I met for our daily check-in. As customary, he grabbed my wrist and pressed firmly, closing his eyes, and whispered to himself. Before this, I filled out a questionnaire that asked about my diet, meat intake, exercise, and how I felt in certain climates. Was my hair thick or fine? My skin, dry or oily?

Any issues surrounding "bed pleasures?" Dr. Patesh opened his eyes and gently let go of my wrist, exclaiming,
"Pitta-Vata!"
"Okay, and what does that mean, exactly?"
"My dear boy, it means you have the fire of Lord Shiva running through your veins! It will be my job to cool you," he said as he laughed.
"Yeah, I run pretty hot, Dr. Patesh."
"Very hot! You are a passionate lover, my boy!" He snickered.
I looked down and giggled shyly.
"You are not vegetarian, no?"
"No. Well, I've not had meat for over a month, and I won't be eating any in India. But I feel like I need it."
"Need?" he asked, perplexed.
"Well, I'm a physical person, and being a total vegetarian at this stage in life doesn't feel right. It will weaken me."
Dr. Patesh sat upright, a skeptical expression clearly visible.
"The American diet is most toxic. Too much meat, too much refined sugar, too much salt, and too much in general. Excessive! Your organs are healthy, your muscles supple, but you have to cool your body, or you will develop health issues later. And I will recommend when you return to America to eat less meat."
"Like, what kind of issues?" I asked, distracted by his comment.
Dr. Patesh took hold of my wrist again and pushed down firmly with his fingertips.
"Fire, what we call *agni*. It is a problem for Pittas. Temper short. Hot climate, alcohol, spicy food, all produce agni. The Vata is nerves. The anxious mind that never slows. Sleep disturbance, fidgety, talks too much, forgets to, how do you say, 'smell the roses.'"
Then he added, "Most intellectuals have Vata imbalance. Moving the body is most critical to channel that energy."
I nodded, impressed.
"Your body is healthy, but as you age, you will need the yoga and *pranyama*. Do you drink coffee? Your blood pressure is a tad high, yes?"
"Well, I've not had much on this trip, but I do love my coffee. And, yes, my blood pressure has always been high. It runs in my family, on my father's side."
"Yes, yes, you Americans and Europeans like your coffee. I will recommend you drink only Vata tea, lukewarm. It is much better. The coffee angers your blood pressure and heats you up."

Ayurveda

"And what kind of health issues could I be susceptible for?" I repeated, my natural nervousness showing.

"Hard to say, but not too serious. Your liver needs to be detoxified, from your heat. Then we will build your *ojas* to strengthen your body."

As I sat in his humid office, beads of sweat trickled down my forehead. I wiped my face with my sleeve. Seeing this, Dr. Patesh laughed heartily.

"My dear boy, you will use your heat to light many beautiful fires for God. But first, we cool you down. This morning, a peppermint steam bath with herbs and then a sesame oil massage."

I rose from the chair, reflecting on evenings at the bar, baskets of spicy chicken wings, and ice-cold IPAs. Sometimes it was festive, other times, work recovery. Our emotions and diets are certainly linked.

The lack of a physical outlet, aside from yoga, and the absence of a phone and Internet slowed time considerably. Between treatments, I walked the dusty paths into Rishikesh and across the iconic Lakshman Jhula bridge, into a busier sector of town. Sadhus seated on the bridge held tridents and begging bowls as collections of black-faced monkeys perched and angrily screeched at tourists making eye contact. Below, a dozen yellow rafts drifted down the clean, refreshingly cool river. Whitewater rafting was recommended by a European guest at the clinic, and I made note to check it out.

It was in Rishikesh that serenity lingered. My first four days were languidly pleasant, as I dipped into the river to purify. On one occasion, I brought a prasad of fruit and flowers, and donated them to the fast current. Upon releasing the offering, a large cow walked toward me. I stared into its kind eyes as it inched closer, eventually collapsing its head into my shoulder, remaining still. I embraced it for several seconds, remembering my beloved sheltie, MacGuyver, who could read my energy so clearly. On particularly stressful days, he'd saunter close, collapsing onto me for cuddles. This mysterious cow remained clutched, as collections of Indians strolling the beach spoke rapidly to one another, some snapping pictures with their phones.

The daily rations were minimal, primarily vegetable broths and bland liquids. The midday meal was the heartiest because it had two chapatis smeared with ghee, though it still didn't break five hundred calories. I cinched my shorts tightly before yoga and rubbed my hand over my bony hip. The day before my first basti, I fasted as requested. As the technician readied the concoction and lubed up the plastic tube, I noticed a digital scale tucked underneath the table. He smiled when

I pulled it out, turning it on for me and switching the kilo button to pounds. To my astonishment it read 195. I had lost approximately thirty-five pounds since my arrival in Bangkok nearly eight months earlier. *Detach from the body. Detach from vanity. It is just the shell, Nick.*

The evening after my basti, I sat in the downstairs lounge with a noticeably docile mind. My forehead dry, I sank into the other frame of India. The clinic was like a library after the young tourists left, though their spark was missed. The fierce giggles that emanated over morning tea, and the shine they brought back after rigorous hours of yoga. It was all silence now, except for the jungle critters. The inner work and literal purges taking place required levity for balance, and they were the salt that made the watery broth more palatable. Under the dim lighting, I journaled. I looked at my shins and ran my fingers over certain scars. I considered the eight months away; an unplanned montage of physical tests at camps and along steep mountainous trails. Conversations and meals shared with perfect strangers. Internal shifts and planted seeds that I knew confidently would germinate and eventually heal old wounds. Then thoughts went to Varanasi; the burning ghats and sting of punching poverty. Single mothers and lepers. Did they really accept their existence as mere karma, so casually stated by Rishi and other wise ones?

The previous day, I went to the balcony with Swami-ji for what was supposed to be a thirty-minute astrological reading. I remained in the high nook with Swami for nearly three hours.

"Welcome back to your true home. Mother India has missed you, my dear child."

Swami-ji, only using my requisite birth information, proceeded to mention periods of significant life events; my parents' divorce at thirteen, then leaving high school at sixteen. He told me that I was in a "death period" from thirteen to twenty-three, and that my antics could have resulted in the end, or at least the loss of a limb. But I was now in a much safer period. He pinpointed my three significant relationships, including my most recent, the beautiful and kind Christian realtor, D, whom I continued to think of. It took significant willpower to not reach out to her, especially in moments of loneliness or reminiscence. I sometimes awoke in the early hours, temporarily adrift, though wondering if she was beside me. As waking reality took over, a wash of longing hovered.

"Your chart is a most fascinating one. You have some of the most beautiful yogas, though it also shows difficulties and many fluctuations.

You are very much a monk, but your karma places you on a stage of some kind."

I leaned closer.

"You will not become the next Brad Pitt I'm afraid, but your chart is most beautifully unfolding toward career fame of some kind. I sense you had a most stressful career change occur in the late part of 2018, though it was a blessing, my child. There was a necessary shift that stripped you of many attachments you no longer need. Is what I say correct?"

I had not mentioned my work, or job loss, to anyone at the clinic.

"Your life has been one of motion, much like the waves that form when Mother Ganga comes down the mountain. She is coldest and more aggressive. But she softens the further she flows. Your life has been a series of movements. You have come down the mountain quite forcefully. You are ready to flow, yes?"

I nodded.

"Will it always be like that, Swami-ji? The movement, I mean. I am a bit burdened by all of that, and ..."

He let out a belly roar that echoed off the top deck. Faceless creatures in the jungle stirred below.

"God will give you exactly what you need when you need it, my child. But your astrology is such that the first forty-five years are chaotic. You are forty-one, so it may be like this another few years."

"And then?"

"And then you should begin a more stable time."

I hesitated to ask about love and marriage, embarrassed that I was continuing to place my trust in mystics about it.

Swami-ji looked intently at my chart, as a soft hum or prayer mantra descended from his lips. He repeated it, then stared into the chart without saying anything for several seconds.

"You are to be married this life, my child. Were you married in 2006?" he asked.

I thought of my first love. We didn't talk about it much, but the energy was certainly there.

"No. But I was with someone special."

"Mm."

"Can you say more, Swami-ji? I mean, more about that time frame and her."

"Well, it was best you did not marry. You were not ready."

I thought of her and her son. A loving warmth breezed through the balcony.

"Do you sense a time frame when I will meet a potential wife?"

Swami-ji continued to inspect my chart, his eyes not leaving the spotted white paper.

"It is quite strange, my child. I do not see a formal marriage for a couple years, though I sense you have already met a significant person. I also see a foreigner, perhaps."

"Foreigner?"

"Yes, someone different; maybe from a different country or caste. Something distinctively different from you. Have you met such a person on your travels?"

I sorted through a handful of shared dinners and walks with attractive, kind women. They were platonic, though. A brief image of Brooke and the Gili fiasco flashed by, bringing excited energies in its wake. A hopeful wonder if a great white chomped Scott while he was diving. I struggled to remember if I'd given her my contact info. Then, I thought of D. Was it my destiny to return to her?

"Swami-ji, can you elaborate?"

"The timing, my dear child, is perplexing. There are windows, pockets of time for meeting someone most significant over the coming years. But I am perplexed you have not met someone on your travels. I cannot sense if this is your bride-to-be, but someone karmic sharing is close by."

"*Karmic sharing?*"

"Past incarnation. A person from your previous life who returns. You will recognize her immediately, most notably her eyes. All relationships, my dear child, are karmic. Some people have karma to marry, to have children, to be fulfilled, or to be anguished by a most unfortunate relationship. That is their karmic contract. Some have karma to be Sadhus; married to God, living a chaste life. You have many Sadhu qualities, but …" Swami-ji paused, then released another roar that rattled the jungle pests.

"… But you have karma with women! I will not ask if you've lived a chaste life, as God is listening."

I joined Swami-ji with unrestrained laughter, though bewildered of the possibility of a mysterious woman from a previous life showing up. I considered the mystics of my past and their predictions of my love life. Some were correct, most were not. As we finished on the balcony, Swami-ji stated that he was somewhat astonished that I'd been born in America instead of India. He warned delicately that I would

Ayurveda

struggle to find balance juggling a spiritual and solitude path, with a career and family. He lightened though, telling me it didn't have to be one or the other, but to be cautious about neglecting my relationship responsibilities. I reverently touched the top of his feet at the end of our session, and to my surprise he waved his hand when I asked how much I owed him.

******

The clinic locked its doors at ten to persuade guests to follow an early bedtime. Around a quarter till, I rose from the long couch and stretched, then poured a cup of tepid tea. I thought about the last leg of the trip, which would finish with six weeks in Chiang Mai. Images of running through fragrant streets, skipping rope, and dodging punches sparked a welcomed fire. I was ready to test again. With my arms extended, I inspected my knuckles. The first two protruded distinctively, as if perpetually swollen. I missed the smell of rubber mats and the anxious fluttering walking into a new gym. India was less physically strenuous, though the stretch manifested in other ways. Profound, mystical ones.

The front door chimed lightly, prompting me to sit up on the couch. I expected the night watchman to soon enter and pour himself a tea. He was a sickly thin man, with droopy eyes. His short wooden baton resembled a half-broken baseball bat. A silver whistle on a dark cord hung around his pencil neck. On previous evenings, we'd sit on the same couch and enjoy the serenity together before he ascended the steps to make his nightly rounds. But it wasn't the security guard. A tall, fast-moving figure bolted into the room, then stopped immediately. In the washed light, she had long flowing black hair that shined, and her features and skin looked Indian. It wasn't unusual for locals to stop in after hours to speak with Dr. Patesh. He was a revered doctor, I learned, and India's work hours were elusive.

"I was afraid the doors were locked," the figure said to no one in particular.

I placed my journal on the table. As my eyes focused, the figure moved under a more generous light. Indeed, she was tall. And thin, with sculpted arms and shapely legs. Through her designer yoga pants, her calves looked like diamonds cut by a laser. She had the lean sinewy cut of a high-level athlete.

A Ronin's Tale

"Are you staying here at Shanti?" she asked.

"I am," I said, the words barely escaping my lips.

I took an extended gulp of tea to moisten the inside of my mouth. Under the chandelier, a radiance of some kind shot out and spun around me like a translucent web.

"Are you checking in?"

She walked closer.

"I just finished teacher training up in the mountain. Patesh was gracious to store my luggage while I was away."

"Teacher training?" I asked.

"For yoga," she smiled.

Her eyes stared intently into mine. For the briefest second, I considered a most heinous thought that I was chest high in another one of India's elaborate scams. This one orchestrated by Swami-ji, and perhaps Dr. Patesh. Would she soon tell me she was stranded and needed money? Would she slip something into my tea, then harvest my organs? Who was this luminous figure that just stumbled in with a strange accent?

She descended the shallow steps, then sat on the edge of the couch with her hands folded. Effortlessly, she kicked her legs up and crossed them.

"I'm Nick," I said.

"Hello, Nick. I am Simone."

I looked down, then discretely scanned her fingers for a ring.

"So, you do yoga?" I asked. It was the best I could muster.

She smiled, perhaps sensing she was in the presence of a schoolboy.

"Yes," she answered and nodded.

"Cool," I said, looking straight ahead.

"I teach yoga in my home in Stuttgart. I came to Rishikesh last year for training, then returned for a more advanced one."

"That's impressive. So, you're German?"

"Yes, I am German."

"You look kind of Indian, actually. Not what a stereotypical German looks like."

Shut up, Nick! You're ruining it! Play it cool. Relax. Relax. Relax.

She giggled.

"I am part Hungarian and Mongolian. On my mother's side. Many people ask of my heritage."

"You'd make a good spy," I said. "You could blend into a lot of places." *Stop talking!*

Ayurveda

I adjusted my position on the couch, attempting to sit upright. My hands fidgeted across my lap, then made small circles on my thighs. She continued to sit in full lotus, like a tree undisturbed by a gale wind.

"So, are you doing Ayurvedic treatment now, I mean, now that you're training is finished?"

"Yes."

Her eyes didn't stop looking at me. Even as I looked away and anxiously scanned the room, her gaze was fixed. As I began to soften into the moment, I turned, and our eyes locked. We stared at each other for an extended breath, then she smiled and looked away.

"Your accent, you are American, yes?"

"Mm hmm. Been traveling. Got to India a little less than a month ago."

A sound emanated from the stairwell around the corner. Simone turned, her elongated neck revealing a silver chain.

"Oh, still up?"

A different voice, though familiar, broke the enchanted circle. This one owned by an overly chatty Greek in his late forties. His short, stocky frame and head of thick black hair made its way into the room.

"Hello, Demetrius," I greeted him and sighed.

As he walked closer, he stopped immediately, then looked at the foreign figure.

"*Oh, hello,*" he said, grinning, then offering his hand.

Wasting no time, Demetrius poured himself a cup.

"Who are you?" he asked.

"My name is Simone."

"Oh, a beautiful name. And where is Simone from?"

"Germany."

"Germany. Ah, great music you got there in Berlin."

Simone nodded, but said nothing.

Demetrius steadied his cup of lukewarm tea, then sat in the middle of the couch, facing Simone.

"So, staying here now, at the Shanti?"

She nodded, though this time more shallowly.

"I've been here three weeks today, lost nearly five kilos already. I cheat a little, though. Walk into town for an extra meal somewhere. I need more than what they give us here. Patesh knows I bend the rules, but so what."

Demetrius continued with incessant chatter. He quizzed Simone, though admittedly, I enjoyed his sleuthing and insolent approach. She had a son who'd recently started college. Her age was unclear, though I suspected it was only a few years older than mine. She studied under a renown yoga instructor in Rishikesh, who had a global following.

Then, the front door chimed. The watchman entered with Dr. Patesh close behind.

"Oh, hello, my friends," he said, surprised. "Are we having a party I was not invited to?"

Dr. Patesh descended the tile steps.

"Oh, Simone, I did not see you there. How was your retreat?"

"Hello, Dr. Patesh," she said warmly. "It was magnificent."

"Here for your bags, I assume?" Dr. Patesh turned to the watchman and barked in quick Hindi, pointing to the storage closet.

"Actually ..." she began.

Simone rose, then gracefully walked away with Dr. Patesh. She began to whisper. The watchman poured himself a cup, then took Simone's place on the couch.

The following morning after yoga, I went downstairs to the lounge. A morning ritual was that most of the guests, about twenty in total, meandered on the various chairs and couches, sipping tea, and talking. We waited for our meager rations, before being whisked away for treatment, or a personal consultation with Dr. Patesh.

As I cleared the last of the steps, I said hello to the staff behind the counter, then turned the corner toward the lounge. To my delight, Simone's flowing hair, even shinier in the daylight, cascaded to the small of her back, as she poured tea. Turning around, she smiled radiantly.

"Good morning, Nick. How was your rest?" she asked.

I nodded as if giving a slight bow, then sat on a vacant couch. She walked over and sat beside me. From two or three feet away her radiance was more powerful than the previous evening. We didn't say much, electing to observe instead. Then Demetrius picked up his tray and scurried over.

"Mind if I join?" he asked.

Simone glanced at me, then grinned slightly.

Fuck off, Demetrius! Take your tray with your double rations and go outside and eat with the monkeys and the scorpions!

"Sure, Demetrius, we would love that," I said.

"So, staying with us now?" Demetrius asked, his back fully turned.

"Yes," Simone said.

"Excellent!"

"But, only for a few days. I head home to Germany in a week."

"So, you teach yoga?"

"Yes, but mainly as a hobby. I own a studio."

"Just a hobby? Well, what do you do for your work?"

Simone placed her hands on her lap and sat up even more erect than before.

"I've been a professional model since I was seventeen," she said, matter of fact.

Demetrius fluttered excitedly, sending shockwaves through the couch.

"Yeah, I can tell you're a model. Who do you model for, like what brands? Mainly Europe, or all over?"

Before Simone could answer, he transitioned again.

"I'm heading to the Beatles Ashram later, you should come with me," he continued.

"Oh, thank you, but I have my treatments this afternoon," Simone said.

"Well, maybe some other time then. There's a lot to see here. And you're here for a week, so ..."

"How about you, Nick? You follow the Maharishi. Want to go to his ashram together?"

"Uh, I'd love to, but I have treatment, too," I lied.

Simone looked over and winked.

"Demetrius, can you please grab that chair over there and sit here?" Simone asked. "That way, we can all see each other."

As if ordered by the general, Demetrius popped up quickly and fetched a chair. We sat in a trine, the holiest of shapes.

"You practice transcendental meditation?" Simone asked.

"Yes. I was sort of raised in it, really. In Iowa, where the headquarters is."

"That is interesting. I do a meditation, but not the same one."

"Yeah, me too," Demetrius added.

"I do a couple different kinds. Learned them on YouTube for free. Heard TM was a cult, like people think they can lift up in the air and fly around. Nonsense!"

"It's the full moon, you know. Tonight," I said.

"Yes, I know." Simone smiled.

"A good night for setting intention; asking the universe what you want and saying thanks."

Simone took a deep breath from her perfect model nose, then exhaled slowly. She looked at me.

"I heard you and that girl, I think she is Canadian maybe. You were discussing astrology. Are you traveling with her? Together, I mean?"

"Oh, you mean Terry? No, no," I said quickly. "We met here, at the clinic. Dr. Patesh recommended Guru-ji, an astrologer, then told her I knew a little bit about Jyotish and had met with him."

Simone nodded.

"I only know little things, like the sun and moon. Generic things, like the sun is masculine, the moon is feminine. But I don't know so much about the planets or their significance," she said.

"What do you think about the full moon, the one this evening?"

"I don't really know," I confided truthfully.

"The moon brings things into the light, though. Like it illuminates things we might not see or don't want to look at within ourselves. It can enhance our intuition, or ..."

"I am ready for some different food," Demetrius barked, cutting off my lecture.

"I like it here, but the food is not satisfying. It is not healthy to eat so little, for so long."

Demetrius gawked at Simone.

"So, you're here for a week, Simone. Any sites you want to see, places to visit? I am renting a car. With a driver."

Dr. Patesh walked into the room.

"Good morning, my beautiful guests. I hope my family is most fulfilled." He scanned the room, then moved closer.

"Demetrius, I have been waiting in my office for the past ten minutes. Please come."

A current of light filled the room, as Demetrius steadied his tray on the table, then rose from his chair.

"Okay, I am off to treatment. We will talk later. Hope to see you soon," he said, looking at Simone.

As Demetrius left the room, Simone shifted her posture back toward me. We sat similarly; mirror images on the couch. The sun and moon. I thought about the divine balance of masculine and feminine energy, as depicted by *Shiva-Shakti*. One cannot exist without the other, at least not well. The universe was showing me what that meant. I was in the presence of a significant soul, a woman with immeasurable grace and power. A little less than half of the guests were male, but I watched each take a turn with Simone in his own way. Under a spell of sorts. An elderly woman with an accent I didn't recognize told Simone she was the most beautiful woman she'd ever seen.

"Are you doing anything for the moon, tonight?" Simone asked.

The warmth of her question cascaded like honey. I could smell jasmine and lavender.

"I haven't thought about it but was thinking I should. Some of the kids in the market sell prasad boats for *arti,* and I have some blessed incense I brought with me from Varanasi. Why do you ask?"

"Maybe we should meet on the balcony this evening. Together. And, I have chocolate hidden in my bag," she confided and then laughed.

Yes!

"Chocolate, huh? Well, I guess you can count me in then," I said, coolly.

Then I inched closer to Simone.

"That sounds nice. I've actually been planning to do a ritual."

"Well, I must go. I have yoga. We will meet on the balcony at eight o'clock, okay?"

As Simone rose from the couch, she picked up her tray from the floor and leaned over, placing it on the table. Then she glided past, touching my shoulder slightly as she walked away. I sat on the couch, swimming in some sort of golden light.

I began in my journal.

Rishi said something about "The message being delivered," when I told him about Guru-ji mentioning Ayurveda. The balcony this evening. What is this about?

Chapter 43

LOVE

Fall 2017, A Classroom in the Midwest

Raise your hand if you've ever been in love. Okay, good, we've all experienced it. It's magical, yeah? Daniel glimpses love through his girlfriend, Ali. They're in high school and haven't dated long, but that excited buzz has planted its seeds. Life can be a whole other reality when we're in love, especially in its beginning. But our journey and soul's curriculum, although we can share it with others in part, is ultimately an individual experience. A large part of the hero's journey is finding that love within ourselves. That might entail forgiveness for things we're not proud of. Letting go of regret, guilt, past behaviors, etc. It also entails forgiving those we believe wronged us. Remember, according to this mythological work, even the people who hurt us are our teachers. They are aspects of ourselves, and the qualities that we're not at peace with. They show us what still needs to be addressed and healed. Sometimes the mythological world continues to bring a bad relationship into our life. Some of us know people like that; they are always in dramatic or unhealthy relationships, one after the other. Toxic. If we follow the essence of this work, it could be construed that the person is failing to learn certain lessons, so the teachers keep showing up giving them the same curriculum over and over.

    I, personally, believe that the hero's journey is rooted in love. It's the glue of the whole show. Love from a divine force that pushes and protects the Hero, but also the Hero's own maturation that produces self-love and love for others. Now, when I say "self-love" we don't want to confuse that with narcissism. It is about acknowledging and embracing our faults and the things we beat ourselves up over. Instead of trying to be Johnny Tough Guy who always appears to have his shit together, or who answers most questions with, "I'm fine," we become comfortable with vulnerability. We become more expressive and emotionally literate, challenging the things that our society tells us is weakness.

Our society sends us many confusing messages, and love is no exception. I believe in our culture, we have this confusing, though romantic concept, about finding "the one." It sort of assumes that once we find this magical soul, everything falls into place. I love that story, and I love its symbolism, but I don't think it's that easy. I think we have the potential to meet many wonderful mates, though we still have to own that we have a considerable amount of personal work that never ends. In other words, when we meet this great person, we can't just say, "oh good, I found them, now I can just drink beer, watch sports, and have fun." For me, balanced love is finding someone who will continue to challenge me and help me grow. A person who sees my potential and lovingly chips away the rough edges to help me become a better version of myself. And ideally, I am doing the same thing for her. At some point you will meet people who have been together for a very long time, but who have grown differently over those years. That can strain a relationship; when people grow differently, or one person takes off in some way and their partner is stuck.

I don't want to spend too much time on love, but it's important that we acknowledge its place within this larger framework of the story. Also, most of you are at the age, and being students, where you could very easily find a mate. To close, I will share a few quotes from Campbell and what he says about love.

> When seeking your partner, if your intuition is a virtuous one, you will find him or her. If not, you'll keep finding the wrong person.
>
> If you marry only for the love affair, that will not last. You must also marry on another level, to reconstruct the androgyne, to make the perfect whole, male and female.[31]

---

31   Osbon, *Reflections on the Art of Living.*

Chapter 44

CHOCOLATE

October 2019, Rishikesh, India

> Tradition is not the worship of ashes, but the preservation of fire.[32]
>
> —Gustav Mahler

Around six-thirty, I sat shirtless at my little table, journaling. I had a lot to say. Beads of sweat descended from my armpits, at times, dripping onto the top of my feet. The Ayurvedic treatment cooled, but this new fire was different from the poisonous agni. It was Dionysian; raw, passionate heat that rose from benevolent embers. Throughout the day, my posture was straighter than usual. I felt purposeful in my stride, as a bubbling confidence assured that everything in my life would be fine. It is guided by an invisible force, God, who loves me, and would never seek to hurt or embarrass me. Indeed, God is real. Yeah, I'm still weird. Yeah, I don't really fit into the mainstream culture and never have. But that's okay. It's my own trip. This magical seed, somehow related to Simone, was not about romantic love necessarily. It was something further. Something beyond and related to absolute faith and divine order. And it came when I needed it most; on the tail end of the journey, having logged many months on the road. I needed a lift of the heart after purging so much and negotiating bouts of loneliness.

I brushed my teeth three times before I ascended the steps to the balcony. I had been up there before, sometimes drinking tea in the

---

[32]   Gustav Mahler quote sourced from the Mahler Foundation, https://mahlerfoundation.org/.

stillness. Nobody had ever bothered me there, so it felt like the right place for gazing at the moon together. I took the thin blanket off my bed, and a pillow, then ventured up early. The balcony was usually pitch black, facing a dense jungle. On this evening, however, the moon's grace illuminated it. I paced for a while, and waved my flashlight looking for scorpions. Guilt about my ex wafted by, momentarily. We'd not had much correspondence since I left, and my abrupt departure overseas gave me enough distraction to keep the thoughts at bay. My patterning still very much alive. I was still in love with her, too.

Not long after eight, I heard sandals delicately tap against the concrete steps. My heartbeat fluttered, as I breathed slowly through my nose and out my mouth. The sounds grew near, though I leaned against the balcony with my back to the stairwell. Seconds later, a soft hand touched my shoulder and stayed there for a moment. Then, a lean next to me, our hips gently touching. Neither one of us said anything as we swam to the moon. I thought about first dates and client meetings. Incessant chatter and questions. Filling up space with small talk and empty words. All that fluff was gone on the balcony.

"What a magnificent evening," I finally whispered.

Simone nodded, though didn't say anything. Her hip inched closer.

I wanted to place my hand on the back of her head and feel her hair. I could smell the earthy sandalwood of her shampoo and Ayurvedic soap. Occasionally, we'd break from the luminescent rays and gaze at each other. A heart language.

"You have amazing power, Nick," she said silently.

"Thank you," I said, a bit taken back. "So do you," I said truthfully.

"I felt it immediately when you walked in the other night."

We stood pressed, literally joined at the hip for several minutes before I lit a stick of temple incense I'd purchased earlier in the day. I waved it circularly, then held it upward toward the moon. Simone slid her hand off the railing, then clasped it into mine as she chanted a mantra softly. I'd heard it many times. It was part of the puja the slender man sang at my fifth birthday, before giving me my mantra. An energetic current transferred through us. We stood still, listening to the jungle creatures and the distant chaos of scooter horns. I moved behind, wrapping my arms around her shoulders, then lower around her stomach. She sank backward into me, and I rested my chin on the top of her head. With closed eyes, I inhaled and gently kissed the back of her ear, then her neck. I transported to fourteen, shortly after my parents' divorce. I was visiting Dad on the weekend in his trailer. A friend of his loaned him a book on Kama Sutra, and I scoured its pages when he fell asleep. Earlier that day, Dad showed me the book and said, "One day you'll be doing this." Then he laughed.

More than the positions of the sex itself, it was the colorful imagery; the way the lovers embraced that captivated most. Each picture was like a statue of a holy scene. Dr. Patesh talked about *ojas* as the essential life force to health. Our goal, he said, was to build our body up with them. There were things that produced ojas, and things that consequently took them away. Love, for instance, was one of the big producers. Conversely, excessive, or the wrong intention around sex was a no-no. That's why many men feel drained afterward, he said. They lost their precious life force. My memory bank flooded through a nauseating slideshow of mischief. Bouncing days, drunken moments in dive bars, stoned with women friends. The images went on. I had acted on so many raw fantasies. Debaucheries that were self-serving and at times, hurtful. I lost a lot of ojas, rarely stopping to consider how the women felt. Now I bowed before the moon, listening, as she telepathically spoke through Simone. It wasn't so much an admonishment or reprimand, but more a disappointment. There were higher expectations, and I was out of gimmicks at this stage.

At some point we transitioned from the rail, to the makeshift bed. I pulled Simone on top of my crossed legs, and we held each other. I don't how much time lapsed, as I was in that place where time is irrelevant. Each second was fullness. We kissed tenderly, but it was the holding and breathing in union that I remember most.

"Try this," Simone whispered, as she placed a small piece of chocolate into my mouth. I had been without sugar for weeks, and the chocolate slowly melted, jumpstarting endorphins.

"Wooowww," I gasped.

"Mm hmm. From Germany," she said and winked.

The higher Self whispered; *this is what we told you it would be. When you do the work, you can manifest whatever your heart desires. When you serve God, you are always guided. Always.* I thought about the physicality of the journey. The grueling putting out in Thailand and Vietnam. The treks to summits, and the deep bucketing and soul purges in Indonesia. Then, a nearly month-long slog above eighteen thousand feet in Nepal, culminating with the extended fasting and ceremonies in India. I was living from the strands that have always existed inside. The Warrior, the Lover, the Shaman, and now the King. They were like best friend playmates in the innocent years, pulling their favorite toys from the chest. But the ego was there, too. Most men I know want the most attractive woman in the room captivated on them. Even if they're happily married or coupled up, they want it. We all need it to some degree for wholeness; the juiciness of being noticed. It's part of our survival wiring, to be selected for procreation. To be chosen as a protector. Here I was, literally with a model; a model who worked at renown agencies, donning the major brands that my sister proudly hung in her closet. Simone had been all over the world doing her craft. And here she was taking a break from that reality, on the final chapter of her yoga retreat, stumbling in for luggage. *She chose me. She chose me. She chose me.*

The next morning, we sat on the couch sipping tea, smiling and sharing a secret. It felt like the entire room stared. Even Dr. Patesh wasn't immune to the wellspring of ojas in the air.

"My goodness, you both look radiant this morning! The treatments are working." He beamed as he spoke.

Simone smiled, then winked at me.

"Have you been to the *arti*?"

Arti is a ceremony that represents light. As with most wisdom traditions, there is no exact translation. The puja is conducted to offer gratitude to the various deities, which are different aspects of God. In Varanasi, I attended the nightly arti at Dashashwamedh Ghat, on the banks of the Ganges. The elaborate offering was conducted by multiple Brahmin priests who chanted and waved large brass cobra statues with fire emanating from the top. Eventually, they passed the statues among the hundreds of attendees, who took every opportunity to bask in the sacred smoke and wave it over them. I had heard about the evening arti in Rishikesh, also on the Ganges and near a large Shiva statue.

"Yes, I went to arti in Varanasi, and I plan to go in Haridwar when I leave here."

"Oh, we must go together. We must do this. Tonight?" Simone asked excitedly.

"Absolutely. Should we invite Demetrius?" I snickered.

Simone rolled her eyes.

"I need to walk to town. I want to find some prayer bowls to take home. Shall we go together, after your treatment?"

I nodded, feeling the electric buzz of romantic seeds beginning their maturation.

"Oh, yeah, I meant to ask yesterday, how was the Beatles Ashram?"

Simone grinned widely.

A Ronin's Tale

"Nick, you must go! Oh, I so want to take you. The Maharishi, you could feel his presence there. The Beatles ... oh, it was so great."

"Tell me about it."

"There was this incredible silence there. The, how you say, *structures*, you know, the buildings, were not so good, but you could feel the power. Here, here, let me show you."

Simone slid closer, our knees touching, and retrieved her phone from her designer purse. It was a famous French brand, and when I asked about it, she laughed and rolled her eyes.

"Yes, I modeled for them, and get for free. Would never pay two thousand Euro for such a silly thing. Come closer, look at this painting of the Maharishi."

Eyes in the room continued to fixate on us.

"These are fantastic. They remind me of the commune, in Utopia Park," I said.

"Yes, I knew you would like them. You must go, Nick. Maybe we can squeeze time for it? I cannot believe I meet you now, but then go home in four days. Not fair."

A fogginess from Simone's words temporarily hovered.

"Well, we'll make this time special no matter what."

Her right knee rubbed mine, then she leaned her shoulder in.

"Oh my God, I must tell you. Guess who was at the Ashram, too."

"Hmm," I said, sitting back and touching my chin. I thought of hummus and olives.

"Could it be a certain Greek man, perhaps? About this tall, with thick black hair. Someone who doesn't stop talking? Someone who would love for me to accidentally drown in the Ganga?"

We both laughed.

"Yes! I think he followed me, Nick. I hid from him. The Ashram is big, but it was like that game you do as a kid; *hide and seek*, yes? It was like that, but only I was the one hiding."

"I got to get ready for treatment. Let's plan for the arti, then have dinner at the Beatles Café. I heard the food is good."

"Yes, it is good. Okay, after treatment we walk to town."

The treatment continued to cool my system considerably. Strangely, I would occasionally be placed inside a steam chamber that resembled a large wooden wine barrel. My head protruded above, while a thick cloth wrapped around my neck trapped the heat below. A concoction of fragrant herbs rose from the wooden cauldron, steaming into my sinuses and opening them. The herbal magic felt like swimming in a

Chocolate

bath of peppermint. Thoughts of Simone entertained, but I was savvy enough to recognize that I hardly knew her. I was riding a wave of endorphins and celibacy, but I was also conflicted about my ex. I started an email to her just a couple days before Simone and I met. I didn't have any motivation other than to tell her I missed her. Before I left, she generously offered an opportunity to come back to Illinois; to learn the craft of real estate and work together. To be together. I held that image of finally being at peace with my wanderings and being ready to commit. But I never sent the email.

I met Simone in the lobby, refreshed, both of us donning sunglasses. Hers a major brand, mine a new counterfeit. The main room was sparse, with only a cluster of patients we didn't know. As we walked toward the main road, Simone reached down and grabbed my hand. Different people hanging out stared. A Sadhu cackled, then smiled widely. The congestion of bodies increased as we neared town. The café where I snuck off for coffee had dozens of people. Each turned and looked. At first, I wondered if what I witnessed was real, then Simone giggled.

"Everyone is staring at us, Nick."

"I know!" I replied, incredulously.

"They see *it*," Simone waxed, wisely.

"Yes. It's radiating off us."

She squeezed my hand, then turned her head and smiled with her eyes. We sauntered dreamily across the Laxshman Jula bridge, carefully stepping over beggars and avoiding eye contact with the monkeys. Toward the end of the bridge, an elderly Indian man held his hand up.

"My goodness, what a beautiful couple. You are like the great king and queen. May I take your photo?"

Simone leaned in and stared like a model, while I fumbled with a half-cocked grin that probably looked lame. We walked down a set of steep stairs to a section of vacant beach where I purchased two prasad packets from an English-speaking street kid who spoke jive particularly well. The floating sacraments had the requisite candle, small cube of candy, and a flower. All for God. My feeble handful of matches failed, so we cast our wishes down Mother Ganga with a dry fuse. Although the current varied in different sections, our boats stayed intimately close to each other. Simone stood tall on the riverbank, her eyes closed in prayer. I watched her lips move delicately and wondered about her thoughts. Was I a part of them?

"Nick, I want to ask you something, okay?"

"Of course," I said.

"I leave for Germany in a few days. Do you think we will see each other again? I mean, would you like to see me again?"

It was a question I had been sitting with, too. The magical part of travel is that flings and short-lived affairs arise, though I had never had an experience with someone in this way. So fast, yet genuine. She confided that she had separated from her husband of many years after having an intensive spiritual breakthrough. I didn't press for details, though I intuited that her awakening was not congruent to the spiritual leanings of her husband. Perhaps it was a projection, too, as I had failed to connect with my loves in that manner.

"I would love to see you again, but I don't even know what that means, and I realize we live far apart," she began. Then she continued, "When I first saw you, there was something about you that I just knew was familiar. I can't explain it, and it's not because I don't know the word in English, it's just …"

"I understand," I said. "It's something kind of beyond words, really."

"When I meet you, I was getting my luggage. But then I saw you. And I don't know. I tell Patesh to book me a room, even though I already have a place to stay."

I laughed and pulled Simone toward me, then kissed her forehead.

Our walk through town garnered more looks. Simone could pass for part Indian, but that wasn't it. The electricity that love vibrates is noticeable to others. Like darker emotions, and anger, people perceive these energies, even if unconsciously. We stopped at a little café on the edge of town and shared a *thali*, a plate filled with different vegetarian dishes, our hands serving as utensils. We could faintly see the flowing Ganga, and the cows that meandered with their unclipped hoofs that curved upward. I was being rewarded. For whatever reason, this ending leg of my journey was about receiving treasure.

Later that evening, we met in the lobby, before darting off in our sunglasses. I have always been private about my personal life, and part of this showed itself by not wanting the staff or other guests to know about Simone and me. It was *our* thing. There was a younger woman there who expressed interest in me early on. The woman from Canada, Terry. It happened after the first yoga session. She sat next to me during our morning meal. We even went for a few walks and talked about astrology, though I distanced myself as her flirtations increased. It went without saying that every man at the clinic was under Simone's spell. She just had that quality that not only commanded a room, but fully

Chocolate

took it over. Although we said we would not hide it, we agreed to not openly flaunt it inside the compound.

The arti took place on the Mother, in front of a large, blue Shiva statue, about a twenty-minute walk from where we stayed. As we strolled with our hands interlocked, a current of energy flooded my body. I took a breath, as the sensation reverberated up and down, inwardly.

"Can you feel it, it's like a bolt of lightning?" I whispered, expecting a confused expression.

"Yes, yes. It is giving me goosebumps," Simone confirmed.

About two hundred people, mostly Indians, congregated the concrete area. Three priests sat on rugs with their assortment of sanctified items nearby. I scanned the crowd, again, perplexed by the eyes upon us. *This has got to be a joke. This is just too outrageous.* We sat with our new sets of prasad next to us, and I reached into my pocket for a lighter.

"Simone, do you notice ..."

Before I finished, she interrupted.

"The stares? Oh my, yes," she laughed.

"I think it's because I'm with a model. Maybe we can tell people I'm your baggage handler, or your bodyguard."

She turned and looked into my eyes, then kissed me on the lips. We leaned closer, temporarily embracing, before being rocked back to waking reality.

"My friend, my friend, please ..." an Indian man shouted. I looked up, confused. He was dressed in some sort of formal attire, and inched toward us, quickly. I momentarily wondered if public affection was a no-no, and we were to be admonished for our transgression.

"Please, please. Come with me," he said, motioning us to follow.

Simone looked at me puzzled, and I raised my eyebrows and made a face. The man waded effortlessly through groups of seated devotees, snaking around them, before clearing a space right next to the priests.

"Please, sit here," he said.

I shook my head, then turned to the Shiva statue and winked. *Thank you.*

A young boy, not far from us, stood with a weathered microphone. He began a blissful song that immediately transported me away. His song was a long one, then transitioned into different mantras. At some point, the priests assumed command, bellowing their chants, and lighting ghee lamps. Periodically, I cracked my eyelids, noticing that Simone was somewhere else as well. At times, the only indication of her presence was a subtle brushing; a shallow hand that touched my thighs, an elbow that delicately swayed next to mine. She was journeying somewhere. The fragrant scents of the ceremonial rites rose into the air. The serpent gyrations followed, as my spine fluttered back and forth. A picture of a royal couple came into focus. He was tall and dressed vibrantly with different markings on his forehead. His long hair and dark beard added to his regality. His bride was even more impressive, donning an assortment of jewels and gold. They were young and very much in love. It was all shown through their eyes, and the subtle smiles they passively dropped to each other. The time frame was unclear, but it was a long time ago. They walked toward an elephant.

"Nick, are you okay?" Simone whispered, taking my hand.

My eyes still closed, I nodded. I followed the Raja and his beautiful Queen, as they walked past the elephant toward a dense jungle. Then, they vanished. When my eyes opened, the tall blue Shiva looked back.

I took some full breaths, as my soul attached back into the body. Briefly, I reassessed where I was. The priests chanted quietly, and the crowd appeared lost in their own trance. Then the priests lit the cobras and waved them in the air. A wave of commotion circulated, as clusters of devotees moved closer. The sacred bronze snakes were held upright, then passed on. I immediately grabbed one from the nearby priest, and swayed it back and forth, as people rose above, fanning the smoke over their bodies. More movement and commotion unfolded behind, as Simone and I laughed hysterically. I passed the snake to her, and she sang a beautiful chant she'd learned at her retreat. *This is it, Nick. There is no time. There is no past, nor future. You are here. This moment is all there is.*

After passing the sacrament, we inched toward the bank and rolled up our pant legs. Slowly, I entered the water, my shins temporarily numbed. I retrieved the lighter and handed Simone her prasad bundle. It was wrapped in some sort of leaf that made it float. With a few flicks the flame sprung to life, then glowed. We closed our eyes. The boats were carefully placed in the water, with the candles upright. A couple strokes with my hand created subtle waves that set them toward the fast current. Soon after, they briskly took off together, never straying more than a few inches apart. I got out of the water and stood on the concrete. Simone wrapped her arms around me. We watched intently, as our boats descended down the Ganga, eventually disappearing entirely. In spite of a moderate breeze, the candles stayed lit.

Chocolate

******

"The veggie burger platter is the best, huh?" I asked, trying to remember the last time I had fries.

"Oh, yes, you will enjoy it," Simone confirmed.

"Let's feast tonight. We've earned it," I said.

The Beatles Café was suspended high on a hill, providing a magnificent view of the Ganges and Rishikesh's vast colors. The moon, although not full, added a luminescent backdrop to an already ethereal scene. We got comfy on the cushions at a large table, Simone leaning into me. Iconic pictures of the Fab Four during their transcendent days, along with Maharishi, were plastered on the walls. I had grown up seeing pictures of him everywhere on the campus and at school. His joyful smile and radiance clear, even from a photo. I smiled, inwardly laughing that he was witnessing all of it. We ordered health shakes with different fruits and herbs. Then, dessert. I was still very much in the mode of a Raja, enjoying a carefree existence of opulence.

"Simone, will you tell me more about what you felt at Shanti, when we first met?"

She paused reflectively, looking out toward the Ganges. I took a sip of water and stared at a black-and-white picture of John Lennon with Maharishi.

"I just came back to civilization, you know, from the ashram in the mountains. Six weeks doing intensive yoga. I didn't want to see or meet anybody since it was late and I was tired. When I walked inside Shanti, I didn't expect anybody downstairs at that moment, and there was you."

She paused, then continued.

"After we talked, I knew that I needed to spend time with you. I can't explain it. I went upstairs and showered. I felt so pure; so … I don't know the word in English. I go straight to my bed, and it felt like a magic carpet."

Neither one of us said anything for a few minutes. The sand in the hourglass of our pending separation was moving closer.

"So, tell me, you leave Rishikesh and then to Haridwar? What else?" Simone asked.

"There are several Shiva temples in Haridwar I want to see, and the arti, of course. Then I am renting a car and driver for Delhi, so that I can head to Agra for the Taj Mahal. After that, back to Chiang Mai for

another six or seven weeks. Then home, I guess. Or maybe I'll just stay on the road," I mused.
"Or ..." Simone said.
"Or what?"
"Or come to Germany and see me."
Simone sat up excitedly, waving her hands.
"Have you been to Portugal?"
"Not yet, but ..." I began.
"Oh, Nick! You would love it. It is so magical."
I took a long pull of the medicinal drink and licked my lips.
"Maybe Portugal is in the future then."
We moved to a balcony where a breeze shied the sweat beads off my forehead. Simone sat between my legs, her back pressed against my chest. I draped my arms, resting on her lap like a seatbelt on a plane. Flicks of light bounced from the river, as India's festive noises continued. I had no idea what my future looked like, in any regard. But I knew I would be okay.
"Oh, what time is it?" Simone asked, leaning forward.
"About nine-forty-five," I said.
"Oh, we need to call Shanti."
"Right, right," I said, coming back to earth.
Simone pulled her cellphone from her purse, and within a minute was laughing with the night watchman. I paid the bill, then stared at the miscellaneous photos on the wall. Our hands clasped together, we moved slowly through quieter streets. We didn't talk on the way home, instead electing to absorb the fullness of each step. Before we reached Shanti, I pulled Simone close and kissed her. We giggled like school kids, then knocked on the door. Since a large group of Chinese tourists departed, the lounge and lobby were desolate by ten. It was nearly ten-thirty, so we walked into the lobby holding hands. As we turned the corner and looked into the vast room, more than a dozen heads froze in place. Time temporarily ceased, as mixtures of idyllic smiles and eye daggers from the Canadian woman, and Demetrius, shot toward us.
"Oh, hello, everyone," I said, grinning widely. "We're just coming back from arti. Was beautiful."
Silence.
"Well, goodnight." Simone smiled at the crowd before parting.
We darted up the stairs laughing, then went to my room and made a bed on the floor. Simone retrieved more of her contraband chocolate. The following day we checked out of Shanti. I found a quaint hotel on

Chocolate

the other side of the river yet within walking distance to the good stuff. Those last days and nights clarified the kind of man I was transitioning toward. I thought mostly about how I'd run from love for so long. The hurt I'd caused. Although the rational mind shrugged Simone off in part as another whirlwind romance, spicier because it involved a model, the initiated part knew she was a teacher. This was a significant person, and I met her as I was leaving the forest, preparing for my reward. The reward was a combination of things, but mostly it was about healing wounds so that I could finally, one day, embrace love.

Part 3
The Return Home

I am not looking to escape my darkness; I am learning to love myself there.[33]

—Rune Lazuli

---

33 Rune Lazuli quote retrieved from <u>Rune Lazuli | SpiritualCleansing. Org - Love, Wisdom, Inspirational Quotes & Images</u> on October 4, 2023.

Chapter 45

HOMECOMING

Fall 2017, A Classroom in the Midwest

The journey forces the Hero to see himself in a more truthful way, doesn't it? He must have this clarity if he is to return to the Ordinary World again. He was asleep the last time he was there, and he won't go back and live that same life. Many of us would like a re-set in some way, yes? A chance to hit "start over" and redo things differently. We wish the relationship we were in would be less complicated, or just go away. Or our job would change, or just go away, too. We convince ourselves that a certain salary will improve it all. Or life will get more exciting once the kids are grown and out of the house. We ponder our choices, wondering whether we made the right ones. Regret, shame, what ifs, and the wheel of emotions flood around it all. We direct jealousy and hostility at others we sense have it easier. We creep on the Internet at night, wondering what our ex-lovers are up to. Maybe all the face tattoos and piercings, and the shrine of pictures on our social media that scream, "LOOK AT ME," "LOOK AT ME," "LOOK AT ME," are the unfinished parts of ourselves, crying out for something sacred? The Hero cannot return to that existence again because he's seen behind the curtain. Those old parts of him died. He wants to return with fire in his belly so that he can bring the world his deepest gifts and live from his center. But that means the hard work must continue. Campbell actually says that the return is more difficult than the plunge into the adventure.

 We don't get a lot of time to come up for air in our culture, do we? Our schedules are full, our pace frantic. The Hero is wired like we are. When he lays in bed, anxious thoughts keep him awake. In his slumber, the number of women he hooks up with or the brand of bourbon he drinks take on meaning. The Hero is us. He wants to awaken because the foggy existence of the uninitiated reality is shallow and not enough for what his soul asks of him. Most of us know where we need to grow and where changes need to be made. There is some inner guidance or tone that emerges, even if in a subtle way. It whispers things more truthfully. But the openness to receive the messages doesn't happen easily. Like us, the Hero is stubborn. He has to pay his dues in the Special World; to be tested in some profound way. He has to surrender to find humility, and that doesn't happen casually. If it's casual, it's not a true test. So, this is why the Special World is so potent. It's where the teabag steeps and where the Hero cuts his teeth.

One of the reasons I travel alone is to have time to be tested, and to reflect on the ways I am held back from my fuller potential. So, the medium of travel becomes a chance to step out of my familiar routine, away from the distractions of the Ordinary World. Tests are a vital part of it. At the very least, I have to figure out where I am going, where I will sleep, what food is safe to eat. I have to navigate the logistics of getting around, without a cell phone and sometimes with thick language barriers. On occasion there are scams and risks; dangerous situations I find myself in. And loneliness, too. But these moments serve as wisdom producers. You don't need to go overseas necessarily, but you have to find a way to continue testing yourself to stay primed. Although the particular journey ends, the Hero acknowledges that he must live and embody his new wisdom. The Hero similarly returns to the Ordinary World with new priorities. And they encompass everything from a physical routine, to the development of his spiritual growth, the foods he eats, and the company he keeps. His mission is wholeness. To integrate the gifts bestowed upon him, knowing in time that he will again be cast on another journey, and expected to rise. And this last point is key. This is from Campbell, and it's a tall order, but a profound one. When we think of our lives and what it means to live mythologically, we shouldn't make the mistake of seeing it as separate from our ordinary reality. The real work of the Hero is to live from this place of balance, engaged in the world, but continually drawing from his Source. This is what it means to live life at 200 percent.

> The two worlds, the divine and the human, can be pictured only as distinct from each other, different as life and death, as day and night. Nevertheless, here is a great

Homecoming

key to the understanding of myth and symbol. The two kingdoms are actually one. The realm of the gods is a forgotten dimension of the world we know.[34]

---

[34] Osbon, *Reflections on the Art of Living.*

Chapter 46

THESE SHADOWS

December 2019, Chiang Mai, Thailand

> There is in every one of us, even those who seem to be most moderate, a type of desire that is terrible, wild, and lawless.[35]
>
> —Plato

It's hotter than usual, and it's getting dark. Slews of vendors wheel their goods onto the sidewalk, as mixtures of Thais and tourists zigzag in between. I pick up a blue soccer jersey with a small Thai flag sewn on the sleeve and a black kickboxing shirt for my nephew after a short barter. I pay more than I should, but I don't care. The stand is next to a collection of framed insects. A long scorpion looks back, and I think of Rishikesh. I follow the smell of pungent spices and listen to the sizzle of heated woks as I enter the food court. There's a lot to choose from, but I'm burned out on noodles and rice. An electric green Chang sign buzzes back and forth. Damn, I would love a beer. Especially now. I settle into the mellow night wearing the afterglow that follows a rigorous workout. I look at my knuckles and shins, smiling at the battle scars.

"You don't look like the type a guy to drink a slushie. All those tattoos, and those shoulders. Gee whiz, you an athlete?"

I scan the vast open room, looking for the voice. Then I notice a figure. The accent is definitely American, from somewhere east.

"No, too old and uncoordinated for the sport game. Just finished

---

[35]   Plato, *The Republic* (Penguin Classics, 2007).

These Shadows

a workout down the street. Now a protein shake," I said, raising my plastic cup.

"A fighter, eh, like those guys in the cage?"

I laugh. "No. Too delicate for that game. Just trying to stay in shape. And look good when I'm naked, I suppose."

The figure returns an honest laugh and asks if he can join me. As the man approaches, he's a little above six feet tall, in the two-twenty to two-forty range. Solidly built, with large hands and tan olive skin. His bluish short-sleeve button-up shirt and khaki pants contour nicely to his frame. I don't notice a wedding ring; just a gold watch with diamonds.

"I'm Franke. You Australian?"

"No, from the states," I reply, as we shake hands. The handshake is firm and extends momentarily.

"Ah, you look Aussie. That's a compliment, mind you. Where in the states?"

"That's tricky to answer, but northern California is what I've always considered home. Around Sonoma, an hour or so north of the city."

"Ah, practically neighbors. I lived some years in Napa and over twenty in LA. Got a place in San Pedro now I rent to some young couple. Been here about seven years."

"Seven years in Chiang Mai, huh?"

"Yeah."

The trepidation of my karmic history, trapped in conversation with everyday oddballs hovers, but doesn't last long. There is something inviting about Franke, and it comes from an interior sensation. This whole journey has sharpened my radar. I tune into him. A confident radiance that isn't showboating shines through. It's reminiscent of a man who's been through some journeys and reached a point where he's comfortable in his own skin. It's visible how he sits in his chair. He sinks into it, naturally, relaxed. He spreads his arms wide across the table, owning his territory. I'm with a lion.

"Lived back east in Jersey and got the fuck outta there in the seventies. Smartest thing I ever did. Not now, though. Too many crazies in California. You got the hard drug dopers and the loafers. Mental whackos. You got the illegals, and the traffic. The homeless shittin' in the streets. And of course, the quakes. A mess. No thank you."

"And the fires," I add.

A salt-and-pepper-haired man comes over and places a beautiful plate in front of me. It's become a ritual. After a grueling two-hour

A Ronin's Tale

workout, I sit in the humid sauna of the open-air night market. But the reprieve is solid Middle Eastern food. His faded white shirt is soaked in sweat, his torso visible. A hairy neck continues south, congregating in swirls on his back. A couple dolma hang off the edge of the plate. He and Franke speak a language I don't recognize, but there is history there. Franke isn't faking his way through basic greetings, like my failed attempts at Spanish or Thai, or any other language besides English. He converses effortlessly. The sweaty man places a hand on Franke's shoulder and leaves it there before returning to his inferno kitchen.

"You chose a good one here. This place," he says, his large finger tapping the table.

"Wait 'til you taste the hummus. That guy's Turkish, and I'm three-quarters Syrian and a quarter Italian, so I know food and call bullshit when it ain't done right. I don't leave home much, but when I come to town, this is it. The only place."

As we converse, collections of attractive Thais and foreigners walk by, one after the other. The scene, busy. Franke makes eye contact with a few, sometimes chatting with a hello, or shaking his head as they glide by.

"Jesus H. Christ. What's a man to do, huh?"

"I got to ask, Franke. What brought you to Chiang Mai seven years ago?"

Without pause, he replies matter of fact.

"I moved here for the pussy, kid," pointing toward the women. Then adds, "And a lot fewer headaches."

"Headaches?"

"Nowadays, you meet a woman, and the first two or three dates are unpaid therapy. You listen, you nod, you act interested when you're thinking about other things. But you tell yourself it's just a phase. It'll get better. Before you know what hit you, their hooks are in, and you realize you're signed up for a lot of unhappy nights."

"Unhappy nights?"

"Yeah. No freedom, lots of rules, the sex gets stale or dries up. You help her friends move. Your weekends are filled with weddings and other bullshit. Plus, you pick up the tab for most everything." Franke pauses reflectively, then finishes with, "A lot of these broads think they need a man when what they really need is a damn life coach ... or a pooch."

"Interesting," I say.

"Mmm hmm. And these millennials are even worse. I doubt any of these girls cook for their man. It's ingrained in them, like it's a bad thing to cook or to please your man. A hate crime or somethin'. Everything's off now, kid."

Franke surveys the scene of new women circulating close by. There's a stage twenty yards away. A slender, attractive Thai directs a group of traditionally dressed teenagers who are practicing some sort of formal dance. The pink and purplish colors are vibrant; their faces painted white. An empty see-through pitcher rests on both sides of the stage for tips.

"And I don't really like people to be honest. I'm a recluse. I should introduce ya to a guy I know here. Big black guy from Oakland. Does the fight thing. You two would hit it off."

"You've never married? Kids?" I ask.

Franke scoffs.

"Thank the good Lord, no. That's a bullet I dodged. Had a lot of women though, and maybe a few I could've hitched, but losing freedom was too much."

"I can relate to the freedom."

"Yeah?"

"Yeah. I'd say it's one of the big reasons I've had some issues dating," I confess.

"Well, women are wired for security, and men for freedom. That's like oil and water, kid. It's a tough act. So, eventually, I just became a crumb man."

"Crumb man?" I ask.

"A man who only gave crumbs. A man who gives just enough to keep the woman interested and hoping for more, but in the end, he does nothing but disappoint. It's not intentional, just happens. And it sure ain't a good way to live."

As I attempt to ask Franke a question, he interrupts.

"Plus, we're just wired to fuck. I mean honestly, I've had some beauties in my day. Women I cared for. Sex was great, conversation stimulating. The whole chemistry thing, but you know what?" Franke stops talking and stares at a long-legged woman ordering noodles.

"A few hours after I come, I could just as easily go to a bar and take home some trashy chick. I mean that. Now, I still love the woman back home, but it don't matter. Men can compartmentalize like that, whereas women are all emotional about it."

I try to speak, but Franke keeps going.

"In fact … I have friends the same way. Love their wives, never lay a hand on them, pay all the bills, you know. But once a month, they like those Asian massages in the seedy neighborhoods."

"I hear what you're saying, but I don't know. I guess ..." my words trail off.

"Remember that British actor guy, kind of a cocksucker actually. Had a beautiful woman, then got arrested with some black hooker. This was years ago, all over the tabloids."

"Hugh Grant?" I ask.

"Yeah, yeah. Him. I mean, the guy's famous, he's got bucks, and a gorgeous skirt, but then he does what he does. Part of the rush is the adventure of being bad. You know, like the ritual of going to a cathouse. That's hardwired in us, kid. We're different creatures than women. This whole equality thing will never work. Shit, we have kids now who don't even know if they're boys or girls."

"Do you believe love is a real thing, like a couple can be together and help each other grow?"

Franke laughs, and I regret my wording.

"You sound like a Sonoma therapist." He snickers.

"Humor me. You don't think a couple can be genuinely happy?"

"I didn't say that. But what happens is that most people go into this thing they think is love, thinkin' the person they're with is a certain way. They see them the way they *want* to see them, rather than the way they *are*. Over time, that wound starts to gush."

I briefly think of Simone and wonder if what I saw was real.

"Say more. And I'm not asking as a therapist."

Franke sits up, and shakes his shoulders, then repositions into his seat.

"Well, they try to change you, or you try to change them, 'cuz you expect them to be a certain way. Then resentment comes along 'cuz they're not, and probably never will be."

"Interesting."

I sit in the brief silence, recalling conversations with jaded exes. Words like *narcissist, selfish, you've changed, I didn't sign up for this*, float by like wounded musical notes.

"And the cutsie-cutsie stuff in the beginning, all that becomes the stuff later on that annoys the shit outta you. It's the kind of stuff you think about when considering upping the insurance policy and calling a hitman."

"A little extreme, maybe," I add.

"I know a few guys so beaten down, that they just hand their balls

These Shadows

over on a silver platter with a big red bow. They live like fuckin' eunuchs just to keep some semblance of peace. Maybe if they're lucky they have a garage to retreat to, and some good scotch hidden. But some of these poor bastards can't even order their own meal in a restaurant."

"You're not lonely? I mean, living this way, you're okay with it?"

"I got women here, but on different terms. By the way, you friends with Glen?"

"Glen?" I ask, perplexed.

With a sheepish grin, Franke fumbles with a brown paper bag hidden under the seat next to him. He pulls from the bag a green bottle of Glenlivet scotch and places it firmly on the table. Almost on cue, the sweaty man arrives with Franke's dinner and a cocktail glass filled with ice. Franke pours the equivalent of two and a half shots.

"No, thank you. I'm doing the whole training thing and I've been clean for several months. Trying for another month if I can," I say, feeling a need to explain myself.

"Good on you, kid. The drink is the surest way to ruin a man. That, and a bad woman. But those usually go hand in hand. My real pleasure these days is cannabis oil. I make my own, actually."

"Really?" I ask, surprised. I take Franke for a drinker who despises anything liberal, including weed.

"You bet. Just wish I weren't in my sixties when I discovered it. Miracle drug is what it is. That's why it was illegal for so long, you know. Those big pharmaceutical schmucks don't want you goin' off the res to get stuff that actually works. Those are the *real* drug dealers. What a racket," he says, shaking his head.

"You get it locally?"

"Oh, no. That'd be suicide. I buy a kilo of some okay buds up near Burma, then make oil that'll last a whole year. You should come out to the house for breakfast, and I'll give ya some. It'll help them bruises. By the way, don't buy anything from them damn Tuk Tuk mopes or cabbies."

"No?"

"Hell, no. They'll offer you all kinds of shit, then turn you in. The cops here are corrupt bastards. They'll just shake you down for some money, but if you're a wise ass or they think you got dough, they'll haul you in and then it gets expensive."

"Really?"

"Really. They even traffic kids. I'm telling ya, the rules are different out here. Real cowboy shit. Don't let the smiles and all the Buddhas fool you."

In the twenty minutes we're together, I witness a European couple stand at a table adjacent to ours, listening. Shortly after, the man shakes his head toward his wife, and they walk away with full trays. As our conversation spans prostitutes, drugs, and police corruption, an exit strategy is paramount.

"Franke, you got the time?"

"Yeah, it's about quarter to seven."

"Okay. I got a lady coming to my hotel at eight, but we're good."

"A lady? Like a working girl?"

"Yeah. I had a massage last night on Kumpangdin Road, and she and I negotiated an outcall."

"What price?"

I had his full attention.

"Uh, fifteen hundred baht for two hours."

"One shot or multiple?" he quizzes.

"What do you mean?"

"You blow once or do you get to blow more than once?" he clarifies, like a medical professional.

"I don't know. We didn't get that far into the contract. I'll have to check the print," I quip.

"Wise ass! But fifteen hundred ain't bad. I got about five or six ladies I should turn you onto. Decent ones. They come over, cook me breakfast, we mess around. I give 'em like a thousand, sometimes more. You don't strike me as the type to pay for it."

"Thanks," I reply, with a nervous laughter. "I think it was Charlie Sheen who said something about not paying for sex but paying to leave. Or maybe he pays them to leave. Somebody leaves, anyway."

"You resemble him, kinda. When he was younger, like his *Platoon* days. Before the tiger blood and his haram of crack whores. Anyone ever tell ya that?"

"Actually, yeah. When I was younger, I got it quite a bit."

"I like Charlie. He has a code, you know. A good black sheep for our times."

"Code?"

"A man's got to have a code," Franke states boldly, pausing for a long pull on his drink.

"A lot of those Hollywood pansies are all about what's trendy. Like Leo, with the global warming bullshit. These jokers say this and that, but behind the doors of the castle they're doing lines and touchin'

These Shadows

underage boys. No code. Hollywood is filled with satanists."

"I see."

"Yeah. But Charlie owns it. He tells the world who he is, and he doesn't apologize for it. Speakin' of our neck of the woods, I think he actually got the bug from a lady-boy, or a tranny. Don't know if it's true, but read that somewhere."

"Well, I appreciate the comparison to him now more than ever. Speaking of celebrities, I got to admit, Franke, you've got the whole Tony Soprano thing going for you. Being from Jersey isn't helping your case, either. You a retired outfit guy?"

The first silence hangs long enough that the Glen is merely a shallow puddle. Franke slurps some of the melted ice water, then raises his glass and shakes it.

"I ran bars and clubs, but never got into the strippies. Too many drugs and jealous tricks in that racket. Made a little coin. And that's about all you need to know. At my peak, I nearly bought Kerouac's bar … the bar he frequented, anyway."

"Fair enough. That's interesting on Kerouac. Been reading a good bit of Bukowski on this trip. I never read his work until now, but it's entertaining."

Taking a last sip, and swirling an ice cube in his mouth, Franke nods slowly before spitting it back into his glass.

"I called him up once, must have been in the seventies. We were living close to each other, and I read his weekly newspaper stuff that was actually pretty good."

"No shit?" I inquire, excitedly.

"No shit. I was friends with a famous musician, well, wasn't famous at the time, but you don't need all the details. Anyway, we were drinking one night. A lot. And we started talkin' 'bout Bukowski and what dumb luck this guy must've had. You know, he was an ugly guy … acne scars, dad used to beat him, no confidence, what have you. But he could write. He worked a bunch of odd jobs, then wrote that postal book and some others, and his star rose, then money, women … well, you probably know all this."

"So, you're drinking with the mystery musician, and you just decide to open the phone book and randomly call *Charles Bukowski*?"

"Yeah. Pretty much. We didn't talk long, maybe ten minutes, but the guy's straight. What you see is what you get. We were all shitfaced, and I don't remember one damn thing he said, which is a shame. But, his writing, you know, is him. His character … what's his name?"

"Chinaski," I offer.

"Yeah, Henry Chinaski. That's him. I know people who knew him personally and they said the guy was Chinaski in real life. Drank, womanized, spent time at the track."

I read five of Bukowski's books on the trip. At various times, it was as if my shadow were whispering pieces of my soul. In Franke's presence, I see it again. The unhealed parts literally right in front, staring back like a mirror.

"Bukowski was old school. Seemed authentic, like he owned who he was. A lot of men I meet today repress that stuff, but it has to be there. I think it's in all of us to some degree. What I consider to be *shadows*."

"You can say that again. I'll be chattin' with St. Peter for quite a while before he flips his coin," Franke says.

"You know, Franke, it's strange. I've worked a lot of environments, like as a military officer, academic; what many consider 'grown-up jobs.' I had this colleague who was a therapist. Gay guy. About twenty years older. Real nice. We became friends, and eventually he confides that he's been hosting orgies at work. On a regular basis."

"No shit?" Franke says, excitedly.

"Seriously. He tells me that once a month or so, a group of guys he's met online go to our work site, and right there, in the group therapy room no less, it's the last days of Rome. He even told me that many guys he meets online are married."

"Good story, kid."

"I actually find it kind of tragic, to be truthful."

"These shadows, or whatever you call them. If you don't make peace with them, they wage war with you, kid. It's the really nice ones; the non-boat-rocker types who smell just a bit too sweet, those are the ones where they find bodies in the basement."

Franke jumps to his next philosophy, hitting stride.

"Problem is now, everyone is competing to show themselves a certain way, instead of just being who they are. It's creatin' chaos."

"How so?" I ask.

"I saw a kid in LA a few years back with a purse, and what are those jeans they wear now ... *skinny jeans*," he states incredulously.

"I feel that way about guys with fanny packs."

"AMEN, kid."

"When I worked at a university, it was eye-opening."

"God bless you, kid," Franke says, as he raises his glass.

These Shadows

"My first week on the job, and keep in mind I'm working with veterans. I have the American flag, and all the different service flags in my office, displayed on the wall. The big boss comes in, looks around, and almost in a whisper asks me if the American flag might send a *hostile* message to some of the students and staff."

I stare at the Glen, tempted to pour a glass and feel its smokiness around my lips. Then pour a little more, and revisit old chambers. There is still tenderness around the wound.

"So, a few months later, I'm in another meeting. And this professor goes off on a rant. Just yelling, unhinged. She's demanding we adorn our office doors with different types of activist posters to show solidarity with various marginalized groups."

Franke stares, nodding slowly. He leans closer, almost paternal in posture. Then whispers, "Mm hmm … .and that was the beginning."

"Beginning?"

"The moment you were seen as not one of *them*. Different from the tribe. And different means problem, yeah?"

Franke takes another moment, then offers, "A lot of people are sheep, kid. On their phones, snappin' pics for Facebook, or whatever. Tellin' the world how great they got it. But it's all bullshit. They don't realize there's a …"

He pauses.

"A malicious force."

"Malicious force?"

"Yeah. An evil that controls what they read, what they see, how they should think, what to be offended by. These young kids are spoon-fed a lot of nonsense in college. There's parallels you know, taking place, that remind me of the Nazis. The media, the propaganda and censorship, keeping people in conflict with each other. It's a mess. That's the other part of why I'm here. But you, you were in the factory where a lot of that shit's made."

"You just had enough?" I ask.

"America?"

"Mm hmm."

"I love it, kid, but it's all emotion now."

Franke pours more Glen into his new glass. He sits upright, shoulders back and wide.

"But the colleges; Jesus H. Christ. When you have kids fetal, cryin' over spilt milk, and every group under the sun offended, well, you're just enabling them to be jerk offs. No wonder the women ain't cooking.

They don't feel safe ... or inspired."

I nod, though I don't want to go further down this path with Franke. I'm committed to move beyond that time in my life. The inner wisdom chimes: *Be the chalkboard, Nick. Don't dwell on the writing that's on it. That's the illusion. Franke sees the illusion. Get beyond that.*

Perhaps sensing my discomfort, Franke changes subjects and invites me to join him on a motorcycle trip the following day. It's a nine-hour slog he explains, to a town near the Laos border. He promises he'll get me laid. I deflect.

"Suit yourself, kid. You want to sweat with a bunch of dudes rather than some skirt, be my guest."

At one point in the conversation, Franke said something surprising. He was waxing about his move from the East coast to California and stated that something inside him, or beyond him, forced him to do it. I don't recall his exact wording, but I asked him to elaborate.

"It was after the acid tests, and the hippies realized they had to go work. Things were changing in the country. But something kept telling me go to California. It kept me awake at night. I finally told my brother I was going, and he says he's wantin' a change too, so we pack our stuff and drive out less than a week later. Now mind you, we're not college educated, but we're good with people. We sort of pump each other up on the drive. We pull into LA, and within a week we're working and drinking in a bar and sort of trying to figure out what just happened."

"I like that story, Franke. It reminds me of what Joseph Campbell said about, 'follow your bliss.'"

Franke perks up and grins.

"Campbell. Campbell. Now that's a name I haven't heard in a while. He's dead, right?"

I nod.

"I remember him on Bill Moyers. Man, that shit was deep. You know, Luke Skywalker came from him? The concept, I mean."

A comfortable silence slows the evening. Franke stares into his glass. It's hard to decipher what he's thinking, and the line of Glen left in the bottle is shallow.

"You're alright, kid. You read and shit, and you take care of yourself. And I can tell you're nice ..." His words trail off.

"Yeah, definitely come by the house while you're here."

I rise to get a napkin and pen from one of the cashiers to take down Franke's information. But hesitation forms. For a brief moment, I'm transported to the nightclub days. The tight black shirt; the sour acidic smell of booze and sick in the bathroom. It's an unhurried evening; reggae and joints. Customers you can smell. A regular couple is at the front lower bar away from the concert room, looking out of place. Early forties her, and mid-fifties him. Smartly dressed, and I once saw them drive away in a newer Lexus. I was emptying the trash, trying to avoid puke droplets from landing on my boots. The man slipped me a twenty once when leaving. His wife held eye contact for lengths that made me uncomfortable.

He wrote his phone number on a napkin and slipped it to me one evening. The offer was generous: to screw his wife.

"I promise, I won't touch you," he said, nervously. "I just like to watch. You can come over and have drinks, and if you don't feel it, no pressure."

The interior world is layered. We all have demons. I am ready to leave the shadowlands, though.

I take the pen from the kind-eyed cashier; an early thirties Thai woman, dressed in a Burka. I return to Franke, my mind electric with images of the random strangers throughout my travels. The expats, by and large, are a broken bunch. Their stories rife with pain and bitterness. Their loneliness, palpable and exposed. But I feel this way about most of the folks in the TM commune, too. And the academics at the university. Is it me? Are they reflections of my own toxicity? I ruminate briefly, then conclude these messengers are mirrors. This is what I could become if I don't do the work. I will become just another shell walking the earth awaiting death. I will live without wholeness. I will become Franke. Or Charlie.

I take my seat across from Franke, then slide his information into my damp short pockets.

"Hey, Franke, can I ask you something?"

"Shoot."

"Do you ever get lonely? I mean, I know you have women, but don't you ever want something more ..."

"Like love?"

"Yeah. Exactly."

"I hate three things in life, kid: condoms are the first. But even more than condoms, I hate pregnancy tests," Franke laughs.

"And the third?" I ask.

Franke fidgets in his chair, and extends his arms in front, cracking his knuckles. Then he rolls his head in a circular motion.

"This thing we call *love*."

"So, you don't believe in it?"

"I gave up on love a long time ago. It wasn't what I thought. You sound like you haven't, though, yeah?"

"No. But I don't think I was ready for love. At least until recently, maybe. I had some shit to figure out."

"Say more."

"It may sound stupid or corny, but I've been alone most my life. I mean, I have a great family. I've had my share of relationships, and other arrangements. Too many probably. But I've loved very few women. Just a handful. They all seemed to come about in times when I was possessed by this thing I call the Search. And I cared more about that than I did them. Selfish, I know, but it's how I felt. The Search came first, before them. Always."

"Search?"

"I won't go into it, but it's like something spiritual that guides. It is like a thirst that only gets quenched through lived experiences. A lot of experiences, really. Preferably adventurous and dangerous ones. But it's related to God, too. It's complicated, but …"

"Okay. I think I got it."

"Well, over the past nine months, I sit around, and I think about having a family. I *want* a family. I want a wife and a home. Maybe even kids. I have this fantasy, all of us sitting around watching a movie together, and the doorbell rings and this fat guy is standing outside holding a pizza. I pay the fat guy and go back into the living room and everyone cheers and runs toward me. We're all there just …"

There is an internal silence that wells up by the image, as a pang of wretched loneliness surrounds me. I glimpse what life will be like if I stay on this solo ride too long. Franke gazes with paternal kindness, as light exudes from his eyes. He gifts me a few breaths and lets me continue.

"I just feel like I am nearly through the forest, and I can honestly state what it is that I want now. I want a woman to grow old with. I want another career. One I truly believe in. I am ready to be a different man. I think I can find real happiness through simplicity and the mundane, because I'm at peace with myself now. That's what had to change."

Franke crumples the paper bag on his lap and pours the remaining drops of Glen into his glass. He looks me in the eyes again, then raises his glass.

"You know the story about the two birds?"

"Refresh my memory."

These Shadows

"So, there's a bird outside the window of a home. Flappin' around, all wild like, doing its thing. It rests on a branch for a minute and looks through the window, because on the other side of that window is a big bird cage. With me?"

"Yes."

"Okay. So, inside that bird cage is a beautiful bird that sings, and it has an owner that brings it clean water every day. It gets fresh birdseed, and sometimes the owner pops a cracker through the bars to nibble on. Shit like that. The point is that the bird is loved. It has everything taken care of, right?"

"Right."

"But that's not the whole story. You see, the bird inside the cage is actually a miserable fuck. He stares out that window every day and watches while all the other birds fly around. His song is actually a song of pain. He sings the blues. Now sometimes he sings happy stuff, but mostly that caged bird is just sitting there hopeless. He doesn't have the freedom that the other birds have. Understand?"

"I think so."

"The bottom line is that the birds outside envy the bird inside. They see his home, and the love he receives and that he doesn't have to worry about predators or go searchin' for his food. Security. But the bird inside is envious of those guys outside because they're free. And let's admit, me and you are a couple of outside birds, and we know what being free is all about. We know adventure. We know exploring and risk. We know the rush you get walking down the street in some foreign place that smells funny, or the rush you get when the massage girl rolls you over and her hands start moving toward Mr. Willie. But it sounds like you're ready to go inside now. You're ready to be indoors. And I don't think the cage will be a prison for you, like it is for most. I don't think the song you sing will be a somber one. You just know what you want, now."

An attractive blonde who walked by earlier and dropped a warm smile circles by again. She remarks how good the hummus looks, and she has a cute boy in tow. She smiles again, and almost on cue, Franke pounces.

"Whoa, whoa, beautiful. You can't keep walking by us like that. You're getting the kid here too excited. What's your name, gorgeous?" It turns out I'm the kid in this story.

I feel a quick surge in my heartbeat. The attractive woman stops and greets us, warmly.

"Hello, I'm Christina." She glows with a soothing Australian accent.

"And who is the little guy, here? He looks like Casper," Franke inquires, pointing at her son, a handsome boy with bright blue eyes and shaggy blond hair that resembles Julian Assange in color. His skin is even whiter.

"This is Malcom. He's nearly four."

The young boy is occupied with an action figure, happily making sounds as the figure jumps off the table and bounces on the cool cement floor.

"You need to put that kid in the sun, darling. He's white as a ghost. You married to an albino, or a polar bear?"

I wait for Christina to walk away, but being true Australian, she lets out a hearty laugh. Franke has radiance, for sure. Just a few moments with him, and you're under his spell.

"We're here on holiday for three months, just Malcolm and I."

"No man? Or did you leave hubby at home to work, while you and the kid play?"

"I'm actually retired," she reveals.

"Get outta here. You're too young for that. Married a man with money, you smart one."

Christina only looks toward me a few times. Her tall body is cocked at an angle with her left shoulder aligned to my torso. Her dark blonde hair is wrapped cleanly in a ponytail, and she doesn't wear makeup. She has an athletic body and straight posture, a combination of strength and femininity. There is a quality about her. Knowing she's married has curbed my interest, though. Aside from her beauty, there is something cool about the way she carries herself. I noticed it the first time she walked by. Not in a hurry. Savoring moments.

"I'm forty-four," she states, before continuing, "and, I'm actually the one with the money. We started a construction business years ago, so he works while I take holiday. Six years of marriage, together for ten. You need breaks."

Franke looks over at me and says with raised hands, "Sorry, kid. Sounds like she's got a good thing going."

Franke invites Christina and her little ghost to join us, and I take the opportunity to make a clean exit.

"Well, I need to get going. Christina, it was a pleasure meeting you and I hope you enjoy your time here. Franke … it's been …" I pause.

"A good conversation with a good bird," Franke interrupts.

These Shadows

He rises from his seat, standing tall in front of me. As we shake hands, he places his left hand on top and looks far into my eyes. His thin gold bracelet rests on top of my wrist. I think of the cobra in Varanasi.

"Remember to live with a code, Nick. Don't get caught up in other peoples' bullshit. Most of them are asleep and aren't really livin'."

I nod as he sits back down and fumbles with his empty cup.

"We'll be in touch, Franke."

"I hope so, kid. Enjoy the massage. I hope it's not a lady-boy either, but sometimes you get surprised once the panties come off. A moment each man has to get honest with himself."

As I turn to walk away, Franke shouts, "Eh, tell me a Campbell story before you go. Something quick, though, cuz I got a lady here with me."

I sort through my internal database of things that stuck over the years, honing onto something fitting.

"Joseph Campbell talked a bit about his later years when he moved to Hawaii with his wife. They didn't have any children, and at this stage he had already made a big name for himself. So, they moved to Hawaii, and he's just writing for the pure joy of it. They live in a retirement community on the ocean, around other couples. Campbell muses about how all the couples have been married for a long time and they've reached a point in their lives where after navigating the rough waters, they're now like ships coming into the harbor, floating comfortably with all kinds of sea stories. I like it because it embodies what it means to be an elder. And I think you're pretty damn close, Franke. Even if your path has been an unorthodox one."

Franke smiles and raises the empty Glen, as I turn my back and walk away. Then, he yells, "Sea stories, mate. Stay salty, sailor!"

I wade through the mix of tourists and touts through the sweltering evening. My time in the forest is nearly finished. I pass by blocks of massage parlors and devious temptations, smiling at some of the faces, wondering of their internal dialogue. I smell pungent garlic and ginger from a small food cart. Each moment is full, like a photograph. It doesn't take long to get to my apartment. As I strip to my underwear and turn on the air con, I lay on my big bed. Then I turn on my laptop and check email. It's been several days, and a dozen messages sit unread. I see Simone's name, and click on that one first.

Good evening, Nick. I want to see you. Even if only for a few days before you fly home. I will fly from Germany to

A Ronin's Tale

*Bangkok. It is far, but I will do it. Do you want to see me?
I hope so. Let me know.*

Love, Simone.

Chapter 47

Be Artists

Fall 2017, A Classroom in the Midwest

As you progress through your time at the university, life will speed up. You will take on internships, tweak your resume and social media, and meet employers. Dare I say it, but you may even buy a suit. Some of you will go further with your education. These are excellent pursuits, and I hope that you will maximize every opportunity offered here. I know that the sexy career titles, money, and glitz of the material world are seductive. I'm attached, too. But as you promote and ascend throughout your life, make time for your art. That's a takeaway I want from this course. When I say art, I mean the ingredients that make your life flavorful. The things that drive and punch from your soul in all the right ways, slow the time down and prioritize that. Remember that it never has to be one or the other. Find that balance.

When people make drastic moves at a certain stage, they're often dismissed as having a midlife crisis. There's a cliché of the working man who's had enough at fifty and is burned out. He subsequently buys a Harley, leaves his wife, and runs off with his much younger secretary. Maybe he gets back in the gym, or he takes up boxing, or gets his first tattoo. The point is that he feels disconnected in some way, and he is searching for an edge that's missing. Even though this is an archetypal story, it's a weak one. It's the story of a man, in my estimate, who didn't find that balance. He didn't do the hard work asked of him, to continually better himself through death and rebirth. He got lost somewhere on the journey, or perhaps he never knew about it to begin with, so his shadows overpowered him. Life became about the wheel's rim, rather than the center.

A Ronin's Tale

Another archetypal story is the wisdom of elders. Now, this is a story I like. At a later stage, things like work and raising a family will be finished, so more free time is available to ponder and play. To take up hobbies, or to simply glide through the day on a slower schedule. Many older people I know have a peace about them. They don't get worked up over details. Their days are usually not overbooked or packed with noise. And many successful ones I meet, all tell me the same thing: that they wished they'd worked less and played more. That was their one regret—they sacrificed their art.

Part of my goal through this course was to sharpen your critical thinking skills, and to expose you to nonlinear knowledge. But of equal significance, it is to encourage you to not wait until you're older to access that reservoir of wisdom that's inside, waiting to flourish. I don't want you buying the Harley. Instead, my desire is for each of us here to live 200 percent; to savor each day as a gift with gratitude, and to help spread light to others. Remember, the people we meet, we have no idea what's going on in their inner world. We have no idea what their journey looks like. And the ones who irritate and frustrate us, what aspect of ourselves are they showing? What I say here is a lot to ask, I know, especially since most of you are under thirty, and you're hungry. I get it. But I believe it's possible. I believe that the mythological lens keeps us balanced and on course, particularly when life feels like it's slipped out of our hands. It's those uncertain moments, and the painful ones, where our deepest wisdom is cultivated. The understanding doesn't happen in the moment, but eventually it will come. Get mentally prepared now, if you haven't already, that your life will be a circus of epic proportion. Part brilliant, and many parts something else. It will go as planned to some degree, and follow its own rhythm regardless of what you want. Getting caught in a big wave is both frightening and exhilarating, so surrendering to the ocean is a must. You will be fine, nonetheless. That much I know. I want to close with this:

At some point, physical death comes for all of us. What will they say about you when your time comes? When the grief stricken stand in front and say their words, what will they say? When life is measured out, it is never about the titles, the money, or the power that counts. Those things won't be mentioned. It's about the hearts you touch, and your love. The love you project out to others. The grace you give yourself, and the gold you put into the world, that's what matters. You have it in you to live from this initiated place. The world needs you in your most balanced form. The world needs Heroes. Now, go get dirty.

Be Artists

******

There is nothing noble in being superior to your fellow man. True nobility is being superior to your former self.[36]
—Ernest Hemingway

---

36   Retrieved from Quote by Ernest Hemingway: "There is nothing noble in being superior to you..." (goodreads.com) on November 7, 2023.

Afterword

Reintegration

The anticipation of approaching the majestic Golden Gate Bridge standing quietly as a gatekeeper to my favorite city was a boyhood delicacy. The suspense rose, as we held our breath through the rainbow tunnel just before its regal pillars came to view. It was my favorite landmark, only recently losing its esteemed standing to the tragically romantic Taj Mahal. Our station wagon purred along Highway 101 from the sleepy rural farmlands of Sonoma, as we languidly crept toward the city for a special Saturday. The Japanese Tea Garden in Golden Gate Park and a bay cruise off Pier 39 created enough tattoo memories that I can still see what I was wearing, even to this day.

The woman who died in the military, lived off the 101, just north of the bridge. At the time, I was up in the foggy outlaw paradise of Humboldt. We'd take turns making the long trip, sometimes just for a night. About a year after our breakup, I met Aimee, who became my first true love. Ironically, Aimee lived just off the 101, less than a quarter mile from my ex.

I cut my grown-up teeth on that highway. The biker bar. The nightclub just yards away, where I walked through a plume of marijuana smoke and haram of patchouli fragrant hippie chicks, delicately informing Mr. Eek-A-Mouse that he was overdue on stage. The commute to my military work, mostly taken on it. Sometimes in foreign places, I closed my eyes and traced it, familiar beauty unfolding like still frames. It calmed in those moments abroad when the walls were a little tighter; when the loneliness banshees danced.

Interstate 74 became another mysterious landmark in my hero's journey. As an undergraduate in North Carolina, I made the thirteen-

Reintegration

hour trek to visit my father and to work a summer job with foster kids, never once feeling premonition of the influence it would one day wield. A decade later, it would be my regular route as a company man for the university. Seventy-four marked the complicated layers of my existence. At times it was an ominous marker, a starting point toward Chicago. Donning a suit and with minty breath, I massaged the powerful in an attempt to schmooze donor dollars and endorsements. I drove it, more freely, to the humble and nondescript Hindu temple just north of town; a bouquet of flowers fragrantly riding shotgun along with dreams of India. At times it was a steppingstone to a quieter country road, where I therapeutically fired guns and cleansed myself of university noise. But it was also a soothing Cupid's path to my last love, D.

In early 2022, some years after returning from abroad, I walked into her home. A familiar smell greeted me like an old friend. I scanned the surroundings from the entryway, though every inch of the space was imprinted. I placed my hand on the top of her couch, steadying, while I removed my shoes. We made love for the first time on it. We retired there most evenings, watching HGTV, our hands interlaced. We cried on that couch my last day there. I didn't think I would ever sit on it again, yet here I was, looking at the fireplace, assorted memories frozen in each brick.

Truths shared by the wise caution against visiting old flames. Preserving the sacrament memories on the altar, untouched, is the preferred medium. But while visiting Becki, D randomly texted out of the blue, perhaps sensing I was close by.

Embracing, the familiar curvature of her body wrapped effortlessly around mine like a completed puzzle. I pushed back an unexpected surge of emotion, closing my mouth and opting to wink instead. She looked good. She looked the same. Behind her, my eye caught an array of sparkling appliances.

"Those are new," I said, pointing at the stainless items.

I needed safe talk.

"You don't miss much," she said as she laughed. "I just got them, actually."

I grabbed her again, wrapping my arms tighter this time, then kissed her forehead. The floral scent of her hair and body familiar like the home, but different too. We stood in her living room, as two young puppies dashed toward us, barking and filled with suspicion.

"These are Nash and Knox," she said, as they sniffed and barked wildly.

I crouched to the floor, extending my hand. I stretched a little, mostly to move energy, while D sat on the couch. Something inside called for distance. We made more small talk; she jubilantly shared of her recent and well-deserved promotion. We gave casual updates on our families, as I scanned a stack of leadership books neatly placed next to her laptop. Other recognizable landmarks scattered across the room looked back. Had it really been three years? A part of me never left.

After sitting briefly, I rose and walked the narrow hallway to the bathroom. I turned on the fan and light, its memorable hum whirling different realities. Then I glanced at the off-color marking on the laminate counter. We had lit a candle, then forgot about it as we made love. At some point it melted down. I peed, sinking into a complex spell; familiar ease and separation. I knew D hurt when I left. So did I. But true to pattern, I simply immersed myself into distractions and stuffed it. Then hit the road. Things were beginning to leak, though. The shift from the journey revealing its accountability. More insignificant talk occupied the living room before we decided to drive to Homer for a walk.

Subtle lines cast from quiet fishermen reflected off the glassy surface. The stillness that slowed time and balanced me in the past was still there in the park, offering its magic.

"Before I came to your place, I took Curtis exit, then some back roads."

Our hands organically touched and then clasped.

"I went by the dojo, then to the old neighborhood. I knocked on Trent's door to surprise him, but nobody was home. Eventually I made my way to the condo before coming to see you."

D nodded.

"None of it was planned really. I just … uh …" my words trailed.

More synchronicities. It had been exactly three years to the day that we sat next to each other in a sterile conference room, signing papers for the sale of my condo. The bittersweetness to all of it; a modest check that would finance my Asian odyssey, but a complete severing of us. Just fourteen months before I handed over my condo keys, D and I met for the first time. Although she didn't cover that particular area, my real estate inquiry was somehow passed to her. We went for a celebratory dinner after I purchased it, surprised I was finally rooting.

"Mexico was special, huh," I said, squeezing her hand.

Anonymous faces at the resort gleefully divulging how radiant and in love we looked produced an inner smile. A comedic scenario of D and I hiding from a swinger couple from New York widened it.

The safe familiarity of Homer Lake released the tension in my shoulders. The stiffness in my neck began to wane, as the abundant fresh air opened my lungs and heart.

"Mexico was *amazing*!" D beamed, returning the squeeze.

Then a slight breeze blew through, the kind that chilled.

"I actually took R (her daughter) there, the following year. The same place we stayed. I needed a new memory. I also went to Starved Rock with a friend for the same reason."

We walked silently, as clusters of happy people regaled themselves in the crisp dusk. A faint smell of marijuana, recently legalized, wafted past. Then she spoke.

"So, I can't imagine there hasn't been *someone* in your life."

Our hands separated, as our pace quickened.

I ruminated on Simone, wondering what to say, if anything. But before I uttered a word, D continued.

"I had someone. I mean, I was with someone. We were off and on."

A choking sensation expanded throughout my throat. My chest tightened. *We* implied union. More than casual.

"Oh really," I muttered.

I looked ahead for oncoming cars. Then my gaze went further into the naked trees patiently awaiting spring. My logical mind assured me it was inevitable. Healthy, even. To move on. I wondered at times, secretly hoping as most every man hopes, that she was chaste in spite of my carefree galivanting. But still, I couldn't swallow.

"I was really sad when you left. Like, heartbroken, Nick. And I ..."

"Did you love him?" I asked, feebly.

D paused. I looked to the lake, then to blurry faces that stood around a barbecue.

"I thought I did, but ... I don't know."

Maybe it is instinctual or rooted in a part of our DNA that prioritizes survival, but a dart covered with a small bit of poison on the tip shot from my lips. It was impulsive and reactionary, a knee that thumps when struck by the doctor's little hammer. Suddenly I had less reservation for secrets.

"I did meet someone, actually. While I was away. It was brief ... but powerful," I confessed truthfully.

"Oh ..."

"Yeah. She's German. A professional model. She was doing a yoga retreat in Rishikesh, and I, we, well ..."

I was momentarily adrift in the emotional tides, as painful images of D with another man circulated. Had they slept on our couch? Her bed, her ethereal chamber where we exchanged massages and shared secrets, what happened there?

The next morning, her early alarm sprung to life. I sat upward, groggily, to meditate. Within seconds of awakening, the cloud cover sheened the room with suffocating fury. I positioned oversized pillows against the small of my back, as D readied herself for work. We'd only slept a few hours, but it wasn't fatigue.

I waited until she left. Though still a struggle, the gift of release symbolized hopeful light that a new Hero had indeed emerged. Still not perfect by a long shot, but at least congruent to the soul language; at least open now to vulnerability and the heart medicine. Still, the ego's tears rained first.

She knew him a while, even when we were together. Was she attracted to him then? Was he a better lover? Did he have a big dick? When she got into bed at night, did she think of him?

The ego's tears dried, as the unabashed pain was given free reign. It was a moment of pure ownership of my mistreatment of women and selfish patterns. Hurt and devastation I inflicted that I never intended. The mixed messages, the confusing signals, the lack of commitment; the guttural toxins our most truthful moments spotlight. I confronted it overseas, but sitting on the bed of my beloved, knowing that another man had been there, put me atop the glowing embers. I loved D. I had never stopped loving D. The Hero nodded his approval to grieve, and I accepted.

I wept for many things; for my strange upbringing and inability to have a conventional life. For my self-centeredness and combative nature. I wept for having lost everything I owned, and that D had only known me in a transitional place, never experiencing when I stood tall with purpose. Indeed, I had grown considerably, but I had little materially to show for it.

Yet in the midst of the cleanse, a silver lining that God's grace was somehow behind it all, watching from above, pulled me to the surface for breath. The realization that I was a good man. I AM a good man. The remembrance that faith was at the crux of the journey brought me back to center. I needed to lose everything so that I could gain everything. Everything that mattered.

There was no clear reason why I went to see D, at least consciously. Just before I left, she told me to take the time I needed over there, then

Reintegration

come back and she would teach me the real estate trade. We would be a powerful team. I thought about it a good bit overseas; the pizza man ringing the doorbell, as we sank into the couch and talked about our day. I wondered, at times, if we were really finished. I missed our Rummikub battles, and our opposing but respectful spiritual differences. I missed our sacred intimacy. Now three years later, our natural rhythms, in spite of the passing time and new lovers didn't degrade what was still there. She opened her home and arms, showering me with kindness and effortlessly brushing off pains of the past. But in spite of her colossal wisdom and generosity, and in spite of our interwoven hearts, I knew it could never be. *We* could never be. The tears baptized this truth.

I wiped my puffy eyes, then slowly composed as the weight dissipated. It wasn't D that brought the clarity. I felt it driving into town the day before. The foreignness of it all. The dojo, the Brooklyn Building on Oregon Street. My condo, and favorite bar. Perhaps I came wondering if stray ghosts were still lingering about. But no part of my spirit was there. Not an ounce. It was finished, and I was merely a stranger now, cruising the streets of some random American town as a spectator. I *had* died overseas, and the new man couldn't go back. But D's family, her numerous friends, and her successful career were embedded there. D's life was there. Mine was not.

******

The great masters and initiated ones remind us that the world is filled with duality. Light and dark, good and evil. There is our external reality, and the softer inner one we conceal from others. Our thoughts, actions, and, for some, even our astrological charts determine reality and how we navigate its unstable waters. And sometimes it is through our deepest sorrow that our greatest light emerges. Although the hero's journey rarely unfolds cleanly in real life, the shift that occurred opened my heart in ways I never thought possible.

I try to consider how to share it with others. The grand adventure, that is. For some outsiders it was merely a midlife crisis. To others, an extended holiday without rules. To Troy, it was the Big Orgasm. The necessary spiritual release of poisons before the seeds of commitment and domestic life root. Some shared that I looked younger; that I seemed more at peace. I sit with it in meditation and quieter moods, mainly musing on the crystal truth that my life had lost something; something vitally important for my long-term health and sanity. A need to be stripped and exposed before God to see what's real.

The matrix is seductive. Tech addiction. Porn. Craft bourbons. Sensual pleasures. Overly filled plates with helpings of what one is supposed to be. Constant messages and bombardments mostly to consume. Get a bigger home. Get a better-looking partner. If you're 401(k) doesn't have this by fifty, you're screwed. More, more, more, and we'll give you free shipping. As we fatigue and wear down, our grasp of center is lost. But they have pills for that in the matrix. Many of them. It was time to begin healing all that. So my life was beautifully shaken up.

As I close, I want to emphasize that there are far worse fates than losing a career and having the ego tarnished. Just ask any parent camped in the room of a children's cancer ward. A staggering number of the world's population does not have access to clean drinking water. Among the grand symphony, my story doesn't evoke any authentic blip on the radar. Yet, our suffering is still our suffering. Our inner worlds, delicate. Trusting that the divine knows what it's doing and has a plan for each of us is key. And for whatever reason they conspired to awaken me, they rattled my Wild Man's cage and simply demanded that I was capable of better. A better version of myself was possible, but only if I trusted and did the work.

Upon landing on U.S. soil after my time away, I spent a month in California, contemplating if the Golden State was still golden. Sitting in bumper-to-bumper traffic a block from the club I bounced at, I witnessed a hard-living woman insert a needle into her bruised sinewy arm on the sidewalk of an underpass as a seminaked man close to her yelled at invisible entities. So, I made my way back to Iowa, resolved to quieter pastures. I made health my priority; a morning routine of box jumps, sled pushes, squats, and deadlifts overseen by a beautiful young couple who took my training to new heights. Then I came across a wise, prodigious professional fighter, whom I continue to douse in sweat as he patiently teaches me to strike and strangle. The allies continue to show up.

Free time lingered after my travels, unstructured time with Dad and Troy, and other ghosts of the past. Walks and drives along languid country roads. I resumed meditation in the dome, smiling at the khaki-clad warriors who were even thinner and more hunched over. Notices of community deaths, with sweet messages, adorned the dome's entrance.

I recognized some of those faces from the Utopia Park days. The elders were finishing their work and checking out. An entire subculture few knew about were disappearing into the ether.

My life right now is a humble one. A small, tidy room in an ashram in the country. I sip coffee most mornings, looking out over an overgrown field filled with deer and assorted wildlife. Many days I walk in nature or burn sage and frankincense at the river. The past four summers, I've escaped to Colorado to camp and conquer a 14er mountain. But the summits are different now. Mostly inward.

Although I feel things will soon shift, I take solace that my routine is healthy. I take solace that my blood pressure is normal and that I sleep through most nights. Eventually the career and material front will rise again. Eventually I will be called to another adventure, perhaps an even tougher one. And perhaps I will finally have my moment when the doorbell rings and the pizza man extends his hand for a tip. But instead of forcing it all, instead of trying to figure it all out, or the *when*, finding fullness in the mundane and embracing gratitude are the waves I ride these days. Staying plugged into the Source as best I can, and just like the mantra, taking each day as it comes. As a better man.

Nick Osborne, January 2024
Fairfield, Iowa

> There is a knighthood of the 21st century whose riders do not ride through the darkness of physical forests as of old, but through the forest of darkened minds. They are armed with a spiritual armor and an inner sun makes them radiant. Out of them shines healing, healing that flows from the knowledge of the human being as a spiritual being. They must create inner order, inner justice, peace and conviction in the darkness of our time.[37]
>
> —Karl Konig

---

[37] Retrieved from the Anthroposophical Society in America, Mysteries of the Holy Grail from Arthur and Parzival to Modern Initiation – Anthroposophical Society in America (anthroposophy.org) on April 26, 2022.

Bibliography

12 of the best Bas Rutten quotes for MMA and life. www.budodragon.com. August 26, 2021.

Addison Allen, S. *The Girl Who Chased the Moon: A Novel.* Bantam Books, 2011.

Cameron, A. *Cult or Culture? How to Avoid the Kool-Aid Effect.* Cult or Culture? How to avoid the Kool-Aid effect (linkedin.com), April 10, 2017.

Daczynski, V. *Tat Wale Baba: Rishi of the Himalayas.* Yogi Vince Books, 2022.

Dass, R. *Dealing with Fear.* Retrieved from the Ram Dass Foundation on June 3, 2023. www.ramdass.org.

Hesse, H. *Siddhartha: A Novel.* Bantam Books, 1982.

The Karate Kid, Columbia Pictures, June 22, 1984.

Krakauer, J. *Into the Wild.* Anchor Books, 1997.

Lamott, A. *12 Truths I Learned from Life and Writing.* Ted Talk, Anne Lamott: 12 truths I learned from life and writing | TED Talk, April 2017.

Leopold, A. *A Sand County Almanac: And Sketches Here and There.* Oxford University Press, 2020.

Mafi, M. *Rumi's Little Book of Wisdom.* Hampton Roads Publishing, 2021.

Mahler, Gustav. Mahler Foundation, https://mahlerfoundation.org/.

Osbon, Diane K. *Reflections on the Art of Living: A Joseph Campbell Companion.* New York: Harper-Collins, 1991.

Plato. *The Republic.* Penguin Classics, 2007.

Sakugawa, Y. Personal Blog: https://www.yumisakugawa.com/post/13759359719, December 4, 2011.

Solzhenitsyn, A. "A World Split Apart." *Solzhenitsyn's Commencement Address Harvard University.* June 8, 1978.

Thompson, H. *Fear and Loathing in Las Vegas: A Savage Journey to the Heart of the American Dream.* Warner Books, 1982.

Watts, A. *The Joyous Cosmology: Adventures in the Chemistry of Consciousness.* New World Library, 2013.

Wilde, O. *Oscar Wilde's Wit and Wisdom: A Book of Quotations.* Dover Publications, 1998.

Yukteswar, S. *The Holy Science.* Self-Realization Fellowship Press, 1990.

About the Author

Dr. Nick Osborne is a former bar bouncer, military officer, and university administrator. Growing up in a transcendental meditation commune in the Midwest, his writing focuses on spirituality, masculinity, and mythology. Nick has completed numerous workshops on male initiation and facilitated discussions on rites of passage. An intrepid solo traveler and adventurist, after losing his job in academia, Nick went abroad to study martial arts and to trek in the Himalayas, culminating with a pilgrimage to India. He is a nationally recognized expert on veterans in higher education and holds a doctorate from the University of California at Davis.

He may be reached at nickronin78@gmail.com.

Other Books by Ozark Mountain Publishing, Inc.

Dolores Cannon
A Soul Remembers Hiroshima
Between Death and Life
Conversations with Nostradamus,
   Volume I, II, III
The Convoluted Universe -Book One,
   Two, Three, Four, Five
The Custodians
Five Lives Remembered
Horns of the Goddess
Jesus and the Essenes
Keepers of the Garden
Legacy from the Stars
The Legend of Starcrash
The Search for Hidden Sacred
   Knowledge
They Walked with Jesus
The Three Waves of Volunteers and the
   New Earth
A Very Special Friend
Aron Abrahamsen
Holiday in Heaven
James Ream Adams
Little Steps
Justine Alessi & M. E. McMillan
Rebirth of the Oracle
Kathryn Andries
Time: The Second Secret
Will Alexander
Call Me Jonah
Cat Baldwin
Divine Gifts of Healing
The Forgiveness Workshop
Penny Barron
The Oracle of UR
P.E. Berg & Amanda Hemmingsen
The Birthmark Scar
Dan Bird
Finding Your Way in the Spiritual Age
Waking Up in the Spiritual Age
Julia Cannon
Soul Speak – The Language of Your
   Body
Jack Cauley
Journey for Life
Ronald Chapman
Seeing True
Jack Churchward
Lifting the Veil on the Lost
   Continent of Mu
The Stone Tablets of Mu
Carolyn Greer Daly
Opening to Fullness of Spirit
Patrick De Haan
The Alien Handbook
Paulinne Delcour-Min
Divine Fire
Holly Ice
Spiritual Gold
Anthony DeNino
The Power of Giving and Gratitude
Joanne DiMaggio
Edgar Cayce and the Unfulfilled
   Destiny of Thomas Jefferson
   Reborn
Paul Fisher
Like a River to the Sea
Anita Holmes
Twidders
Aaron Hoopes
Reconnecting to the Earth
Edin Huskovic
God is a Woman
Patricia Irvine
In Light and In Shade
Kevin Killen
Ghosts and Me
Susan Linville
Blessings from Agnes
Donna Lynn
From Fear to Love
Curt Melliger
Heaven Here on Earth
Where the Weeds Grow
Henry Michaelson
And Jesus Said – A Conversation
Andy Myers
Not Your Average Angel Book
Holly Nadler
The Hobo Diaries
Guy Needler
The Anne Dialogues
Avoiding Karma
Beyond the Source – Book 1, Book 2
The Curators
The History of God
The OM
The Origin Speaks

For more information about any of the above titles, soon to be released titles,
or other items in our catalog, write, phone or visit our website:
PO Box 754, Huntsville, AR 72740|479-738-2348|800-935-0045|www.ozarkmt.com

Other Books by Ozark Mountain Publishing, Inc.

Psycho Spiritual Healing
James Nussbaumer
And Then I Knew My Abundance
Each of You
Living Your Dram, Not Someone Else's
The Master of Everything
Mastering Your Own Spiritual Freedom
Sherry O'Brian
Peaks and Valley's
Gabrielle Orr
Akashic Records: One True Love
Let Miracles Happen
Nikki Pattillo
Children of the Stars
A Golden Compass
Victoria Pendragon
Being In A Body
Sleep Magic
The Sleeping Phoenix
Alexander Quinn
Starseeds What's It All About
Debra Rayburn
Let's Get Natural with Herbs
Charmian Redwood
A New Earth Rising
Coming Home to Lemuria
David Rousseau
Beyond Our World, Book 1
Richard Rowe
Exploring the Divine Library
Imagining the Unimaginable
Garnet Schulhauser
Dance of Eternal Rapture
Dance of Heavenly Bliss
Dancing Forever with Spirit
Dancing on a Stamp
Dancing with Angels in Heaven
Annie Stillwater Gray
The Dawn Book
Education of a Guardian Angel
Joys of a Guardian Angel
Work of a Guardian Angel
Manuella Stoerzer

Headless Chicken
Blair Styra
Don't Change the Channel
Who Catharted
Natalie Sudman
Application of Impossible Things
L.R. Sumpter
Judy's Story
The Old is New
We Are the Creators
Artur Tradevosyan
Croton
Croton II
Jim Thomas
Tales from the Trance
Jolene and Jason Tierney
A Quest of Transcendence
Paul Travers
Dancing with the Mountains
Nicholas Vesey
Living the Life-Force
Dennis Wheatley/ Maria Wheatley
The Essential Dowsing Guide
Maria Wheatley
Druidic Soul Star Astrology
Sherry Wilde
The Forgotten Promise
Lyn Willmott
A Small Book of Comfort
Beyond all Boundaries Book 1
Beyond all Boundaries Book 2
Beyond all Boundaries Book 3
D. Arthur Wilson
You Selfish Bastard
Stuart Wilson & Joanna Prentis
Atlantis and the New Consciousness
Beyond Limitations
The Essenes -Children of the Light
The Magdalene Version
Power of the Magdalene
Sally Wolf
Life of a Military Psychologist

For more information about any of the above titles, soon to be released titles,
or other items in our catalog, write, phone or visit our website:
PO Box 754, Huntsville, AR 72740|479-738-2348/800-935-0045|www.ozarkmt.com